DEFINING BOUNDARIES
IN AL-ANDALUS

DEFINING BOUNDARIES IN AL-ANDALUS

MUSLIMS, CHRISTIANS, AND JEWS IN ISLAMIC IBERIA

JANINA M. SAFRAN

CORNELL UNIVERSITY PRESS

Ithaca and London

First published 2013 by Cornell University Press
First printing, Cornell Paperbacks, 2015

Printed in the United States of America

Library of Congress Cataloging-in-Publication Data

Safran, Janina M.
Defining boundaries in al-Andalus : Muslims, Christians, and Jews in Islamic Iberia / Janina M. Safran.
      p. cm.
   Includes bibliographical references and index.
   ISBN: 978-0-8014-5183-6 (cloth : alk. paper)
   ISBN: 978-1-5017-0074-3 (pbk. : alk. paper)
   1. Andalusia (Spain)—Ethnic relations.   2. Dhimmis (Islamic law)—Spain—Andalusia—History—To 1500.
3. Islamic law—Spain—Andalusia—History—To 1500.
4. Islam—Relations—Christianity—History—To 1500.
5. Christianity and other religions—Islam—History—To 1500.   6. Islam—Relations—Judaism—History—To 1500.   7. Judaism—Relations—Islam—History—To 1500.   8. Spain—Civilization—711–1516.   I. Title.
   DP302.A468S24 2013
   946.8'02—dc23
                                        2012029369

Cornell University Press strives to use environmentally responsible suppliers and materials to the fullest extent possible in the publishing of its books. Such materials include vegetable-based, low-VOC inks and acid-free papers that are recycled, totally chlorine-free, or partly composed of nonwood fibers. For further information, visit our website at www.cornellpress.cornell.edu.

Cloth printing   10 9 8 7 6 5 4 3 2 1
Paperback printing   10 9 8 7 6 5 4 3 2 1

To Dan and Anna

Contents

ACKNOWLEDGMENTS

I am grateful to the National Endowment for the Humanities for generous fellowship support for this project. I also owe a debt of gratitude to the Institute for the Arts and Humanities at the Pennsylvania State University for granting me a resident scholarship for one semester, and the College of the Liberal Arts at the Pennsylvania State University for a sabbatical granting me time away from teaching and administrative responsibilities to learn, research, and write more intensively.

I learned about Islamic law, the Maliki *madhhab* (school of law), and Andalusi and Maghribi jurists and texts from the work of a number of eminent scholars and benefited tremendously over the years it took to develop this project from the well-directed references, perceptive questions, and comments of many scholars and students. These include the comments of anonymous readers for articles I wrote along the way, and the recommendations of the editors of *Speculum*, *History of Religions*, and *Comparative Islamic Studies*. Thank you, all. I would like to single out for acknowledgment four scholars who read the manuscript in different stages of its development with thoughtful attention and provided me with guidance: David S. Powers, Simon R. Doubleday, David J. Wasserstein, and Thomas F. Glick. The book is far better for their care, and its shortcomings are my own. Two workshops at different ends of the writing process helped me formulate my approach and my conclusions: the Medieval and Early Modern History Workshop at Brown University and a workshop in Madrid on the legal status of *dhimmīs* in the Muslim West sponsored by two European Research Council Seventh Framework Programme Advanced Research Grants (one directed by Maribel Fierro, the other by John Tolan), and hosted by the Consejo Superior de Investigaciones Científicas and by the Casa de Velázquez. I would like to thank Tara Nummedal and Caroline Castiglione for inviting me to the first, John Tolan and Maribel Fierro for inviting me to the second, and all involved for such stimulating occasions for discussion.

Family provides special support, and that, too, merits acknowledgment. Heartfelt thanks to Dan and Anna, and Anita, Liz, and Abby.

DEFINING BOUNDARIES
IN AL-ANDALUS

The identification of the text with the caliph ʿUmar ibn al-Khattab is not clearly established, and its characterization as an original pact of surrender has long been subject to criticism. These concerns in themselves have already had serious implications for the way historians interpret its significance. In his 1930 study *The Caliphs and Their Non-Muslim Subjects*, A. S. Tritton argued that the "Pact of ʿUmar" resembles a pattern treaty like the one preserved in al-Shafiʿi's *Kitab al-umm* rather than an actual surrender treaty, which would have been short and simple. He observed that the text "presupposes closer intercourse between Christians and Muslims than was possible in the early days of the conquest."[20] Antoine Fattal took up the interrogation of the text and suggested that the "Pact of ʿUmar" represents an amalgamation of conditions of surrender and restrictions imposed periodically on dhimmis during the first three centuries of Islam (notably by the Umayyad caliph ʿUmar ibn ʿAbd al-ʿAziz, r. 717–720, and later the Abbasid caliph al-Mutawakkil, r. 847–861) that were retroactively attributed to ʿUmar ibn al-Khattab.[21] For example, he identifies restrictions against elevating voices during prayer and ringing church bells, riding on saddles, and wearing certain clothes with ʿUmar ibn ʿAbd al-ʿAziz. Fattal shows that the earliest extant text of a treaty between ʿUmar ibn al-Khattab and the Christians of Syria is quite simple and directly reflects immediate postconquest interests. In comparison with the versions of the "Pact of ʿUmar" referred to by modern historians, it lacks many social distinctions and restrictions. The surrender treaty, recorded in a work commissioned by the Abbasid caliph Harun al-Rashid (r. 786–809), basically states the aid the Christians of Syria were required to provide the Muslims, including three days' pasturage,

---

so on the grounds of the Pact [of ʿUmar]." Rustow also observes that new houses of worship were built in her discussion of the circumstances of Jewish communities after al-Hakim's destruction of synagogues. Rustow, *Heresy and the Politics of Community*, 119–125 (quotation 122–123), 184–185; see also S. D. Goitein, *A Mediterranean Society: Volume 2: The Community* (Berkeley: University of California Press, 1971), 286.

20. A. S. Tritton, *The Caliphs and Their Non-Muslim Subjects: A Critical Study of the Covenant of Umar* (1930; repr., London: Frank Cass, 1970), 5–17 (quotation, 10).

21. Antoine Fattal, *Le statut légal des non-musulmans en pays d'Islam* (Beirut: Imprimerie Catholique, 1958), 68–69, 96–99. Fattal provides a complex view of the status of dhimmis based primarily on legal and judicial sources; Yohanan Friedmann also investigates the corpus of legal sources to discuss interfaith relations in Islam in *Tolerance and Coercion in Islam: Interfaith Relations in Muslim Tradition* (Cambridge: Cambridge University Press, 2003). Both authors include in their discussions variations across and within the different schools of law. However, these studies also have limitations for historical analysis; they tend to draw on opinions, positions, and sources from a span of centuries to characterize, in the case of Fattal, the legal status of dhimmis in the Islamic world from 622 to 1517 or, in the case of Friedmann, to investigate the "ethos" of tolerance and coercion in traditional Islam, providing only limited guidance for understanding juridical developments in sociohistorical context.

the construction of bridges, and the lighting of signals for Muslim combatants. They were not to injure or strike a Muslim or reveal points of vulnerability to their enemies. The treaty also established the security of churches, required that the beating of clappers (*nāqūs*, pl. *nawāqīs*) not take place before or during the Muslim call to prayer, and prohibited the display of banners and the carrying of arms in the celebration of feasts.[22]

Albrecht Noth also compares the *shurūṭ ʿUmariyya* or "ordinances of ʿUmar" with early examples of surrender treaties but does not find the differences to be significant. He argues that the few ordinances with no parallels in surrender treaties (such as those having to do with dress) derived from the immediate postconquest period, perhaps even the period of ʿUmar ibn al-Khattab's rule, although he explicitly avoids drawing conclusions about the date of the text's composition.[23]

Mark R. Cohen, who has examined "approximately thirty specimens of the "Pact of ʿUmar" in medieval Arabic sources," argues that the literary form of the text follows that of a petition rather than a surrender treaty. In his view, the text is a "pseudoepigraphic invention" that grew out of the conquest treaties but "incorporates features that are characteristic, not of the conquest situation, but of the administrative procedures of the developed Muslim state, wherein decrees were issued in response to petitions." The date of the text remains unfixed; Cohen notes that al-Shafiʿi's treatment of the status of dhimmis and al-Mutawakkil's decrees suggest awareness or promotion of stipulations similar to the "Pact of ʿUmar" in the early ninth century, but he finds the earliest example of the text with its characteristic elements in Abu Bakr al-Khallal's (d. 923) collection of the opinions of Ahmad ibn Hanbal (d. 855).[24]

Milka Levy-Rubin, following Fattal and Cohen, situates the invention of the "Pact of ʿUmar" in the postconquest period. She reads the text as the

---

22. Fattal, *Statut légal*, 60–69.

23. Albrecht Noth, "Problems of Differentiation between Muslims and Non-Muslims: Re-reading the Ordinances of ʿUmar (al-Shurut al-ʿUmariyya)," in *Muslims and Others in Early Islamic Society*, ed. Robert Hoyland (Aldershot: Ashgate, 2004), 103–124.

24. Mark R. Cohen, *Under Crescent and Cross* (Princeton, NJ: Princeton University Press, 1994), 55–57; Cohen, "What Was the Pact of ʿUmar?," *Jerusalem Studies in Arabic and Islam* 23 (1999): 100–133 (quotation, 128); al-Khallal, *Ahkam ahl al-milal min al-jamaʿ li-masaʾil al-imam Ahmad ibn Hanbal*, ed. Kisrawi Hasan (Beirut: Dar al-Kutub al-ʿIlmiyya, 1993), 357–359. Matthias Lehmann has also revisited the debate about the "Pact of ʿUmar." He considers the text to be a legal fiction (based on capitulation treaties) that has the form of a model treaty rather than a petition. See Matthias Lehmann, "Islamic Legal Consultation and the Jewish-Muslim 'Convivencia,'" *Jewish Studies Quarterly* 6 (1999): 25–54.

product of an effort in the eighth and early ninth centuries to establish an agreed-on "uniform set of regulations applicable to all *dhimmīs* living under Muslim rule" that would override all the previous diverse and outmoded conquest agreements. The effort emerged out of protracted experience of coexistence and amid burgeoning juridical debates about the social and legal status of dhimmis and resulted in various formulations, including two by the eminent jurists Abu Yusuf and al-Shafi'i, as well as the "Pact of 'Umar." At the core of the "Pact of 'Umar" and more evident than in the other two formulations are the restrictions about *ghiyār* (distinguishing marks) that symbolize the social subordination of dhimmis and that Levy-Rubin finds rooted in Sasanian concepts, values, and status symbols. The assertion of such restrictions began with the caliph 'Umar ibn 'Abd al-'Aziz and found fuller expression in the set of restrictions promulgated by al-Mutawwakil. In Levy-Rubin's opinion, al-Mutawwakil's restrictions may have followed, rather than preceded, formulation of the text of the "Pact of 'Umar." In any case, from al-Mutawwakil's reign forward, she argues, the "Pact of 'Umar" "acquired priority" and became "canonic."[25]

All the discussion centered on the dating, form, and dissemination of the basic text of the "Pact of 'Umar" is pertinent to, but cannot resolve, the matter of its application as a legal standard and its usefulness for understanding relations between Muslims and dhimmis. To some extent I am writing against a conception of the pact as a universally agreed-on and applied code and against the relevance of the pact for understanding law and society in al-Andalus in the Umayyad period. To turn briefly to the evidence of al-Andalus, the recorded text of a surrender treaty in al-Andalus between 'Abd al-'Aziz ibn Musa and the Christian lord of Murcia, Theodemir, dated 713, is simple in its terms and in this way appears remote from the extant versions of the "Pact of 'Umar" (as one might expect from the arguments originating with Tritton). The text guarantees the lives of the men and women of the seven towns under Theodemir's control and promises that the inhabitants "will not be coerced in matters of religion, their churches will not be burned, nor will sacred objects be taken from the realm." In exchange, Theodemir "will not give shelter to fugitives, nor to our enemies, nor encourage any protected person to fear us, nor conceal news of our enemies. He and [each of] his men shall [also] pay one dinar every year, together with four measures of wheat, four measures of barley, four liquid measures

---

25. Levy-Rubin, *Non-Muslims in the Early Islamic Empire*, 68 (quotation); she notes that if the *isnāds* (chains of transmission) are reliable, the text may have existed in some form in the mid-eighth century, but it was not yet established as canonical (61–62).

of concentrated fruit juice, four liquid measures of vinegar, four of honey, and four of olive oil. Slaves must each pay half of this amount."[26]

Andalusi historical texts provide narrative evidence that treaties such as that between Theodemir and ʿAbd al-ʿAziz ibn Musa, that between the Visigothic prince Artabas and the conqueror Tariq ibn Ziyad (reportedly confirmed by the caliph al-Walid), or those stipulating the terms of capitulation of Cordoba and other cities were abrogated. Treaty arrangements in al-Andalus, contracted between individuals, could be, and were, renegotiated. Interpretations of how modes of submission applied in specific circumstances were subject to debate, and adjudication took place on a case-by-case basis. Much of the legal discourse that pertains to dhimmis centers on matters of individual Muslim-dhimmi interaction. In evaluating the meaning of protected legal status it is important to investigate, alongside stipulations presented by treaties or by official decrees, the jurisprudence regarding Christians and Jews and their relations with Muslims that developed over the centuries after the conquests and, to the extent possible, accounts of legal decisions and practice. Well beyond the mid-ninth century, jurists expressed legal opinions that were part of a process of negotiation and contestation in the interpretation of dhimma. It is important to note that Maliki jurists of the ninth and tenth centuries, in the texts I have examined, do not refer to the "Pact of ʿUmar" or shurūṭ ʿUmariyya (in this regard the text does not appear to be "canonic"), nor do they detail comparably specific terms of any other surrender treaty or contract of protection between Muslims and Christians and Jews.[27] They do occasionally refer to statements by ʿUmar

---

26. Translation by Olivia R. Constable, "The Treaty of Tudmir," in *Medieval Iberia: Readings from Christian, Muslim, and Jewish Sources*, ed. Olivia Remie Constable (Philadelphia: University of Pennsylvania Press, 1997), 37–38; Arabic text: al-Dabbi, *Bughyat al-multamis fi ta'rikh rijal ahl al-Andalus*, ed. F. Codera and J. Ribera, *Bibliotheca Arabico-Hispana 3* (Madrid: Josephum de Rojas, 1885), 259.

27. Mark Cohen, "What Was the Pact of ʿUmar?," 121–122, points out that the Zahiri jurist Ibn Hazm included versions of the "Pact of ʿUmar" in *Kitab al-muhalla* and in *Maratib al-ʾijma*. Lehmann identifies two references to the shurūṭ ʿUmariyya in two fatwas in al-Wansharisi, *al-Miʿyar al-muʿrib wa-l-jamiʿ al-mughrib* (Rabat: Dar al-Gharb al-Islami, 1981–1983), 2:254–255, 214–253. The older reference comes from an unnamed jurist from Tangier at the turn of the twelfth century. In his response to a question about a Jewish doctor named Ibn Qanbal who reportedly dressed like Muslim notables (or better), the jurist quotes the shurūṭ ʿUmariyya about showing respect for the Muslims and agreeing not to resemble the Muslims in dress and in other ways. The other reference comes from al-Wansharisi himself in his long fatwa on the synagogues of Touat, in which he provides the full text of al-Turtushi's rendition of the "Pact of ʿUmar" (2:237–238). (The shurūṭ quoted by the unnamed jurist and the corresponding passages in the full text do not match exactly; also, al-Wansharisi's version differs slightly from the version in the edition of al-Turtushi's *Siraj al-muluk* [Cairo: Bulaq, 1872], 229–230, translated by Lewis in *Islam* and by Stillman in *Jews of Arab Lands*.) Lehmann, "Islamic Legal Consultation and the Jewish-Muslim 'Convivencia,'" 28–41,

or about the practice of ʿUmar or to the abstract ʿahd al-dhimma, invoke the circumstances of conquest (whether a town was taken by treaty or by force), and address specific issues common to the text of the "Pact of ʿUmar," such as the construction of new churches and synagogues, the public display of religion, and the selling of wine, in a number of juridical contexts, but we should consider their engagement in these matters independently of the template of the "Pact of ʿUmar." This point will be revisited in the conclusion of this book in light of the fuller analysis.

The "Pact of ʿUmar" has become the dominant lens among modern scholars for viewing the status of Christians and Jews in an undifferentiated Islamic world; its paradigmatic use masks a historical complexity that is admittedly elusive. Generally speaking, the legal status of dhimmis must be investigated locally and historically from a variety of types of evidence and vantage points. The approach of this book is to turn away from the question whether the terms of the "Pact of ʿUmar" were applied in al-Andalus between the eighth and eleventh centuries and to investigate how the impulse to define boundaries between Muslims and dhimmis identifiable in the "Pact of ʿUmar" drove the elaboration and complication of legal opinion and the mediation of practice. As Noth writes of the shurūṭ ʿUmariyya: "All these regulations show that Muslims strove to draw a very clear distinction between the spheres of both groups [Muslims and non-Muslims], with the aim of protecting Muslim minorities in a new and alien environment, who had to be careful not to lose their (not yet fully developed) identity."[28] Noth locates the "problem of differentiation" in the immediate postconquest period, but I argue that the "problem" was mutative, became more fully realized in the context of transculturation and conversion and the development of distinct legal traditions, and evolved over centuries in al-Andalus. A "clear

---

discusses both the fifteenth-century case of the synagogues of Touat and the case of a synagogue in tenth-century Cordoba that is enfolded in the fatwa as examples of conflict over the application of the terms of the "Pact of ʿUmar." Al-Wansharisi's citation of al-Turtushi's version of the "Pact of ʿUmar" is evidence for a relatively late application of the text as a standard. The discussion of the Cordoban case suggests, in contrast, a process of working out what capitulation to Muslim rule and the ʿahd al-dhimma allowed or prohibited with regard to the construction or repair of houses of worship (rather than the application of the "Pact of ʿUmar," which is not mentioned in the Cordoban fatwa, as a standard). For further discussion of the fifteenth-century fatwa in its historical context, see John O. Hunwick, "Al-Maghili and the Jews of Tuwat: The Demise of a Community," *Studia Islamica* 61 (1985): 155–183; and Hunwick, "The Rights of *Dhimmīs* to Maintain a Place of Worship: A 15th Century *Fatwā* from Tlemçen," *al-Qantara* 12 (1991): 133–155; for a history of the Jews of Touat, see Jacob Oliel, *Les juifs au Sahara: Le Touat au Moyen Âge* (Paris: CNRS Editions, 1994).

28. Noth, "Problems of Differentiation," 122.

distinction between the spheres of both groups" was an ideal; the evidence of ninth- and tenth-century Maliki legal texts reveals a discursive negotiation of principles of difference and separation in contingent circumstances of social interaction and intimacy between Muslims and dhimmis. Boundary making was an act of engagement with the other, and the "problem" of differentiation looks like a process of accommodation of practice in these sources.

Muslim political and religious authorities defined their leadership and roles in terms of Islam and presided over a conceptually universal Muslim community. At the same time, they asserted authority over a plural society and recognized a political and religious commitment to the welfare of the non-Muslims living under their rule. The act of conquest created a large subject population, and the legal-religious scholars named and created, through their jurisprudence, a new category of people, the *ahl al-dhimma*. The process of determining and articulating the proper way of life for Muslims involved consideration of the rights and obligations of dhimmis and the appropriate forms and limits of interactions between Muslims and dhimmis. What this meant in specific regions and periods has yet to be fully explored. I hope that the effort to focus my study on al-Andalus and this book's concentration on (developing) Maliki law will, in turn, prompt further investigation of the development of law as boundary making among different traditions or madhhabs of Islamic law in different and varied historical contexts. Boundary making differentiated Muslims from non-Muslims (and engaged Muslims with non-Muslims) as part of a process whereby jurists differentiated madhhabs from one another.

The normative quality of much legal-juridical writing directs us to approach the sources creatively as evidence of boundary making and negotiation. These texts are part of a diffuse and multivocal discourse about how to be Muslim and who is and who is not Muslim in a context of cross-confessional interaction, intermarriage, and conversion, or, more broadly, social differentiation and cultural transmutation. Although the process of boundary making strove to separate communities, it in fact involved the recognition and accommodation of new social categories and relationships and multiple roles for individuals.

The anthropologist Fredrik Barth has drawn attention to the importance of social (as opposed to territorial) boundaries for the continuity of ascriptive and exclusive groups (ethnic groups), especially where people of different cultures interact, and his work has profoundly informed subsequent studies of ethnicity and plural societies. As he observes, group identity depends fundamentally on the "dichotomization between members and outsiders." This dichotomization or differentiation involves "criteria and signals

of identification" and also "a structuring of interaction which allows the persistence of cultural differences." Stable interethnic relations thus require prescriptions and proscriptions governing situations of contact to protect or insulate the cultures of the ethnic groups from confrontation or modification. The social boundaries Barth describes are dynamic and adaptable to circumstances and contingencies. They both differentiate and allow for interaction.[29]

Thomas F. Glick and Oriol Pi-Sunyer affirm the importance of the structure of interaction and boundary making for understanding intergroup relations and acculturation in Spanish history in an article published in 1969. They ask and address a series of questions: "What were the mechanisms by which the cultural blocs themselves and the enclaves within them—Muslim, Christian, Jewish—maintained their cultural integrity? What were the rules in each culture governing, for example, change of religion? How receptive was each to learning the other's language (or extirpating it)?"[30]

The dominant direction of cultural change in al-Andalus was toward the adoption of the Arabic language and Arabic-Islamic cultural norms, and Islamic law served as a significant boundary-making mechanism that protected the integrity of the Muslim community from external influences, from acculturation. In Glick and Pi-Sunyer's estimation, the dominant culture bloc in al-Andalus was largely resistant to cultural change, at least in part, because "the acculturation of the indigenous population was sharply structured, the rules for conversion or for coexistence with 'People of the Book' (Christians and Jews, categorized as dhimmis, or protected people) being prescribed by Islamic law."[31]

The structuring of intercommunal relations in al-Andalus was an ongoing process in a context of social change. The concept of dhimma provided a basic framework for understanding and defining intercommunal relations and preceded the Muslim conquest of the Iberian Peninsula; however, the vast corpus of legal opinion pertaining to intercommunal relations and relationships developed only in the context of proximity, interaction, transculturation, and conversion in the following centuries. Boundary making was

---

29. Fredrik Barth, introduction to *Ethnic Groups and Boundaries: The Social Organization of Cultural Difference*, ed. Fredrik Barth (Boston: Little, Brown and Company, 1969), 9–38 (quotations and paraphrasing, 14–16).

30. Thomas F. Glick and Oriol Pi-Sunyer, "Acculturation as an Explanatory Concept in Spanish History," *Comparative Studies in Society and History* 11 (1969): 150.

31. Glick and Pi-Sunyer, "Acculturation as an Explanatory Concept in Spanish History," 142.

an extended, extensive, and diffuse process. Ninth- and tenth-century jurisprudence developed as an engagement with social transformation, and the
legal-juridical literature is diverse and contradictory; in many ways the indefinite qualities of Islamic law and jurisprudence in this period contributed to the predominant direction of cultural change and conversion in
al-Andalus, and the flexibility, permeability, and refinability (and contest-
ability) of boundaries were as important as the structure they provided for
understanding social and cultural developments.

The term "Islamic law" may thus be misleading; it should not be understood as a legal code universally and uniformly applied by agents of the regime or the religious establishment when it is applied to al-Andalus in the
three centuries after the Islamic conquest. In this period jurisprudence was
an emerging field developed by religious scholars largely independent of
rulers in informal association with one another through personal connections,
networks of students, and generations of transmitted opinions and commentary. Scholars in al-Andalus, as part of a larger community of Muslim
scholars who actively engaged in collecting, transmitting, offering, and contesting legal opinions about how to worship and live as Muslims, played an
essential role in integrating the Muslim communities of al-Andalus, the
Maghrib, and the central Islamic lands. Judges (appointed by rulers) acted in
response to particular complaints and often consulted jurists before render-
ing legal decisions. Legal-juridical consensus informed and was informed by
the administration of justice and was part of the process of discussion and
contestation among scholars who were interested in determining the Islamic "way." As jurists and judges responded to challenges and demands
posed by specific individuals and relationships, they participated in negotiation with (often unwitting) boundary testers, commonly Muslims but also
Christians and Jews. Jurists and judges considered extenuating circumstances
and conditions, as well as exceptions. Given the legal complications of interfaith marriage and conversion and the multiple occasions for interaction
and engagement among Muslims, Christians, and Jews, legal boundary making was contingent and associational, flexible and negotiable. Jurists considered matters of formal law, such as crimes and punishments and contracts
and legal obligations, but their purview also extended to matters of informal
interaction, such as manners and etiquette, and into the domain of symbolic
differentiation. The ruler, for his part, played a role in the administration
of justice through his appointment of judges and (from the mid-ninth century) official jurisconsults (fuqahāʾ mushāwarūn; s. faqīh mushāwar) and sometimes had a political interest and influence in judicial outcomes. The ruler
also promulgated occasional edicts regarding matters of public concern and

governed according to administrative conventions and standards developed primarily at court.

The authority asserted over individuals and communities by rulers and by the legal-religious scholars is idealized and exaggerated in the texts they produced, and it is hard to assess how it was actually experienced across time and place. Some of the insights of Postcolonial theory about the negotiation and transformation of power and culture in a context of domination and resistance inform my perspective on the evidence, which bears in mind that the definition and exercise of power in the premodern Islamic context was markedly different from and much less effective than that of the modern colonial context. One may observe that in the process of asserting Islamic rule and dominion (or idealized "hegemony") the dominant elite emphasized alterity and dedicated efforts to the production of cultural differentiation.[32] If identities are multiple (there are many forms of identification), social, and hierarchical, the definition of "us" as opposed to "them" produced not a simple binary opposition but a shifting hierarchy of communal references and "belongings," some articulated by terms such as *dhimmī*, *mawlā*, and *muwallad* (to be discussed), others less definite.

One could argue that the space between the culture(s) of the conquerors and the culture(s) of the conquered became a space for cultural "hybridity" without connoting cultural synthesis.[33] The assertion of hegemony by the conqueror transformed the culture of both the conquered and the conqueror and contributed to a multiplication of cultural forms and social

---

32. These observations are based on Homi Bhabha's work, in particular, the introduction and chapters 1, 2, and 6 in *The Location of Culture* (London: Routledge, 1994); and Etienne Balibar, *Politics and the Other Scene*, trans. Christine Jones, James Swenson, and Chris Turner (London: Verso, 2002), chaps. 3 and 4. On the application of Postcolonial theory to the medieval context, see Jeffrey Jerome Cohen, ed., *The Postcolonial Middle Ages* (New York: St. Martin's Press, 2000); Ananya Jahanara Kabir and Deanne Williams, eds., *Postcolonial Approaches to the European Middle Ages* (Cambridge: Cambridge University Press, 2005); Bruce Holsinger, "Medieval Studies, Postcolonial Studies, and the Genealogies of Critique," *Speculum* 77 (2002): 1195–1227; and Nadia R. Altschul, "Postcolonialism and the Study of the Middle Ages," *History Compass* 6 (2008): 588–606. On the application of Postcolonial theory to medieval Iberia, see Altschul, "The Future of Postcolonial Approaches to Medieval Iberian Studies," *Journal of Medieval Iberian Studies* 1 (2007): 5–17. Altschul, arguing against the idea that Postcolonial theory is anachronistic in medieval studies, explains that "postcolonialism engages with the myriad effects and interstices produced on all sides and between all elements of hierarchically uneven cultural contacts, and is engaged not only with the resistances but also with the collaborations, contradictions and legacies produced by colonial encounters" (7).

33. Ragnhild Johnsrud Zorgati explores issues of cultural change and identity in medieval Spain and the concept of hybridity in "Beyond Boundaries: Islamic and Christian Legal Texts Dealing with Conversion and Mixed Marriages in Medieval Iberia" (Ph.D. dissertation, Faculty of Humanities, University of Oslo, 2007).

diversification in al-Andalus in the ninth and tenth centuries. Conversion contributed to close interaction between Muslims and non-Muslims, and the incorporation of converts and their descendants into the reticulated Muslim community further stimulated social and cultural diversity. Engagement with the other and the process of differentiation were not unidirectional and not comfortable. In this context, as in others, power relations were ambivalent and ambiguous, and we can recognize that the words and actions of political and legal-religious authorities in al-Andalus reflect an anxiety about social and cultural change. The efforts of rulers and scholars to control social relations through limits and restrictions (and force, if necessary), using the language of religion, shared community, and normative practice, were a response to perceived and real disorder and danger.

This book may be said to undertake the project proposed by Jeffrey Jerome Cohen to "destabilize hegemonic identities . . . by detailing historical contingency." It treats Islam in this period as he would Christianity in medieval studies as "a conflicted nexus of discourses, lacking uniformity and full cohesion, mutable over time."[34] The interest in contingency and the delineation of discourses encompasses consideration of the authority of the regime and judges and jurists and of their engagement with those over whom they had authority. The focus, because of the source and nature of much of the (limited) evidence, tends to be from the perspective of the conqueror, but boundary making is part of the dynamic engagement between the assertion of hegemony and resistance to it. This is often played out, or at least represented, in terms of personal relationships and interpersonal practice.

A few observations can be made about how the regime defined insiders and outsiders and how jurists addressed intercommunal relations. In both contexts the focus of attention was the actions of individuals and their relations to others. The ruler defined membership in and integration into the political community in terms of loyalty to himself, and because he represented, and was responsible for, the unity and integrity of the Muslim community, political opposition was equated with religious deviance, and religious deviation from the consensus of the Andalusi ʿulamaʾ (as upheld by the ruler) with political rebellion. Boundary making by Muslim jurists was informed by the fundamental premise that Muslims were distinct from Christians and Jews by their recognition of the Qurʾan as God's revelation and Muhammad as God's Messenger. The way jurists articulated boundaries,

---

34. Jeffrey Jerome Cohen, "Introduction: Midcolonial," in Cohen, *Postcolonial Middle Ages*, 1–17 (quotations, 7).

however, commonly had little to do with belief—they directed themselves to matters of ritual and everyday practice and interaction. Many of the legal opinions I discuss in this book have to do with the limits of engagement and personal interaction between Muslims and non-Muslims. Jurists identified people in terms of legal categories and capacities and investigated legal obligations between individuals. Questions about kinship, clientage, and neighborly obligations between Muslims and non-Muslims described a network of social relationships that extended outward from the most immediate relationships of the family. Legal opinions addressing matters between Muslims and non-Muslims often had to do with social obligation and social positioning as much as with the formal enactment of law (such as the contracting of a marriage or the distribution of an inheritance).

Jurists opined on matters of social mores and etiquette, conceiving of Islamic law as an embodiment of "being Muslim." Their opinions conjure up social roles and conventions, a system of identity signifiers and modes. Erving Goffman's insight about the way the self is defined through engagement with others in a variety of contexts and roles directs our attention to identity as social practice and suggests how intercommunal relations could be understood or experienced as the playing out of roles. With this insight, one may more readily appreciate the dislocation experienced by individuals and social groups in contexts of personal change (such as conversion), social differentiation, and transculturation. As Goffman describes, individuals put together clues about other people that guide them in their own behavior. Individuals are able to assess appearances and manners in any given situation because they have stereotyped expectations and because "performance is socialized," and they act accordingly for the same reasons.[35] In a sense, by using the evidence of the Islamic legal sources, we can approach the world of the everyday from another direction than Goffman—jurists addressed questions that had to do with interactions between individuals and contributed, in the process, to the socialization of practice. The involvement of jurists in matters of appearance and manners, addressing questions about how certain types of individuals should act, for example, at a funeral, and what they should say in a variety of social situations, for example, in the exchange of greetings or on occasions of condolences, is part of the socialization of expectation and performance. In the context of social and cultural change, when signs of identity could be unfamiliar, inconsistent, and contradictory, their interest and involvement reflected and expressed the

---

35. Erving Goffman, *The Presentation of Self in Everyday Life* (Garden City, NY: Doubleday, 1959).

elaboration of orienting norms that facilitated communication among communities.

Pierre Bourdieu's concept of "habitus" provides a way to characterize this socialization process. As jurists addressed questions having to do with roles, manners, and signifiers of cultural value, they contributed recursively to the shaping of the hegemonic culture, the evolving Muslim habitus—the predispositions and habits that structured how people lived and assessed the social and cultural values of others. His conception of a "linguistic habitus" is particularly relevant to the analysis later in this book of how jurists discussed proper speech and conduct.[36]

The way Muslims in al-Andalus understood themselves to be Muslim and different from Christians and Jews was not simply a straightforward matter of belief and ritual practice or adherence to Islamic law but a matter of culture and social practice that was situational and associational. Anthony Cohen observes that although the boundary a community presents to the outside world may be symbolically simple, the boundary of a community from within is symbolically complex and an object of internal discourse. The simple boundary of the "public face" defines community in a way that "incorporates and encloses difference." Members participate in the conceptualization and symbolization of their community boundary in terms of their own experiences.[37] In Umayyad al-Andalus boundaries between "us" and "them" were understood and recognized in simple symbolic terms— "we" (Muslim men) go to the mosque on Fridays, but "they" (Christians and Jews) do not—but they were also expressed and understood in contextual and symbolic terms in different ways by various individuals. Differences in conceptualization and symbolization of community boundaries proliferated in the context of conversion with diversification of social categories and shifting markers of social status. The discourse about community boundaries (about identity) recorded in the Andalusi legal literature is part of a larger discourse (largely inaccessible to us) that the jurists participated in and tried to shape.

Al-Andalus offers certain advantages as a locus of study of how Muslim political and religious authorities represented and responded to cultural

36. Pierre Bourdieu, *Language and Symbolic Power*, ed. John B. Thompson, trans. Gino Raymond and Matthew Adamson (Cambridge, MA: Harvard University Press, 1991); see Thompson's introduction for concise explications of "habitus" (12–14) and "linguistic habitus" (17–22).

37. Anthony P. Cohen, "Of Symbols and Boundaries; or, Does Erties's Greatcoat Hold the Key?" in *Symbolising Boundaries: Identity and Diversity in British Cultures*, ed. Anthony P. Cohen (Manchester: Manchester University Press, 1986), 1–19 (paraphrase of Cohen's summation on 13).

change and conversion in the first centuries of Islam, how they participated in the structuring of Muslim practice and Muslim interactions with non-Muslims, and how they interpreted dhimma in a period of formative legal development because of its discrete political history and its almost exclusive adherence to the developing Maliki madhhab. The focus of this book is the period of Umayyad rule in large part because the dynamism of social and cultural change in the formative period of legal development generated a range and variety of legal opinions and positions, and because the period of Umayyad rule provided a more or less stable political structure for the jurists engaged in boundary making. The fragmentation of political authority under the *ṭā'ifa* (party) rulers that followed Umayyad rule, the subsequent introduction and consolidation of Almoravid and Almohad rule, frontier warfare, and the impact of Christian conquests all add further complications to this kind of investigation.

The challenge for the historian working with legal-juridical texts that claim universal authority is to read the universal in relation to the local. Al-Andalus may be regarded as an extension and local field of interpretation of Arabic-Islamic culture that emanated from the political-cultural centers and nodes of learning in the East. Religious and juridical scholars from the peninsula pursued learning in the Maghrib, Egypt, and the Hijaz, and then transmitted this learning to their circles of students back home. Andalusi jurists in the first half of the ninth century, notably Yahya ibn Yahya (d. 848), 'Isa ibn Dinar (d. 827), 'Abd al-Malik ibn Habib (d. 853), and Muhammad al-'Utbi (d. 869), in consultation with contemporaries elsewhere (most commonly Sahnun ibn Sa'id in Qayrawan), and the students who followed them in succeeding generations promoted the legal opinions of the Medinan authority Malik ibn Anas as a source for developing jurisprudence and the legal tradition of al-Andalus. They did so by transmitting Malik's opinions, as heard from his students, and by using his opinions (and those of his students), sometimes with reference to the Qur'an and the example of the Prophet and his companions, to articulate legal questions and formulate positions. Their efforts reflect an early stage in a process of developing and establishing a legal tradition that eventually would acquire a hermeneutical logic and involve a systematic ramification of juridical subjects. This process was related to, in part derived from, and in part shaped social concerns and a social experience.

Our understanding of the relationship between legal opinions and social life informs how we interpret the extant texts from this period as a source for boundary making and intercommunal relations in al-Andalus. It might be argued that Malik's opinions are external to and are not generated

by the social realities of al-Andalus. However, opinions taught, actively discussed, and evaluated in al-Andalus engaged Andalusi jurists at least in part
because of a perceived social relevance. In the eighth century Malik (who
lived in Medina) and his students addressed questions arising from the experience of Muslims in Syria and Egypt, both with predominantly Christian populations. These questions were relevant in al-Andalus a century
later. More significantly, Andalusi students and scholars actively consulted
Malik's students about questions pertinent to their legal interests and social
environment.

An anecdote in the biography of Muhammad ibn Bashir, *qāḍī* (judge) of
Cordoba under the amir al-Hakam I (r. 796–822), illustrates how Andalusi
jurists transmitted and applied Malik's opinions in al-Andalus. We are told
that whenever a difference of opinion arose between the qadi (Ibn Bashir)
and the *fuqahā'* (jurists), or a complicated matter required elucidation, the
qadi (who had once studied with Malik) used to write to ʿAbd al-Rahman
ibn al-Qasim (d. 806) and ʿAbd Allah ibn Wahb (Malik's disciples) in Egypt.
In this connection the text cites a story the prominent Andalusi jurist Yahya
ibn Yahya told his son ʿUbayd Allah (who also became a notable jurist).
According to Yahya, Ibn Bashir sent him to Egypt to consult with Ibn al-
Qasim about certain legal questions (*masā'il*; s. *mas'ala*) and also Muhammad
ibn Khalid ibn Martinil (d. 835 or 838). He arrived in Egypt first, asked the
questions, and wrote down Ibn al-Qasim's responses. After Muhammad ibn
Khalid arrived (having gone to Medina first) and met with Ibn al-Qasim,
the two Andalusis compared notes. Yahya found that Ibn al-Qasim had responded differently to each of them. He sought out Ibn al-Qasim again and
explained the situation: "If we go back home with different answers, they
will doubt our transmission from you, and the judge will have to write to
you again." Ibn al-Qasim called for Muhammad ibn Khalid and told him,
"When I replied to your questions, I was preoccupied—rewrite the responses according to what Yahya wrote down." And so the two returned to
al-Andalus with their answers in agreement.[38] This anecdote describes a process of consultation between Andalusi judges and Maliki authorities in the
East—Ibn Bashir had specific questions he wanted Ibn al-Qasim to address.
We can see how this process of consultation developed into a series of transmissions from Malik's disciples to Andalusi scholars. The story's account of
Yahya's observation of differences between Ibn al-Qasim's responses to

---

38. Al-Khushani, *Kitab al-qudat bi-Qurtuba (Historia de los jueces de Córdoba)*, ed. and trans. (into
Spanish) Julián Ribera (Madrid: Maestre, 1914), Arabic, 62–63; Spanish, 77–79.

him and to Muhammad showcases Yahya's particular attention to the accuracy of his transmission and establishes the authority of the masa'il he discussed and transmitted from Ibn al-Qasim (and reflects apparent divergences in records of legal opinions). Yahya's transmissions of masa'il, of legal questions and responses, from Ibn al-Qasim, in fact, are among our most important sources for the investigation of boundary making in ninth-century al-Andalus.

Ana Fernández Félix has shown how al-ʿUtbi's *Mustakhraja* is important for understanding ninth-century Andalusi society and suggests its relevance to the determination of boundaries between Muslims and dhimmis, informing our perspective on how juridical opinion structures meaning and practice.[39] She considers the main impetus behind al-ʿUtbi's work to be the establishment of Islamic norms of conduct based on the opinions of Malik and his disciples; in this way she sees the text as a form of the structuring of society. Some of the questions and opinions cited in al-ʿUtbi's text are those of fellow Andalusis (notably al-ʿUtbi's teacher Yahya ibn Yahya), men who had tremendous influence in al-Andalus and probably effected the application of these norms.[40] She demonstrates the popularity of al-ʿUtbi's *Mustakhraja* from the ninth century to the middle of the twelfth century, a period when, along with Malik's *Muwatta'* and Sahnun's *Mudawwana*, it was one of the essential works studied and consulted by Andalusi legists.[41]

The relevance of the legal opinions of Malik and his disciples can be inferred from the interest of the Andalusi jurists in seeking them and their engagement in the process of collecting and transmitting them (with questions asked and answered). The radiation of transmitted opinions from town to town and the enduring popularity of transmissions across generations suggest continued relevance into the tenth century. Our reading of the legal opinions as socially and historically relevant is informed by an understanding of the relationship between the paradigmatic modes of structuring the legal opinions represent and the patterning of social relations in time and space. Giddens's theory of structuration emphasizes that "rules" do not exist

---

39. Ana Fernández Félix, *Cuestiones legales del islam temprano: La ʿUtbiyya y el proceso de formación de la sociedad islámica Andalusi* (Madrid: Consejo Superior de Investigaciones Científicas, 2003); chapters 5 and 6 and the appendixes specifically identify masa'il in al-ʿUtbi's text relevant to al-Andalus and to the subject of dhimmis.

40. Fernández Félix, *Cuestiones legales del islam temprano*, 410–413; see also 20–21, 118–120, and appendix B, "Cuestiones planteadas por alfaquies Andalusis y sus *aqwāl*," 505–548.

41. Fernández Félix, *Cuestiones legales del islam temprano*, 199–257, 282–294.

independently of social practices but are reproduced recursively: "Structure exists, as time-space presence, only in its instantiations in such practices and as memory traces orienting the conduct of knowledgeable human agents."[42] The evidence for the currency of opinions and texts as they are reproduced, discussed, and challenged suggests relevance to and engagement with social practice. Locating the problems discussed in the masa'il in the Andalusi historical context is, of course, important to our assessment of historical relevance, and there are enough points of contact with other genres of historical evidence to support the argument that conversion, transculturation, intermarriage, and interrelations were matters of compelling interest and practice. Opinions that appear in the masa'il can be related to fatwas more firmly located in time and place, and the subjects of the masa'il can be identified with circumstances and sometimes situations described in other sources, for example, the martyrologies.

The dynamic role of practice in the intersection between juridical opinion and everyday life is apparent in legal boundary testing. One might expect legal boundary testing in a context of multiple legal systems (Islamic, Christian, Jewish) and statuses (legal status in Islamic law depends on whether one is Muslim or dhimmi, adult or a minor, male or female, slave or free, or mentally competent or incompetent). Boundary testing involves cases on the margins where jurisdictions are unclear or more than one legal concept may apply. For example, what if the husband of a Christian marriage converts to Islam (or both spouses convert), and part of the bridal dower (ṣadāq) included wine and pigs?[43] This question highlights the fact that the convert has crossed from one legal system to another. What may be legal in a Christian marriage may not be in an Islamic marriage. We do not know how likely it is that wine and pigs were part of a dower, but they were anathema in Islam and would invalidate a marriage contract between two Muslims—hence the matter for discussion. A marriage could be invalidated by conversion if it were the Christian or Jewish wife who converted and the husband did not. As Maya Shatzmiller points out, the legal discussion appended to tenth-century Cordoban conversion formularies is primarily concerned with how conversion might affect the status of a marriage. It was up to the notary to determine whether the marriage should be confirmed or annulled, and his decision depended on the religious status of the spouse,

---

42. Giddens, *Constitution of Society*, chap. 1, "Elements of the Theory of Structuration," 1–40 (quotation, 17).

43. Al-Qayrawani, *Nawadir wa-ziyadat*, 3:339–340, 4:594–96; Ibn Rushd, *Bayan*, 4:185–186; Sahnun, *Mudawwana*, 2:297.

whether he or she was free or slave, and whether the marriage was between individuals within the prohibited degrees defined by Islam.[44]

The process of the systematization of law structured society and culture in ways ranging from fundamental to subtly nuanced. Questions posed and answered in legal-juridical works of the ninth and tenth centuries were occasions for early legal casuistry; in some instances issues seem contrived to test the boundaries of legal concepts.[45] The impression of casuistry is strongest when questions and opinions about a legal matter are pursued to the utmost limits. This might be the result of the prodding of a particular questioner, like Sahnun ibn Sa'id in his *Mudawwana*, or the effect of a combination of multiple legal positions under one rubric, as when Ibn Abi Zayd al-Qayrawani devotes a few pages in *al-Nawadir wa-l-ziyadat* to accusations of adultery under the following circumstances: when the wife is a child, a Christian, deaf, blind, or a slave; or when the husband is a slave, a child, an old man, impotent, a eunuch, a mute, or a fool.[46]

Baber Johansen argues that casuistry is "a way of reconciling the requirements of practical life with those of legal doctrine."[47] In his view, casuistry is an outgrowth of and contributes to "a process of social differentiation that renders the universal validity of norms socially implausible."[48] Johansen provides the example of a shift from a universal norm, land tenancy based on contract, to a detailed and refined casuistry in which the variety of forms of land tenure that had emerged during the classical period are treated as particular instances of a new legal concept of rent-yielding property for the benefit of new elites.[49]

Johansen's focus is on the classical (tenth to twelfth centuries) and post-classical periods of Islamic law, but we can apply his approach of examining

---

44. Maya Shatzmiller, "Marriage, Family, and the Faith: Women's Conversion to Islam," *Journal of Family History* 21 (1996): 235–266.

45. The discussion of casuistry here owes much to Baber Johansen, "Casuistry: Between Legal Concept and Social Praxis," *Islamic Law and Society* 2 (1995): 135–156.

46. Al-Qayrawani, *Nawadir wa-ziyadat*, 5:345–347. *Al-Nawadir wa-l-ziyadat* is a work for specialists, for the fuqaha', in contrast to the same author's more famous and concise *al-Risala*, a manual of instruction for Muslims on religious obligations: "What tongues should say, hearts believe, and limbs perform"; al-Qayrawani, *La Risala; ou, Epître sur les éléments du dogme et de la loi de l'islam selon le rite Malikite*, Arabic text with French translation by Leon Bercher (Algiers: Editions Populaires de l'Armée, 1968). Both genres of legal writing express an interest in defining, refining, shaping, and clarifying what it means to be a Muslim.

47. Johansen, "Casuistry," 149.

48. Johansen, "Casuistry," 133.

49. Johansen, "Casuistry," 141–142.

casuistry in both legal and social contexts when we look at ninth- and tenth-century legal-juridical texts. Casuistry as boundary testing and exception making is identified with many of the legal questions having to do with Muslims and their relations with dhimmis or with liminal persons, such as converts and apostates. The legal questions about individuals on the margins or straddling legal categories and social roles have social significance in their affirmation of boundaries, on the one hand, and their accommodation of nuances, on the other. Casuistry grew out of and contributed to the process of identity differentiation in an increasingly complex social environment and provided room in which to maneuver.

Many of the distinctive qualities of the Arabic legal texts will become apparent in specific examples discussed in this book; these examples convey some of the contexts of intercommunal interaction and the significance of boundaries and their breaching for all the communities involved. Here I will identify and briefly describe only the most important legal-juridical sources for my study. The most important are the compendia of masa'il (questions and answers about specific issues): al-'Utbi's *Mustakhraja*, Sahnun's *Mudawwana*, and Ibn Abi Zayd al-Qayrawani's *Nawadir wa-ziyadat*. The commentary on al-'Utbi's *Mustakhraja* by Ibn Rushd (d. 1126) (grandfather of the philosopher of the same name) titled *al-Bayan wa-l-tahsil* and another work of his, *al-Muqaddamat al-mumahhadat*, represent a later systematization of the law. Ibn Rushd was a Maliki jurist and qadi in Cordoba, and his *Bayan* is particularly useful (not only for providing al-'Utbi's text) because his commentary includes juridical opinions from a variety of sources, including citations of works no longer extant, and delineates the issues at hand and the differences and discrepancies among the early generations of jurists.

Of the three main compendia, *al-Mustakhraja*, *al-Mudawwana*, and *al-Nawadir wa-l-ziyadat*, al-'Utbi's text is the most relevant for my investigation of ninth-century al-Andalus and is also, in its current form, the most accessible, in part because of Ibn Rushd's commentary and in part thanks to the work of Ana Fernández Félix.[50] The text is organized into books or chapters on specific legal subjects (starting with ritual purification, ritual prayer, and burial rites); each book contains masa'il from Malik and his students according to distinct chains of transmission.[51] Fernández Félix calculates

---

50. Fernández Félix, *Cuestiones legales*, provides a wealth of information about al-'Utbi, his work, his teachers, his peers, his students, the transmission of his text, and its place in the development of Maliki law that is invaluable for anyone working with *al-Mustakhraja*.

51. See Fernández Félix, *Cuestiones legales*, 115–198, for a description and analysis of the organization of al-'Utbi's text and identification of chains of transmission and individual transmitters.

that 72.49 percent of the masa'il in *al-Mustakhraja* follow one of four chains of transmission: (1) Malik to Ibn al-Qasim to Sahnun to al-ʿUtbi; (2) Malik to Ashhab and Ibn Nafiʿ to Sahnun to al-ʿUtbi; (3) Ibn al-Qasim to ʿIsa ibn Dinar to al-ʿUtbi; and (4) Ibn al-Qasim to Yahya ibn Yahya to al-ʿUtbi. The chapter or book on burial rites, for example, includes material from eleven chains of transmission. The Andalusis ʿIsa ibn Dinar, Yahya ibn Yahya, and Muhammad ibn Khalid (who also transmits questions to and answers from Sahnun), as well as Musa ibn Muʿawiya (of Ifriqiyya) and Asbagh ibn al-Faraj (of Fustat and Medina), all transmit questions to and answers from Malik's student Ibn al-Qasim to al-ʿUtbi. The chapter on burial rites also records the Andalusi ʿAbd al-Malik ibn al-Hassan's questions to Ibn Wahb (another student of Malik's) and his replies. The opinions of Malik's Egyptian and Medinan students were a fundamental supplement to Malik's opinions for Andalusi scholars, addressing issues not treated by Malik and occasionally expressing alternative views.[52] A preponderance of masa'il in al-ʿUtbi's *Mustakhraja*, it should be noted, present responses from the Egyptian Ibn al-Qasim, derived through the process of transmission illustrated in the anecdote about Yahya ibn Yahya and Muhammad ibn Khalid and their meetings with him. In the competition among Andalusi transmitters and followers of three preeminent disciples of Malik, Ibn al-Qasim, Ashhab ibn ʿAbd al-ʿAziz al-Amiri, and ʿAbdallah ibn Wahb, the first came to dominate, in part because of the authority of Sahnun's *Mudawwana* (which transmits Malik's opinions from Ibn al-Qasim and Ibn al-Qasim's opinions) and in part because of the prestige of Yahya ibn Yahya.[53] The masa'il recorded by Yahya ibn Yahya and the other Andalusis, such as Muhammad ibn Khalid and ʿIsa ibn Dinar, were probably informed by experience and conform to our composite understanding of the Andalusi social context. Al-ʿUtbi conveyed the masa'il he collected to his peers and students through his transmissions and teachings, and his students imparted them and exercised their

---

52. The opinions thus transmitted from Malik do not derive from *al-Muwatta'* and have little relation to this text (transmitted by the Andalusi Yahya ibn Yahya). *Al-Muwatta'* is anomalous in the way it situates (even subordinates) statements of Malik's *ra'y* (legal opinion) in relation to the Qur'an and hadith. Scholars have different ideas about why this text is so different from the masa'il texts; see Norman Calder, *Studies in Early Muslim Jurisprudence* (Oxford: Oxford University Press, 1993), 1–38; and Yassin Dutton, *The Origins of Islamic Law: The Qur'an, the Muwatta' and Madinan ʿAmal* (Richmond, Surrey: Curzon Press, 1999), 26–27.

53. Maribel Fierro, "Proto-Malikis, Malikis, and Reformed Malikis in al-Andalus," in *The Islamic School of Law: Evolution, Devolution, and Progress*, ed. Peri Bearman, Rudolph Peters, and Frank E. Vogel (Cambridge, MA: Islamic Legal Studies Program of Harvard University, Harvard University Press, 2005), 65–66.

learning in the different towns in al-Andalus where they resided, taught, and perhaps served as judges, as part of their engagement with local practice. This book will focus on the masa'il identified with Andalusi jurists as evidence of their participation in boundary making.

Although Sahnun and Ibn Abi Zayd were based in Qayrawan, the Qayrawani and Cordoban branches of Maliki jurisprudence were closely integrated in the ninth century and, according to Ibn Khaldun, "shunned" the Iraqi branch (an exaggeration).[54] Sahnun, the leading proponent of Maliki jurisprudence of his generation, informed and was informed by juridical developments throughout this Maliki network. Almost every Andalusi who left the peninsula to study went to Qayrawan, and Sahnun was often consulted by Andalusi jurists, including Ibn Habib and Yahya ibn Yahya. Sahnun's *Mudawwana* reads as a series of hypothetical questions, often starting "What is your opinion if." His text is the product of a reworking of a text of the same name compiled by Asad ibn al-Furat (d. 828). Asad asked Ibn al-Qasim to answer a series of questions according to Malik's opinion; Sahnun returned to Ibn al-Qasim with Asad's *Mudawwana*, and the two went over the questions and responses, making changes, and the text evolved further. Sahnun's entries have a casuistic quality, sometimes in the questions asked and especially in the way follow-up questions develop in a series, addressing multiple ramifications.

Ibn Abi Zayd conceived of *al-Nawadir wa-l-ziyadat* as an expansion of Sahnun's *Mudawwana*, and his work brings together the opinions of Malik, his disciples, and later generations of Maliki authorities. His text presents subject headings (sometimes in the form of questions) followed by the opinions of authorities, often in the form of excerpts from their works or as recorded in the works of others. For example, Ibn Abi Zayd presents Sahnun's opinions as transmitted in the writings of his son, Ibn Sahnun (*Kitab ibn Sahnun*), Yahya ibn Yahya's questions to Ibn al-Qasim and his replies, as found in al-*'Utbiyya* (*al-Mustakhraja*), and Ibn Habib's opinions according to his own work, al-*Wadiha*. In this way he pulls together a variety of sources and opinions as a resource and a reference for jurists and judges. His work gives the jurist a range of opinions rather than definitive answers (in contrast to Ibn Rushd, who, in his commentary on al-'Utbi's text, guides his reader to what he considers the most authoritative position). The length of any particular entry and the number of authorities cited and opinions presented

---

54. Ibn Khaldun, *The Muqaddimah*, trans. Franz Rosenthal (London: Routledge and Kegan Paul, 1986), 3:15–16.

vary. Often the subject headings are long because Ibn Abi Zayd combines opinions addressing a number of related masa'il in his entries. What might be a few sentences in al-ʿUtbi's *Mustakhraja*, expanded to two or three pages (of the printed edition) with Ibn Rushd's commentary in *al-Bayan*, may be found in an extensive presentation of opinions pertaining to related issues that fills nine or ten printed pages in *al-Nawadir wa-l-ziyadat*. Ibn Abi Zayd's text integrates Andalusi and Qayrawani juridical writing of the ninth century with the work of other ninth-century Maliki jurists in Medina and Egypt, such as Ibn al-Majishun (d. 829) and Ibn al-Mawwaz (d. 883). Ibn Abi Zayd's engagement with juridical developments in al-Andalus is apparent throughout the text and is also manifest in his transmission of al-ʿUtbi's *Mustakhraja* to North Africa.

Like *al-Bayan*, *al-Mudawwana* and *al-Nawadir wa-l-ziyadat* are organized topically into chapters or books according to a system characteristic of works of *fiqh* (jurisprudence) They begin with matters of ritual purity, prayer, and other acts of ritual devotion and extend to matters of personal status and criminal law, including marriage, divorce, slavery, oaths, slander, contracts, taxation, and corporal and capital punishment. Interactions with dhimmis are treated in the context of these topics and are part of an effort to treat each topic comprehensively. It is significant that the fiqh literature does not dedicate a separate chapter to dhimmis but treats dhimmis in the context of their social relations with Muslims. Dhimmis appear playing different roles, and each role is considered in social context—the definition of dhimma is worked out and negotiated in terms of practice.

As much as possible, I will try to establish connections between legal questions and opinions and historical context through reference to other sources. Some of the fatwas preserved in collections by ʿIsa ibn Sahl (d. 1093) (*al-Ahkam al-kubra*) and al-Wansharisi (d. 1508) (*al-Miʿyar al-muʿrib wa-l-jamiʿ al-mughrib*) refer to specific inquirers and respondents or provide other historically specific details that help the investigator situate the issues under consideration in a specific social context. For example, two fatwas about whether a Muslim qadi has jurisdiction when a dhimmi presents a case to him for adjudication can be fixed in time and place through the names of the jurisconsults (*fuqahāʾ mushāwarūn*) who were consulted and responded. In one case, the jurist and notarial authority Ibn al-ʿAttar (d. 1009) was the mufti (gave the opinion); in another, a number of tenth-century Cordoban jurists responded, including Asbagh ibn Saʿid (d. 968–969), Ibn ʿAbd Rabbihi, Ibn Harith al-Khushani (d. 981), Ibn Maysur, and Ibn Zarb (d. 991). These fatwas, incidently, provide evidence, unsurprisingly, that Jews in tenth-century Cordoba were adept at Arabic, had the ability to marshal documents (watḥāʾiq) in Arabic, could enlist Muslim witnesses, and had access to Islamic courts.[55]

Outside the realm of legal texts, historical chronicles provide political context and meaning to the social changes of the ninth and tenth centuries, while the biographical literature provides insight into the social world and personal and political interests of rulers, judges, and fuqahaʾ. Finally, the polemical interpretations of the "Christian martyrs' movement" in Cordoba written in the ninth century by the priest Eulogius and the layman Paul Albar offer an extraordinary view of Cordoba as a society in the throes of social and cultural change. These Latin texts provide specific evidence of the messiness of intercommunal relations in the mid-ninth century, of conversion to Islam and from Islam to Christianity, of the existence of mixed-faith families and the conflicts that divided them, and of legal and illegal interfaith marriages.

The organization of this book is more thematic than narrative. The chapters relate to one another and build on one another as components of the investigation of intercommunal relations and boundary making to provide a multifaceted view of Andalusi politics and society. Each chapter stands alone, but its meaning is deepened by its connections to the other chapters; the significance of boundary making as a theme develops chapter by chapter. As much as possible, I have quoted from sources to try to bring the subject of study to life. Chapter 1 provides an overview of the structuring of Umayyad authority in al-Andalus in the ninth and tenth centuries, examining how political identity was expressed in religious terms and how the religious and political authorities worked together to define who was an insider and who was an outsider to the community of Muslims. Chapter 2 describes the social and cultural transformation of al-Andalus in the same period. Chapter 3 examines how jurists accommodated close personal relationships between Muslims and dhimmis and at the same time maintained boundaries between communities. The discussion provides insight into how jurists contributed to and conveyed the development of a Muslim habitus—a way of being Muslim—that was culturally comprehensible. Chapter 4 is a bookend to chapter 1, returning to the subject of political authority and boundary making, but in the context of jihad and the borderlands. This chapter, like the first, combines political and legal history but examines how

---

55. Al-Wansharisi, *Miʿyar* 10:56, 128–131. If Ibn Maysur is Muhammad ibn Maysur al-Nahhas (935–1013), it seems unlikely that the Ibn ʿAbd al-Rabbihi here is the court poet and author of *al-ʿIqd al-farid* (who died in 940). Perhaps he is Saʿid ibn Ahmad b. Muhammad ibn ʿAbd Rabbihi, who died in 966 and was a *faqīh mushāwar*; see Ibn al-Faradi, *Taʾrikh ʿulamaʾ al-Andalus*, 1:239–240.

the presence of a military-political and jurisdictional border between the Domain of Islam and the Domain of War informed how jurists evaluated and upheld the social contract between Muslims and dhimmis. The indeterminacy of "the border," the fluidity of life in the borderlands, and the changeability of identity generated complicated legal questions; this chapter adds another dimension to our understanding of the relationship between social change and the development of law. The conclusion returns to the question of the legal status of dhimmis, raised in the introduction, as a way to review the evidence and analysis of the preceding chapters.

CHAPTER 1

The Structuring of Umayyad Rule

> O Assemby of Muslims! You know that here on this peninsula you
> are surrounded by all kinds of polytheists and all types of heretics
> who seek to sow dissension among you and break your community
> apart, to cause you to forsake your religion, dishonor your women,
> and undermine the call of your Prophet.

The words of warning in this chapter's epigraph close a speech Mundhir
ibn Sa'id al-Balluti delivered in praise of the caliph 'Abd al-Rahman III al-
Nasir li-Din Allah during a reception for an embassy from Constantinople
held in the palace (*qasr*) of Cordoba in 949. The thrust of the speech was to
remind the audience of the obedience they owed to the Commander of the
Faithful as defender of the community and of the faith, recalling the trials
they had endured before the triumph of his rule and invoking God's command: "O you who believe! Obey God, and obey the Messenger, and those
charged with authority among you" (Qur'an 4:59).[1]

This chapter is about those in authority among the Muslims in al-Andalus
and their roles in defining insiders and defending them from outsiders. It provides a historical overview of the structuring of Umayyad authority and the
relationship among rulers, judges, and jurists in al-Andalus from the time of
the conquest to the consolidation of the caliphate. The discussion hardly refers to the non-Muslim population, reflecting the Umayyads' construction of
their authority (and the perspective of the sources), although the subject of
conversion does come up in the discussion of social differentiation and its

---

1. Al-Nubahi, *Kitab al-marqaba al-'ulya*, ed. E. Lévi-Provençal (Cairo: Scribe Egyptien, 1948), 26–
28; al-Maqqari, *Nafh al-tib min ghusn al-Andalus al-ratib*, ed. Ihsan 'Abbas (Beirut: Dar Sadir, 1968),
1:368–371.

political significance. This chapter is intended to provide a political context for understanding social and legal boundary making and boundary testing in al-Andalus and at the same time to elucidate the part played by the ruling dynasty in defining political community. A few specific examples will demonstrate how Umayyad concern for boundaries in a variety of situations and interactions was part of a process of enacting authority and building consensus.

The principles of Umayyad dynastic legitimacy and authority and the regime's exercise of power, as well as the contestation of Umayyad legitimacy and authority and resistance to the regime's power, structured Umayyad rule and the political culture of al-Andalus in the ninth and tenth centuries. The Umayyad rulers of al-Andalus defined political community most basically in terms of recognition of and submission to their authority. The amir or (after 929) the caliph became overtly involved in the definition of boundaries when the words and actions of individuals seemed to challenge his authority.[2] In the Umayyads' construction of their authority, a political renegade was, by definition, a religious deviant, and a Muslim recognized to have strayed from the straight path became, by definition, someone in defiance of the authority of the legitimate Muslim ruler. What constituted crossing the line in certain politically sensitive situations could be a matter of judgment involving consultation and collaboration with the *fuqahā'* (jurists) who were also engaged with, and at times politically invested in, determining who was an insider and who was an outsider. In such cases the ruler might not only consult but coerce the fuqaha'; he occasionally chastised some individuals for their opinions and exonerated others.

The Umayyads of al-Andalus, like their Syrian dynastic forebears, affirmed the principle of dynastic authority and based their legitimacy on that of the third rightly guided caliph, 'Uthman. The general terms in which they expressed their legitimacy were similar: the dynasty and the ruler are favored by God and meritorious; the ruler ensures the integrity of the faith and the community by upholding justice and promoting the proper practice of religion; he defends the community against infidels and undertakes the expansion of the domain of Islam.[3] Descriptions of the personal merits of

---

2. See Janina M. Safran, "The Command of the Faithful in al-Andalus: A Study in the Articulation of Caliphal Legitimacy," *International Journal of Middle Eastern Studies* 30 (1998), 183–198 on the Umayyad adoption of caliphal titles and prerogatives in 929.

3. Patricia Crone, *God's Rule: Government and Islam* (New York: Columbia University Press, 2004), 33–47. Patricia Crone and Martin Hinds, *God's Caliph: Religious Authority in the First Centuries of Islam* (Cambridge: Cambridge University Press, 1986), provide a close analysis of (Syrian) Umayyad claims to legitimacy and religious authority. The circumstances of Umayyad rule in al-Andalus from the mid-eighth century until the early eleventh century were, of course, different from those in

the Umayyad amirs in Andalusi texts exemplify their legitimacy. For example, Ibn al-Qutiyya writes of Hisham (r. 788–796) that he looked after his "flock" with kindness, justice, and humility. He visited the sick and attended funerals. He collected the *zakāt* (the legal alms tax) but reduced the *ʿushūr* (tithes) and was frugal in his expenditure on dress and horse.[4] Of his successor al-Hakam I (r. 796–822) Ibn al-Qutiyya begins by reporting that he (too) conducted himself well with his subjects. He was selective in his appointments (he appointed the best judge in al-Andalus, Muhammad ibn Bashir) and governed as a believer, waging jihad repeatedly.[5] We can discern how the Andalusi Umayyad amirs enacted their right to rule in accounts of their actions (leading military campaigns against the "unbelievers," suppressing revolts and uprisings that threatened the security of the community and the faith, choosing the best men to serve as commanders and ministers, appointing upright and learned judges, and undertaking public works). We have more abundant evidence for the caliphal period of how the Umayyad rulers and their officials, courtiers, and subordinates articulated, displayed, demonstrated, and enacted the principles of their legitimacy. The evidence describes a much more hierarchical and complex regime than in the days of Amir Hisham. Ibn al-Qutiyya describes the amir as modest in his public presentation, and his involvement in the lives of others was personal and unmediated; in contrast, Ibn Hayyan's history of the reign of al-Hakam II describes a formal style of rule where highly developed protocol governed interactions between ruler and ruled.[6]

Syria and changed over time; Andalusi-Umayyad claims to religious authority were expressed at the same time at which traditions of legal-religious scholarship emerged on the peninsula, and, especially from the ninth century on, in connection with the authority of the fuqaha'. Some of the discussion of Andalusi-Umayyad legitimacy and political culture in this chapter is developed in Janina M. Safran, *The Second Umayyad Caliphate*, (Cambridge, MA: Harvard University Press, 2000).

4. Ibn al-Qutiyya, *Ta'rikh iftitah al-Andalus (Historia de la conquista de España de Abenalcotía el Cordobés)*, ed. and trans. (into Spanish) Julián Ribera (Madrid: Revista Archivos, 1926), Arabic, 42; Spanish, 33; English translation, David James, *Early Islamic Spain: The "History" of Ibn al-Qutiya* (London: Routledge, 2009), 82–85. The unknown author of *Akhbar majmu'a* praises Hisham for his defense of the borderlands, his commitment to justice, and his promotion of the faith (sending money to be distributed in the mosques on nights of inclement weather to encourage attendance). Such was Hisham's reputation that he was reportedly praised by the great Malik ibn Anas of Medina. See *Akhbar majmuʿa fi fath al-Andalus*, ed. and trans. Emilio Lafuente y Alcantara (Madrid: Real Academia de la Historia, 1867), Arabic, 120–124; Spanish, 109–112.

5. Ibn al-Qutiyya, *Ta'rikh iftitah*, Arabic, 45; Spanish, 35; James, *Early Islamic Spain*, 86–94. See also *Akhbar majmuʿa*, Arabic, 124–125; Spanish, 112–113.

6. Ibn Hayyan, *al-Muqtabis fi akhbar balad al-Andalus (Muqtabis VII)*, ed. A. A. Hajji (Beirut: Dar al-Thaqafa, 1965); Spanish translation, *Anales palatinos del califa de Córdoba al-Hakam II por ʿIsa ibn Ahmad al-Razi*, trans. Emilio García Gómez (Madrid: Sociedad de Estudios y Publicaciones, 1967).

The sources for the caliphal era show how principles of Umayyad legitimacy were repeatedly expressed to particular audiences, on specific occasions, and in a variety of forms. The context for the expression of legitimacy could be circumscribed, as in communications between officials, or directed toward the Muslim community as a whole, as in sermons and announcements read in the mosques. The participation of officials in service to the ruler in formal ceremonies to celebrate the annual feasts, to welcome embassies, or to recognize the submission of former rebels enacted the recognition of the legitimacy of the ruler, affirmed bonds of loyalty, and articulated the hierarchy of the ruling elite. Expressions of legitimacy, authority, and power were both verbal and symbolic and could take the form of public display, as in the expansion and embellishment of the congregational mosque in Cordoba and the construction of the palace city of Madinat al-Zahra', the military cavalcades that left for campaign and returned to the capital triumphant, and the display of the crucified corpses of individuals declared to be enemies of the faith and the community. Symbolic acts and constructions were often accompanied by explicating texts, such as proclamations, inscriptions, and commemorative poetry. Poetry extolled the achievements of Umayyad rulers and celebrated their merits, and dynastic histories provided the narrative of dynastic rule, demonstrating continuity and confirming Umayyad dedication to the principles of legitimate rule. Everyone who participated in Umayyad rule in the caliphal period understood and communicated in an idiom that affirmed the principles of Umayyad caliphal legitimacy.

The Umayyads of al-Andalus exercised their power and authority through individuals bound to them by ties of kinship, patronage, and alliance. As the administration expanded and the regime became more hierarchical, the network of individuals who exercised power on behalf of the ruler became more extensive, and individuals in certain positions wielded significant power; competition between individuals and families involved great stakes. The ruler's ability to govern depended on his political astuteness, the loyalty he cultivated to his person, family, and office, and his command of the military. The centralization of Umayyad power, characterized by the development of a standing army and the expansion of the administration, began in the ninth century but derailed with the rebellions that broke out in the second half of the century, which were directed, in part, against the centralizing process. This period is dominated in all historical accounts of Umayyad rule in al-Andalus by the rebellion of 'Umar ibn Hafsun and his sons and the threat it posed to the regime. 'Abd al-Rahman III's accession in 912 and his success in extinguishing the rebellion in 928 mark a significant turning point in the history of Umayyad rule and Umayyad political culture. The Umayyad regime was put to the test by the rebellions; reasserting its sovereignty reinforced both territorial and political boundaries in ways that involved changes in the practice of rule and the conception and integration of the political community.

The discussion of Ibn Hafsun's rebellion is at the center of an analytic time frame that extends from the foundation of Umayyad rule to the consolidation of the Umayyad caliphate. This chapter thus begins with a brief historical narrative of the reign of the amirs to sketch the development of the regime and the organization of power, devoting attention to relations between the ruler and the fuqaha'. This leads to a discussion of accusations of blasphemy and *zandaqa* (secret apostasy) and the instantiation of the amirs' authority in legal-religious (as well as political) boundary making. These cases against Muslims were more or less contemporary with charges of blasphemy and apostasy brought against a number of individual Christians in the 850s who defiantly challenged the terms of coexistence between Muslims and Christians (the Christian martyrs to be discussed later). In all these cases the amirs were involved in the judicial process, in consultation with the *qāḍī* (judge), and in the execution of judgment. The ruler performed and enacted his authority on these occasions before those subject to his rule in the circle of the court and beyond to the street. The final determination by the ruler that an individual was a blasphemer or a secret apostate secured the accused's public and exemplary punishment.

The identification of political allegiance with religious orthodoxy informs the representation of Ibn Hafsun's rebellion and the meaning of his defeat as described by the regime and its chroniclers. His command over Muslim and Christian populations in the central lands of al-Andalus posed both a real threat and a conceptual challenge to the regime. Ibn Hafsun's designation as a *muwallad* rebel, that is, as an indigenous Muslim without Arab or Berber lineage or client status, is central to our understanding of the significance of his rebellion. The discussion of this chapter thus transitions from the cases of blasphemy and apostasy during the reigns of the amirs ʿAbd al-Rahman II, Muhammad, and ʿAbd Allah and the breakdown of political order at the end of Muhammad's reign to a brief discussion of the term *muwallad* (pl. *muwalladūn*) and the categories of social differentiation that appear in accounts of the rebellions of the second half of the ninth century. In this period a number of warlords of different ethnic identities established themselves as petty rulers, sometimes at war with one another, as well as in rebellion from Cordoba, and sometimes in alliance with one another; the regime's inability to collect taxes or tribute from these regions or to overcome the armies of the rebel leaders imperiled Umayyad rule. From the Umayyad perspective, this was a state of *fitna* or civil war, and the rebels, in defiance of the ruler's legitimate dynastic authority, fractured and factionalized the community and threatened the integrity of the faith. Ibn Hafsun looms large in Andalusi historiography because the long-lived rebellion of the Banu Hafsun (878–928) was the last great rebellion extinguished by 'Abd al-Rahman III and because at the height of his rebellion, 'Umar ibn Hafsun's forces threatened the very gates of the capital. 'Abd al-Rahman III's suppression of the fitna entailed the reincorporation of a large number of formerly dissident subjects, a challenge he addressed, in part, with the declaration of the caliphate in 929. Broadly speaking, he restored the bonds and the boundaries of the political community practically, with military success, and politically, with his (re)assertion of the Umayyad caliphate of his forefathers who had ruled from Damascus. 'Abd al-Rahman III promoted an idiom for the communication and enactment of political authority and allegiance, employed in multiple forms and contexts, that encompassed all Muslims and served in the restructuring of Umayyad rule after a period of profound political dislocation.

This chapter concludes with discussion of two later legal cases against "outsiders" deemed a danger to the community and the faith that exemplify the exercise of Umayyad rule in the caliphal period and how the caliphs promoted communal identity. 'Abd al-Rahman III and, after him, al-Hakam II each took advantage of charges of heresy and unbelief brought against particular individuals to assert and affirm their authority. 'Abd al-Rahman III confirmed the legitimacy of his caliphate and his role in the integration of the community of Muslims in his suppression of Ibn Masarra's heresy and consolidated his rule. Al-Hakam II secured his own rule shortly after his father's death with his public condemnation and execution of a man characterized as the personification of evil.

When 'Abd al-Rahman (I) ibn Mu'awiya (r. 756–788), grandson of the Syrian Umayyad caliph Hisham, established his rule in al-Andalus after fleeing from the 'Abbasid revolution and the massacre of his kinsmen in Syria, his primary supporters were *mawālī* (clients; s. *mawlā*,) of the Umayyad family who traveled with him or had already settled in al-Andalus. The mawali of the Umayyad dynasty in the early period were commonly affiliated with their patrons by clientage due to contractual ties (*walā' al-muwālāt*), and manumission (*walā' al-'itq*), that is, bonds of clientage established when they themselves were manumitted or when an ancestor was manumitted by a member of the dynasty, and, more rarely, *walā' al-Islām*, clientage established through conversion. In due course only the patron–client relationship established by manumission was recognized as legal practice.[7] Ibn al-Qutiyya describes how ʿAbd al-Rahman's freedman, Badr, prepared the way for his former master's arrival in al-Andalus from his refuge with the Nafza Berbers: he first contacted the leader of the Umayyad mawali, Abu ʿUthman, and Abu ʿUthman and his son-in-law, ʿAbd Allah ibn Khalid, made contact with other local power brokers and secured their participation in a conspiracy against the governor, Yusuf al-Fihri, in support of the Umayyad scion.[8] The Umayyad mawali became the foundation of ʿAbd al-Rahman I's rule, and their descendants played an important role in the support and service of the dynasty as military and administrative officials. Mohamed Meouak's study of the 273 men he was able to identify in service to the Umayyad regime suggests that ten families of mawali (of mostly *sharqī* or eastern origin with a clientage relationship to the Umayyad dynasty extending back to Umayyad rule in Syria) dominated the central administration throughout the period of Umayyad rule in al-Andalus. Meouak argues that these mawali of eastern origin provided a certain continuity and stability to the regime; although rivalries emerged among them, they were also an influential political elite interested in protecting their privileged status.[9]

During the thirty-two years after the establishment of his amirate in 756, ʿAbd al-Rahman I struggled to secure Umayyad rule against the Fihris and their allies and other local rivals and to assert Umayyad dominance over the commanders of the Syrian regiments (*ajnād*; s. *jund*) who had

---

7. Dolores Oliver Pérez cautions that the term *mawlā* (pl. *mawālī*) as it appears in historical accounts must be understood in context and that sometimes the usage does not strictly conform to the legal definition. For example, she argues that in accounts describing the history of the peninsula before the arrival of ʿAbd al-Rahman I, *mawālī* may sometimes refer to collateral tribes. In accounts of the period of the Umayyad amirate and caliphate, she suggests that mawali may include clients with ties of *walā* of different historical origins and also relatives of the Umayyads, notably males related to the dynasty through their women. She argues that by the tenth century in al-Andalus the term *mawālī* came to refer almost exclusively to individuals associated with the Umayyad dynasty. See Dolores Oliver Pérez, "Sobre el significado de *mawlā* en la historia Omeya de al-Andalus," *Al-Qantara* 22 (2001): 321–344. See also Maribel Fierro, "*Mawālī* and *Muwalladūn* in al-Andalus (Second/Eighth–Fourth/Tenth Centuries)," in *Patronate and Patronage in Early Classical Islam*, ed. Monique Bernards and John Nawas (Leiden: E. J. Brill, 2005), 195–245, esp. 211–218. Fierro points out that only *walāʾ al-ʿitq* was recognized by the Maliki madhhab, and practice changed as the madhhab developed. She traced information on nineteen clients ʿAbd al-Rahman I inherited from his Umayyad family and on twenty-two clients he established himself and was able to determine that of the twenty-two, seven were clients out of manumission and two were cases of contractual ties. See Fierro, "Los *mawālī* de ʿAbd al-Rahman I," *Al-Qantara* 20 (1999): 65–97.

8. Ibn al-Qutiyya, *Taʾrikh iftitah*, Arabic, 21; Spanish, 16; James, *Early Islamic Spain*, 67–68.

9. Mohamed Meouak, *Pouvoir souverain, administration centrale et élites politiques dans l'Espagne Umayyade (iie–ive/viiie–xe siècles)* (Helsinki: Academia Scientiarum Fennica, 1999), 70–163.

settled in al-Andalus in the decade before his arrival, originally landing in al-Andalus in 742 to suppress a Berber uprising (each jund had been assigned to a specific district and was supported by the revenues of the district). From the perspective of Andalusi Umayyad dynastic history, ʿAbd al-Rahman I "al-Dakhil" (commonly translated as "the Immigrant") is a heroic figure.[10] A survivor of the ʿAbbasid usurpation and massacre, he took possession of al-Andalus for his dynasty, defended his reign against all challengers (including, in 763, al-Aʿla ibn Mughith of Beja, who fought under an ʿAbbasid standard and boasted a deed of investiture from the ʿAbbasid caliph al-Mansur), and firmly established the seat of Umayyad rule in the West. It is striking to note that the main opponents of ʿAbd al-Rahman I's rule were fellow Muslims, and that from the perspective of Umayyad dynastic history, the main challenge ʿAbd al-Rahman and his immediate successors faced was not rule over a subjugated indigenous non-Muslim population but how to maintain the loyalty of the Umayyad clan and clients and secure stable alliances among various notables and their clans. The names of a few notable Christians, such as the descendants of the former Visigothic king Witiza, appear in the chronicles in reference to such alliances, and frontier lords in this period included Christians and newly converted Muslims. An anecdote about ʿAbd al-Rahman I's conflict with Artabas, a son of King Witiza, tells the story of the renewal of an alliance and may also describe the inception of an office dedicated to the governance of the Christians (unfortunately, we have only scant evidence for and no description of the office). The two matched wits after the amir confiscated lands formally deeded to the Visigothic prince at the time of the Muslim conquest (Artabas and his two brothers had at that time reportedly agreed to betray King Roderick, Witiza's successor, if they could be confirmed in the title to their father's estates and had secured a formal document attesting to their agreement from the caliph in Damascus, al-Walid). The amir's intention to consolidate a territorial base of revenue and power came up against Artabas's dependence on his estates and determination to hold on to them, and he invoked his rights. The two men ended up acknowledging each other's situation and that they had no choice but to accommodate their changed circumstances. A new arrangement was made: in exchange for guidance and advice, presumably regarding the amir's rule over the Christians, ʿAbd al-Rahman I granted Artabas the return of twenty of his estates, as well as gifts and new clothes, and appointed him to the office of count (*qūmis*).[11]

---

10. See *Akhbar majmuʿa*, Arabic, 46–56, 117–119; Spanish, 55–62, 106–108.

11. Ibn al-Qutiyya, *Taʾrikh iftitah*, Arabic, 36–37; Spanish, 28–29; James, *Early Islamic Spain*, 75–76.

'Abd al-Rahman I's son and successor Hisham I (r. 788–796) secured his ascension against the opposition of two of his brothers, and his decadelong rule was relatively stable. The process of centralization proceeded under the rule of his son and successor, al-Hakam I (r. 796–822), who determined to collect taxes and secure his rule with the development of the *ḥasham*, a professional unit under the command of an officer of the court in direct service to the ruler that was distinct from the tribal armies of the ajnad and the volunteer recruits. He placed the initial unit of this new guard under the command of a Christian, al-Rabiʿ ibn Theodulfo. Al-Hakam proved ruthless in his suppression of opposition. Most notably, he had 72 men (or by another account 140) whom he accused of conspiring to replace him with a paternal cousin crucified in the capital in 805; in 818 he massacred many of the opponents to his rule who marched on the palace from the suburb of Shaqunda, just across the Guadalquivir. He razed the suburb, which was inhabited by merchants, craftsmen, religious scholars, and students, and sent most of its population into exile.[12]

Al-Hakam's successor, ʿAbd al-Rahman II (r. 822–852), is credited with the transformation of the Andalusi-Umayyad administration and style of rule, going further than his father in his efforts to secure the fiscal and military foundations of the regime. He created a hierarchy of officials headed by the chamberlain (*ḥājib*) and expanded his administration through the establishment of ministries; his expansion of court culture and elaboration of protocol further enhanced his personal and dynastic prestige and reinforced loyalty to the regime. The efforts of the Umayyad amirs of al-Andalus to achieve greater control over their subject population and revenues and to assert their authority through the creation of a more hierarchical and differentiated system of offices seems to have corresponded to a shift away from dependence on the Syrian ajnad and their Arab commanders; ʿAbd al-Rahman II designated a commander responsible for the security of the capital (*ṣāḥib al-madīna*), and the hasham served as the basis for control within al-Andalus; during the reign of Amir Muhammad (852–886), campaigns on the frontiers

---

12. Ibn al-Qutiyya, *Taʾrikh iftitah*, Arabic, 50–57; Spanish, 40–46; James, *Early Islamic Spain*, 88–89; Ibn Hayyan, *Crónica de los emires Alhakam I yʿAbdarrahman II entre los años 796 y 847 (al-Muqtabis II-1)*, trans. Mahmud ʿAli Makki and Federico Corriente from the manuscript (Zaragoza: Instituto de Estudios Islámicos y del Oriente Próximo, 2001), 40–45, 55–85. I will cite this text as *Muqtabis II-1*. A facsimile of the manuscript by Joaquín Vallvé Bermejo has been published: Ibn Hayyan, *Muqtabis II* (Madrid: Real Academia de la Historia, 1999). In a circular al-Hakam I sent to all the provinces announcing the suppression of the rebellion, the amir clearly defines the rebels as enemies of the legitimate ruler (the imam) and of God. He declares that although he has the right to their property, women, and children, he will forfeit that right (57–58).

relied increasingly on volunteer levies.[13] Muhammad was responsible, in this connection, with the redesignation of the principal judge of al-Andalus from the *qāḍī al-jund* to the judge of the community (*qāḍī al-jamāʿa*).

The conspiracy against al-Hakam I in 805 involved a number of the notables of Cordoba; al-Hakam I's forceful response put important *ʿulamā* (religious scholars) like ʿIsa ibn Dinar, Talut ibn ʿAbd al-Jabbar, and Yahya ibn Yahya to flight and resulted in the execution of (among others) Yahya ibn Mudar, a noted scholar and teacher. The revolt of the suburb a dozen years later may have been fueled by resentment of the amir's ruthless punishment of those he suspected in the plot against him and others who crossed him, with simmering grievances exacerbated by the drought of 814.[14] Al-Hakam's successor took immediate action to restore the regime's legitimacy. Upon taking the oath of allegiance, ʿAbd al-Rahman II had Rabiʿ ibn Theodulfo removed from his command and executed for abuse of office (he was responsible for tax collection) and also ordered the destruction of the wine market of Cordoba, two acts of symbolic significance that asserted Islamic principles and Muslim domination.[15] More substantively, ʿAbd al-Rahman II

---

13. The hasham is described variously in modern accounts as a slave guard or a mercenary army; by the time al-Jilliqi and Ibn Hafsun were enrolled, it must have become a mercenary (or mixed?) army. The sources are not precise, and it may be that al-Hakam created a special palace guard, referred to as *al-khāṣṣa*, as well as a mercenary army, or one may have led to the development of the other. Ibn Hayyan reports that Count Rabiʿa was in charge of the destruction of Shaqunda and that he was head of a special guard of slaves (*ghilmān*) called the "mute" (because they did not speak Arabic). After the suppression of the revolt, al-Hakam I reportedly freed all the slaves of the special guard. He also reportedly recruited a new guard of slaves and freemen who were paid salaries from a tithe the amir instituted; see Ibn Hayyan, *Muqtabis II-1*, 63, 67, 75. On the Andalusi-Umayyad military in this period, see Évariste Lévi-Provençal, *L'Espagne musulmane au xe siècle* (1932; new ed., Paris: Maisonneuve et Larose, 2002), 127–136; Lévi-Provençal, *Histoire de l'Espagne musulmane* (Paris: Maisonneuve, 1950), 3:67–76; and Hugh Kennedy, *Muslim Spain and Portugal: A Political History of al-Andalus* (London: Longman, 1996), 50, 65–67.

14. On the revolt and its possible causes, see Lévi-Provençal, *Histoire de l'Espagne musulmane*, 1:160–173. Maribel Fierro argues that Lévi-Provençal's emphasis on the role of the ʿulama' in leading or inciting the revolt is not clearly supported by the evidence; Yahya ibn Yahya and his brother Fath, for example, fled Cordoba after the revolt of the suburb, but this does not necessarily implicate them as its instigators. See Fierro, "El alfaqui beréber Yahya b. Yahya al-Laythi (m. 234/848), 'El inteligente de al-Andalus,'" in *Estudios onomástico-biográficos de al-Andalus*, vol. 8, ed. María Luísa Ávila and Manuela Marín (Madrid: Consejo Superior de Investigaciones Científicas, 1997), 289–293.

15. Although we cannot date his opinion and directly tie it to the destruction of the wine market, at some point Yahya ibn Yahya approved the destruction of the house of a wine merchant, citing Malik's approval of burning down the house of a Muslim who sells wine and of a Christian who habitually sells wine to Muslims; al-Wansharisi, *Al-Miʿyar al-muʿrib wa-l-jamiʿ al-mughrib* (Rabat: Dar al-Gharb al-Islami, 1981–1983), 2:409. The clampdown on wine merchants did not have long-term consequences; al-Khushani reports a few anecdotes about drunks and observes that generally speaking, Andalusi judges tended to close their eyes to drunkenness; al-Khushani, *Kitab al-qudat*

also created a council of jurisconsults, the *shūrā*, to assist the qadi of Cordoba and ensure that justice was administered according to the standards of the eminent fuqaha' of the time. The amir thus integrated the leading fuqaha' into his rule and promoted the collaboration of jurists and the regime. Through the shura the Andalusi-Umayyad rulers institutionalized the exercise of their authority as guardians of the faith and yoked the development of Islamic law, as well as the exercise of justice, to the regime. This collaboration contributed to regime stability and relative coherence of legal interpretation and practice.[16]

The first and second generations of *fuqahā' mushāwarūn*, the jurisconsults who served in the shura during the reigns of 'Abd al-Rahman II and Muhammad I, included compilers and transmitters of *masā'il* (legal questions and opinions) from Malik's disciples: Yahya ibn Yahya, 'Isa ibn Dinar, 'Abd al-Malik ibn Habib, Muhammad ibn Ahmad al-'Utbi, and Yahya ibn Ibrahim al-Muzayn. The jurisconsults were in a privileged position to apply and disseminate their learning.[17] Maribel Fierro and Manuela Marín, drawing on evidence in biographical dictionaries, observe that it is in this period, the mid-ninth century, that we see Cordoba emerge as the predominant seat of learning in al-Andalus and the hub of a network of scholars and legal-judicial functionaries. Until this period 'ulama' from provincial Andalusi towns often received their training in Qayrawan, Medina, and Fustat (Egypt), bypassing Cordoba.[18] By the tenth century a jurisconsult like Muhammad ibn 'Umar ibn Lubaba (838–926), renowned for his fatwas, could study and transmit the fundamental Maliki texts of juridical opinion, *al-Muwatta'*, *al-Mudawwana*, and al-'Utbi's *Mustakhraja*, without leaving al-Andalus.[19]

---

bi-Qurtuba (Historia de los jueces de Córdoba), ed. and trans. (into Spanish) Julián Ribera (Madrid: Maestre, 1914), Arabic, 103–105; Spanish, 126–127; see also al-Nubahi, *Kitab al-marqaba al-'ulya*, 61–63.

16. See Hussain Monès, "Le rôle des hommes de religion dans l'histoire de l'Espagne musulmane jusqu'à la fin du califat," *Studia Islamica* 20 (1964): 47–88; trans. John Smedley, "The Role of Men of Religion in the History of Muslim Spain up to the End of the Caliphate," in *The Formation of al-Andalus*, ed. Maribel Fierro and Julio Samsó (Aldershot: Ashgate-Variorum, 1998), 2:51–84; Hady-Roger Idris, "Réflexions sur le Malikisme sous les Umayyades d'Espagne," *Atti del 3 Congresso di Studi Arabi e Islamici (Ravello 1966)* (Naples: Istituto Universitario Orientale, 1967), 397–414; trans. John Smedley, "Reflections on Malikism under the Umayyads of Spain," in Fierro and Samsó, *Formation of al-Andalus*, 2:85–101; and Manuela Marín, "Šūrá et al-šūrá dans al-Andalus," *Studia Islamica* 62 (1985): 25–51.

17. Ana Fernández Félix, *Cuestiones legales del islam temprano: La 'Utbiyya y el proceso de formación de la sociedad islámica Andalusi* (Madrid: Consejo Superior de Investigaciones Científicas, 2003), 331–332.

18. Maribel Fierro and Manuela Marín, "La islamicización de las ciudades Andalusies a través de sus ulamas (s. ii/viii–comienzos s. iv/x)," in *Genèse de la ville islamique en al-Andalus et au Maghreb occidental*, ed. Patrice Cressier and Mercedes García Arenal with Mohammed Meouak (Madrid: Casa Velázquez, 1998), 65–97.

19. Fernández Félix, *Cuestiones legales*, 47–48.

In the tenth century the Andalusi-Umayyad caliphs emphasized their adherence to, and promotion of, the *madhhab* or "way" of Malik as transmitted and interpreted by his disciples as an expression of their dedication to upholding the true faith and guidance of the community of believers. In light of this representation of Umayyad legitimacy, chronicles of Umayyad rule project a close association with Malik further back than the mid-ninth century that may be more legendary than historical. The Medinan and Egyptian juridical tradition associated with Malik probably edged out the appeal of the doctrines of the Syrian al-Awza'i (d. 774), popular among the Muslim Arab soldiers of the ajnad, only during the first half of the ninth century, when Andalusi fuqaha' traveled east and returned with transmissions of the teachings of Malik and his disciples.[20] Umayyad patronage of jurists like Yahya ibn Yahya and others who based their judgments on the opinions of Malik and his followers contributed to the predominance of the *ra'y* (legal opinion) of Malik and the development of the Maliki madhhab in al-Andalus as the transmitters themselves became authorities for successive generations of fuqaha'. The jurisconsults and judges of al-Andalus of the ninth century often competed with one another in ways that influenced directions of legal interpretation. For example, Yahya ibn Yahya was a partisan of Malik's disciple Ibn al-Qasim; his relationship with the amir, his influence over his contemporaries, and the prominence of his students played a role in the privileging of Ibn al-Qasim's transmissions and opinions in Cordoba over those of Ashhab and Ibn Wahb and in diminishing the authority of his own rivals. Fierro calculates that Yahya ibn Yahya had 58 students (including his son, 'Ubayd Allah), Ibn Habib 43, Sa'id ibn Hassan 24, and 'Isa ibn Dinar 13.[21] It is striking that one of Yahya's students, al-'Utbi, does not transmit anything from Ibn Habib in his *Mustakhraja* (although Ibn Habib's *Wadiha* is cited frequently by other jurists in other legal texts).[22]

The fuqaha' occasionally deployed accusations of blasphemy and zandaqa against one another when personal and professional interests were threatened, prompting the ruler to intervene.[23] Late in the reign of 'Abd al-Rahman II, 'Abd al-Malik ibn Habib had to defend his brother Harun against charges

---

20. According to Ibn 'Abd al-Barr, as reported by Ibn Hayyan, the shift to Malik from al-Awza'i took place during the reign of al-Hakam I; Ibn Hayyan, *Muqtabis II-1*, 104.

21. Fierro, "El alfaqui beréber Yahya b. Yahya al-Laythi," 306.

22. Fernández Félix, *Cuestiones legales*, 22, 329.

23. Maribel Fierro points out that an accusation that did not have legal consequences could nonetheless serve as a way of excluding and isolating an individual; see Fierro, "Religious Dissension in al-Andalus: Ways of Exclusion and Inclusion," *Al-Qantara* 22 (2001): 463–487.

of blasphemy.[24] Harun was charged with two incidents of blasphemy. On one occasion he allegedly refused to lend a man a ladder in order to repair a mosque, saying that he would be willing to lend him the ladder if he would use it to repair a church. When the man questioned him, Harun retorted that those who cling to God are forsaken, while others prosper. On another occasion, after falling ill, Harun reportedly remarked that he would not have deserved to suffer as much if he had killed Abu Bakr and ʿUmar (the first two caliphs). When a number of ʿAbd al-Malik's colleagues in the shura took the charges seriously and called for punishment (even death), ʿAbd al-Malik wrote to the amir and accused them of conspiring against him, pointing out that they had long harbored hostility toward him; he reminded the amir of their bonds of *walāʾ* (patronage-clientage) and challenged him to consider why he had appointed him to the shura in the first place. In fact, there was a backstory. Earlier in his reign the amir had appointed an outsider (from the district of Elvira) as qadi of Cordoba, Ibn Maʿmar (or Muʿammar). The judge maintained his distance from the jurists of Cordoba; rather than consult with them, he wrote to Asbagh ibn al-Faraj (d. 839) in Egypt if he had questions about a decision (Asbagh had studied with Ibn al-Qasim, Ibn Wahb, and Ashhab). Tensions escalated as complaints circulated regarding the performance of his duties—reportedly the judge tended not to rule in favor of petitioners. Reacting to the hostility of the fuqahaʾ, the judge registered complaints against seventeen of them. The matter came to a head when the amir, presented with written testimonies against the judge and evidence of widespread animosity toward him among the leading men of the city, sought the opinion of Yahya ibn Yahya (who had been careful to protect his appearance of impartiality). Yahya observed pointedly that he had no personal knowledge of Ibn Maʿmar's conduct as judge because he did not attend his court and was never consulted for his juridical opinions, but in his view the testimonies against the judge were overwhelming. ʿAbd al-Rahman II dismissed Ibn Maʿmar the same day. Later the amir came to realize that the denunciations of the judge were false and determined to reappoint him. Once again in office, Ibn Maʿmar refused to consult with Yahya ibn Yahya or his faction and recommended that

---

24. ʿIyad ibn Musa, *Tartib al-madarik wa-taqrib al-masalik li-maʿarifat aʿlam madhhab Malik* (Rabat: Wizarat al-Awqaf wa-al-Shuʾun al-Islamiyya, 1965–1983), 4:133–138; Ibn Hayyan, *Muqtabis II-1*, 281–282. See Isabel [Maribel] Fierro, "Andalusian ʿFatāwāʾ on Blasphemy," *Annales islamologiques* 25 (1990): 103–117; also Fierro, *La heterodoxia en al-Andalus durante el periodo Omeya* (Madrid: Instituto Hispano-Arabe de Cultura, 1987), 63–70; and Jorge Aguadé's introduction to his edition of Ibn Habib's *Taʾrikh* (Madrid: Consejo Superior de Investigaciones Científicas, 1991), 32–41.

a fellow Elviran, Ibn Habib, be brought to Cordoba as jurisconsult. Ibn Habib's claim to the amir that the fuqaha' of Cordoba were hostile to him was not unfounded.[25]

The ruler was responsible for executing the punishments determined by jurists and imposed by judges, but in matters where a punishment was not prescribed or in specific situations when the jurisconsults were of differing opinions about how a case should be decided or disagreed over the determination of a punishment, he had discretion. In this case the amir supported 'Abd al-Malik ibn Habib's opinion and ruled in Harun's favor. Baber Johansen observes that one of the effects of casuistry and the multiplication of divergent opinions is expanded scope for the discretion of the qadi, who can adjudicate cases more closely on the merits as he sees them.[26] In this case the divergence of opinion concerned whether Harun's statements were blasphemous and how, and if his blasphemy could be demonstrated, what the appropriate punishment should be. The qadi Sa'id ibn Sulayman al-Balluti did not initially find Harun's statements to be so clearly insulting as to merit the death penalty, but Ibrahim ibn Husayn ibn Khalid argued that Harun impugned God's justice in his complaints and should suffer death. In this situation the amir stepped in to exercise his discretion. He manipulated the differences of juridical opinion to serve his ends, contributing by his actions to juridical debates about blasphemy. The charges of blasphemy against Harun ibn Habib, whether concocted as part of a conspiracy against his brother or seized on by 'Abd al-Malik's enemies as an opportunity to aggress against him, tested the boundaries of correct speech. The amir's support for his protégé gave substance to the legal opinions expressed by 'Abd al-Malik in defense of his brother that in accusations of blasphemy the statements of the accused should be unambiguous in their offensive nature, and that the testimony of more than one witness was required.

The professional histories of Andalusi fuqaha' suggest in a number of examples how the parameters of legal-religious consensus were imposed (and sometimes challenged) by men of legal-religious authority and political influence. Someone who asserted his independence in the formation of legal opinions could find himself subjected to pressure to conform or face dismissal from office or worse. If we take a look at the start of Ibn Habib's

---

25. Al-Khushani, *Kitab al-qudat bi-Qurtuba*, Arabic, 80–85, 87–89; Spanish, 98–105, 106–110; al-Nubahi, *Kitab al-marqaba al-'ulya*, 44–45. Both sources ascribe the campaign against Ibn Ma'mar to Yahya ibn Yahya.

26. Baber Johansen, "Casuistry: Between Legal Concept and Social Praxis," *Islamic Law and Society* 2 (1995): 154.

career in Cordoba, we see that when he tried to assert himself and challenged Ibn Ma'mar to determine his decisions according to the statements (*qawl*) of Ashhab rather than of Ibn al-Qasim, the judge insisted that the consensus of the men of learning in al-Andalus was the qawl of Ibn al-Qasim, and he would not go against it (even though Ibn Ma'mar had himself studied with Ashhab in Egypt).[27] Ibn Habib's initiation into the conventions of the shura also involved confrontation with Yahya ibn Yahya and Sa'id ibn Hassan, who resented his fatwas expressing positions opposing theirs and hatched a plan to put him in his place (this occurred sometime before the case against Harun).[28] Ibn Habib referred to the opinions of the Egyptian jurist Asbagh ibn al-Faraj in a number of his fatwas. His two rivals determined to undermine his authority and did so by embarrassing him in front of the judge. They enlisted 'Abd al-A'la ibn Wahb, who had studied with Asbagh, to demonstrate that Ibn Habib misremembered or distorted Asbagh's opinion about a particular question. Ibn Habib wrote to Amir 'Abd al-Rahman II to complain, pointing out that the judge had consulted with 'Abd al-A'la without the amir's approval; 'Abd al-A'la, in turn, wrote to defend himself and secured a spot on the shura (but not Ibn Habib's dismissal). Alliances among jurists could shift; 'Abd al-A'la eventually found himself accused of zandaqa by Yahya ibn Yahya, Ibn Habib, and Ibrahim ibn Husayn ibn 'Asim for his reported interest in *kalām* (rational disputation) and the books of the Mu'tazila and his belief that spirits die; he survived the charges and continued to serve as a jurisconsult until his death during the reign of Muhammad, another example of a reputable jurist enduring "correction" by his peers.[29]

---

27. Al-Khushani, *Kitab al-qudat bi-Qurtuba*, Arabic, 88; Spanish, 108.

28. In another story the faqih Asbagh ibn Khalil (d. 886) helps a man outwit these two when they act obstructively; see al-Khushani, *Akhbar al-fuqaha' wa-l-muhaddathin*, ed. M. Luisa Ávila and Luis Molina (Madrid: Consejo Superior de Investigaciones Científicas, 1992), no. 41.

29. 'Iyad, *Tartib al-madarik*, 4:245–248; Ibn al-Faradi, *Ta'rikh 'ulama' al-Andalus*, ed. Bashar 'Awad Ma'rouf (Tunis: Dar al-Gharb al-Islami, 2008), 1:370–372; Fierro, *Heterodoxia*, 49–53, 189–192. Sometimes the fuqaha' rose above their rivalries, even though their grudges could be enduring. When 'Abd al-Rahman II consulted Ibn Habib about suspicions he had about the close relationship between Yahya ibn Yahya and the judge Ibrahim ibn al-'Abbas of the Quraysh (the amir feared a plot to seize the throne), Ibn Habib assured him of Yahya's loyalty to the regime despite their mutual animosity. Baqi ibn Makhlad also took the high ground when the former judge 'Amr ibn 'Abd Allah was confronted with serious questions about his probate records and insinuations of embezzlement; although the judge had supported the accusations of zandaqa against him, Baqi deterred the fuqaha' from requiring that the judge swear his innocence on the Qur'an (al-Khushani, *Kitab al-qudat bi-Qurtuba*, Arabic, 93, 144–149; Spanish, 112–113, 178–184). Ibn Ma'mar was less forgiving of his treatment by Yahya ibn Yahya; approaching death, he asked a confidant to convey a warning to his rival about the fate of those who commit injustices: "Assailants know what vicissitudes their affairs will take!" (Qur'an 26:227) (al-Khushani, *Kitab al-qudat bi-Qurtuba*, Arabic, 89; Spanish, 109).

The ruler, generally speaking, presided over the judicial system and occasionally played an active role as arbiter of legal opinion. His involvement in the rivalries of the fuqaha' and their legal-religious disputes proved integral to the process of consensus building, even if his interest in legal interpretation could be secondary to his political interests, as is suggested in the case against Harun ibn Habib. Another case illustrates the point further.

In his history of the judges of Cordoba, the jurist and judge Ibn Harith al-Khushani (d. 971) tells the story of how Muhammad ibn Ziyad, a reputable judge, came to be dismissed from office over his handling of an accusation of blasphemy against the nephew of 'Ajab, one of al-Hakam I's favorite concubines. When witnesses came forward against the accused, the amir 'Abd al-Rahman II had him imprisoned, and when 'Ajab sought his release, the amir determined that he would evaluate the opinions of the judge and the shura and act accordingly. In this case the ruler intervened not on the side of clemency (as he did in the case against Harun) but rather in support of the harshest penalty. After reviewing all the fatwas issued by the shura, 'Abd al-Rahman II dismissed the presiding judge (Muhammad ibn Ziyad) and rebuked three of the jurists (including 'Abd al-A'la, whose opinion he said he dismissed because of the accusations of zandaqa previously directed against him). He decided to follow the recommendations of Ibn Habib and Asbagh ibn Khalil for execution. Al-Khushani's account suggests that the ruler acted forcefully to uphold justice; al-Khushani, himself a jurist and judge, does not criticize any of the principals (their professional reputations survived), but he does record the amir's rebukes to 'Abd al-A'la (reminding him of the zandaqa accusations) and Aban ibn 'Isa (to whom he remarked that he was either untruthful or had a lot to learn about issuing fatwas).[30]

The legal principle upheld in this case is not obvious. The statement made by the accused, recorded in other sources, is obscure: on a cloudy day he allegedly said, "The cobbler has started to water his skins." Some of the jurists took these to be inappropriate words of jest; others heard them as insulting God.[31] Ibn Habib's determination of blasphemy and call for execution here (and the amir's support of his position) are difficult to reconcile with his defense of his brother and his position that the punishment of death should be avoided when the interpretation of the words of the accused is ambiguous (the two blasphemy cases occurred close to each other

---

30. Al-Khushani, *Kitab al-qudat bi-Qurtuba*, Arabic, 104–105; Spanish, 127–129.

31. 'Iyad, *Tartib al-madarik*, 4:132–133; Ibn Hayyan, *Muqtabis II-1*, 278–281; al-Nubahi, *Kitab al-marqaba al-'ulya*, 55–56; al-Wansharisi, *Mi'yar*, 2:362.

in time, but the chronology is not definite).[32] It may be that this particular accusation against 'Ajab's nephew has survived in the historical record as a legal oddity and was originally accompanied by other accusations. The historian 'Isa ibn Ahmad al-Razi's summary of the case suggests that the accused had been the subject of a number of complaints and was finally seized and brought before the gate of the qasr by the many people incited against him (for mocking the religion and denigrating the mission of the Prophet), among them 'Abd al-Malik ibn Habib.[33] The amir thus may have been pressed to pursue the case; in any event he treated it as an opportunity to demonstrate his vigilance in protecting the standards of the faith. Rejecting 'Ajab's initial request that her nephew be released from prison, the amir reportedly took the high ground: "The fear we inspire in the hearts of our enemies depends on our enforcing the *ḥudūd* [statutory penalties], strengthening God's religion, and waging holy war against his enemies, averting deviant tendencies and dangerous innovations." The case had political significance for the amir, and he refers to the accused as *al-fāsiq* (the iniquitous), confirming that he was someone outside the bounds of the faith and the community. The case also had significance in the amir's relationship with the judge and the shura (particularly if Ibn Habib initiated the case), and he made a choice to support Ibn Habib (perhaps also responding to popular opinion) and thereby dismiss the judge and chastise the three jurisconsults who counseled leniency. The accused ended up being escorted by the sahib al-madina, the two jurisconsults who called for his death, and a contingent of forty soldiers. He was raised on a cross of wood and stabbed to death, and his body was left on display.

The part played by the ruler as arbiter imposed consensus but at the same time could allow for some diversity of opinion among the fuqaha' because the amir might intervene to prevent any particular jurist from dominating his colleagues. The intervention of Amir Muhammad on behalf of Baqi ibn Makhlad (d. 889) may have defused tensions among the Andalusi fuqaha' arising from the introduction of the science of hadith ('*ilm al-ḥadīth*) in

---

32. 'Isa al-Razi, as cited by Ibn Hayyan, indicates that the case against Harun ibn Habib preceded the case against 'Ajab's nephew, but 'Iyad reverses the order. Both cases seem to have taken place in 851, but no account of either case mentions the other. For discussion of the dates of the cases and the sequence, see Fierro, "Andalusian 'Fatāwā' on Blasphemy," and Fierro, *Heterodoxia*, 57–63.

33. 'Isa al-Razi as cited by Ibn Hayyan, *Muqtabis II-1*, 278. In this excerpt 'Isa does not mention the differences of opinion among the fuqaha'; rather, he suggests that they were uniform in the call for the death penalty. 'Isa also reports that 'Ajab's nephew (whom he identifies as Yahya ibn Zakariyya') was crucified at the end of 'Abd al-Rahman II's reign along with the astrologer Muhammad ibn 'Abd Allah ibn al-'Adra' (279).

al-Andalus and an approach to jurisprudence that featured hadiths as a primary source (aṣl) of fiqh.[34] Baqi traveled to the East for study, to Egypt, the
Hijaz, Syria (Damascus), and Iraq (Kufa, Basra, Wasit, and Baghdad), and
brought back to Cordoba texts dedicated to juridical differences of opinion
(ikhtilāf), collections of hadith, and al-Shafiʿi's Risala.[35] After a long sojourn
abroad, Baqi shook things up among the learned circles of Cordoba. He
actively disseminated his learning to a circle of students (over the course of
his professional career he wrote a commentary on the Qur'an and compiled
a collection of hadith organized by both transmitters and topics useful for
the application of hadith to juridical questions). Baqi came into conflict
with the leading fuqaha' because he challenged the priority the Andalusis
gave to the opinions of Malik and the authority of their own tradition of
transmission. Other Andalusi jurists had transmitted hadiths in the course of
their teaching and writing—for example, Yahya ibn Yahya transmitted Layth
ibn Saʿd's (d. 791) collection of hadiths and Malik's Muwatta', and ʿAbd al-
Malik ibn Habib transmitted hadiths—but they had also been involved since
the first part of the ninth century in the transmission of the ra'y of Malik
and the teachings of Malik's disciples and were in the process of assimilating
the various transmissions through application, as well as through contestation
and competition among themselves, as we have seen.[36] Two jurists, ʿAbd

---

34. See María Isabel Fierro Bello [Maribel Fierro], "Accusations of 'Zandaqa' in al-Andalus," Quaderni di Studi Arabi 5–6 (1987–1988): 251–258 on the charges against ʿAbd al-Aʿla ibn Wahb and Baqi
ibn Makhlad. Fierro also discusses the case against Baqi ibn Makhlad and the sources describing it
in Heterodoxia, 80–88. She discusses the conflict between the ahl al-ra'y (partisans of ra'y) and the ahl
al-ḥadīth (partisans of hadith) in al-Andalus and the eventual integration of ʿilm al-ḥadīth into the
Maliki tradition in other studies as well. See Maribel Fierro, "El derecho Maliki en al-Andalus: Ss.
II/VIII–V/XI," Al-Qantara 12 (1991): 119–132; Fierro, "Proto-Malikis, Malikis, and Reformed
Malikis in al-Andalus," in The Islamic School of Law: Evolution, Devolution, and Progress, ed. Peri Bearman, Rudolph Peters, and Frank E. Vogel (Cambridge, MA: Harvard University Press, 2005), 57–
76; and Maribel Fierro with Julio Samsó, introduction to Fierro and Samsó, Formation of al-Andalus,
2:xix–xxvi.

35. See Manuela Marín, "Baqi b. Majlad y la introducción del hadit en al-Andalus," Al-Qantara 1
(1980): 165–208; and María Luisa Ávila, "Nuevos datos sobre la biografía de Baqi b. Majlad," Al-
Qantara 6 (1985): 321–367.

36. Yahya ibn Yahya's student Ibn Waddah corrected errors he found in Yahya's transmission of al-
Muwatta'; on the transmission of hadith by Yahya ibn Yahya and Ibn Waddah, see Fierro, "El alfaqui
beréber Yahya b. Yahya al-Laythi," 307–313. Later scholars disparaged Ibn Habib's transmissions of
hadith because they did not conform to subsequent norms of hadith criticism; see Aguadé's introduction to Ibn Habib, Ta'rikh, 41–46. Biographical accounts suggest that scholars tended to be
critical of one another's work, and later generations often evaluated the work of their forefathers by
the standards of their own time. For example, ʿIyad records criticisms of al-ʿUtbi's Mustakhraja by Ibn
Waddah, Muhammad ibn ʿAbd al-Hakam (d. 882) (as expressed to Aslam ibn ʿAbd al-ʿAziz when
the latter studied with him in Egypt), and Ahmad ibn Khalid (as expressed to Ibn Lubaba, who
taught al-Mustakhraja); ʿIyad, Tartib al-madarik, 4:254. Muhammad ibn ʿAbd al-Hakam appears in a

Allah ibn Muhammad ibn Khalid ibn Martanil (d. 869 or 874) and Abu Zayd ʿAbd al-Rahman b. Ibrahim (d. 871 or 872) led the charge against Baqi with accusations of *bidʿa* (innovation) and zandaqa.[37] Eminent fuqaha' were asked to bear witness against him, and Muhammad ibn Yusuf ibn Matruh (d. 884), ʿUbayd Allah ibn Yahya (d. 910), Asbagh ibn Khalil (d. 886), and Muhammad ibn Waddah (d. 900) all did so; ʿAbd al-Aʿla refused— perhaps after his own experience he was reluctant to condemn others.

Baqi's life was in jeopardy. The support of the amir and the commander Hashim ibn ʿAbd al-ʿAziz (who reportedly drew the amir's attention to the case) ensured Baqi's immediate survival. In one account Hashim advised the amir to dismiss the judge presiding over the case against Baqi and thus halt the proceedings; in this way the amir could spare the life of a good man and avoid confrontation with the fuqaha'. Baqi's personal reputation as an upright and pious Muslim and his ability to come to some sort of accommodation with the leading fuqaha' ultimately ensured his political survival; he remained active as a jurist and a teacher in Cordoba and later was approached for the office of qadi of Cordoba by the amir al-Mundhir (Baqi declined the offer).[38] Although hostility persisted between Baqi and his detractors, and ʿUbayd Allah ibn Yahya and Baqi steered clear of each other, the amir ʿAbd Allah was able to effectuate reconciliation when he brought

---

number of anecdotes in judgment of Andalusi scholars. He is critical of al-ʿUtbi's *Mustakhraja* but esteems Asbagh ibn Khalil's work on documents (*wathāʾiq*); see al-Khushani, *Akhbar al-fuqaha'*, nos. 133, 41. Ibn al-Faradi notes that his teacher Ibn al-Qutiyya was not authoritative in his transmission of hadith and *fiqh* (jurisprudence) (but he was learned in grammar and the accounts [*akhbār*] of the rulers, jurists, and poets of al-Andalus); al-Faradi, *Ta'rikh ʿulama' al-Andalus*, 1:102–103.

37. In their opinions and writings in this period, jurists tested and contested the finer lines between belief and unbelief: What if someone says that he does not pray? Or says that he does not perform ablutions before prayer? Or says that he does not pay the zakat? Or says that he will not perform the pilgrimage? (See Ibn Rushd [al-Jadd], *Al-Bayan wa-l-tahsil wa-l-sharh wa-l-tawjih wa-l-taʿlil fi masa'il al-Mustakhraja*, ed. Muhammad Hajji [Beirut: Dar al-Gharb al-Islami, 1984–1987], 16:393–396.) The fuqaha' wrestled with whether major sinners, innovators (*ahl al-bidʿa*), and heretics (*ahl al-ahwāʾ*) were outside the community and the implications of their exclusion: Who inherited from them? Were their marriages valid? Could they be buried as Muslims in Muslim cemeteries? Must prayer behind them be repeated? See Ibn Sahl, *al-Ahkam al-kubra*, excerpted and edited by M. ʿAbd al-Wahhab Khallaf, *Thalath wathaʿiq fi muharabat al-ahwa' wa al-bidaʿ fi al-Andalus* (Cairo, 1981), 17–38. Ibn Rushd provides further examples of these kinds of issues, considering the legal implications of an apostate's actions (crimes or legal commitments) and of his repentance, in *Bayan*, 16:390, 406– 409, 409–413, 421–426, 427–432, 436–437. Ibn Waddah's (d. 900) treatise on "innovations" is an example of concern to determine the boundaries of proper belief and practice: Ibn Waddah, *Kitab al-bidaʿ*, ed. Maribel Fierro (Madrid: Consejo Superior de Investigaciones Científicas, 1998). See Maribel Fierro, "The Treatises against Innovations (*Kutub al-Bidaʿ*)," *Der Islam* 69 (1992): 204–246.

38. Baqi's son Ahmad said, recalling his father, that he did not criticize the madhhab of Malik to others and did not argue with his colleagues about it; he understood that judicial decisions in al-Andalus were made according to the madhhab of Malik; al-Khushani, *Akhbar al-fuqaha'*, no. 58.

Baqi's son Ahmad and ʿUbayd Allah ibn Yahya together in consultation.[39] Ahmad ibn Baqi became a leading jurist and served as prayer leader and judge in Cordoba during the reign of ʿAbd al-Rahman III.[40]

The case against Baqi may have confirmed for others interested in ʿilm al-hadith and *uṣūl al-fiqh* the importance of accommodation to the leading fuqaha' and the prevailing legal conventions, and the amir's intervention made such accommodation possible (*uṣūl al-fiqh* translates as "the sources of jurisprudence"—in this context it refers to an approach to jurisprudence originally identified with al-Shafiʿi centered on the Qur'an and hadith and not on the ra'y of scholarly authorities like Malik). The amir reportedly examined a text meant to support the charge of zandaqa against Baqi and found it exculpatory—the text is identified variously as either al-Shafiʿi's *Risala* or *al-Musannaf* of Ibn Abi Shayba (by one account, the amir ordered that a copy of *al-Musannaf* be made for his library).[41] Muhammad ibn Waddah had studied with some of the same teachers in Iraq as Baqi and was pressured to bear witness against him; in the long run Ibn Waddah successfully integrated his hadith scholarship with his career as a prominent member of the shura and as a scholar and influential teacher.[42] By the time Ibn al-Faradi (962–1013) compiled his biographical dictionary, the heat of the controversy over hadith had largely abated, and hadith had become integrated with ra'y among the fuqaha' of al-Andalus. Ibn al-Faradi observes that Baqi survived the opposition of his Andalusi colleagues (due to divine favor) and transmitted hadith so that it spread in al-Andalus; Ibn Waddah followed Baqi in the promotion of hadith, and subsequently al-Andalus became an "abode of hadith and *isnād*" whereas before it had been

---

39. Al-Khushani, *Akhbar al-fuqaha'*, no. 310; al-Khushani, *Kitab al-qudat bi-Qurtuba*, Arabic, 193; Spanish, 240; Ibn al-Faradi, *Ta'rikh ʿulama' al-Andalus*, 1:336–337; ʿIyad, *Tartib al-madarik*, 4:421–423.

40. Al-Khushani, *Kitab al-qudat bi-Qurtuba*, Arabic, 125–126, 147–148, 154, 191–201; Spanish, 154–155, 181–184, 191, 238–251; ʿIyad, *Tartib al-madarik*, 5:200–209.

41. Asbagh ibn Khalil, one of the witnesses against Baqi and a staunch partisan of the ra'y of Malik and his disciples, especially Ibn al-Qasim, remained hostile to hadith and its proponents. He reportedly said that he would rather be buried with the head of a pig than with the *musnad* (hadith collection organized by chains of transmission) of Ibn Abi Shayba. Although Asbagh issued fatwas in Cordoba for fifty years, his reputation was tarnished when he allegedly fabricated a hadith to support his opinion against raising the hands in prayer (in opposition to Baqi). The efforts of an opponent of the use of hadith to use hadith himself in disputation with those who referred to hadith as a source of law (and who proved able to detect his fabrication) are suggestive of the impact of the introduction of ʿilm al-ḥadīth in al-Andalus. See al-Khushani, *Akhbar al-fuqaha'*, no. 41; Ibn al-Faradi, *Ta'rikh ʿulama' al-Andalus*, 1:129–131; ʿIyad, *Tartib al-madarik*, 4:250–252.

42. See Fierro's introduction to her edition and translation of Ibn Waddah's *Kitab al-bidaʿ*, 9–57.

dominated by the learning and transmission of the ra'y of Malik and his disciples.[43]

Ana Fernández Félix suggests that the confrontation between the *ahl al-ra'y* or the "partisans of ra'y" and the *ahl al-ḥadīth* or "partisans of hadith" in al-Andalus, evident in the case against Baqi ibn Makhlad, contributed to the development of the concept of the Maliki madhhab as a madhhab and a more comprehensive approach to the teachings of Malik, stimulating the collation of the transmissions and opinions of Malik's disciples and the bridging of differences among the various partisans of different disciples.[44] Malikis could not ignore, and came to assimilate, the use of hadith, although some were more ready to do so than others.[45] Ultimately, Ibn Rushd used methods of usul al-fiqh to clarify and explain ambiguities in the opinions of Malik and his disciples in regard to particular legal questions, to reconcile apparent contradictions, and to indicate preferred opinions in his commentary on al-ʿUtbi's *Mustakhraja*. His *Bayan wa-tahsil* both supplanted *al-Mustakhraja* and ensured its survival (since he reproduced its content in his commentary), bringing the Maliki madhhab into closer alignment or correspondence with the jurisprudence of the other schools of law.

The amir could handle the trespasses of individuals on a case-by-case basis in a judicial forum. The regime handled large-scale social conflicts and rebellion with a combination of force and diplomacy, and the language of exclusion and inclusion took different forms. To the extent that chronicles describe the motives of rebel leaders, they seem to be opportunistic. At the same time, chroniclers represent large-scale social upheaval in the ninth century in terms of ethnic and factional conflict. This suggests the exploitation by men of ambition, at least in some cases, of underlying social tensions. For example, Ibn al-Qutiyya reports that a man named Qa'nab fomented fitna between the Arabs and the mawali and between the Butr Berbers and

---

43. Ibn al-Faradi, *Ta'rikh ʿulamaʾ al-Andalus*, 1:143–145. Ibn al-Faradi's linkage of "hadith and *isnād*" is a way of asserting that Andalusis had taken up ʿilm al-ḥadith with its concern for authoritative chains of transmission (*isnād*) and followed its methods.

44. Fernández Félix, *Cuestiones legales*, 332–348.

45. In his chapters on the practice of justice, Ibn Abi Zayd al-Qayrawani cites Malik and his disciples in their opinions that a judge should have knowledge of hadith as well as fiqh. Some of the statements (anachronistically) attributed to Malik and his disciples outline the methodology of *uṣūl al-fiqh*, summarized as follows: the judge should rule according to the book of God first, and if the ruling is not apparent in the Qur'an, the sunna of the Messenger of God; if necessary, he should turn to the statements of the Messenger's companions and consensus; finally (as necessary) the judge may use his reasoned opinion, seeking an analogy from the sources, drawing on past decisions, and seeking consultation with others. See Ibn Abi Zayd al-Qayrawani, *al-Nawadir wa-l-ziyadat*, ed. ʿAbd al-Fattah Muhammad al-Hulw, et al. (Beirut: Dar al-Gharb al-Islami, 1999), 8:10–17.

the Baranis Berbers in the region of Moron and then between the Berbers and the muwalladun in Merida. I use this example because it pairs groups likely to be economic and social rivals in a political system dominated by the Umayyads and their mawali and because of the appearance of the term *muwalladūn*. The term appears in chronicles of Umayyad rule as a label for an emergent social category: converted Muslims and their descendants, indigenous Muslims who were not affiliated by ties of clientage to the Umayyad house or other prominent Arab families.[46] The use of this term (a usage peculiar to al-Andalus) suggests that indigenous Muslims had become a significant social group that did not fit in other categories (it is important to state that *muwallad* describes a social and not a legal category). Muslims, generally speaking, were the dominant social group among Muslims, Christians, and Jews, but the social ranks of the Muslims were complicated by conversion. Mawali, in particular, especially those of Andalusi origin, may have been most concerned to differentiate themselves from other Muslims who were not of Arab lineage. The mawali at times experienced stigmatization by those who claimed Arab descent because of their clientage status, and differentiation from the muwalladun enhanced their prestige and served in the defense of their status. It is notable that Ibn al-Qutiyya and other chroniclers of Andalusi-Umayyad history who employ the term *muwalladūn* were themselves mawali of the Umayyad house.

The stigma experienced by Andalusi mawali in some circles and contexts in the ninth century is conveyed in the story about the appointment of a mawla 'Amr ibn 'Abd Allah (d. 886), to the office of qadi in Cordoba. Al-Khushani reports that 'Amr was the first mawla to be named to this office; he was descended from a mawla of the daughter of 'Abd al-Rahman I, the founder of Umayyad rule on the peninsula. 'Amr had served as secretary to the qadi of Cordoba, Ahmad ibn Ziyad, and as qadi of Ecija before his appointment to the judgeship of the capital; in other words, he was qualified

---

46. Maribel Fierro defines *muwalladūn* differently in "*Mawālī* and *Muwalladūn* in al-Andalus," 195–245, esp. 227–231. She identifies muwalladun as "Arabized indigenous inhabitants of the Iberian peninsula whose Islamization came about as a result of that Arabization." She includes Arabized Christians in this category but acknowledges that over time, as linguistic and cultural assimilation led to religious assimilation, the original meaning of the word as "Arabized indigenous inhabitants" was lost, and the term came to signify indigenous Muslim converts. See also Fierro, "Cuatro preguntas en torno a Ibn Hafsun," *Al-Qantara* 16 (1995): 221–257; trans. Michael Kennedy, "Four Questions in Connection with Ibn Hafsun," in Manuela Marín, *Formation of al-Andalus*, 1:291–328 (specifically 1:307–310, 316–318). I find this definition unwieldy and will refer to muwalladun as Andalusi converts and their immediate descendants; I agree that the term *muwallad* captures the liminal status and mutative culture of a growing social group of partially Islamized and Arabized Muslim converts and their families and immediate descendants.

for his position. The appointment, however, aroused criticism from "the Arabs," who informed the amir that although they would accept 'Amr's appointment to the office of qadi, they objected to his serving as prayer leader—they refused to pray behind a mawla. The amir Muhammad deferred to their pride and appointed 'Abd Allah ibn al-Faraj al-Numari as imam. 'Amr, whom al-Khushani describes as an exemplary judge, was subsequently dismissed from office at the suggestion of Hashim ibn 'Abd al-'Aziz as a way to defuse the case against Baqi ibn Makhlad, but after an interval he was reappointed (he served as judge in Cordoba for two terms, 864–866 and 873–876).[47]

None of the judges in al-Khushani's history of the judges of Cordoba are muwalladun, although the subject does come up in the context of al-Khushani's account of the career of a descendant of a client of the third rightly guided caliph, 'Uthman. Aslam ibn 'Abd al-'Aziz (d. 929) (brother of Hashim ibn 'Abd al-'Aziz) served 'Abd al-Rahman III as qadi of Cordoba for two terms (912–921 and 924–926). One of the candidates for his replacement after he requested retirement after his first nine years of service, was someone identified as having 'ajam parentage ('ajam is a term used to refer to Persians in the eastern Islamic world and might be translated as "foreign"; the term was used in al-Andalus as an ethnic designation for the local Romance-speaking population). 'Abd al-Rahman III ultimately chose to

---

47. Al-Khushani, *Kitab al-qudat bi-Qurtuba*, Arabic, 117–126, 141–144; Spanish, 144–155, 175–177. Al-Khushani reports that Yahya ibn Yahya declined the position of judge when it was offered to him by 'Abd al-Rahman II (Arabic, 11–12; Spanish, 13), but Fierro questions whether Yahya would actually have been offered the appointment considering his lineage—descent from a Berber mawla—no matter how strong his reputation for fiqh (Fierro, "El alfaqui beréber Yahya b. Yahya al-Laythi," 294–296). Ibn al-Qutiyya notes that 'Amr ibn 'Abd Allah was the first to be appointed *qāḍī al-jamā'a* (judge of the community); the designation of the chief qadi and the qadi of Cordoba had previously been *qāḍī al-jund* (judge of the army), and qadis had been selected from the Arab armies; see Ibn al-Qutiyya, *Ta'rikh iftitah*, Arabic, 71–73; Spanish, 57–59; James, *Early Islamic Spain*, 109–110 (note that Ibn al-Qutiyya's account of 'Amr's two tenures as qadi of Cordoba differs from al-Khushani's). It is possible that the resentment by the "Arabs" of 'Amr's appointment had to do with this restructuring of the office of the qadi. See also Luis Molina, "Un árabe entre muladíes: Muhammad b. 'Abd al-Salam al-Jusani," *Estudios onomástico-biográficos de al-Andalus*, vol. 6, ed. Manuela Marín (Madrid: Consejo Superior de Investigaciones Científicas, 1994), 337–351; trans. Michael Kennedy, "An Arab among Muwallads: Muhammad Ibn 'Abd al-Salam al-Khushani," in Marín, *Formation of al-Andalus*, 1:115–128. Molina discusses the attitudes of a contemporary of 'Amr ibn 'Abd Allah, Muhammad ibn 'Abd al-Salam al-Khushani (d. 899), who claimed an illustrious Arab lineage from both parents. Ibn 'Abd al-Salam harbored "hatred of the descendants of converts and *mawālī*" and made malicious allusions to Muhammad ibn Waddah, in particular, who was descended from a mawla of the Umayyad amir 'Abd al-Rahman I. Ibn 'Abd al-Salam got caught in the conflict between Baqi ibn Makhlad and the leading fuqaha' of Cordoba and spent a few days in prison. Molina points out that divisions in this conflict were personal and intellectual and were not drawn along ethnic lines.

appoint Ahmad ibn Muhammad ibn Ziyad for a second term. When the appointment was made, Aslam approved and reportedly praised God for making him someone who descended from "one who says there is no god but God," a statement that expresses his appreciation for, and affirms, his status as an Umayyad client from a family with a long history of association with the ruling house, in contrast to the lowly status of the nameless candidate of 'ajam descent.[48]

Clientage with the Umayyads did confer prestige, and many mawali held positions of power, as we have seen, from the earliest days of Umayyad rule. When 'Abd al-Rahman III ascended the throne after his grandfather's death, the first to formally swear the oath of allegiance to him were his uncles and other members of the Umayyad family, the Arabs of the Quraysh, and the Umayyad mawali. Two stories highlight the significance of clientage with the ruling dynasty by describing the extreme measures individuals might take to secure such a relationship. The frontier lord Muhammad ibn Lubb of the Banu Qasi purportedly murdered the son of a former qadi of Zaragoza when rumors circulated that Ibn Lubb's ancestor, Casius, had been converted to Islam by that qadi rather than by the Umayyad caliph in Damascus, al-Walid. Such a rumor would have greatly undermined his claims to privilege.[49] The story that the eunuch Nasr (whose father was a convert from Carmona) entered palace service when his family surrendered him to slave status and castration illustrates the advantages of personal affiliation to the ruling house. Nasr became a close adviser to 'Abd al-Rahman II and commander of his armies before his involvement in a conspiracy led to his demise.[50]

The muwalladun were not in an enviable position in the competition for status and privilege in the social and political order, but a man with military and political skills could raise a local army and establish regional autonomy.

---

48. Al-Khushani, *Kitab al-qudat bi-Qurtuba*, Arabic, 187–188; Spanish, 233–234.

49. Fierro, "*Mawālī* and *Muwalladūn* in al-Andalus," 213–214.

50. Ibn Hayyan, *al-Muqtabis min anba ahl al-Andalus*, ed. Muhammad Ali Makki (Cairo: Matabi' al-Ahram al-Tijariyya, 1971), 156. Ibn al-Qutiyya reports that Nasr became involved in conspiracies to secure the succession for 'Abd al-Rahman II's son 'Abd Allah (at the instigation of 'Abd Allah's mother, the concubine Tarub). He tried to poison 'Abd al-Rahman II but was forced to drink the poison himself; Ibn al-Qutiyya, *Ta'rikh iftitah*, Arabic, 76–77; Spanish, 61–62; James, *Early Islamic Spain*, 112. Al-Khushani reports that during the reign of al-Hakam I a number of slaves gathered outside the qasr clamoring to be purchased from their masters and entered into the service of the ruler; see *Kitab al-qudat bi-Qurtuba*, Arabic, 50; Spanish, 61. Ibn Hazm reports that after the revolt of the suburb, al-Hakam I recruited (and castrated) Cordobans for service, among them Nasr; Ibn Hazm, *Jamharat ansab al-'Arab*, ed. E. Lévi-Provençal (Cairo: Dar al-Ma'arif, 1948), 87–88. See Joaquín Vallvé, "Nasr, el Valido de 'Abd al-Rahman II," *Al-Qantara* 6 (1985): 179–197.

'Abd al-Rahman ibn Marwan al-Jilliqi (the Galician) was able to secure recognition of his independent rule in Merida (west of the Guadiana River) in
the region of the lower march in this way. He recruited an army and in alliance with Alfonso III of Asturias (866–910) defeated the Umayyad army
led by Muhammad's son and heir apparent, al-Mundhir, and Hashim ibn
'Abd al-Aziz (Hashim was taken captive and held in Asturias for two years
until a heavy ransom secured his release). Muwalladun like the Banu al-
Jilliqi, Banu 'Amrus, and Banu Qasi were able to take command in the
marches and, in exchange for formal allegiance, retain the revenues of their
regions until and unless a new campaign from Cordoba changed the terms.
According to tenth-century accounts, Ibn Marwan al-Jilliqi and his ally
Sa'dun ibn Fath al-Surunbaqi became leaders of the muwalladun in the
west; 'Isa ibn Ahmad al-Razi (as cited by Ibn Hayyan) reported that al-Jilliqi
appealed to the solidarity ('aṣabiyya) of the muwalladun against the Arabs.[51]
Such accounts suggest that the rebellion had a social dimension, but it is
hard to interpret what this meant politically. Did Ibn Marwan al-Jilliqi
emerge as a leader of muwalladun (and others) who were alienated from the
regime, or in the context of the frontier did he (and before him, his father,
who had been governor of Merida) effectively recruit men to Islam as a
marker of allegiance to him (rather than to rival Christian rulers) and as
a means to maintain their allegiance? The question of identity in the borderlands is the subject of chapter 4 ("Borders and Boundaries"), but this
particular question is not resolved. For our purposes, it is significant that
al-Jilliqi is identified as a leader of the muwalladun. The muwalladun who
supported his rebellion did not recognize the authority of the Umayyad regime; when al-Jilliqi agreed to recognize Muhammad's suzerainty, they
were brought into the political community.

The tenth-century historian 'Isa ibn Ahmad al-Razi portrays 'Umar ibn
Hafsun as the leader of a movement inspired by a cause when he refers to
the unity and solidarity 'Umar inspired among the muwalladun and the
'ajam against the Arabs.[52] The terms da'wa, which connotes a religious "call,"
and 'aṣabiyya, which connotes tribal solidarity, are potent with meaning and
suggest that al-Jilliqi and Ibn Hafsun were charismatic leaders who inspired
deeply felt loyalty. Ibn 'Idhari quotes Ibn Hafsun's declamation to his supporters: "Too long . . . already have you borne the yoke of this sultan [ruler]

---

51. Ibn al-Qutiyya, Ta'rikh iftitah, Arabic, 88–90; Spanish, 74–76; James, Early Islamic Spain, 118–
119; Ibn Hayyan, al-Muqtabis III: Chronique du règne du calife Umaiyade 'Abd Allah a Cordoue, ed.
Melchor M. Antuña (Paris: Paul Geuthner, 1937), 15, 23.

52. Ibn Hayyan, Muqtabis III, 24.

who seizes your possessions and crushes you with forced tribute. Will you allow yourselves to be trampled underfoot by the Arabs, who regard you as slaves? . . . Do not believe that it is ambition that makes me speak thus; no, I have no other ambition than to avenge you and deliver you from servitude!"[53] One might expect that converts who were not of Arab lineage in al-Andalus, as elsewhere in the Islamic world, came to challenge the status quo as their numbers became significant, putting pressure on and clashing with the political system and engaging with and contesting the social order. From this perspective, it seems reasonable to conclude that the muwalladun harbored grievances and experienced frustrations and disadvantages that were expressed in their participation in revolts against the regime.[54] In the rural context, if the Syrian ajnad were supported (at least in part) by the revenues derived from taxes on the Christian population, we can imagine tensions and conflict erupting over the assessment and collection of revenues as a consequence of widespread conversion, with converts to Islam resisting payment. Rebellion involving Christians and muwalladun together expressed a common resistance to supporting the Arabs of the ajnad and of the regime. Such conflicts may have been one reason, among others, that the amirs relied increasingly on volunteer levies for specific military campaigns. Meanwhile, in the capital, in the ranks of service, and in professional contexts, individual converts may have experienced personal discrimination and prejudice.

The naming of the recently converted indigenous Muslims as a social group, the muwalladun, reflects the interest of the more advantaged to maintain their privileges and may have fostered the development of a distinctive identity among what must have been a socially diverse population. Pierre Bourdieu writes that the imposition of a name (to describe a "social essence") "is to *signify* to someone what he is and how he should conduct himself as a

---

53. Fierro's translation in "Four Questions in Connection with Ibn Hafsun," 300 n. 35 (English trans. Kennedy), and in "*Mawālī* and *Muwalladūn*," 220–221. See Ibn Idhari, *Kitab al-bayan al-mughrib fi akhbar al-Andalus wa-l-Maghrib*, ed. G. S. Colin and E. Lévi-Provençal (Leiden: E. J. Brill, 1948–1952), 2:114; French translation, *Histoire de l'Afrique et de l'Espagne intitulée al-Bayano l-mogrib*, trans. E. Fagnan (Algiers: Imprimerie Orientale P. Fontana, 1901–1904), 2:108.

54. Thomas F. Glick, *Islamic and Christian Spain in the Early Middle Ages* (Princeton, NJ: Princeton University Press, 1979), 188–191. Fierro suggests that Ibn Hafsun's biography may personify muwallad grievances. The immediate cause for the uprising in his home district of Rayya, she proposes, may have been an exhorbitant increase in taxes to pay for the ransom of Hashim ibn ʿAbd al-ʿAziz, who was held in captivity by the king of Asturias from 876 to 878. Efforts to reconcile Ibn Hafsun to the regime and incorporate him into the hasham failed because converts were precluded from the highest ranks and stipends. Fierro, "Four Questions in Connection with Ibn Hafsun," 298–312.

consequence."[55] The muwalladun had a social identity conferred on them that reinforced an emergent social division. Among Muslims in al-Andalus there were at least four major categories (with subcategories): Arabs, Berbers, mawali, and muwalladun. At the same time, it must be acknowledged that the motives of the muwalladun who led or participated in uprisings in the ninth century were likely to have been varied, divided, circumstantial, and changeable. We do not know what muwallad identity meant or how strong any bond among the muwalladun was.[56]

Ibn al-Qutiyya's account of Ibn Hafsun's rebellion draws on legendary stories and offers a glimpse of what might have been a popular sympathetic view of the rebel leader. Read this way, the historian's narrative supports the idea that ʿUmar ibn Hafsun had a charismatic or ideological appeal that set him apart from other rebels. ʿUmar ibn Hafsun is identified by signs and prophecies as a man with a destiny (opposition to Umayyad rule) that he cannot avoid.[57] The trajectory of Ibn Hafsun's story follows a heroic pattern: he leaves his home as an outcast and goes into exile, returning when his destiny calls him to take up arms against the oppressor. Ultimately, he comes to terms with the limits of his power—he meets his match.[58]

---

55. Pierre Bourdieu, *Language and Symbolic Power*, trans. Gino Raymond and Matthew Adamson (Cambridge, MA: Harvard University Press, 1991), 120; he continues, "To institute, to give a social definition, an identity, is to impose *boundaries*."

56. Manuel Acién Almansa rejects the argument that Ibn Hafsun's rebellion was inspired by a common cause based on ethnic or religious identity. He points out that alliances among those who opposed or supported the regime cut across ethnic and religious lines, and he questions the popular appeal of rebel leaders. He also proposes an interpretation of ʿUmar ibn Hafsun's rebellion that is difficult to prove. In his view, ʿUmar ibn Hafsun and other rebel leaders were fighting to defend their prestige as descendants of the Visigothic nobility and asserted their dominance of the countryside as feudal lords against Umayyad centralization; see Acién Almansa, *Entre el feudalismo y el Islam: ʿUmar ibn Hafsun en los historiadores, en las fuentes y en la historia* (Jaen: Universidad de Jaen, 1994), 66–81. Maribel Fierro defends the idea of ʿUmar ibn Hafsun as a muwallad rebel who appealed to other muwalladun in terms of a cause and group solidarity. She considers Ibn Hafsun and his contemporary, Ibn Marwan al-Jilliqi, to be adventurers who took advantage of local opportunities to establish themselves as petty rulers, rejecting the idea that they were upholders of Visigothic feudal lordship; see Fierro, "Four Questions in Connection with Ibn Hafsun," 291–328. David J. Wasserstein, "Inventing Tradition and Constructing Identity: The Genealogy of ʿUmar ibn Hafsun between Christianity and Islam," *Al-Qantara* 23 (2002): 269–297, demonstrates how the scant evidence of ʿUmar ibn Hafsun's purported noble lineage is suspect.

57. Fierro, "Four Questions in Connection with Ibn Hafsun," 322–326, suggests that messianic expectations of the period became focused on Ibn Hafsun, and that the legends about him did not fully develop or endure because of subsequent events. She also notes a parallel between this episode and the story of ʿAbd al-Rahman I's legendary crossing from North Africa to al-Andalus to found a new dynasty and forge a new destiny.

58. On Arabic-Islamic heroic narratives, see John Renard, *Islam and the Heroic Image: Themes in Literature and the Visual Arts* (Macon, GA: Mercer University Press, 1999), 26–29, 43. I discuss

Ibn al-Qutiyya's narrative has two cycles; perhaps he has combined two versions of the origins of Ibn Hafsun's revolt.[59] The first cycle, which tells a story of exile and return, insult and vindication, clearly identifies 'Umar as the hero with a portended destiny. We are told that the cause of 'Umar's revolt was the unjust action of the governor of his home province of Rayya (Malaga), who had him seized and whipped. 'Umar flees across the sea to Tahart, where he works for a tailor who is also from Rayya. One day an old man enters the shop, and the tailor introduces him to his assistant simply as his compatriot. The old man asks him, as someone who has recently arrived from Rayya, if he is familiar with Bobastro and if he knows any indications of a movement (haraka) there. 'Umar replies that he lived at the foot of the mountain of Bobastro and that he had not observed anything out of the ordinary. The old man assures him that something will soon occur. He then asks, "Do you know of a man from the region named 'Umar ibn Hafsun?" Before 'Umar can answer, the old man realizes to whom he is speaking. He urges 'Umar to give up sewing and go home, telling him, "You will be master of the Banu Umayya; they will meet ruin by your hands and you will rule over a great kingdom."

'Umar returns home, not to the house of his father, with whom he has had a falling out, but to the house of his uncle. He tells his uncle of the old man's words, the uncle affirms them, and together they raise some forty men and take control of the mountain of Bobastro. This cycle in the narration ends with the amir's commander, Hashim ibn 'Abd al-'Aziz, forcing 'Umar (and two other rebels in the mountains of Algeciras) down from the mountains. Ibn al-Qutiyya's narrative continues, relating another story of an insult, a journey, a prophecy, and a return to Bobastro in a different sequence.

Hashim enrolls 'Umar in the hasham and takes him on campaign to the frontier. They confront the enemy in fierce battle, and 'Umar proves himself on the field. He attracts the attention of some of the shaykhs of the frontier, who approach him and tell him: "Return to the fortress you descended from. Nothing will bring you down from it again but death. You will become master of a great portion of al-Andalus and shall fight to the very gates of Cordoba."

'Umar returns to Cordoba from this journey to the frontier and there suffers the abuse that causes him to return to Bobastro and take up arms. The

---

Ibn al-Qutiyya's narration of 'Umar ibn Hafsun's revolt in Safran, *Second Umayyad Caliphate,* 114–115.

59. Ibn al-Qutiyya, *Ta'rikh iftitah,* Arabic, 90–94; Spanish, 76–79; James, *Early Islamic Spain,* 119–121.

prefect of the city (*walī al-madīna, ṣāḥib al-madīna*) is an enemy of Hashim's and takes out his hostility on Ibn Hafsun. He forces him to move from residence to residence and has the worst wheat allotted to him. Ibn al-Qutiyya relates the denouement in the words of ʿUmar himself (as reported by Ahmad ibn Maslama): "I took bread made from this wheat and went to Ibn Ghanim, sahib al-madina, and told him: 'May God have mercy upon you; how can one live on this?' He replied, 'Who the devil are you?' I left him and found Hashim on his way to the qasr. I told him what happened and he said: 'The people are ignorant of you. Make them know who you are.' So I went to my companions and told them all this and left Cordoba on that day. I went to my uncle and told him what this one and that one had said."

The story ends with ʿUmar ibn Hafsun reclaiming Bobastro and "making himself known." From Bobastro he establishes dominion over all the territory between Algeciras and Tudmir. Ibn al-Qutiyya's text describes a figure who really seems to belong in another narrative, culminating in his triumph rather than in a dynastic history of Umayyad rule.

Ibn Hayyan's history, which draws on a number of sources, describes Ibn Hafsun as the enemy in no uncertain terms. He is the enemy of the faith, the agent of the disorder and strife (*fitna*) associated with the Final Hour. The chronicles refer to him as the renegade (*al-māriq*), the rebel (*al-marīd*), the evil or filthy one (*al-khabīth*), the iniquitous or godless one (*al-fāsiq*), the profligate (*al-fājir*), the amir of error (*amīr al-ḍalāla*), the enemy of God (*ʿadūww Allāh*), the apostate or heretic (*al-mulḥid*), the imam of criminals (*imām al-mujrimīn*), and the most extreme of those who disagree (*ashadd al-mukhtalifīn*). ʿUmar's sons, who rebel in turn, are condemned in the same terms.[60]

Ibn Hayyan devotes considerable attention to ʿAbd al-Rahman III's capture and destruction of Bobastro, the mountain stronghold of the Banu Hafsun, in his account of ʿAbd al-Rahman III's reconquest of al-Andalus. He presents the texts of the ruler's pronouncements about the significance of the event, which were read to the public in all the congregational mosques of the realm. ʿAbd al-Rahman III presents himself as heir to the legitimate caliphs (the rightly guided caliphs followed by the Umayyads) and

---

60. Ibn Hayyan, *Muqtabis III*, 9, 50, 52–53, 82–83, 89, 93, 104, 107–108, 128, 139–140; Ibn Hayyan, *al-Muqtabis [V] de Ibn Hayyan*, ed. P. Chalmeta, F. Corriente, and M. Subh (Madrid: Instituto Hispano-Arabe de Cultura, 1979), (Arabic) 61, 65, 67, 71, 76, 101, 114, 138, 147–149, 151, 153, 160–161, 168, 172, 180, 181, 204–207, 209–237; Spanish translation, *Crónica del califa Abdarrahman III an-Nasir entre los años 912 y 942 (al-Muqtabis V)*, trans. María Jesús Viguera and Federico Corriente (Zaragoza: Instituto Hispano-Arabe de Cultura, 1981), 57, 60, 62, 64, 75, 86, 95, 113, 119–121, 122, 123, 124, 127–128, 133, 135, 140, 141, 157–160, 161–181. This evidence is also discussed in Safran, *Second Umayyad Caliphate*.

points to the suppression of the Banu Hafsun as evidence of his mandate. He, like the Umayyad caliphs (of the East) before him, is charged by God with responsibility for maintaining the continuity of the faith by upholding traditions (*sunan*) and by eliminating sedition (*fitan*). He portrays his campaigns against the rebels as holy war against hypocrisy (*nifāq*), schism (*shiqāq*), and polytheism (*shirk*), and his success over Bobastro as the triumph of the true faith. Acting as divine scourge, he has the citadel, mosque, buildings, gardens, and fields of Bobastro razed.[61]

'Umar ibn Hafsun appears in the sources as a man with a calling (da'wa) but also as an opportunist who swears allegiance to both the 'Abbasid caliph and the Fatimid imam successively. From the perspective of the regime, 'Umar's rejection of the authority of the legitimate ruler puts him outside the community. 'Abd al-Rahman III refers to Bobastro in his announcements as "the abode of unbelief and falsehood" (*dār al-kufr wa-l-ifk*), "the locus of error" (*buq'at al-ḍalāla*), "the den of iniquity" (*ma'din al-ghawāya*), and "the pulpit of discord" (*minbar al-khilāf*).[62]

'Umar ibn Hafsun's identity, like his loyalty, seems uncertain and unstable. His exploration of the possibility of securing a bond of "allegiance" to the 'Abbasid caliph in 891 and his reported acknowledgment of the legitimacy of the Fatimid imam in 909 suggests his Muslim identity and interest in Islamic legitimacy. Some of the pejorative terms used to refer to him echo terms used by the Umayyad rulers to describe the Fatimid imams in the tenth century: he is the "Imam of Error" who leads the Muslims astray, the agent of fitna that tears apart the community of believers. On the other hand, 'Abd al-Rahman III also identifies Bobastro as the base of polytheism and the strength and refuge of Christianity. Between 891, when Ibn Hafsun may have acknowleged the 'Abbasid caliph, and 909, when he may have acknowleged the Fatimid imam, he purportedly announced his conversion to Christianity (899)—did he then revert to Islam? In 915 'Umar agreed to submit to 'Abd al-Rahman III for a grant of security and remained obedient (presumably as a Muslim) until his death in 918. 'Umar's son, Ja'far, who also purportedly announced his conversion to Christianity, remained in Bobastro and agreed to pay tribute (after 'Umar's death) only after 'Abd al-Rahman III's army appeared before the walls of his fortress, having secured the defeat of Belda, a town in the region under Ja'far's control (the Muslims of the town agreed to surrender, but the Christians

61. Ibn Hayyan, *Muqtabis [V]*, Arabic, 226–231, 232–237; Spanish, 173–177, 178–181.

62. Ibn Hayyan, *Muqtabis [V]*, Arabic, 226–231; Spanish, 173–177.

refused and were subsequently decapitated). After Ja'far was killed in 920 by some Christians (perhaps for agreeing to pay tribute to Cordoba), his brother Sulayman assumed control of Bobastro and renounced Umayyad authority, while another brother, 'Abd al-Rahman, ruled in Torrox; after Sulayman's death in 926, his brother Hafs assumed control of Bobastro and the remaining Hafsunid lands; he finally surrendered Bobastro in 928.

'Umar ibn Hafsun appears in this account of his rebellion as an elusive figure; his identity, the nature of his authority, and his motivations for rebellion are difficult to interpret, perhaps because he was difficult for contemporaries to define. The uncertainty about 'Umar's identity, whether he was a Muslim or a Christian or changed back and forth, may reflect the way his leadership defied categorization by the Umayyad regime and its chroniclers. His ruling circle included Christians as well as Muslims, and his domains included significant populations of both Christians and Muslims. His identification as a muwallad rebel, to begin with, expresses a differentiation between him (and his followers) and other Muslims (the regime). The fact that the majority of muwalladun had converted from Christianity may have made their identity and loyalties suspect when they so clearly intermingled with Christians. The social and political perspectives of the Banu Hafsun and their allies were alien, if not unfathomable, to the Umayyad regime. The historical narrative does end with resolution: the disinterment of the bodies of 'Umar and Ja'far after the final surrender of Bobastro is said to have confirmed, for all who saw them, that they were Christian (it is explained that they were buried in the Christian manner, facing east, with the hands folded across the chest). (Ibn Hayyan also considered the fact that the churches were in much better repair than the mosques to be proof of 'Umar's apostasy).[63] 'Abd al-Rahman III had the corpses of the officially declared apostates transported back to Cordoba and displayed on al-Sudda gate.[64] The insistence on the significance of 'Umar's identity and the conclusion that he died an apostate (with "clear" evidence) should draw our attention to how unbounded the political community and Muslim society had become in the latter part of the ninth century.

A practical expression of this unboundedness is the question whether and how Islamic law applied in the territories under rebellion. There is evidence to suggest that the fuqaha' supported the Umayyad regime's identification

---

63. Ibn Hayyan, *Muqtabis [V]*, Arabic, 217; Spanish, 167. On the subject of churches in the domains of the Banu Hafsun, see Fernando Arce Sainz, "Arquitectura y rebelión: Construcción de iglesias durante la revuelta de 'Umar ibn Hafsun," *Al-Qantara* 22 (2001): 121–145.

64. Ibn Hayyan, *Muqtabis [V]*, Arabic, 216–217; Spanish, 166.

of the Banu Hafsun as illegitimate rulers, maybe even non-Muslim, and issued fatwas pertaining to some of the legal and religious implications this had for Muslims living in their domains. In the context of a question about Muslims in Sicily living under Norman rule, al-Wansharisi refers to a fatwa the fuqaha' of al-Andalus issued declaring that the testimony of those who were affiliated with the rebel and renegade 'Umar ibn Hafsun was invalid, and that the judgments of his qadis were not legally acceptable.[65] Ibn Zarb observes in a fatwa regarding the status of a slave who claimed to be a free-man unjustly sold as a slave that many of the men sold in the lands of Ibn Hafsun during his rebellion were properly free men. The jurists of al-Andalus addressed this matter, tasking the master (in such circumstances) to present evidence (such as a bill of sale) attesting to the soundness of his purchase and that the slave was the property of the seller.[66]

The Cordoban jurisconsult Muhammad ibn 'Umar ibn Lubaba addressed a hypothetical situation that conjures up the fuqaha' considering the legal-religious significance of Ibn Hafsun's alleged apostasy for Muslims who lived in his domains. The situation presented to the jurist was this: A man acted as prayer leader during Ramadan. He had a Qur'an, led the community in prayer, and presided over the Qur'anic recitations for the entire month. When Ramadan was over, he told the community, "I led you in prayer, and I am a Christian." He then disappeared. Most immediately, this situation raises the question of the validity of the community's observance of Ramadan. Ibn Lubaba opined that the community should repeat the recitations of the Qur'an but not the supererogatory prayers. As for the fraud, Ibn Lubaba stated that if they should get hold of the man, they should ask him to repent and put him to death should he refuse.[67]

---

65. Al-Wansharisi, *Mi'yar*, 2:134.

66. Al-Wansharisi, *Mi'yar*, 9:219–220. The shura of Cordoba considered claims by a man that his female slave had been taken from him in Bobastro by Ibn Hafsun, who then married her; in their fatwa the jurists (Ayyub ibn Sulayman, Muhammad ibn Ghalib, 'Ubayd Allah ibn Yahya, Ahmad ibn Yahya, Ibn Lubaba, Muhammad ibn Walid, Yahya ibn 'Abd al-'Aziz, and Sa'd ibn Mu'adh) emphasized that the laws of Islam did not apply in regions loyal to Ibn Hafsun (considered Dar al-Harb [the Domain of War]); see Ibn Sahl in M. Abdel Wahhab Khallaf, *Watha'iq fi ahkam qada' ahl al-dhimma fi-l-Andalus* (Cairo: al-Markaz al-'Arabi al-Dawli li-l-I'lam, 1980), 83–86. 'Iyad reports that the fate of some captives thought to have been partisans of Ibn Hafsun was discussed by the shura at the behest of the amir 'Abd Allah. All the jurisconsults except Ahmad ibn Baqi, who remained silent, agreed that the captives should be killed as people of fitna and *fasad* (corruption). When pressed, the newly appointed jurisconsult recommended that each captive be interrogated so that those who truly supported Ibn Hafsun and had left the community of Muslims could be executed and those who might simply have been living in his domains could be spared and released; 'Iyad ibn Musa, *Tartib al-madarik*, 5:203.

67. Al-Wansharisi, *Mi'yar*, 1:156.

The fatwa may be another iteration of a question posed to Malik, related by Ibn al-Qasim to Yahya ibn Yahya, and recorded in the masa'il literature. Malik was asked about a Christian who befriended the Muslims, prayed with them for a few days, and then revealed his true identity. Malik said that in such a case the Muslims should make up all the prayers they had performed in his presence. When he was asked whether the man should be killed for pretending to be a Muslim and concealing his unbelief, Malik replied in the negative. Al-'Utbi reports that Sahnun was posed the same question about a deceitful Christian and responded that whether he should be killed depended on circumstances. If the Christian feared for his life or his property (and this caused his deceit), then nothing should be done to him. If he was under no such constraints, he should be invited to Islam and be decapitated should he refuse.[68]

The jurists in these examples were asked to address specific legal questions in extreme circumstances that probably did not describe real situations. Nonetheless, questions about a Ramadan prayer leader who turns out to be Christian and a companion in prayer who turns out to be Christian suggest an anxiety about identity and social practice. The men who acted fraudulently in these scenarios, pretending to be Muslims, were impostors who abused the trust granted to them through their deceit. Erving Goffman articulates the fear impostors generate sociologically: "When we discover that someone with whom we have dealings is an impostor and out-and-out fraud, we are discovering that he did not have the right to play the part he played. . . . The more closely the impostor's performance approximates the real thing, the more intensely we may be threatened, for a competent performance by someone who proves to be an impostor may weaken in our minds the moral connection between legitimate authority to play a part and the capacity to play it."[69]

One might consider that the insecurity generated by the fitna of the ninth century was profoundly disturbing to the Umayyad establishment in ways conjured up by the impostor, and that metaphorically the new caliph dedicated himself to the defeat of the impostor. The regime's interpretation of the fitna after 'Abd al-Rahman III's final triumph over Bobastro was defined by imperatives of boundary making in a context of shifting identity markers in al-Andalus and in opposition to Fatimid claims to the definition of the true faith and who was or was not a member of the Muslim community.

---

68. Ibn Rushd, *Bayan*, 16:426; see also al-Qayrawani, *Nawadir wa-ziyadat*, 1:290, where Ibn Habib's *Wadiha* is also cited for the example of the person who leads a group in prayer while they are traveling and who turns out to be a Christian. He should be offered repentance like an apostate (*ka-l-murtadd*).

69. Erving Goffman, *The Presentation of Self in Everyday Life* (New York: Doubleday, 1959), 59.

'Abd al-Rahman III (r. 912–961) is styled the second founder of Umayyad rule in al-Andalus because he, like his eponymous ancestor, (re)conquered the kingdom and (re)established Umayyad rule.[70] The restoration of the political community and the reintegration of the Muslims depended first on the recovery of the central domains of al-Andalus. 'Abd al-Rahman III came to power at the age of twenty-one without incident and enjoyed the allegiance of families who had served the dynasty for generations. He set about reclaiming his patrimony with strategically targeted campaigns to the immediate north and south of Cordoba, and from there his campaigns ventured further, taking fortresses and towns in the regions of Jaen and Granada, then Seville, and then Malaga (where Bobastro was located). Rebel leaders who agreed to submit to the amir and swear their obedience were sent to Cordoba and eventually allowed to return to their former domains in service to the regime (some who rebelled again were brought captive to Cordoba and executed, and their bodies were left on display). When Hafs ibn 'Umar ibn Hafsun agreed to submit to the amir, he was enrolled in the hasham, like his father before him. The razing of Bobastro in 928 symbolized the culmination of 'Abd al-Rahman III's effort to secure the Andalusi interior; by this time he had already become involved in efforts to secure the northern frontiers against the independence of the frontier lords and in campaigns to counter incursions by the armies of Navarre, Leon, and Castile. 'Abd al-Rahman III first responded to appeals by Berber chiefs across the Straits of Gibraltar for support against the Fatimids in 917, and his involvement intensified after his victory at Bobastro and his declared revival of the Umayyad caliphate. Campaigns in both the northern and southern frontiers continued under his successors, al-Hakam II and the chamberlain Ibn Abi Amir al-Mansur, who ruled in the name of the caliph Hisham II.

'Abd al-Rahman III presented his reconquest of the peninsula as evidence of his divine favor, "He has shown his preference for us," and as the enactment of divine will, "He has achieved his wishes through our rule." These were his words in a letter sent to all his governors in which he announced his adoption of the title Commander of the Faithful and honorific name, al-Nasir li-Din Allah, "Champion of the Religion of God." 'Abd al-Rahman III's reestablishment of Umayyad political authority is characterized as divine grace, "He has hung the hope of the two worlds [this one and the next] on us and brought those who deviated back to us so that they

---

70. Maribel Fierro has published a biography, *'Abd al-Rahman III: The First Cordoban Caliph* (Oxford: Oneworld Publications, 2005).

rejoiced in the shadow of our rule," and he used his success to assert a grander claim to legitimacy: "Anyone else who uses the title [Commander of the Faithful] is an impostor who appropriates what is not rightly his"—a reference both to the Fatimid imam al-Mahdi (r. 909–934) and the ʿAbbasid caliph al-Muqtadir (r. 908–932).[71] ʿAbd al-Rahman III's "restoration" of the Umayyad caliphate or reclamation of Umayyad caliphal legitimacy emerged from and addressed Andalusi politics both in local terms and in terms of the wider Islamic political context, the rise of the Fatimids and the relative weakness of the ʿAbbasids. ʿAbd al-Rahman III's achievement in restoring Umayyad rule in al-Andalus gave him a foundation for the assertion of his legitimate command, and his rivalry with the Fatimids deepened his claims to leadership of the faithful; the local and universal dimensions of his caliphal ideology intertwined. The caliph elaborated on his divine favor, his dynastic legitimacy, his triumph over fitna, his commitment to upholding the true faith, and his leadership of jihad in the context of his rule in the peninsula and his rivalry with the Fatimids in the Maghrib.

After the model of his caliphal rivals, the Andalusi-Umayyad caliph established a new seat of rule in the palace-city of Madinat al-Zahra' but retained his qasr in Cordoba and traveled between the two. He greatly expanded the offices of palace, government, and military service, reflected in the descriptions of all the ranks in attendance on ceremonial occasions, especially when all the men in his service lined up for the entrance of a special dignitary or in the context of a formal enactment of obeisance. The inner circle expanded to include, in addition to men from client families who had served the Umayyads for generations, an increased number of eunuchs and freedmen referred to as the ṣaqāliba (the term refers to their "Slavic" identity—most were originally slaves from central and eastern Europe). Some of the Saqaliba were freedmen clients of the caliphs themselves and served in the highest offices, such as the military commander Ghalib ibn ʿAbd al-Rahman (his patronym is that of his master and patron ʿAbd al-Rahman III) and Jaʿfar ibn ʿAbd al-Rahman (III) al-Nasir (another freedman of ʿAbd al-Rahman III), who held the title of chamberlain.[72]

---

71. *Crónica anónima de ʿAbd al-Rahman III al-Nasir*, ed. and trans. E. Lévi-Provençal and E. García Gómez (Madrid: Consejo Superior de Investigaciones Científicas, 1950), Arabic, 79; Spanish, 152–153.

72. See Lévi-Provençal, *Espagne musulmane*, chaps. 2 and 3, on the government and administration of the caliphate, for discussion of the multiplication of offices; and Mohamad Meouak, *Ṣaqāliba, eunuques et esclaves à la conquête du pouvoir* (Helsinki: Academia Scientiarum Fennica, 2004), on the ṣaqāliba in al-Andalus.

The caliph's judicial appointments were an important function of his rule as Commander of the Faithful. Al-Khushani, who wrote his history of judges at the behest of ʿAbd al-Rahman III's heir apparent, al-Hakam (II), makes clear the caliph's careful consideration of his choices and describes how the caliph instructed each appointment in the duties of his office. ʿAbd al-Rahman III's first judicial appointment was Aslam ibn ʿAbd al-ʿAziz, a man of prominent mawla lineage (he was descended from a client of the third rightly guided caliph) who, like his ancestors and family, was loyal to the Umayyad dynasty. Aware of their role as representatives of his legitimate rule and of the caliphate (after 929), the caliph chose judges who were not only scholars (of breadth as well as depth) but also notable for their eloquence in writing and in speech; Mundhir ibn Saʿid al-Balluti reportedly attracted the caliph's attention when he stepped forward to deliver a rousing oration in praise of the caliph during a reception of envoys from the Byzantine emperor, as described at the beginning of this chapter.[73] The symbolic role of the judge, enhanced during the caliphate, elevated him above the other fuqaha' as his participation in more fully elaborated public ceremonies transformed the office. ʿAbd al-Rahman III, for example, invited the qadi Aslam ibn ʿAbd al-ʿAziz to stand on the balcony of the qasr in his symbolic place when he himself led the cavalcade out of the city for a campaign.

The judges who served during ʿAbd al-Rahman III's reign were not necessarily of Arab lineage; for example, Muhammad ibn Abi ʿIsa and Mundhir ibn Saʿid were of Berber lineage, Aslam ibn ʿAbd al-Aziz descended from an early Umayyad client, and Ahmad ibn Baqi descended from an Andalusi mawla affiliated with the Umayyad family.[74] Many, however, were members of families with enduring connections to the Umayyad dynasty.[75] Training in hadith scholarship as well as in the ra'y of Malik and his disciples did not

---

73. Al-Khushani's history of judges ends with brief mention of ʿAbd al-Rahman III's last judicial appointment, Mundhir ibn Saʿid ibn ʿAbd Allah al-Balluti, in 950 and al-Hakam II's first judicial appointment as caliph (after Mundhir ibn Saʿid al-Balluti's death), Muhammad ibn Ishaq ibn al-Salim, at the end of 966; see al-Khushani, *Kitab al-qudat bi-Qurtuba*, Arabic, 182–207; Spanish, 225–257. See also al-Nubahi, *Kitab al-marqaba*, 69–75; and al-Maqqari, *Nafh al-tib*, 1:364–371.

74. Al-Khushani reports that Baqi ibn Makhlad was the descendant of a mawla of a woman from Jaen, but Fierro suggests that Baqi was a muwallad rather than a mawla. She argues that sources identify him as a mawla in recognition of his merits as a scholar but could not go so far as to attribute an Arab *nisba* or lineage to him. See Maribel Fierro, "Árabes, beréberes, muladíes y *mawālī*: Algunas reflexiones sobre los datos de los diccionarios biográficos Andalusíes," *Estudios onomastico-biograficos de al-Andalus*, vol. 7, ed. Manuela Marín and Helena de Felipe (Madrid: Consejo Superior de Investigaciones Científicas, 1995), 49.

75. Muhammad ibn ʿAbd Allah ibn Abi ʿIsa (d. 950) was a descendant of Yahya ibn Yahya. The caliph named him to a number of offices, both civilian and military, in addition to his role as qadi of

hinder their professional advancement. Mundhir ibn Saʿid al-Balluti was a Zahiri (a partisan of a madhhab that emphasized literal interpretation of the Qurʾan and hadith as the basis for jurisprudence), although he adjudicated according to the madhhab of Malik.[76]

The caliphal commitment to the Maliki madhhab and the personal and professional integration of Andalusi fuqahaʾ into Umayyad rule is evident in an emergent tradition of learning in the Umayyad house. ʿAbd al-Rahman III reportedly learned (heard and recorded) Malik's *Muwatta*ʾ with ʿUbayd Allah ibn Yahya ibn Yahya (who learned it from his father); al-Hakam II then studied the text with Ahmad ibn Muttarif ibn al-Mashshat (who also studied with and transmitted from ʿUbayd Allah ibn Yahya); al-Hakam II, in turn, brought Yahya ibn ʿAbd Allah (great-grandson of Yahya ibn Yahya and brother of Muhammad, the qadi of Cordoba mentioned earlier) to court to instruct his son, the future Hisham II al-Muʿayyad Billah.[77]

Jurists in this generation were bound together more closely by scholarly lineages as the network of Andalusi scholars expanded. Many Andalusi fuqahaʾ learned from shared teachers and taught students in common. When those in the inner circle in Cordoba felt threatened by those they deemed outsiders, they enlisted the support of the caliph. The caliph responded to their complaints about the followers of Ibn Masarra (d. 931) as mediator and consensus builder among the legal-religious scholars and because this was an opportunity to demonstrate his commitment to the true faith to his community and, more broadly, to project his authority in opposition to the claims of the Fatimid imam.

The teachings of Ibn Masarra seem to have been informed by Neoplatonic ideas and an interest in reconciling revelation and philosophy. He was exposed to Muʿtazili thought by his father and also to the instruction of the Sufis Dhu al-Nun, Abu Yaʿqub al-Nahrajuri, and Sahl al-Tustari during his travels in the East, and these ideas informed his outlook.[78] The contemporary

---

Cordoba and prayer leader. See Manuela Marín, "Los Banu Abi ʿIsa: Una familia de ʿulamaʾ Cordobeses," *Al-Qantara* 6 (1985): 291–320.

76. Fierro suggests that ʿAbd al-Rahman III's appointment of a Zahiri as qadi of Cordoba was a way to assert the Sunnism of his regime in opposition to the Shiʾism of the Fatimids, and that the caliph had an interest in Sunni pluralism; see Fierro, ʿ*Abd al-Rahman III*, 125–131. It may be that ʿAbd al-Rahman III chose his judges with the shura in mind and with an interest in preserving his role as arbiter.

77. Ibn Hayyan, *Muqtabis [V]*, Arabic, 216–217; Spanish, 256–258.

78. Some of Ibn Masarra's writings have been published; see Muhammad Kamal Ibrahim Jaʿfar, *Min qadaya-l-fikr al-Islami* (Cairo: Maktabat Dar al-ʿUlum, 1978), 310–360; and Emilio Tornero, "Noticia sobre la publicación de obras inéditas de Ibn Masarra," *Al-Qantara* 14 (1993): 47–64. On ʿAbd

historian al-Razi reports that Ibn Masarra retreated from Cordoba to an estate outside the city where he conducted his teachings and ensnared the unsuspecting with his clever talk, committing his followers to secrecy. Al-Razi gives the official view of Ibn Masarra's heretical views: he believed in the createdness of the Qur'an and human free will and did not believe in the intercession of the Prophet on behalf of the repentant sinner.[79] Ibn Masarra had been a student of Ibn Waddah and al-Khushani before he traveled east to expand his learning; there he sought out experts in kalam and became associated with the Mu'tazila.[80] His ideas were criticized by some in his day, but others too were criticized for their interest in kalam and Mu'tazili ideas without dire consequences. It was only some twenty years after his death that the caliph undertook to respond to the appeals of the fuqaha' and formally suppress his teachings.[81] The proclamations against Ibn Masarra's followers issued in the Great Mosque of Cordoba in 952, 956, and 957 and read in the provinces articulated and demonstrated the caliph's defense of the straight path and his caliphal legitimacy and became an occasion to assert these claims most pointedly against his caliphal rivals.[82] 'Abd al-Rahman III used the persecution of Ibn Masarra's followers to assert his claim to leadership of the Sunni community (in opposition to the 'Abbasids) at the same time at which he had the Shi'a cursed publicly from all the *minbars* (pulpits) of al-Andalus and pursued his anti-Fatimid campaign in North Africa.

The caliph authorized an investigation of all those suspected of innovation and heresy among the disciples of Ibn Masarra and dedicated himself to the elimination of this emergent sect (*firqa*). In the course of the campaign,

---

al-Rahman III's persecution of Ibn Masarra's followers, see M. Cruz Hernández, "La Persecución anti-Masarri durante el reinado de 'Abd al-Rahman III al-Nasir li-Din Allah, según Ibn Hayyan," *Al-Qantara* 2 (1981): 51–67; Fierro, *Heterodoxia*, 113–118, 132–140; and Maribel Fierro, "La política religiosa de Abd al-Rahman III," *Al-Qantara* 25 (2004): 133–137.

79. Ibn Hayyan, *Muqtabis [V]*, Arabic, 20–24; Spanish, 25–30.

80. Ibn Hayyan, *Muqtabis [V]*, Arabic, 30–36; Spanish, 35–39 (citing Ibn al-Faradi).

81. Al-Wansharisi records a question posed to the Cordoban jurist Abu Ishaq ibn Ibrahim and his reply, discussing two debatable points of difference between Ibn Masarra's followers and the Cordoban fuqaha'. The former accused the latter of innovation in the arbitration of marriage disputes and in the rejection of the proof of a single testimony with an oath; see al-Wansharisi, *Mi'yar*, 2:443–445. For discussion of differences of opinion about the arbitration of marriage disputes (whether two arbiters were required), including discussion of this fatwa, see María Isabel (Maribel) Fierro, "Los Malikíes de al-Andalus y los dos arbitros," *Al-Qantara* 6 (1985): 79–102.

82. Ibn Hayyan, *Muqtabis [V]*, Arabic, 24–30; Spanish, 30–35. The suppression of Ibn Masarra's followers was protracted. In 961 the future qadi Muhammad ibn Zarb held a public burning of Ibn Masarra's writings outside the congregational mosque, attended by a group he had persuaded to repent. Ibn Zarb also composed a refutation of Ibn Masarra's "madhhab"; he was qadi of Cordoba from 978 until his death in 991. See al-Nubahi, *Kitab al-marqaba*, 78.

he affirmed his commitment to the madhhab of Malik and also to the sunna of the Prophet and the pious ancestors, bringing them together with references to the sunna of Medina and to Medina as the "nest of the faith" and refuge of the Prophet. In his proclamations the caliph described his commitment to bring back to the fold those who had been led astray by those who themselves had been led astray by books they did not understand, by those who disputed the verses of the Qur'an (a reference to Qur'an 40:69–72), twisted the interpretation of the hadiths of the Prophet, and insulted the upright ancestors and transmitters of hadith. The caliph pointed out that the members of this firqa had deviated so much from the norms of the community (and identification with the community) that they no longer returned the greetings of Muslims (a reference to Qur'an 4:86). They had withdrawn from the faith and the pious community and proclaimed themselves to be at war; in the caliph's words, they declared the shedding of the blood of Muslim men to be licit, as well as the violation of Muslim women and the enslavement of Muslim children.[83]

In his persecution of Ibn Masarra's sect 'Abd al-Rahman III affirmed the conjunction of interests between the regime and the leading fuqaha' that defined the parameters of Islamic pluralism.[84] Ibn Masarra's withdrawal from society effectively defined him as an outsider; the growth of his following even after his death suggested that his teachings were becoming the basis of a group identity and solidarity independent from his leadership and self-consciously apart from the larger Muslim community. The fuqaha', in essence, considered their ideas and activities to be out of bounds, and the caliph had his own ideological reasons for making a show of their persecution. In the process, both he and the fuqaha' affirmed the custom of Medina and the compatibility of the ra'y of Malik and the hadith of the Prophet and the sunna of the pious ancestors.

Early in his reign al-Hakam II also had an opportunity to demonstrate his commitment to defense of the faith in the prosecution and punishment of an individual, in this case a man called Abu al-Khayr (literally, "Father of Good").[85] The chief of police of Cordoba, Qasim ibn Muhammad, collected over forty testimonies against this individual and presented his report

83. Ibn Hayyan, *Muqtabis [V]*, Arabic, 25–30; Spanish, 31–35.

84. Fierro, "Política religiosa de 'Abd al-Rahman III," 119–156.

85. The case of Abu al-Khayr is most fully preserved by Ibn al-Sahl in *al-Ahkam al-kubra*; see Khallaf, *Thalath watha'iq fi muharabat al-ahwa'*, 57–100. Abu al-Khayr's case is cited by Ibn 'Attab (d. 1069) in the case against Ibn Hatim al-Tulaytuli in 1064; see al-Wansharisi, *Mi'yar* 2:329. See also Fierro, *Heterodoxia*, 149–155.

to the qadi, Mundhir ibn Sa'id al-Balluti, the prayer leader, Ahmad ibn Mutarrif, the jurisconsult Ishaq ibn Ibrahim, and other jurisconsults in the hall of the ministers (bayt al-wuzarā') in the palace. They all found Abu al-Khayr to be a godless unbeliever (mulḥid kāfir) and called for his death. Qa-sim ibn Muhammad, Mundhir ibn Sa'id, Ahmad ibn Mutarrif, and Ishaq ibn Ibrahim all agreed that he should not be given an opportunity to defend himself, but others (not named) disagreed.[86] The caliph rendered the final judgment: he ordered that in defense of God, his Book, and his Messenger, Abu al-Khayr should be crucified without opportunity for defense.[87]

If the recorded testimonies against Abu al-Khayr are to be believed, he was a provocateur whose statements were deliberately out of bounds. Some of his reported statements were politically defiant: he insulted the first three caliphs and the Prophet's wife, 'A'isha, and claimed that 'Ali was the true messenger of God; he reviled the caliphs and their ancestors and descen-dants and called for jihad against them.[88] When Muhammad ibn 'Abd Allah al-Tujibi, in conversation with the accused, described the caliph al-Hakam II as the shadow of God on earth where all the oppressed found refuge, Abu al-Khayr replied that his great ambition was to lead five thousand horsemen to the caliphal city of Madinat al-Zahra', kill the people there, and establish the mission of Abu Tamim (the Fatimid caliph al-Mu'izz). Al-Tujibi de-clared him outside Islam in accordance with the words of the Prophet that "those who bear arms against us are not of us."[89]

Abu al-Khayr was not simply or obviously a partisan of the Fatimid cause, according to the other testimonies against him. He made other state-ments considered outrageous by religious orthodoxy. In another exchange, this time with Muhammad ibn Ayyub ibn Sulayman ibn Rabi'a, Abu al-Khayr compared people to plants and insinuated that people were not ac-

<hr/>

86. Ibn Sahl in Khallaf, Thalath watha'iq fi muharabat al-ahwa', 82–84

87. Ibn Sahl in Khallaf, Thalath watha'iq fi muharabat al-ahwa', 62–63; Ishaq ibn Ibrahim's position is presented at 91–100. The jurist cites the opinions of Malik and Ibn al-Qasim and hadiths from al-Muwatta' in support of his argument that defense is precluded because of the preponderance of reliable testimonies.

88. Ibn Sahl in Khallaf, Thalath watha'iq fi muharabat al-ahwa', 60, 62, 63, 65, 68, 70, 71, 74, 76, 77, 78, 79. Al-'Utbi records the question posed to Ibn al-Qasim whether someone who says, "Gabriel made a mistake in the revelation, and the true prophet should have been 'Ali ibn Abi Talib" should be offered the chance to repent or should be killed outright. Ibn al-Qasim replied that he should be offered repentance and killed if he did not repent. Ibn Rushd considers such a statement to be in-novation (bid'a) that crosses into patent unbelief. See Bayan, 16:320. Ibn Sahl also identifies this as an example of innovation that expresses clear unbelief (as opposed to other examples of innovation that do not transgress into unbelief); see Ibn Sahl in Khallaf, Thalath watha'iq fi muharabat al-ahwa', 17–38.

89. Ibn Sahl in Khallaf, Thalath watha'iq fi muharabat al-ahwa', 57.

countable for their actions. Muhammad ibn Ayyub challenged him with the Qur'an: "A portion [of people] goes to the Garden, a portion to the Fire" (Qur'an 42:7) Abu al-Khayr responded by disparaging the Qur'an as superstition and nonsense.[90] Saʿd ibn Saʿid testified that Abu al-Khayr told him that half the Qur'an was fables and that he could recite a better one if he wanted to.[91] Another witness reported that Abu al-Khayr claimed to know the capacity of the seas, the weight of the mountains, and the number of particles in the universe.[92]

Abu al-Khayr was accused of mocking the religion, and the evidence was copious against him; additional reports of his statements were provocative because of his apparent defiance of Islamic proscriptions and prescriptions. Many witnesses reported that he claimed that the drinking of wine and sodomy (*liwāṭ*) were permissible; for example, according to testimony, Abu al-Khayr confronted ʿAli ibn ʿAbd Allah al-Hujari about the latter's previous statements against him: "I heard what you testified against me, that I commit illicit and homosexual acts and drink wine and listen to the *ʿūd* (lute)." He then told him that he concurred with this testimony and would tell the authorities about it himself.[93] When Masʿud ibn ʿAbd Allah al-Umawi found Abu al-Khayr drunk, he reported, the reprobate asked that when he died, the ritual lustration of his body should be performed with wine rather than water.[94] By other accounts, Abu al-Khayr referred to the hajj as foolishness and made fun of people in prayer; A witness testified that he heard Abu al-Khayr comment on the people in prayer in *ʿajamiyya* (local Romance): "O, People! They raise their buttocks and lower their heads!"[95] He himself reportedly did not perform the daily or Friday prayers. Another witness overheard Abu al-Khayr asking a Christian for some pork, and when the Christian questioned him, he replied, "I do not follow the religion of Muhammad or believe in it."[96] Asbagh ibn ʿIsa al-ʿAyni testified that he

---

90. Ibn Sahl in Khallaf, *Thalath watha'iq fi muharabat al-ahwa'*, 60.

91. Ibn Sahl in Khallaf, *Thalath watha'iq fi muharabat al-ahwa'*, 61. David J. Wasserstein finds a close similarity between another statement of Abu al-Khayr reported by Saʿd ibn Saʿid and Abot 1:3 and proposes that this may be a bit of evidence that part of the Mishnah or the Talmud was translated and available in Arabic, perhaps in the library of al-Hakam II. See Wasserstein, "An Arabic Version of Abot 1:3 from Umayyad Spain," *Arabica* 34 (1987): 370–374; and Wasserstein, "Encore un fois 'Abot' 1:3 dans l'Espagne Omeyyade," *Arabica* 38 (1991): 275–277.

92. Ibn Sahl in Khallaf, *Thalath watha'iq fi muharabat al-ahwa'*, 75.

93. Ibn Sahl in Khallaf, *Thalath watha'iq fi muharabat al-ahwa'*, 62–63.

94. Ibn Sahl in Khallaf, *Thalath watha'iq fi muharabat al-ahwa'*, 76.

95. Ibn Sahl in Khallaf, *Thalath watha'iq fi muharabat al-ahwa'*, 64.

96. Ibn Sahl in Khallaf, *Thalath watha'iq fi muharabat al-ahwa'*, 66.

heard Abu al-Khayr say, "If I could destroy the ka'ba and leave the Muslims without a *qibla* [an orientation for prayer], I would do it."[97]

Unfortunately, we do not have enough information to assess adequately whether the collected testimonies against Abu al-Khayr were sound (the chief of police personally affirmed the testimony of eighteen of the witnesses). If the testimonies did reflect the statements of the accused, it is difficult to discern his motivations—why was he determined to provoke the leading men of the community (why was he called Abu al-Khayr)? If the recorded testimonies were part of a plot contrived against him, the motives behind such a plot are opaque. It may well be that he was a Fatimid sympathizer, and the additional accusations were the result of a piling up of evidence against him, or perhaps he was an antinomian *bāṭinī* (believer in the inner or esoteric meaning of revelation), an Isma'ili but not necessarily a Fatimid partisan, stirring up trouble and delighting in his defiance of conventional Islamic belief and practice.[98]

The testimonies against Abu al-Khayr, whether concocted or not, describe very clear boundaries. His reported transgressions were indisputably beyond the limits of acceptable speech and behavior. The recording and presentation of the testimonies against this "godless unbeliever" and his condemnation and crucifixion reinforced the experience of community and the role of the caliph as defender of the faith. Ishaq ibn Ibrahim reported to the caliph of the "joy" of the people of Cordoba (both high-ranking and common) at his execution. In his letter to the caliph he celebrated the fact that the first bloodshed of the new reign was out of rage on behalf of God, his Book, and his Messenger against someone who made light of God's greatness. Ishaq ibn Ibrahim observed how grateful the caliph's subjects (flock) were for his rule and for his extirpation of the heretic "Abu al-Sharr" ("Father of Evil") and revivification of the sunna (*iḥyā' al-sunna*).[99] The bloodshed of the evildoer stirred emotions and, as the jurist described, promoted group solidarity and obedience to the new caliph.

Al-Hakam II, having recently assumed the throne, acted to demonstrate his authority broadly, to all his subjects, projecting his legitimacy near and

---

97. Ibn Sahl in Khallaf, *Thalath watha'iq fi muharabat al-ahwa'*, 67

98. Khallaf suggests that Abu al-Khayr was a Fatimid missionary; Khallaf, *Thalath watha'iq fi muharabat al-ahwa'*, 48–51. See also Farhat Dachraoui, "Tentative d'infiltration S[h]i'ite en Espagne musulmane sous le règne de al-Hakam II," *Al-Andalus* 23 (1958): 97–106. Crone describes Isma'ili antinomianism and arrests for openly defying Islamic prohibitions in this period—perhaps this is an example? See Crone, *God's Rule*, 207–211.

99. Ibn Sahl in Khallaf, *Thalath watha'iq fi muharabat al-ahwa'*, 84–89.

far. He also took care to assert his authority to the more circumscribed circles of the court and the legal-judicial establishment. He wrote to his minister 'Isa ibn Futays of his decision in the case against Abu al-Khayr. In this context he declared that the madhhab of Malik and his disciples was the best and conformed completely to *al-sunna wa-l-jamāʿa*, that is, to Sunni (rather than Shiʿi) Islam, and he urged that the fuqahaʾ adhere to it.[100] He made a similar statement in his correspondence with Ishaq ibn Ibrahim, disparaging those who diverged from the madhhab of Malik in their fatwas. In his decision about Abu al-Khayrʾs case, the caliph made clear that the preclusion of defense in circumstances like these was the position of the Maliki madhhab. His judgment and his support of the fatwas of those who argued this position involved him in legal interpretation.[101] In this connection al-Hakam IIʾs assertion of the primacy of the Maliki madhhab was in part an assertion of his authority among the fuqahaʾ. Al-Hakam II was well known for the depth and breadth of his intellectual interests—he was an avid patron of learning and culture as heir apparent and had already founded his great library. Perhaps because of this reputation, as Commander of the Faithful he declaratively established his commitment to the Maliki madhhab in the administration of justice.[102]

Al-Hakam II ruled for fifteen years, and during that time two judges presided over Cordoba: Mundhir ibn Saʿid al-Balluti, who died in office in 966 at age eighty-two, and Abu Bakr Muhammad ibn Ishaq ibn al-Salim, who also died in office in 977. With only one exception (Ahmad ibn ʿAbd Allah al-Asbahi, who died in office after two years of service), all the Cordoban judges of the caliphal period until al-Mansurʾs death in 1002 held their positions for a decade or longer, indicating continuity in the practice of justice and suggesting political stability among the fuqahaʾ.

In summary, one may observe that the extension and expansion of Umayyad rule in the caliphal period secured stability in the tenth century, quite different from the situation in the ninth. In the ninth century rebellion persistently challenged the Umayyad regime. The fickle loyalties of the Banu

---

100. Ibn Sahl in Khallaf, *Thalath watha'iq fi muharabat al-ahwa'*, 83–84, 89–91.

101. Al-Hakam appointed Muhammad ibn Salim as qadi after the death of Mundhir ibn Saʿid and instructed him to apprise him of any difficult or ambiguous cases so that he could offer his opinion. Al-Nubahi includes the text of Ibn Salimʾs appointment in his biographical entry; see al-Nubahi, *Kitab al-marqaba*, 75–77.

102. See David J. Wasserstein, "The Library of al-Hakam II al-Mustansir and the Culture of Islamic Spain," *Manuscripts of the Middle East* 5 (1990–1991): 99–105.

Hafsun and the questionable religious identities of 'Umar and his son Ja'far exemplify a kind of unboundedness in politics, society, and religion. The Umayyad amirs' reincorporation of former rebels into the political community and their system of rule as border lords or members of the hasham suggests that they were flexible in their determination of insiders and outsiders, perhaps as a function of their relatively limited coercive and persuasive power. In the domain of law and justice, Andalusi fuqaha' and judges in the ninth century were acquiring and testing their expertise and status and participated through competition and with the consensus building of the amir in the negotiation of legal opinions and decisions. They negotiated boundaries of acceptable expression in the cases of blasphemy against Harun ibn Habib and 'Ajab's nephew, and of the domain of Andalusi jurisprudence in the dropped charges of zandaqa against 'Abd al-A'la and Baqi ibn Makhlad. The burgeoning of a large reticulated professional class of Maliki fuqaha' who studied and taught an emergent canon of Maliki texts in al-Andalus suggests different issues and stakes in the development of consensus and perhaps greater likelihood of conformity and continuity of practice in the tenth century than in the ninth. The persecution of Ibn Masarra's followers and the case against Abu al-Khayr were less matters of internal politicking or debates about points of law than they were occasions for the projection of the caliph's authority and the identification of his rule with the mutual support of the Maliki fuqaha'. The trial of Abu al-Khayr, in particular, was performative and predictable in its outcome.

The numbers of jurists multiplied between the ninth and tenth centuries, and so did judicial offices. The provinces and the marches all had judges in the major towns; some also had minor district judges (ḥukkām; s.ḥākim) who resolved simple matters in local quarters. A variety of judicial offices with specialized jurisdictions emerged as part of the extension of caliphal authority, such as chief of (the court of) complaints (ṣāḥib al-radd or ṣāḥib al-maẓālim) and market inspector (ṣāḥib al-sūq or muḥtasib). The administration of justice also became more routinized, with insistence on written opinions (by the judge Ahmad ibn Muhammad ibn Ziyad, who served twice as qadi of Cordoba in the early tenth century), the publication of notarial books, and the formalization of testimony.[103] Jurists circulated through various judicial offices in the provinces and the capital and became

---

103. Al-Khushani, *Kitab al-qudat bi-Qurtuba*, Arabic, 176; Spanish, 217. Ibn al-'Attar provided instructions for the issuing of documents in his tenth-century notarial handbook *Kitab al-watha'iq wa-l-sijillat*, ed. P. Chalmeta and F. Corriente (Madrid: Academia Matritense del Notariado, Instituto Hispano-Arabe de Cultura, 1983), 642.

functionaries of the regime in a number of capacities. Muhammad ibn Abi 'Amir (al-Mansur), who effectively usurped Umayyad rule in the last quarter of the tenth century, was himself a faqih and served as chief judge of Seville and of the Maghrib for al-Hakam II (he was at the same time chief of police, the administrator of unclaimed inheritances, and the official in charge of the mint) before he insinuated himself into the court of Hisham II.

The chapter concludes with a brief reference to Ibn Abi 'Amir's assumption of power as majordomo acting in the name of the caliph Hisham II (who ascended the throne as a boy) and with the manipulation of the symbols of the Umayyad caliphate. For five years after the death of al-Hakam II (from 976 to 981), Ibn Abi 'Amir deftly played one of the former caliph's officials against another until he himself dominated the court as hajib or chamberlain (to a caliph he had sequestered), the administration (with the appointment of his close supporters),[104] and the military (with his elimination of al-Hakam II's commander in chief and importation of Berber armies). According to Ibn 'Idhari, he eventually replaced the Andalusi ajnad with Berber armies and created his own guard, eliminating that of al-Hakam II.[105] In this connection it is worth observing that the office of the qadi of Cordoba may also have eventually come under Ibn Abi 'Amir's sway along with the other pillars supporting Umayyad rule, but also that he respected continuity in the judgeship. Al-Hakam II's qadi Ibn al-Salim remained in office until his death in 977. His successor Muhammad ibn Yabqa ibn Zarb, appointed by Hisham II (presumably with some counsel), was a respected jurist from the shura of Ibn al-Salim's court and an authority on masa'il.[106] Ibn Zarb, who served for thirteen years, was aware of his authority and perhaps attempted to preserve the dignity of his office and that of the caliph in (at least) symbolic ways. He reportedly took care to address the caliph and the hajib appropriately and distinctively in his sermons and issued a fatwa expressing his view that the qadi and the shura should not meet in the new mosque of al-Mansur's palace-city Madinat al-Zahira (in 979 Ibn Abi 'Amir ordered that all official business be conducted there); the

---

104. An anecdote describes Ibn Abi 'Amir's confidence in his eventual mastery over al-Andalus. He asked his friends what positions they would like when he came to power; they laughed but gave their answers, and ultimately he fulfilled their wishes for various offices: 'Amr ibn 'Abd Allah ibn 'Amma became sahib al-madina, Ibn al-Mar'azzi became sahib al-suq, and Ibn al-Hasan became qadi of Rayya. See al-Nubahi, Kitab al-marqaba, 81.

105. Ibn 'Idhari, Kitab al-bayan al-mughrib, Arabic, 2:293; French, 2:489.

106. Hisham II's appointment of the qadi took place before al-Hakam II's chamberlain was arrested (in 978) and perhaps while Ibn Abi 'Amir was on military campaign.

qadi and the shura continued to meet in the congregational mosque of Cordoba until the qadi's death. After Ibn Zarb's death in 991, however, al-Mansur, by now fully secure in his power, appointed his maternal uncle, Muhammad ibn Yahya ibn Zakariyya ibn Bartal, qadi of Cordoba.[107] The same year al-Mansur designated his son ʿAbd al-Malik (al-Muzaffar) as his successor, bestowing on him the title and status of hajib (which henceforth al-Mansur no longer used). Late in al-Mansur's rule, when Ahmad ibn ʿAbd Allah ibn Dhakwan served as qadi of Cordoba for the first time (1001–1004), al-Mansur demonstrated his commitment to orthodoxy and asserted his authority over the fuqaha' by removing all books having to do with philosophy and materialism from al-Hakam II's library and burning them in the presence of the qadi, the jurist ʿAbd Allah ibn Ibrahim al-Asili, and the grammarian (and former tutor to the Umayyad house) Muhammad ibn Hasan al-Zubaydi.[108]

---

107. See al-Nubahi, *Kitab al-marqaba*, 77, 84. Ibn Bartal studied with a number of scholars in the East (especially in Egypt, but also in Mecca, Jerusalem, and Ramallah) and in al-Andalus. ʿAbd al-Rahman III appointed him qadi of Rayya; he served as qadi of Jaen at the start of Hisham II's reign, and after Ibn Zarb's death he was appointed qadi of Cordoba. Ibn al-Faradi studied with him (among other things, al-Bukhari's hadith collection) and portrays him as a man of honesty and impartial justice. See Ibn al-Faradi, *Ta'rikh ʿulama' al-Andalus*, 2:139–141.

108. Ibn ʿIdhari, *Kitab al-bayan al-mughrib*, Arabic, 2:292–293; French, 2:487. According to Ibn al-Faradi, al-Asili studied in the East, returned at the end of al-Hakam II's reign, and served in his shura. He was an authority on hadith and transmitted al-Bukhari's *Sahih*; he also wrote a book on differences of legal opinion among Malik, al-Shafiʿi, and Abu Hanifa. Al-Zubaydi was a grammarian, and al-Hakam II appointed him as tutor to Hisham II. See Ibn al-Faradi, *Ta'rikh ʿulama' al-Andalus*, 1:334–335; 2:120–121. Ibn Dhakwan was the last qadi of Cordoba (second term, 1005–1010) before the fitna that wrought the demise of Hisham II and the ruination of the city.

CHAPTER 2

Society in Transition

In the immediate postconquest era the divide between conquerors and conquered in al-Andalus was marked in a number of ways. The conquerors were distinct by virtue of their origins, religion, language, social organization, manners, and customs. However, with the establishment of Muslim rule, identity markers began to shift. Conquerors and conquered became Muslims and *dhimmīs* ("protected persons"). They inhabited the same polity and lived together in physical proximity in the towns and countryside of the peninsula, and original defining differences mutated. The gradual centralization of political power, changes in patterns of settlement and demography, economy, and culture, interfaith marriage, and conversion pushed the transformation of boundaries over three centuries. The interest in asserting distinctions between Muslim and non-Muslim, between Christian and non-Christian, or between Jew and non-Jew persisted on all sides for those who saw themselves as guardians of their religion and community; distinctions might be nuanced and recognized subtly or on some occasions asserted emphatically. At the same time, as part of the process of transmutation, emerging distinctions within the different confessional communities also became significant as reflected in the emergence of the term *muwalladūn* (s. *muwallad*) to refer to converts of indigenous origins and their descendants.

This chapter describes more fully the social transformation of al-Andalus in the ninth and tenth centuries, and discusses what the Arabic Islamic legal texts and the Latin martyrologies reveal about cultural change, interfaith marriage, and conversion. It begins with an overview of the physical integration of communities, describing patterns of settlement over time, to situate the changing dynamics of intercommunal relations in an evolving and transformative social space.

At the time of the Islamic conquest, the population of the Iberian Peninsula may have been largely rural, with the seat of aristocratic power in the countryside; modern scholars have traditionally described a trend of urban decline in the late Roman era associated with the loss of civic space, although this perspective has come under review.[1] After the Visigoths converted to Catholicism, some previously Roman settlements became the seats of bishoprics and centers of administration, generating a modest urban revival. Notably, Cordoba became a regional center with a governor's palace and the newly constructed Basilica of St. Vincent. The Muslim conquerors directed their campaigns against these cities and in 716 chose Cordoba as the capital. The commanders and their men settled in existing structures in towns primarily in the southeast; other towns were left to decline, or their settlements gradually shifted sites, and new towns were eventually established. In the ninth century the Muslim ruling establishment constructed towns such as Murcia, Ubeda, and Badajoz in strategic locations and rebuilt or fortified others, such as Calatrava, Madrid, Talamanca, Calatayud, Daroca, Huesca, Pechina, Seville (after the Norman attack in 844), Algeciras, and Merida. In the upper march local lords founded Ucles and rebuilt Lerida. The ninth and early tenth centuries saw a period of urban growth that accelerated under the caliphate in the tenth century.[2]

Arabs settled in the countryside as well as in the towns, among the Christian populations in the fertile valley of the Guadalquivir, and around Murcia and Zaragoza, while the Berbers tended to settle in the Meseta, Extremadura, and the Northwest (this region was abandoned in the course

---

1. For a revised history of the Roman cities in Spain in late antiquity and the early Middle Ages based on archaeological as well as textual sources, see Michael Kulikowski, *Late Roman Spain and Its Cities* (Baltimore: Johns Hopkins University Press, 2004).

2. See Pierre Guichard, "Les villes d'al-Andalus et de l'occident musulman aux premiers siècles de leur histoire," in *Genèse de la ville islamique en al-Andalus et au Maghrib occidental*, ed. Patrice Cressier and Mercedes García-Arenal (Madrid: Casa de Velázquez, 1998), 37–52; Hugh Kennedy, "From Antiquity to Islam in the Cities of al-Andalus and al-Mashriq," ibid., 53–64; Christine Mazzoli-Guintard, "L'urbanisation d'al-Andalus au xie siècle: Données chronologiques," ibid., 99–106; Manuel Acién Almansa and Antonio Vallejo Triano, "Urbanismo y estado islámico: De Corduba a Qurtuba-Madinat al-Zahra'," ibid., 107–136; and Sonia Gutiérrez Lloret, "Ciudades y conquista. El fin de las *ciutatis* Visigodas y la génesis de las *mudun* islámicas del sureste de al-Andalus," ibid., 137–158.

of the Berber rebellion of 741). Areas of the countryside may have remained exclusively Christian, perhaps initially under the administration of semiautonomous lords like Theodemir, who collected taxes for the regime. The arrival and settlement of the Syrian armies in the middle of the eighth century to help suppress the Berber rebellion, however, resulted in the restructuring of the rural administration. The armies were assigned a portion of the revenue of various districts that had previously been paid to the treasury, as well as revenues of the towns designated in the surrender treaty between Theodemir and ʿAbd al-ʿAziz ibn Musa (abrogating the treaty). The Syrian armies settled in their assigned districts and became a presence in the landscape.[3] The Muslim government and growing numbers of professionals, craftsmen, and tradesmen lived in towns, although members of the ruling family and elite circle might also be found enjoying a change of scene in their country estates *munan* (s. *munya*). Some towns remained predominantly Christian for a time, notably Toledo, the former Visigothic capital located in the middle march. The accounts of the revolts of the Banu Hafsun and Ibn Marwan al-Jilliqi identify certain regions and towns as Christian in the mid-ninth century. Other towns, such as Merida, were characterized as predominantly muwallad; Seville had a mixed population dominated by an Arab elite.[4]

Cordoba as the capital may have been distinct in the intensity and scope of its urban development but not unique in its general patterns.[5] The core of

3. Acién Almansa and Vallejo Triano, "Urbanismo y estado islámico," 107–136; Eduardo Manzano Moreno, "La conquista de 711: Transformaciones y pervivencias," in *Visigodas y Omeyas: Un debate entre la Antigüedad tardía y la alta Edad Media* (Madrid: Consejo Superior de Investigaciones Científicas and Concorcio de la Ciudad Monumental de Mérida, 2000), 401–414; Hugh Kennedy, *Muslim Spain and Portugal: A Political History of al-Andalus* (London: Longman, 1996), 16–18, 23–29.

4. See Cyrille Aillet, *Les Mozarabes: Christianisme, islamisation et arabisation en péninsule Ibérique (ix–xii siècle)* (Madrid: Casa de Velázquez, 2010), 45–93, for the evolving geography of Christian settlement in al-Andalus. He finds three archbishoprics (centered in Toledo, Seville, and Merida) and twenty bishoprics evident in the middle of the ninth century, but in the caliphal period (after the rebellions of the latter half of the ninth century and first decades of the tenth) Christian institutions seem to have diminished to ten identifiable bishoprics concentrated in the southeast.

5. On the development of Cordoba, see Acién Almansa and Vallejo Triano, "Urbanismo y estado islámico," 107–136; Pedro Marfil Ruiz, "Córdoba de Teodosio a ʿAbd al-Rahman III," in *Visigodas y Omeyas*, 117–141; J. F. Murillo, R. Hidalgo, J. R. Carrillo, A. Vallejo, and A. Ventura, "Córdoba: 300–1236 D.C.: Un milenio de transformaciones urbanas," in *Urbanism in Medieval Europe*, ed. Guy De Boe and Frans Verhaeghe (Zellik: Scientific Institution of the Flemish Community, 1997), 47–60; Peter C. Scales, "Córdoba under the Umayyads, a 'Syrian' Garden City?," ibid., 175–182; Christine Mazzoli-Guintard, *Vivre a Cordoue au Moyen Age: Solidarité citadine en terre d'Islam aux xe–xie siècles* (Rennes: Presses Universitaires de Rennes, 2003); Mazzoli-Guintard, "Remarques sur le fonctionnement d'une capitale à double polarité: Madinat al-Zahra'–Cordoue," *Al-Qantara* 18 (1997): 43–64; and Antonio Arjona Castro, "Urbanismo de la Córdoba califal," *Revista del Instituto Egipcio de Estudios Islámicos en Madrid* 29 (1997): 73–86.

the city was a rectangle of 1,400 by 700 meters defined by the Roman walls, although by the time of the Muslim conquest the ancient street plan had already been lost, and some of the population had shifted outside the city walls. The Muslim governor moved into the Visigothic palace in the southwest, opposite the Basilica of St. Vincent and south of the Roman bridge. The next few years saw the repair of the walls and the bridge, the foundation of a cemetery called Maqbarat al-Rabad, and the creation of an open oratory (*musallā*) used for ritual occasions, such as the breaking of the fast of Ramadan and the feast of the Sacrifice, prayers for rain, and prayers on the occasion of an eclipse. The cemetery and the musalla were laid out across the river in Shaqunda, and another musalla was established in the plain to the west of the city. The palace itself soon had its own burial ground (where all the Umayyad rulers would be buried), and another cemetery was established next to the northwest wall and gate called Maqbarat Bab ʿAmir. Eventually, the city claimed twenty-one cemeteries (four of them major). By all accounts, no mosque was founded until ʿAbd al-Rahman I undertook the institutional and structural development of his amirate. Muslims reportedly shared the Basilica of St. Vincent with Christians until the first Umayyad amir destroyed the church and constructed a congregational mosque on the site in 786.

The development of Cordoba proceeded apace both inside and outside the walls. ʿAbd al-Rahman I established the munya of al-Rusafa on the skirt of the mountains to the northwest of the city, and it and other munan became centers of settlement on the city's perimeter. Mosques, cemeteries, baths, and other pious foundations promoted the settlement of Muslims in underdeveloped districts or largely Christian neighborhoods. The amir Hisham built a mosque in the district of the Church of the Three Martyrs (the Church of San Pedro). After al-Hakam I destroyed Shaqunda, intensive development took place to the west of the city walls, around the mosques and cemeteries established by Mutʿa and ʿAjab, concubines of al-Hakam I, and the mosques established by ʿAbd al-Rahman II's concubine Tarub and favorites Fajr and Shifʾa. The cemetery established (with a mosque) by Umm Salama, one of Amir Muhammad's wives, to the north of Cordoba became the largest, and the neighborhood around it grew quickly in the ninth and tenth centuries. The jurists Ibn Habib and Ibn Waddah, among others, are said to have been buried in Maqbarat Umm Salama (Yahya ibn Yahya and Baqi ibn Makhlad were buried in another cemetery in the east, Maqbarat Ibn ʿAbbas).

ʿAbd al-Rahman II's efforts to professionalize his administration and develop the prestige of his rule were reflected in urban development and expansion. He remodeled the governor's palace (the *qaṣr*) and created a mint and the equivalent of a royal factory dedicated to ceremonial robes and fabrics (*dār al-ṭirāz*); he expanded the congregational mosque significantly; he constructed new palaces, such as Dar al-Kamil; and he may have developed the main market west of the qasr. His associates and favorites enlarged the project of urbanization. In addition to the mosques already mentioned that had been constructed outside the city were the mosques of the "Slav" mamluks Surayf and Tarafa inside the city and Abu Harun's mosque near the Seville gate. Another mamluk, Masrur, founded a charitable establishment, perhaps a hostel for the poor (*dār al-ṣadaqa*).

The expansion of the Great Mosque of Cordoba by ʿAbd al-Rahman II and then again significantly in the tenth century by al-Hakam II and after him by the *ḥājib* (chamberlain) and de facto ruler al-Mansur reflects the growth of the Muslim population (by immigration and conversion as well as natural increase) and symbolizes the regime's promotion of the faith.[6] The major expansions, renovations, and elaborations of the Great Mosque (including galleries for women, a *maqṣūra* or enclosure that set the ruler and his entourage apart from the other worshippers, new ablution basins, a covered walkway connecting the mosque to the qasr, a platform for the call to prayer and then a minaret, a planted courtyard, and the monumental mihrab-maqsura area of al-Hakam II) coincided with a parallel process of the development of the qasr by the amirs and, in the caliphal era, the foundation and development of the palace-cities of Madinat al-Zahra' and Madinat al-Zahira.

ʿAbd al-Rahman III ordered the construction of the palace-city of Madinat al-Zahra' in 936 (or 940), after the consolidation of his rule and the proclamation of his caliphate. The new city symbolized the universal command of the caliph and marked a transformative moment in the history of the Umayyad dynasty. Consciously laid out in three levels, Madinat al-Zahra' served as a stage for the performance of ceremony. Some 5 kilometers from Cordoba, the new city was populated exclusively by those associated with and in the service of the palace and administration. The city on the hill expressed an idealized vision of the caliph's rule and of the organization of society and stood far apart from the fray and the muddles of communal and intercommunal life.

Cordoba continued to thrive as a real and living city and remained central to the regime's identity and exercise of power, as demonstrated in the

---

6. Ibn ʿIdhari notes that al-Mansur expanded the congregational mosque in Cordoba to accommodate the large numbers of Berbers he recruited to his army; Ibn ʿIdhari, *al-Bayan al-mughrib fi akhbar al-Andalus wa-l-Maghrib*, ed. E. Lévi Provençal and G. S. Colin (Leiden: E. J. Brill, 1948–1951), 2:287; French translation, *Histoire de l'Afrique et de l'Espagne intitulée al-Bayano l-Mogrib*, trans. E. Fagnan (Algiers: Imprimerie Orientale P. Fontana, 1901–1904), 2:478.

lavish attention and resources devoted to the expansion of the Great Mosque. Three arteries linked the old capital with the new. The caliphs traveled between their residences in Cordoba and Madinat al-Zahra' and bound the two cities together iconographically (for example, the names of the main gates of Madinat al-Zahra' and Cordoba and of the two palaces were the same) and ritually (the caliphs received audiences in both locations, and processions linked the cities on ceremonial occasions). Supporting the further western expansion of Cordoba, the caliphs also effectively brought the two cities together through physical development and settlement.

As Cordoba developed in the eighth, ninth, and tenth centuries, it became increasingly Islamic, with constructions dedicated to Muslim worship and with the formal development of ritual life under the direction of the regime (especially during the caliphate). The parades of departing and returning armies and the cavalcades escorting prisoners or ambassadors to the palace, which were extravagant affairs, particularly in the tenth century, regularly reminded all Cordobans of the presence and power of Muslim rule. The display of the corpses of vanquished rebels, Christian and Muslim alike, warned of the swift and relentless justice of the regime, as did the public humiliation of offenders against law and order. Thus, for example, the merchant John was lashed and paraded through the city seated backward on an ass for words taken to be disrespectful of the Prophet and Islam; in another example, the chief of police Ibrahim ibn Husayn ibn Khalid paraded a man guilty of false testimony through Cordoba after administering forty lashes. Eleven times between the two prayers the man circulated with his beard shorn and his face blackened, accompanied by a crier who shouted, "This is the punishment of the false witness!"[7] As Cordoba developed as the capital of a more centralized and ideologically defined Islamic rulership, the inhabitants of the city became increasingly aware of their submission to that rule.

Evidence suggests that Christians and Jews also undertook constructions on behalf of their own communities, at least in the amiral period. Christians had established churches and monasteries and settled outside the walls of the old city before the Muslim conquest, and Muslims settled in Christian districts to the west and east near the churches of St. Zoylus, St. Acisclus, and the Three Saints.[8] In the ninth century Christians established at least

---

7. María Jesús Aldana García, *Obras de San Eulogio: Introducción, traducción, y notas* (Córdoba: Servicio de Publicaciones, Universidad de Córdoba, 1998), 134–136; al-Wansharisi, *al-Mi'yar al-mu'rib wa-l-jami' al-mughrib* (Rabat: Dar al-Gharb al-Islami, 1981–1983), 2:415.

8. Sites associated with the ninth-century Christian martyrs of Cordoba include the churches of St. Zoylus, St. Acisclus, the Three Saints, the Church of St. Ciprian, the monastery of St. Felix, the

three new monasteries: Tabanos, Penna Mellaria, and Santa Eulalia of Barcelona. Ibn Ziyad consulted with the jurists of Cordoba at the turn of the tenth century about the destruction of a synagogue alleged to have been newly constructed.[9] Cordoba functioned as an administrative center and cultural magnet for Christians and Jews, attracting immigrants from elsewhere on the peninsula, and in this sense the communities in Cordoba continued to thrive even as the demographic tide worked against them.

Descriptions of the celebrations of the major Islamic feasts in al-Andalus in the Umayyad period are preserved in Ibn Hayyan's transmission of the historian 'Isa ibn Ahmad al-Razi's (d. 989) account of four years of the caliph al-Hakam II's reign. The a'yād (s. 'īd) were occasions for the formal display of the caliph's authority and the ritual submission to his command by officials of the regime and leaders of the community. The caliphs expressed their legitimacy as Commanders of the Faithful in commemorations of the Sacrifice and the Breaking of the Fast at a remove from the majority of the population, who went to pray in one of the outdoor prayer grounds and shared their feasts with family, friends, and neighbors and with the poor, Muslims and dhimmis.[10]

In times of drought the entire community of Cordoba may have turned out for processions for the prayers for rain. A reference suggests that Christians too conducted public prayers for rain, but whether they did so in conjunction with the Muslims is uncertain.[11] The story of how Ibn Habib convinced the amir 'Abd al-Rahman II that the procession should go to Musalla al-Musara rather than Musalla al-Rabad provides a glimpse of the

---

monastery of Tabanos, the convent dedicated to Mary in the village of Cuteclara, west of Cordoba, the monastery of St. Christopher downriver from Cordoba, the monastery of St. Martin at Rojana in the mountains above Cordoba, the monastery of St. Justus and St. Pastor, also in the mountains some fifteen miles north of Cordoba, and the monastery of San Salvador at Pinna Mellaria.

9. See al-Wansharisi, *Mi'yar*, 2:246; Ibn Sahl in M. 'Abd al-Wahhab Khallaf, *Watha'iq fi ahkam qada' ahl al-dhimma fi al-Andalus* (Cairo: al-Markaz al-'Arabi al-Dawli li-l-I'lam, 1980), 77–80 (hereafter cited as Khallaf, *Ahl al-dhimma*); Matthias Lehmann, "Islamic Legal Consultation and the Jewish-Muslim 'Convivencia,'" *Jewish Studies Quarterly* 6 (1999): 34–36. Ibn Sahl describes another case pertaining to a synagogue in Cordoba about which he was consulted (late eleventh century); see Ibn Sahl in Khallaf, *Ahl al-dhimma*, 60–65. See also Sally Garen, "Santa Maria de Melque and Church Construction under Muslim Rule," *Journal of the Society of Architectural Historians* 51 (1992): 288–305.

10. One presumes that 'Abd al-Rahman III presided over formal celebrations of the a'yād, but there is no extant evidence comparable to evidence of ceremonial in al-Hakam II's reign.

11. Ibn Habib wrote in *al-Wadiha* that it was prohibited for Christians to display their crosses on their holidays and during their prayers (and processions?) for rain; cited in Ibn Abi Zayd al-Qayrawani, *al-Nawadir wa-l-ziyadat*, ed. 'Abd al-Fattah Muhammad al-Hulw, et al. (Beirut: Dar al-Gharb al-Islami, 1999), 3:376.

practice. The palace official in charge of the arrangements, the eunuch al-Nasr, directed the procession to the musalla across the river because it was near his palace there. After he died, Ibn Habib wrote the amir that Musalla al-Musara was safer and more convenient, and he recalled an occasion when crowding on the bridge across the Guadalquivir resulted in a terrible accident and the drowning of many when people fell off the bridge and onto a crowded boat, capsizing it. The amir agreed to the change of venue.[12]

Ibn Habib disapproved of the practice of people parading high and low, in the countryside and the town, with women and children crying and shouting, when they were beseeching God for rain. His opinion is cited in a fatwa responding to a question about the proper practices for the prayers for rain (sunnat al-istisqā'). The jurist who issued the fatwa, Ibn Sarraj, remarks that apart from Ibn Habib, he knows of no scholar who discusses it. He reports a narrative about how Musa ibn Nusayr (one of the conquerors of al-Andalus) led a procession for prayers for rain in Ifriqiyya. Musa had the boys and the men, the girls and the women, and the "people of the (pact of) protection" (ahl al-dhimma) (here clearly participating as members of the larger community) all process separately. Some of the 'ulama' (religious scholars) of Medina approved of this procession because it was intended to stir the hearts of the people.[13]

An entry in Ibn Hayyan's chronicle of 'Abd al-Rahman III's reign reports a dry December in 942 and the decision by the qāḍī (judge) and prayer leader of Cordoba, Muhammad ibn 'Abd Allah ibn Abi 'Isa, to add prayers for rain during the Friday sermon in the mosque. He started on January 7, 943 (the historian provides the date according to both the Islamic and Christian calendars), and continued for two more Fridays, but the drought continued. The people paraded out to Musalla al-Rabad for the first time that year for prayers on Tuesday, January 11. They went again on Monday, January 17, and Thursday, January 20. The following Saturday they went to Musalla al-Musara, and again on Tuesday the 25th and Tuesday, February 1. That day, as the people were returning home, a cold wind came up, and it snowed all morning and sleeted all afternoon, but then the sky cleared. The earth was not saturated, so the qadi resumed the prayers for rain on Friday, February 4, in the mosque. On Saturday, according to the

---

12. Ibn Hayyan, al-Muqtabis min anba' ahl al-Andalus, ed. Mahmud 'Ali Makki (Cairo: Matabi' al-Ahram al-Tijariyya, 1971), 183–184.

13. Al-Wansharisi, Mi'yar, 1:164. The mufti Ibn Sarraj describes the common practice of al-istisqā' as prayer, sermon (khuṭba), supplication (du'ā'), and humility before God with sincerity, repentance, and charity.

account, God brought water to his worshippers with a driving rain, and people began to plant, prices fell, and the alarm dissipated. Abundant rain fell again on Tuesday, February 8.[14]

Drought affected the welfare and livelihood of all of the city's population, and the prayers for rain and processions to the two prayer grounds evoked and displayed communal solidarity, at least among the Muslims. The connection between a common ecology and economy and intercommunal relations is difficult to discern. In many ways space and time were perceived ambiguously as common and markedly different, and the perspective shifted with the observer and the context. The integration of calendars into historical writing, for example, situates events in seasonal (common) time following the solar calendar, as well as in the ritual time of the Islamic calendar. Al-Hakam II seems to have commissioned a calendar noting the Christian holidays, and this too reflects an awareness of temporal differentiation in the context of common time. The extant Latin translation of the calendar attributed to 'Arib ibn Sa'id expresses a specific interest in all the significant holidays and saints' days and also includes astronomical information and references to the annual cycles of planting, taxation, and military provisioning. Here, as elsewhere, January first is identified as the first day of the Christian year, the seventh day after the birth of Jesus, and the day of his circumcision.[15] The commissioning of the calendar of Cordoba, with its focus on cycles of agriculture, revenues, and provisions, reflects the ruler's will to assert authority over his domain; his interest in the Christian festival cycle reflects his interest in extending authority over all his dominion.

Muslims, Christians, and Jews inhabited a common space. Most obviously they lived in the same physical environment and therefore recognized the same seasonal calendar, but they differentiated that space in ways peculiar to their communal lives and confessions and recognized different ritual calendars. Also obviously, the different communities experienced Umayyad rule and understood Umayyad authority differently; occasions of public ceremony and formal ritual clearly delineated the dominant status of Islam and distinguished the privileged category of Muslim from non-Muslim.

14. Ibn Hayyan, *Muqtabis [V] de Ibn Hayyan*, ed. P. Chalmeta, F. Corriente, and M. Subh (Madrid: Instituto Hispano-Árabe de Cultura, 1979), 477–478; Spanish translation, *Crónica del califa Abdarrahman III an-Nasir entre los años 912 y 942 (al-Muqtabis V)*, trans. María Jesús Viguera and Federico Corriente (Zaragoza: Instituto Hispano-Árabe de Cultura, 1981), 357–358.

15. *Le calendrier de Cordoue publié par R. Dozy, nouvelle edition accompagnée d'une traduction française annotée par Charles Pellat* (Leiden: E. J. Brill, 1961); see Ann Christys, *Christians in al-Andalus (711–1000)* (Richmond, Surrey: Curzon Press, 2002), 116–134, for discussion of the attribution of the extant Latin and Arabic texts published by R. Dozy.

However, Muslims and dhimmis were, as subjects of the regime, part of a larger political community; the status of Christians and Jews and their privileges changed over time (as is evident in the disregard of the original treaties of Artabas and Theodemir), but their security was integrally associated with the Islamic legitimacy of Umayyad rule. The Umayyad regime had an interest in the ways in which the protection and the subordination of dhimmis were defined, enacted, and maintained.

Jurists and judges engaged in the formulation and exercise of Islamic law in the ninth and tenth centuries found themselves pressed to address all manner of legal questions having to do with the interactions of individuals of different communities because of the expansion of contexts and occasions for intercommunal interaction, for example, as Muslims settled in the countryside or moved into Christian neighborhoods. Proximity could be experienced in different degrees, and it is the intimacy of contact reflected in the sources that attracts my attention. The sources allow us to descend from the bird's-eye view of a society becoming visibly integrated and to consider when and how Muslims, Christians, and Jews occasionally crossed one another's thresholds. A question posed to Sahnun, for example, is based on the premise that a Muslim and a Jew were staying in the same house in a village: What happens if a house falls on a Muslim and a Jew and kills them, and it is not known which one is which? How should the funerary rites be performed? Sahnun replies that both corpses should be washed, prayed over, and wrapped in shrouds as if they were Muslim. If the question sounds hypothetical, the premise that a Muslim and a Jew might be staying in the same house in the ninth century may nevertheless be plausible.[16] An anecdote used to convey the amir al-Hakam I's remorse over the razing of the suburb of Shaqunda and the exile of its inhabitants might be adduced to support this point, although admittedly the anecdote describes a particular incident of cohabitation in a context of extreme exigency. The jurist Talut ibn 'Abd al-Jabbar al-Ma'afiri fled from his house (near the mosque that bore his name) and hid in the home of a Jew for a year. When the amir heard this, he was ashamed that a Jew risked his possessions and even his life and the lives of his wife and children for the man out of respect for his learning, while he himself had displayed such a lack of respect in his actions. Did the anonymous Jew exist, or was he a symbolic construct? Even if the story is apocryphal, it provides an intimation of the personal intellectual

---

16. Ibn Rushd, *al-Bayan wa-l-tahsil wa-l-sharh wa-l-taujih wa-l-ta'lil fi masa'il al-Mustakhraja*, ed. Muhammad Hajji (Beirut: Dar al-Gharb al-Islami, 1984–1987), 2:284.

exchanges that took place between Muslims and Jews (and may well have involved the crossing of thresholds) but remain largely hidden from view.[17] Most striking in the sources of the ninth century is the evidence for the intensification of intercommunal bonds through marriage and conversion. The crossing of thresholds, for example, might have occurred most commonly in circumstances of mixed marriage and mixed families; practical matters of such circumstances became a concern of jurists. The rest of this chapter will try to capture some of the qualities of this society in transition in the ninth and early tenth centuries with specific attention to the evidence of cultural change, interfaith marriage, and conversion and the "problems" they represented to jurists and judges; the chapter that follows is of a piece in its exemplification of this society in transition but draws closer to the legal discourse, developing the argument for the accommodation of social practice.

The accounts of the Christian martyrs of Cordoba dramatize some of the conflicts precipitated by social change and uncertainties about status and the definition of communal identity in al-Andalus in the ninth century. Jessica Coope writes, "It was the very closeness of Christians and Muslims and the complex and ambivalent nature of their relationships that produced the martyrdoms."[18] The stories of the martyrs exemplify individual cases of boundary crossing and specific circumstances of boundary testing and demonstrate the threat these actions posed for both Christian and Muslim leaders. The martyrologies by the Cordoban priest Eulogius and his friend and memorialist Paul Albar describe Cordoba in crisis, and the texts themselves are part of their authors' efforts to respond to the crisis, crafted to (re)assert boundaries in the service of maintaining—indeed, in the view of Eulogius, of saving—Christian confessional and communal identity.[19] The texts, while

---

17. Ibn al-Qutiyya, *Ta'rikh iftitah al-Andalus (Historia de la conquista de España de Abenalcotía el Cordobés)*, ed. and trans. (into Spanish) Julián Ribera (Madrid: Revista Archivos, 1926), Arabic, 53–55; Spanish, 42–44; English translation, David James, *Early Islamic Spain: The "History" of Ibn al-Qutiya* (London: Routledge, 2009), 89–91; Ibn Hayyan, *Crónica de los emires Alhakam I y ʿAbdarrahman II entre los años 796 y 847 [Muqtabis II-1]*, trans. Mahmud ʿAli Makki and Federico Corriente from the manuscript (Zaragoza: Instituto de Estudios Islámicos y del Oriente Próximo, 2001), 75–78.

18. Jessica A. Coope, *The Martyrs of Cordoba: Community and Family Conflict in an Age of Mass Conversion* (Lincoln: University of Nebraska Press, 1995), 34.

19. Eulogius, *Memoriale sanctorum, Documentum martyriale,* and *Liber apologeticus martyrum,* in *Patrologiae cursus completus,* Series Latina, ed. J. P. Migne (Paris: Garnier Frères, 1852), 115:731–818, 819–834, 852–870; and in *Corpus scriptorum muzarabicorum,* ed. Juan Gil (Madrid: Instituto Antonio de Nebrija, 1973), 2:363–459, 459–475, 475–495. For a Spanish translation of Eulogius's writings, see Aldana García, *Obras completas de San Eulogio.* Paulus Alvarus [Paul Albar], *Vita Eulogii* may be found in Migne, *Patrologiae cursus completus,* Series Latina, 115:705–720, and in Gil, *Corpus scriptorum muzarabicorum,* 1:330–343. Carleton M. Sage, *Paul Albar of Cordoba: Studies on His Life and Writings*

commemorating the faith and deeds of the martyrs, are consciously fashioned denunciations of Muhammad, Islam, and the Islamic regime in al-Andalus; they emphasize the "persecution" of the Christians by the "pagans" and portray the martyrs as "soldiers of God" who gave up their lives on behalf of the faith as "combatants against the enemy of God."[20] Although the stories of the martyrs may be familiar to scholars and readers of medieval Iberian history, in these pages they are considered in the context of an extended period of social transformation in al-Andalus that involved all three religious communities in relation to one another. Distinctive for their descriptions (however brief) of the lives of individuals of different sexes, social ranks, and family backgrounds, the martyrologies provide evidence of intercommunal relations and complicated social ties that correspond to topics addressed by ninth-century Andalusi legal texts and opinions (and those of their Maliki interlocutors), and the two types of sources present a kind of stereoscopic view of Andalusi society.

Eulogius wrote martyrologies of some forty-eight Christians who were executed by order of the amirs ʿAbd al-Rahman II (r. 822–852) and Muhammad I (r. 852–886) between 850 and 858. He composed three texts intended for circulation: the *Memoriale sanctorum* (written in stages between 851 and 856), the *Documentum martyriale* (written in late 851 while he was in prison, in part to provide moral support for his fellow prisoners and martyrs, Flora and Maria), and the *Liberapologeticus martyrum* (written to commemorate the martyrdoms of Rudericus and Salomon in 857). Paul Albar wrote of Eulogius's martyrdom in March 859 and that of Leocritia, a secret Christian who first sought counsel from Eulogius and then took refuge with him and his sister from her Muslim family. Eulogius's accounts of the martyrdoms are polemical; in his ardent affirmation of the truth and justice of Christianity against the falseness and tyranny of Islam, he asserts an absolute boundary. He also harshly criticizes the church establishment and directs some of his later arguments specifically against those who denied that the Christians who sought their deaths by provoking the qadi were martyrs. Concerned to ensure that the martyrs achieve recognition for their sacrifice,

---

(Washington, DC: Catholic University of America Press, 1943), includes an English translation of *Vita Eulogii*, 190–214. Albar also wrote *Indiculus luminosus* (854), a polemical work denouncing Muhammad and exhorting Christians to oppose him in defense of the martyrs.

20. See Kenneth Baxter Wolf, *Christian Martyrs in Muslim Spain* (Cambridge: Cambridge University Press, 1988), 36–47, for a historiographical overview; much of Wolf's monograph discusses the literary qualities of Eulogius's writings. Aldana García provides a literary analysis as well in the introduction to his translation of Eulogius's writings, *Obras completas de San Eulogio*. Christys, *Christians in al-Andalus*, 52–82, discusses the possible fabrication of some of the stories of the martyrs.

Eulogius emphasizes their willing offer of their lives for the faith and the salvation of the community, and some of his stories follow hagiographic conventions, including occasional reports of signs, visions, and miracles (some of the martyrs' stories are quite short, while others are more fully developed narratives). Because the martyrologies are so clearly directed by their authors' interests, they must be read critically; reports of conversations, emotions, motivations, and divine intervention are subject to narrative shaping. The two authors' relationship to each other and to some of the martyrs, their style of writing, and their appeal to their audience are all revealing, particularly for the study of internal Christian relations. For my purposes, the identification of the martyrs by name, sex, and age and the references to places of origin, training, and occupation and to family and personal relationships are particularly useful, identifying specific types of Christians struggling with matters of religious identity and faith. The basic outlines of the martyrs' experiences leading up to and including confrontation with the Muslim authorities, imprisonment, and death are also of interest for our understanding of the exercise of authority and boundary making and can be separated from the disparaging representation of the Muslim actors and the dramatic portrayal of good against evil.

The brief biographies that Eulogius (and Albar) provide indicate that twenty of the martyrs of Cordoba were monks or nuns, and eight were priests. One of the monks and one of the priests had formerly been in service to the amir; another monk had come from the monastery of St. Saba, outside Jerusalem. These, as well as a soldier, three deacons (and a brother of one of these), a Syrian pilgrim, two comrades who had been educated at the Church of St. Cyprian, and an older woman, were all charged with blasphemy and executed when they refused to recant. Thirteen of the martyrs were charged with apostasy as well as blasphemy: three men converted to Islam and then reverted to Christianity (Felix, Witesindus, and Salomon), and a fourth was accused of doing so (Rudericus); the rest were men and women who defined themselves as Christian but were considered legally Muslim by parentage.[21] This group of "apostates" included both secret Christians who chose to make their Christian identity public and face the consequences and Christians who were brought before the Muslim judge

---

21. Wolf, *Christian Martyrs*, 23–35; Coope, *Martyrs of Cordoba*, 70–79. Eleven of the martyrs Eulogius reports on were women (and Albar reports on Leocritia). Eulogius includes in his account of the martyrs of Cordoba the story of the martyrdoms of two sisters, Nunilo and Alodia (born to a Christian mother and a Muslim father), which took place in Bosca. He reports that he knows their story from an account by the bishop of Alcala. See Aldana García, *Obras completas de San Eulogio*, 124–126.

by relatives and chose not to renounce their Christianity when they were offered the chance to save themselves through formal repentance of their errors. Regarding these last cases, Coope observes that "hatred between relatives in mixed families was one of the engines that powered the martyrs' movement."[22] The evidence of conflict within families is clear, but it is worth raising the question whether in one or two of these cases (or in similar situations) the concerns of relatives about the religion and future salvation of close family members may have been genuine. Bringing a family member before the qadi may in some instances have been an act of intervention intended to scare the misguided one straight since typically the judge would offer an opportunity for repentance and reform. Albar describes the efforts of the Muslim parents of Leocritia, who was secretly baptized and introduced to Christianity as a child by a female relative, as earnest and gentle at first (speaking to her), then harsher (beating her); finally, after she ran away, he reports how they became "tortured by despair and grief" and used whatever influence they had with the qadi and the authorities to get them to make arrests and inflict punishments in desperation to bring their daughter back to Islam. His account acknowledges the feelings the parents had for their daughter even as he praises her steadfastness.[23]

The inspiration to insult the Prophet purposely to attain death in this decade of martyrdoms may have originated with the execution of a priest for blaspheming Islam in the spring of 850. The priest, Perfectus, served at the Basilica of St. Acisclus just outside the walls of Cordoba, and Eulogius portrays him as an inspiration (he was a martyr by force of circumstances) for the voluntary martyrs (who actively sought a similar death). According to Eulogius, Perfectus was accosted by a group of Muslims in the street and asked about his beliefs regarding Christ and Muhammad. Speaking in Arabic, he gladly expounded the power and divinity of Christ but refused to state his view of Muhammad, which he knew would upset them, unless they guaranteed his safety. When they agreed, he denounced Muhammad as a false prophet at length and attacked his character and sexual license. Although Perfectus escaped punishment that day, it was not long before he was accused of blasphemy and brought before the qadi, who sentenced him to death. He was publicly executed at the end of Ramadan.[24]

---

22. Coope, *Martyrs of Cordoba*, 29.

23. Sage, *Paul Albar of Cordoba*, 202–203.

24. See Aldana García, *Obras completas de San Eulogio*, 86, 115–120, for the story of Perfectus. Eulogius also describes a merchant called John as an inspiration. He reports that after the secret Christian Aurelius witnessed John's steadfast faith while being lashed for alleged irreverence toward the

Kenneth Baxter Wolf argues that many of the martyrs may have sought their executions as an ultimate penitential act, particularly the martyrs associated with the monastery of Tabanos, which had recently been founded in the hills outside Cordoba (Jeremiah, one of the cofounders, became a martyr in June 851). In his view, the first voluntary martyr initiating the spate of martyrdoms, Isaac, became an exemplar for others who had also retreated from the world (identified with Islamic Cordoba) and saw death as the culmination of their spiritual journey.[25] Isaac had resigned his office in service to the amir and withdrawn to Tabanos three years before he came down from the monastery and approached the qadi of Cordoba in the public square. Isaac told the qadi that he wanted to convert to Islam, and as the qadi was explaining the principles of Islam, Isaac interrupted him. Speaking in Arabic, he vilified the prophet Muhammad and denounced Islam. He warned the qadi that he faced divine punishment and, turning the situation around, asked him why he did not seek the salvation of the Christian faith. The shocked qadi asked Isaac whether he was perhaps drunk or out of his right mind (and hence not legally responsible) and informed him of the penalty of death for blasphemy. Isaac assured the judge that he knew what he was saying and that he accepted his fate. The qadi had Isaac imprisoned and informed the amir, 'Abd al-Rahman II, who ordered him executed. The amir issued an edict announcing the same fate for any Christian who insulted the Prophet. Despite this effort to deter further acts of public blasphemy, seven more Christians came forward within the next four days to denounce the prophet Muhammad before the qadi.

Isaac's public and provocative action inspired others, although we cannot know what motivated each individual. The actions of the Christians who sought their deaths at the hands of the Muslim authorities, as a whole, were not coordinated, but many of them knew one another through an association with Tabanos or through family relations, and in some cases they volunteered for death together. Not a few were closely associated with and counseled by Eulogius himself.

Prophet and mockery of Islam and saw John paraded around the city seated backward on an ass as a warning and an act of public humiliation, he determined to make his Christian identity public and prepare for martyrdom. Aurelius and his wife Sabigotho (also a secret Christian) visited John and Eulogius in prison, and Sabigotho spent time with Flora and Maria (134–136).

25. See Wolf, *Christian Martyrs*, chap. 7, "The Martyrs and Their Motives," 107–119. See also Aldana García, *Obras completas de San Eulogio*, 84–86, for Isaac's story; Eulogius relates Isaac of Tabanos's story to Abraham's (intended) sacrifice of his son Isaac with a story of a dream that a priest in Tabanos had five days after Isaac of Tabanos's execution.

The Christians who insulted the Prophet crossed a line and in doing so attracted attention to the definition of communal boundaries at a time when the boundaries seemed to be shifting and uncertain. Eulogius and Albar used the narrative of the deaths they defined as "martyrdoms" to excoriate their fellow Christians for using Arabic and adopting the sophistications of Arabic-Islamic culture, and to denounce the "accommodationist" policies of the church. The actions of these unofficial martyrs divided the Christian community into those who condemned them as dangerous and sought to conciliate the Muslim regime and a minority like Eulogius who championed their defiance and celebrated the words they used to bring the sword on their necks. In Eulogius's view it was impossible to be a true Christian and simultaneously to accept, even implicitly, the idea that Muhammad was God's Prophet.[26] In other words, he rejected the basis of coexistence under Muslim rule.

There is no Arabic record or reference to the martyrdoms, but the view of the Muslim religious authorities is reflected in a fatwa issued during the reign of the amir 'Abd Allah (r. 888–912) in response to a case that happened decades after the martyrdoms Eulogius and Albar describe. The qadi Ahmad ibn Muhammad ibn Ziyad, nephew of the qadi Ahmad ibn Ziyad whose term as judge (854–864) coincided with some of the martyrdoms, presented the following problem to the jurists of Cordoba. A Christian woman named Dalja (or Dhabha) approached the qadi while he was in session. In the presence of witnesses she swore that she was Christian, that Jesus was God, and that Muhammad lied about being a messenger of God. The jurists 'Ubayd Allah ibn Yahya (d. 910), Muhammad ibn Lubaba (d. 926), Sa'd ibn Mu'adh (d. 920), Muhammad ibn Walid (d. 921), and Ahmad ibn Yahya (d. 910) all agreed that she must be killed and hastened to the fire.[27]

The qadi 'Isa ibn Sahl (d. 1093), in his collection of legal decisions, *al-Ahkam al-kubra*, discusses the jurists' response and situates the problem of blasphemy within the Maliki juridical context.[28] We can see how debates

---

26. Wolf, *Christian Martyrs*, 86–95.

27. Ibn Sahl in Khallaf, *Ahl al-dhimma*, 70–73; al-Wansharisi, *Mi'yar* 2:344–45. Al-Khushani recounts a story of a Christian coming to the court of the qadi Aslam ibn 'Abd al-'Aziz (Ahmad ibn Muhammad ibn Ziyad's successor as qadi of Cordoba), and the exchange he describes between the qadi and the Christian (who sought his own death) conveys the impression that asking for one's own death as a religious act was incomprehensible to the judge; see al-Khushani, *Kitab al-qudat bi-Qurtuba (Historia de los jueces de Cordoba)*, ed. and trans. (into Spanish) Julián Ribera (Madrid: Maestre, 1914), Arabic, 186–187; Spanish, 231–233.

28. Ibn Sahl was an authority on *masa'il* (legal questions and opinions) (he reportedly memorized *al-Mudawwana* and *al-Mustakhraja*) and served as a *faqih mushawar* (jurisconsult) in Cordoba and as qadi when the Banu Jawhar ruled as *ta'ifa* (party) kings. His biography is unclear about his various

about blasphemy (which occupied Muslim jurists across centuries and legal traditions) become occasions to (re)define or clarify boundaries. Ibn Sahl cites Malik's opinion (also recorded in al-'Utbi's *Mustakhraja*) that if a Christian or a Jew says, "Muhammad was not sent to us but to you; our prophet is Jesus or Moses," or something similar, there is no repercussion. But if the Christian or Jew denies that Muhammad was a prophet and a messenger and that the Qur'an was revealed to him, death is obligatory.[29] Cited elsewhere, Muhammad ibn Sahnun states explicitly that insulting the Prophet violates the 'ahd al-dhimma (pact of protection), as does stealing from a Muslim or killing a Muslim.[30]

---

postings, but after he left Cordoba, he also served as judge across the straits in the Maghrib and ended his days in Granada. He compiled *al-Ahkam al-kubra*, a collection of legal opinions and rulings from the records of the qadi court of Cordoba, organizing the material in subject chapters and peppering it with critical commentary. Most of the collection pertains to legal matters in Cordoba from the late ninth and early tenth centuries until the last quarter of the eleventh century. See Thami El-Azemmouri, "Les *Nawāzil* d'Ibn Sahl: Section relative a l'*ihtisāb*," *Hespéris-Tamuda* 14 (1973): 9–17; Rocío Daga Portillo, "Aproximación a la obra *al-Ahkām al-kubrā* del cadi 'Isa ibn Sahl," *Miscelanea de estudios árabes y hebraicas* 36 (1987): 237–249; and Daga Portillo, "Crítica y política en los *Ahkām al-kubrā* de Ibn Sahl," *Boletin de la Asociacion Española de Orientalistas* 28 (1992), 159–165.

29. Ibn Sahl in Khallaf, *Ahl al-dhimma*, 70–73; see also Ibn Rushd, *Bayan*, 16:414; and 'Iyad ibn Musa, *al-Shifa bi ta'rif huquq al-mustafa*, ed. 'Ali Muhammad al-Bajawi (Cairo: 'Isa al-Babi al-Halabi, 1977), 2:976, 1034–1035; in English, *Muhammad Messenger of Allah: Ash-Shifa of Qadi 'Iyad*, trans. Aisha Abdarrahman Bewley (Granada: Madinah Press, 2006), 410, 434–435.

30. 'Iyad ibn Musa, *Shifa*, 2:1036; English, 411. Clearly the problem of blasphemy attracted the attention of ninth-century Maghribi and Andalusi jurists. Al-Qayrawani cites the books of Ibn Habib, Ibn Mawwaz (d. 882), Ibn Sahnun, and al-'Utbi and transmissions of 'Isa ibn Dinar (d. 827) in his chapter on blasphemy; al-Qayrawani, *Nawadir wa-ziyadat*, 14:525–531. The chapter includes discussion of those who insult (*sabba*) God and Muhammad, other prophets and messengers, angels, and the companions of the Prophet; insults by dhimmis; and unintentional insults. The chapter begins with a clarification: Asbagh says, in the book of Ibn Habib, that any Jew or Christian who vilifies God will be put to death. This excludes the basic principle of their unbelief, for example, the belief in God and Son and the Partner, and the like, because this is central to their religion, and they have made a pact (of toleration for their religion) in exchange for the *jizya* (poll tax). Insulting God and other forms of blasphemy violate the pact. (See also 'Iyad ibn Musa, *Shifa*, 2:1034; English, 434.) Qadi 'Iyad's *Shifa* is dedicated to praise of the Prophet and includes a substantial section reporting opinions regarding forms of insults of the Prophet and punishments, with subsections titled "Clarification about Cursing the Prophet or Saying That He Is Imperfect by Allusion or Clear Statement," "The Judgement against Someone Who Curses the Prophet, Reviles Him, Disparages Him or Harms Him, and How Someone Who Does This Should Be Punished; About Calling on Him to Repent and the Status of His Inheritance," and "Concerning the Judgement on Anyone Who Curses Allah, His Angels, His Prophets, His Books, and the Family of the Prophet and His Companions" (Bewley's translation, 373–447). He mentions the fatwa of 'Ubayd Allah, Ibn Lubaba, and the others regarding the case of the Christian woman and indicates the significance of her public manifestation of unbelief (2:1039; English, 434–435). See also al-Wansharisi, *Mi'yar*, 2:351–352. Al-Wansharisi includes some of Ibn Abi Zayd al-Qayrawani's fatwas addressing problems of blasphemy, such as the following: (1) some people were recalling the Prophet's physical appearance, and an individual likened him to a passerby with an ugly face and beard; (2) an individual

'Abd al-Rahman II treated the first voluntary martyr (from his perspective a blasphemous Christian) as an individual outcast and a rebel against the political order. He ordered the body of the offender publicly displayed as a warning, mounted on the bank of the river opposite the amiral palace or qasr and the Great Mosque, a place where the bodies of previous opponents to the regime had been displayed and had rotted. When more martyrs came forward, he treated the problem as a communal problem and pressured the leadership of the church to establish control over its members. First he arrested members of the clerical leadership, who were detained for some months, and then he ordered a church council to convene and act to curtail future acts of provocation. His efforts met with limited success. 'Abd al-Rahman II's successor, Muhammad I, responded more aggressively and issued edicts that punished the community and asserted the Christians' subordination to Islam. Perhaps emulating the 'Abbasid caliph al-Mutawwakil, who issued similar edicts in 850, he expelled Christians from the court, imposed new taxes, and removed Christians from the military pension rolls; he then ordered the destruction of new churches and the removal of any recent ornamentation of old preconquest churches. Eulogius claims that the amir proposed killing the Christian men and enslaving the women and children, but his counselors deterred him.[31] Although it is dubious that Amir Muhammad would thus destabilize his regime, the threat speaks to the idea that the Christians as a community were violating the 'ahd al-dhimma and in such circumstances might lose their right to protection, an idea Amir Muhammad conveyed through his actions and hoped would bring an end to the trouble.

The Cordoban martyrs sought their deaths by challenging the qadi and the authority of the amir in the public square. Their defiant words agitated many of those who heard them, and their public executions were occasions of outrage and violence. The eruptions of violence disturbed the social order but perhaps also expended subterranean tensions and anxieties and allowed for the reformulation of social relations and the establishment of a new modus vivendi.[32] After Eulogius's death the impulse for martyrdom dissipated, at

---

cursed God "unintentionally." Ibn Abi Zayd called for capital punishment in both cases and referred to the case of Harun ibn Habib in the latter (Mi'yar, 2:355, 361). He left punishment to the discretion of the ruler in a case where an individual might say, "God curse the Arabs, God curse the children of Israel, and God curse the children of Adam," specifying that he did not mean the prophets but the oppressors; or where someone said, "God curse whoever forbids intoxicating drink" (Mi'yar, 2:357).

31. Aldana García, *Obras completas de San Eulogio*, 156–157, 161.

32. David Nirenberg has drawn attention to the role violence plays in intercommunal relations in *Communities of Violence: Persecution of Minorities in the Middle Ages* (Princeton, NJ: Princeton Univer-

least for a while, and the moderate majority within the church prevailed. The actions of the martyrs must have fueled the Muslim juridical interest in establishing communal boundaries and determining norms of interaction between Muslims and dhimmis, especially given the evidence of the dangers of mixed marriages and the incidents of conversion away from Islam.

The story of the disputation between the priest Perfectus and the group of Muslims who challenged him demonstrates the significance of particular words (and blasphemy) in the contest between faiths now that the interlocutors spoke the same language. The story of Isaac approaching the qadi with an interest in conversion and then denouncing the Prophet and Islam in Arabic emphatically illustrates that speaking the same language is not the same as sharing the same worldview, and that Arabicization is distinct from Islamization. Indeed, some of the martyrs, like Emila and Hieremias, excelled in Arabic and, by virtue of their knowledge, attacked the Prophet and Islam in particularly inflammatory language and pointed terms.[33] The assertion of difference may have become vitally important when language no longer served as a barrier between communities, and expressions of difference could be more refined and more finely targeted. Those who sought to resist the system of rule and the hegemony of Islamic culture could use the common language of their "oppressors" and their understanding of Islam in overt attacks meant to provoke their enemy. We see in these extreme examples and in other forms and contexts in al-Andalus in our period that when linguistic, cultural, and social boundaries became blurred, the process of differentiation involved deeper engagement with the "other."[34]

At the time of the conquest of al-Andalus, the newly settled Muslims spoke colloquial Arabic and Berber, and the indigenous population, Christian

---

sity Press, 1996). As he puts it, "This book demonstrates that violence was a central and systemic aspect of the coexistence of majority and minorities in medieval Spain, and even suggests that coexistence was in part predicated on such violence" (9).

33. Aldana García, *Obras completas de San Eulogio*, 148.

34. Eulogius certainly engaged with Islam in his polemics against it; he demonizes the Prophet and Islam, but at the same time, some of his statements indicate a greater awareness and understanding of Islam than his outrageous assertions would suggest. He also endeavors to define "true" Christianity in opposition to the false beliefs and behavior of other Christians. For discussion of another interesting and in some ways parallel historical context, see Sidney H. Griffith, *The Church in the Shadow of the Mosque* (Princeton, NJ: Princeton University Press, 2008). Griffith investigates how Christians living under Muslim rule in the Near East and writing in Arabic defended their communities from loss of faith and identity. He shows how they participated in a process of defining their beliefs and practices in relation to Islam (in the form of polemics and apologetics) and to other regional churches. The different denominations of Christianity in the Arabic-Islamic lands defined their mature ecclesiastical identities through an informed engagement with the Muslim "other."

and Jewish, spoke Latin-Romance. The need for communication promoted the bridging of vernacular differences, especially in towns. David J.
Wasserstein suggests that Arabic speakers became bilingual with Latin-
Romance (Berbers perhaps trilingual with Arabic and Latin-Romance), and
Latin-Romance speakers became bilingual with Arabic (the patterns may
have been different for women); conversion confused the connection between linguistic patterns and religious affiliations. By the eleventh century
an Andalusi vernacular Arabic and classical written Arabic predominated in
al-Andalus.[35]

The Muslim rulers and men of letters established classical Arabic (*fuṣḥā*),
the higher register of Arabic, as the dominant written language of al-
Andalus, the language of administration and law, learning, and poetry. Expertise in classical Arabic distinguished the educated elite from the rest of
society and offered a route to advancement for the studious and gifted. The
opportunities afforded by skill in Arabic are evident in accounts of Christian
and Jewish courtiers, and education and expertise in the Arabic and Islamic
sciences opened avenues for converts and their descendants and proved a
means of integration.[36] Maribel Fierro's analysis of names in biographical
dictionaries suggests that about half the 'ulama' notable for inclusion in Ibn
Harith al-Khushani's *Akhbar al-fuqaha' wa-l-muhaddithin* had converted to
Islam or were the descendants of converts.[37]

Stories about ninth-century 'ulama' provide insight into the complexity
and fluidity of the linguistic scene and demonstrate the adaptation of

---

35. The fate of the Berber language is subject to disagreement. See David Wasserstein, "The Language Situation in al-Andalus," in *Studies on the Muwaššaḥ and Kharja*, ed. A. Jones and R. Hitchcock (Reading, England: Ithaca Press, 1991), 1–15; reprinted in *The Formation of al-Andalus*, ed.
Maribel Fierro and Julio Samsó (Aldershot: Ashgate-Variorum, 1998), 2:3–17; and Consuelo
López-Morillas, "Language," in *The Literature of al-Andalus*, ed. Maria Rosa Menocal, Raymond P.
Scheindlin, and Michael Sells (Cambridge: Cambridge University Press, 2000), 33–59. On Arabic
diglossia in al-Andalus, see María Ángeles Gallego, "The Impact of Arabic Diglossia among the Muslims, Jews, and Christians of al-Andalus," in *A Comparative History of Literatures in the Iberian Peninsula*,
ed. Fernando Cabo Aseguinolaza, Anxo Abuín Gonzalez, and César Domínguez (Amsterdam: John
Benjamins, 2007), 351–365. See also Aillet, *Mozarabes*, 128–241 ("Latinité et Arabisation").

36. Ibn Khaldun appreciates the difficulties of learning Arabic as a second language because "language is a habit of the tongue." He observes that nonnative Arabic speakers and writers may become adept through intensive study and practice, but that this is rare. This, he points out, does not
contradict his observation that most Muslim scholars are not Arab because lineage (Arab descent)
and the language one grows up with (Arabic) may be distinct. See Ibn Khaldun, *The Muqaddimah*,
trans. Franz Rosenthal (London: Routledge and Kegan Paul, 1986), 3:311–319.

37. Maribel Fierro, "Árabes, beréberes, muladíes y *mawālī*: Algunas reflexiones sobre los datos de los
diccionarios biográficos Andalusíes," in *Estudios onomastico-biográficos de al-Andalus*, vol. 7, ed. Manuela
Marín and Helena de Felipe (Madrid: Consejo Superior de Investigaciones Científicas, 1995), 41–54.

language to social context. The story of ʿAbd al-Aʿla ibn Wahb's rise to prominence as a jurisconsult and his conspiracy with fellow jurists Yahya ibn Yahya and Saʿid ibn Hassan against ʿAbd al-Malik ibn Habib provides one example of code switching. Shortly after he secured his position in the *shūrā* (council of jurisconsults), perhaps on the occasion of his first attendance at a session in the presence of the amir, ʿAbd al-Aʿla supported Ibn Habib, to the surprise of Yahya and Saʿid (recall the story of how ʿAbd al-Aʿla was recruited by these two to embarrass Ibn Habib on a previous occasion). When they remonstrated with him, he switched from speaking Arabic to Romance to reassure them of his loyalty and explain his actions. Romance appears to be the language of common folk and popular speech in another story where Sulayman ibn Aswad al-Ghafiqi (chief judge for Amir Muhammad) switches to *ʿajamiyya* (foreign language; in this context, Romance) to banter with a woman who has come to see him about her situation. The story, which is meant to be amusing, showcases the judge's linguistic talent: he is a master of high language and knows how to speak to the common folk. In contrast, the qadi of Cordoba, Saʿid ibn Sulayman, disdained to respond directly to the rude demands of the father of the influential eunuch Nasr when he shouted to him in ʿajamiyya. The judge was about to enter his home after presiding at the mosque all morning, and although he seems to have understood what was said to him, he asked his companions to reply in ʿajamiyya that if the man wanted to conduct business with him, he should return to the mosque in the evening, where the judge handled matters for the public.[38]

Mastery of classical Arabic provided access to a diverse textual universe, to the delights and rigors of Arabic poetry, and to a distinctive culture of manners. Paul Albar famously decried the attraction Christian youths felt for this culture and their ability in Arabic language and poetry. Arabicization apparently proceeded so broadly that by the next generation Hafs ibn Albar (d. 889) translated the Psalms into rhymed Arabic prose (*rajaz*) and may

---

38. ʿIyad ibn Musa, *Tartib al-madarik wa-taqrib al-masalik li-maʿarifat aʿlam madhhab Malik* (Rabat: Wizarat al-Awqaf wa-al-Shuʾun al-Islamiyya, 1965–1983), 4:246–248; al-Khushani, *Kitab al-qudat bi-Qurtuba*, Arabic, 138–139; Spanish, 171; Arabic, 111–112; Spanish, 136–137. In the post-Umayyad era composers of strophic poetry demonstrated their virtuosity with a code switch from classical to vernacular language in the final verse. The *muwashshaḥāt* strophic poetry originated in al-Andalus in the eleventh century and became popular in Arabic and Hebrew. Characteristically, the genre combines written language with oral forms. The final couplet or *kharja* of an Arabic *muwashshaḥ*, for example, might be in colloquial Arabic or in Romance or have Romance elements. Hebrew muwashshahat might end in Arabic or Romance couplets. See Tova Rosen, "The Muwashshah," in Menocal, Scheindlin, and Sells, *Literature of al-Andalus*, 165–189.

have written the no-longer-extant *Kitab al-masa'il al-sab'a wa-l-khamsin* (The book of fifty-seven questions), in which he presented his responses to questions about Christian practice and belief; by the tenth century the Gospels had been translated into Arabic.[39] The pull of Arabic as the dominant language of power, social prestige, and culture accounts only generally for the decline of Latin. In contrast, Andalusi Jews experienced a literary efflorescence between 900 and 1300. Jewish scholars developed Hebrew grammar on the basis of their study of Arabic grammatical texts, and Jewish poets deft at fashioning verse in Arabic developed and cultivated Hebrew secular and religious poetry following Arabic metrical patterns and models. In the process they reinforced and elaborated their identity within, and apart from, the dominant society and culture.[40]

---

39. D. M. Dunlop identifies Hafs ibn Albar as the son of Paul Albar; see D. M. Dunlop, "Hafs ibn Albar—The Last of the Goths?," *Journal of the Royal Asiatic Society*, 1954, 137–151; and Dunlop, "Sobre Hafs ibn Albar al-Quti al-Qurtubi," *Al-Andalus* 20 (1955): 211–213. P. Sj. van Koningsveld, "Christian Arabic Literature from Medieval Spain: An Attempt at Periodization," in *Christian Apologetics during the Abbasid Period (750–1250)*, ed. Samir Khalil Samir and Jorgen S. Nielsen (Leiden: E. J. Brill, 1994), 203–224, identifies Hafs as the author of *The Book of Fifty-seven Questions* and describes the references to and quotations from the text found in a thirteenth-century anti-Christian polemic by al-Qurtubi. His chapter provides a brief overview of Christian Arabic literature from the ninth and tenth centuries and argues that the Arabic version of the *Collectio conciliorum* was in circulation in 1049 and may date to the tenth century. He also observes that Arabic translations of Latin texts by Christians, such as Ishaq ibn Balshk's translation of the Gospels, reveal Islamic idiomatic influence. Thomas E. Burman makes the same observation in his close study of Christian polemical texts against Islam in the eleventh and twelfth centuries, *Religious Polemic and the Intellectual History of the Mozarabs, c. 1050–1200* (Leiden: E. J. Brill, 1994). Burman describes Hafs ibn Albar as "the author of the first Christian apologetic treatise against Islam written by a western Christian in the Middle Ages" (14), referring to *The Book of Fifty-Seven Questions*. For surveys of Christian Arabic (Mozarabic) literature, see, for example, Dominque Millet-Gérard, *Chrétiens mozarabes et culture islamique dans l'Espagne des viii–ix siècles* (Paris: Etudes Augustiniennes, 1984); H. D. Miller and Hanna Kassis, "The Mozarabs," in Menocal, Scheindlin, and Sells, *Literature of al-Andalus*, 417–434; and Aillet, *Mozarabes*.

40. On the Andalusi courtier-rabbis and their poetry (with translations), see Raymond P. Scheindlin, *Wine, Women, and Death: Medieval Hebrew Poems on the Good Life* (Philadelphia: Jewish Publication Society of America, 1986); and Scheindlin, *The Gazelle: Medieval Hebrew Poems on God, Israel, and the Soul* (Philadelphia: Jewish Publication Society of America, 1991). Ross Brann discusses the process of Arabization of Andalusi Jews as one of profound acculturation that stimulated creativity and surveys and analyzes Andalusi Jewish literary achievements in both Arabic and Hebrew. See Ross Brann, "The Arabized Jews," in Menocal, Scheindlin, and Sells, *Literature of al-Andalus*, 435–454; also Brann, "Reflexiones sobre el árabe y la identidad literaria de los judíos de al-Andalus," in *Judíos y musulmanes en al-Andalus y el Magreb: Contactos intelectuales*, ed. Maribel Fierro (Madrid: Casa de Velázquez, 2002), 13–28. See Esperanza Alfonso, "La construcción de la identidad judía en al-Andalus en la Edad Media," *El Olivo* 23 (1999): 5–24, for discussion of the ways in which Jewish identity was defined in relation to the Islamic other in al-Andalus between the tenth and the thirteen centuries. She points out that discourses among Jewish writers about Arabic and Hebrew language and models were very much about identity, and that attitudes shifted as sociopolitical circumstances changed. See also Alfonso, "Los límites del saber: Reacción de intelectuales judíos a la cultura de procedencia Islámica," in Fierro, *Judíos y musulmanes*, 59–84.

The communication and access afforded by the transgression of linguistic boundaries threatened communal autonomy and religious integrity in the eyes of those determined to protect them, even within the dominant community. The *fuqahā'* (jurists) denounced a trend they could not stop. Thus Cordoban and Qayrawani jurist-scholars like Ibn Habib (d. 853), al-'Utbi (d. 869), Sahnun (d. 854), and Ibn Abi Zayd al-Qayrawani (d. 996) cited and commented on Malik's opinions against crossing linguistic-communal boundaries. Al-'Utbi, for example, records that according to Ibn al-Qasim, Malik disapproved of a Muslim allowing his son to study *'ajamī* (foreign) writing, and that he disapproved of a Muslim teaching any of the Christians Arabic script. In his commentary Ibn Rushd asserts that there is no benefit or advantage to involvement in the affairs of the *'ajam* (foreigners) and cites a Qur'anic verse (5:51) in warning: "He among you that turns to them (for friendship) [*yatawallahum*] is of them."[41]

The Qur'an calls for a formal separation between Muslims and Christians and Jews in verses like Qur'an 5:51, which begins: "O you who believe! Take not the Jews and the Christians for your friends and protectors [*awliyā'*]; they are but friends and protectors to each other." The mutual obligations of *walā'*, a term that encompasses friendship, patronage, clientage, sponsorship, and guardianship would seem to be reserved for members of one's own faith community, but we will see that this became a matter of discussion among the fuqaha' in matters of specific interest. Marriage with Christian and Jewish women of good reputation is Qur'anically permissible (5:5): "(Lawful to you in marriage) are (not only) chaste women who are believers, but chaste women among the People of the Book—revealed before your time—when you give them their due dowers, and desire chastity, not lewdness, nor secret intrigues." One can see that the two principles asserted here may require accommodation.

Marriage between Christians and non-Christians was prohibited in the Christian kingdoms of the Iberian Peninsula after the" reconquest," but marriage between Muslims and non-Muslims was not prohibited in Islamic al-Andalus or the contemporary Islamic world. The permissibility of marriage between Muslim men and Christian and Jewish women and the prohibition of marriage between Muslim women and Christian and Jewish men asserted the superiority of Islam and the dominant status of Muslim men, but these conditions also provided a mechanism for the inclusion of members of the indigenous population into Muslim religious and cultural life and for the

---

41. Ibn Rushd, *Bayan*, 18:146.

natural expansion of Islam and the Muslim community, since the offspring assumed the father's religion and communal identity, at least legally. Of course, jurists deliberated the requirements for a valid marriage contract in such cases and the circumstances and conditions that might preclude or annul a marriage contract (see chapter 3). Interfaith marriages were commonly a consequence of the husband's conversion. Since a man could convert to Islam without requiring his wife's conversion (with certain exceptions), he did not need to sacrifice his marriage to pursue a change in status and confessional affiliation. Mixed marriages, at least in some circumstances, likely extended circles of close contact between Muslims and Christians and Jews that contributed to other conversions.

Pierre Guichard may have been the first to argue for the significance of the social and familial structure of the Arab and Berber conquerors and settlers for the maintenance and security of their identity until the eleventh century.[42] He developed his argument against the proposition put forth by Claudio Sánchez Albornoz that interfaith marriage was a mechanism for the assimilation of the conquerors to the culture of the indigenous population. In Guichard's view, the contrast between "eastern" and "western" forms of social organization largely precluded marriage between the Arab and Berber tribesmen and the indigenous population. More specifically, the "eastern" or tribal social system, which was patrilineal, patrilocal, agnatic, and segmentary, tended to promote endogamous cousin marriages. In making his case, which he based on the evidence of chronicles, however, Guichard overemphasized the importance of tribal identity and tribal affiliation over time and for the urban context in particular. Evidence in biographical dictionaries, analyzed by Manuela Marín, suggests that marriages between Muslims were not necessarily

---

42. Pierre Guichard, *Al-Andalus: Estructura antropológica de una sociedad islámica en occidente* (Barcelona: Barral, 1976); and Guichard, *Structures sociales "orientales" et "occidentales" dans l'Espagne musulmane* (Paris: Mouton et Co. and Ecole des Hautes Etudes en Sciences Sociales, 1977). In the three decades or so since Guichard published this thesis, the degree, extent, and characteristics of tribalism in al-Andalus have been the subject of debate and have stimulated considerable archaeological investigation and interpretation. For a more recent essay by Guichard in English, see "The Social History of Muslim Spain from the Conquest to the End of the Almohad Regime (Early 2nd/8th–Early 7th/13th Centuries)," in *The Legacy of Muslim Spain*, ed. Salma Khadra Jayyusi (Leiden: E. J. Brill, 1994), 2:679–708. As Guichard explains, he writes against a "traditionalist" perspective on the history of Muslim rule in Spain that sees the continuity of a Western and Hispanic tradition enduring under an alien superstructure. He observes that traditionalists (such as Ramón Menéndez Pidal and Claudio Sánchez Albornoz) consider the Arabization or Islamicization of the peninsula to have been superficial and assert that, on the contrary, the "foreign elements" became hispanicized through intermarriage with native women.

endogamous.[43] The evidence of the martyrologies and the Andalusi legal sources also indicates that interfaith marriage was, in fact, a feature of Andalusi social life in this period. Guichard's argument for the significance of tribal familial structures and endogamous marriage may be relevant in specific contexts. Otherwise, I suggest that we shift attention to the structure provided by (developing) Islamic law beginning in the century after the conquest and refer to "Islamic" familial structures. Muslim jurists generally structured the family along patrilineal, agnatic, and patrilocal lines, for example, in the elaboration of rules of inheritance (men and women both inherited, but in different proportions), marriage, and child custody, but we will see how they did not preclude, and in fact accommodated, familial relations across religious communal boundaries. The legal literature defines and portrays a complex structure of family and social life in al-Andalus in the ninth and tenth centuries. Individuals and families involved in Islamically legal interfaith marriages were drawn into the orbit of Islamic law, but interfaith marriages had social and cultural implications for all three religious communities that pushed against, and caused the reconfiguration of, boundaries. In this regard, defining the direction of change (eastern/western) and the pull of one spouse or another leads to oversimplication of a more complex process of social and cultural change.

We do not have evidence with which to evaluate the extent and circumstances of interfaith marriage, only evidence that testifies to its occurrence.[44] The chronicles of the Muslim conquest and the early history of Umayyad rule in al-Andalus mention a few marriages between elite Christian women and Muslim men that probably functioned as political-social contracts. Thus the first governor, 'Abd al-'Aziz ibn Musa ibn Nusayr, married a noble Christian woman; the Christian count Theodemir married his daughter to a Muslim; and the first Umayyad amir, 'Abd al-Rahman I, arranged the second marriage of a Visigothic noble woman, Sara, to one of his Arab clients (according to the tenth-century Andalusi historian Ibn al-Qutiyya, who claimed descent from Sara and her first husband, whose marriage was arranged by the Umayyad caliph Hisham). At the court Christian concubines

---

43. Manuela Marín's analysis of Andalusi biographical dictionaries shows that Muslims in al-Andalus (at least the 'ulama') married outside their extended families (not marrying cousins) and used marriage to form alliances and strengthen relationships; she demonstrates how the general patterns of marriage Guichard characterizes as "eastern" and "western" break down in light of this specific genre of evidence. See Manuela Marín, "Parentesco simbólico y matrimonio entre los ulemas Andalusíes," *Al-Qantara* 16 (1995): 335–356.

44. On the religion of women in al-Andalus, see Manuela Marín, *Mujeres en al-Andalus* (Madrid: Consejo Superior de Investigaciones Científicas, 2000), 141–147.

(of northern origin) rather than wives became mothers to the amirs and caliphs of al-Andalus.[45] These examples of marriage arrangements and concubinage describe the actions and interests of the ruling class and do not provide a basis for generalization about the rest of society. The accounts of the Christian martyrs, however, offer compelling evidence of mixed marriages in perhaps less exalted social circumstances. For example, before introducing his account of the martyrdoms of Flora and Maria, Eulogius reports, on the authority of Bishop Venerius of Alcalá, the martyrdom of two sisters in Bosca, Nunilo and Alodia, who had a Muslim father and a Christian mother. Flora's father was a Muslim from Seville, and her mother was a Christian noblewoman from a village west of Cordoba. Maria and her brother Walabonsus had a Christian father who married a Muslim (defying Islamic law) whom he introduced to Christianity. Aurelius had a Muslim father and a Christian mother. His father died when he was young, and his mother raised him as a Christian; despite the intervention of his Muslim relatives, who insisted on his proper Islamic education, he chose to remain (secretly) Christian. He married Sabigotho, another secret Christian; she had been born to Muslim parents, but when her father died, her stepfather (in an illicit marriage) introduced her and her mother to Christianity. The martyr Aurea's father was a Muslim of noteworthy Arab lineage, and her mother was a Christian; her two brothers, John and Adulphus, died as martyrs in 822 (the subject of a *vita* by Abbot Esperaindeo no longer extant). Aurea herself lived as a Christian with her mother Artemia in the convent in Cuteclara until her Muslim relatives from Seville discovered her and brought her before the qadi of Cordoba. Interestingly, the qadi was a relative who urged her to return to her religion, and she agreed to do so, only to be brought before him again for reversion to Christianity. She died affirming her Christianity in July 856.

Our understanding of conversion, which was perhaps the most powerful engine of social transformation in al-Andalus, is constrained by the limited evidence. Although it is clear that conversion took place on a large scale in al-Andalus, it is difficult, if not impossible, to quantify. In the late 1970s Richard Bulliet plotted a bell curve and a logistic curve for individual social conversion in al-Andalus based on an admittedly small sample of 154 genealogies of 'ulama', culled from five biographical dictionaries, which began

---

45. See D. Fairchild Ruggles, "Mothers of a Hybrid Dynasty: Race, Genealogy, and Acculturation in al-Andalus," *Journal of Medieval and Early Modern Studies* 34 (2004): 65–94, for discussion of the religious and ethnic backgrounds of the women in the Umayyad dynasty, their political influence, and their patronage of the built environment, literature, and art.

with names he identified as possible converts. According to his analysis, the rate of individual conversion among the peninsular population was slow until the tenth century, when it became explosive; conversion then tapered off by the beginning of the twelfth century. Bulliet locates the midpoint of conversion in 961 (the year marking the death of the caliph ʿAbd al-Rahman III and the accession of al-Hakam II)—at this point half of all conversions to Islam had taken place.[46] His analysis of genealogies of ʿulamaʾ in other regions of the Islamic world yielded similar curves, and he observes that the midpoint of conversion in al-Andalus seems to have occurred about seventy years later than in Egypt, Syria, Iraq, and Tunisia (a lag that reflects the fact that al-Andalus was conquered some seventy-five years later) and almost a century and a half later than in Iran. Bulliet's methodology has come under scrutiny; he himself acknowledges that the evidence for the construction of the conversion curve is limited and flawed. The number of converts in al-Andalus and the rate of conversion remain conjectural, but for the most part, scholars have adopted Bulliet's view that conversion in al-Andalus (and elsewhere) took place over centuries and follow his time frame.[47]

Bulliet proposes that we use the logistic curve to discuss conversion in al-Andalus (and in the Islamic world) phenomenologically, applying insights from the theory of innovation diffusion to conversion. This conceptualization of conversion proposes that individuals converted to Islam for different reasons at different times and had different experiences. Conversion rates were slow initially; the innovators and early adopters were those who perceived that they had much to gain by changing religion. The rate accelerated as contact with Muslims (and converts) increased and the perception of social risk diminished. However, at this point the marginal benefits of conversion may also have diminished, and more recent converts may have faced social stigmatization relative to those with longer lineages.

---

46. Richard Bulliet, *Conversion to Islam in the Medieval Period* (Cambridge, MA: Harvard University Press, 1979), 114–127 (chapter on Spain); he argues that Berber immigrants to al-Andalus constituted an early wave of conversion in the mid-eighth century.

47. Although Bulliet's methodology has come under scrutiny, his hypothesis still enjoys currency. See, for example, David Wasserstein, *The Rise and Fall of the Party-Kings* (Princeton, NJ: Princeton University Press, 1986), 226; Mayte Penelas, "Some Remarks on Conversion to Islam in al-Andalus," *Al-Qantara* 13 (2002): 193–200; Luis Molina, "El estudio de familias de ulemas como fuente para la historia social de al-Andalus," in *Saber religioso y poder político en el Islam* (Madrid: Agencia Española de Cooperación Internacional, 1994), 161–173; Fierro, "Árabes, beréberes, muladíes y *mawālī*," 41–54; Manuela Marín and Heather Ecker, "Archaeology, Arabic Sources and Christian Documents: From Muslim Fortress to Christian Castle; Social and Cultural Change in Medieval Spain," *British Journal of Middle Eastern Studies* 25 (1998): 335–348, esp. 341; and Maya Shatzmiller, "Marriage, Family, and the Faith: Women's Conversion to Islam," *Journal of Family History* 21 (1996): 236.

In Thomas F. Glick's view, "Bulliet's description of the conversion process, while admittedly a hypothesis, provides a compelling framework for analyzing the dynamics of social, political, and cultural change in the emergent societies of the middle ages, and, at the same time, offers a standard by which to assess such developments in any one Islamic society in comparative perspective." He finds that the model correlates well with developments in Andalusi history.[48] Michael G. Morony, in contrast, is skeptical of Bulliet's heuristic model and offers a critique of its application in Iran. He cautions that specific social and historical circumstances may be more relevant for understanding conversion patterns.[49] In this vein, some scholars interested in the problem of conversion in al-Andalus have tried to move away from Bulliet's model because of concerns about regional variation, the impact of patterns of settlement, and economic, military, political, and institutional circumstances. Mikel de Epalza, for example, explores the intriguing question of how the decline of church institutions may have played a role in conversion to Islam.[50] His argument for an early large-scale shift in the religious identity and legal classification of populations from Christian to Muslim, however, has met with criticism for its emphasis on baptism by priests as a requisite for Christian identity and the implication of Muslim identity by default.[51]

The fact remains that there is insufficient evidence to properly map conversion to Islam in al-Andalus. Generally speaking, the Andalusi and Maghribi legal sources do support Bulliet's argument for conversion taking place over time by demonstrating that conversion was a lively and lived issue over a period extending from at least the early ninth century through the tenth century. Bulliet's model is consonant with the evidence for the prevalence

---

48. Thomas F. Glick, *Islamic and Christian Spain in the Early Middle Ages* (Princeton, NJ: Princeton University Press, 1979), 33–42 (quotation, 34). Glick addresses some more recent debates about conversion in al-Andalus in *From Muslim Fortress to Christian Castle: Social and Cultural Change in Medieval Spain* (Manchester: University of Manchester Press, 1995) and continues to support the relevance of Bulliet's hypothesis (51–63).

49. Michael G. Morony, "The Age of Conversions: A Reassessment," in *Conversion and Continuity: Indigenous Christian Communities in Islamic Lands, Eighth to Eighteenth Centuries*, ed. Michael Gervers and Ramzi Jibran Bikhazi (Toronto: Pontifical Institute of Medieval Studies, 1990), 135–150. Bulliet acknowledges Morony's argument and considers the possibility that his onomastic technique may underestimate conversion in rural areas in Iran in *Cotton, Climate, and Camels in Early Iran* (New York: Columbia University Press, 2009), 31–32.

50. Mikel de Epalza, "Mozarabs: An Emblematic Christian Minority," in Jayyusi, *Legacy of Muslim Spain*, 1:154–160; and Epalza, "Falta de obispos y conversion al Islam de los cristianos de al-Andalus," *Al-Qantara* 15 (1994): 385–400; see also Mikel de Epalza and Enrique Llogrebat, "Hubo mozárabes en tierras Valencianas?," *Revista de Estudios Alicantinos* 36 (1982): 7–31.

51. See Glick, *From Muslim Fortress to Christian Castle*, 55–56.

of mixed families in the ninth century (in the early majority phase of conversion) and the conflicts among Arabs (or old Muslims), muwalladun, and
Christians. His focus on individual social conversion and his perspective
on conversion as a social phenomenon that involved individuals in association with other individuals in families and networks over a long period of
time resonate with the sources. Andalusi legal texts delineate the importance of social ties in a number of ways. For example, they provide indications of how the conversion of a man's extended family followed, sometimes
over a generation or two, his own conversion; the texts include evidence
not only of male but also of female, child, slave, and captive converts, and
sometimes of their circumstances and relationships to others.

Conversion stories are rare; in most instances we cannot know the meaning of conversion for the individuals who deliberately chose to identify themselves as Muslim.[52] The opportunity to change or save one's life by changing
legal status was more or less constant. The idea of conversion as an act of
salvation depends on an assessment of what it might mean for an individual
to change his or her legal status in a society in which each community had
largely autonomous jurisdiction over its own people, and legal authorities of
different faiths did not interfere with one another. Conversion could offer
the possibility for escape from constraining legal circumstances. A person
desperate to change his or her legal situation, however, would have to assess
hopes for improvement against the chance that he or she might end up
worse off. A Muslim woman could not legally be married to a non-Muslim
man; would a woman unhappy in her marriage (a Christian woman could
not divorce) convert to Islam so that the qadi who presided over her conversion would annul her marriage? A Christian or Jew could not own a
Muslim slave; might a slave convert to Islam and hope that the forced sale to
a different (Muslim) master might be an improvement (with prospects for
eventual manumission)? A dhimmi found guilty of a capital offense such as
rape might have his life spared through conversion.

The martyrologies offer some scant evidence of conversion to Islam. A
few of the martyrs mentioned in the martyrologies, such as Felix, Witesindus, and Salomon, were Christians who became Muslims (we do not know
why) and then reverted to Christianity, and some of them had family members who converted to Islam. The priest Rudericus mediated between one
brother who was Christian and another who had become Muslim. According

---

52. On this issue, see R. W. Bulliet, "Conversion Stories in Early Islam," in Gervers and Bikhazi,
Conversion and Continuity, 123–133.

to Eulogius, one night the conflict between the two brothers became violent, and when Rudericus tried to intervene they turned on him and beat
him until he was near death. The Muslim brother carried Rudericus's
senseless body through the streets, announcing his conversion to Islam (as a
last act). Rudericus recovered and went into hiding, but some time later his
brother encountered him and brought him before the qadi of Cordoba, ac-
cusing him of apostasy (perhaps as a way to force his conversion).[53] Eulogius
claims that many Christians apostasized (converted to Islam) under the pressure of the amir Muhammad's efforts to stop the martyrdoms in his emphasis of the deleterious effects of the ruler's persecutions.[54]

Early converts included Visigothic lords such as Casius (progenitor of the
Banu Qasi) of Tudela and Amrus of Huesca, who saw political advantages
to conversion. They converted during the Muslim conquest and became
autonomous border lords of wavering loyalty to Cordoba. Military service
may have been an avenue toward conversion through the ninth century and
into the tenth. Some limited evidence suggests that Christian men interested in military service may have enrolled in the *hasham* (the standing mercenary army created by al-Hakam I). The first commander was a Christian,
al-Rabiʿ ibn Theodulfo, and it appears that one of the martyrs, Sanctius,
had been a soldier of the hasham.[55] A fatwa dating from the mid-tenth century mentions a Christian man serving in the hasham who converted to
Islam.[56] The hasham served a socially integrative function for men with
military ability; former rebels of convert background (and others) such as
Lubb (Lope) ibn Mandaril and ʿUmar ibn Hafsun, and perhaps their men
too, were enrolled in the hasham in the mid-ninth century as a way to bring
them into the service of the regime. Of course, the integration could prove
ephemeral: Ibn Hafsun broke away to revolt again, and Ibn Marwan al-Jilliqi
(the Galician) left the hasham with a contingent of men to assert his dominion in the western part of the peninsula, in rebellion against the regime. Ibn
al-Qutiyya, describing later events, reports that ʿAbd al-Rahman III, triumphant in his efforts to reassert Umayyad sovereignty, brought all the defeated
and now-submissive rebels into the hasham.[57]

---

53. Aldana García, *Obras completas de San Eulogio*, 202–208.

54. Aldana García, *Obras completas de San Eulogio*, 150–159.

55. Aldana García, *Obras completas de San Eulogio*, 121.

56. Al-Wansharisi, *Miʿyar*, 2:347–348.

57. Ibn al-Qutiyya, *Taʾrikh iftitah*, Arabic, 88, 92, 114; Spanish, 74, 77, 99; James, *Early Islamic Spain*, 118, 120, 140.

The story of Qumis (Count) ibn Antonian provides an example of conversion as professional opportunity in the mid-ninth century and also an example of the disdain to which a convert could be subjected.[58] Ibn al-Qutiyya relates that the Christian rose through the ranks of service to the court by virtue of his talents. When the amir Muhammad's chief secretary ʿAbd Allah ibn Umayya ibn Yazid became ill, Qumis was designated his substitute; when Ibn Umayya died, the amir remarked that if only Qumis were Muslim, he would keep him in the position. On learning of this, Qumis testified to Islam. In his position as secretary, Qumis frequently crossed the powerful commander Hashim ibn ʿAbd al-ʿAziz and aroused his hostility. One day, the commander Ibn Abi ʿAbda recalled, Hashim brought the subject of Qumis's appointment to the attention of Muhammad ibn al-Kawthar: "Is it not one of the strange things of our times that a person like you, with your ability and parentage and lineage, is excluded from the administration, and instead the most important wielder of the pen for the Umayyads, their chief secretary, is Qumis the Christian, son of Antonian?" The shaykh (Ibn al-Kawthar) wrote to the amir, urged him to replace Qumis with someone of noble lineage (like himself) who would grace the office, and provided the names of several candidates. Appealing to Umayyad pride, he remarked, "How amazing it would be if the ʿAbbasid caliphs in the East learned that the Umayyads in the West were obliged to appoint Qumis the Christian, son of Antonian, son of Juliana, the Christian woman, to the highest secretarial office!"[59] The amir subsequently replaced Qumis with Hamid al-Zajjali.

Ibn Harith al-Khushani reports in his biographical work on the judges of Cordoba that when Qumis died, Hashim collected testimonial evidence from the notables of the capital attesting to the fact that he had died a Christian, in the hope of despoiling his heirs of their inheritance (an apostate's estate belongs to the treasury). Only one man, the *faqīh mushāwar*

---

58. Aldana García identifies the unnamed Christian official whom Eulogius describes as his nemesis as Qumis. Eulogius reports that a Christian (in name only, he qualifies) acting on behalf of Amir Muhammad spoke against Eulogius at a special council of bishops and ordered the bishops to issue a public denunciation of the martyrs' actions. Later in the text (the *Memoriale sanctorum*), Eulogius describes how this official apostatized in order to continue to work for the regime. See Aldana García, *Obras completas de San Eulogio*, 151–152 and n. 262, 156–157.

59. Ibn al-Qutiyya, *Ta'rikh iftitah*, Arabic, 82–83; Spanish, 67–68; my interpretation of who speaks and writes differs from James, *Early Islamic Spain*, 115–116. Hashim also makes a disparaging remark about Qumis's religion, which is not clear from the text; James suggests Qumis is described as someone "who has abandoned his religion for that of God Most High"; see James 115 and 127 n. 30. The story of Qumis's conversion parallels the outline of the story of the conversion of the Jewish courtier Ibn Killis in Egypt (tenth century); see S. D. Goitein, *A Mediterranean Society*, vol. 1, *Economic Foundations* (Berkeley: University of California Press, 1967), 33.

(jurisconsult) and prayer leader at the congregational mosque of Cordoba Muhammad ibn Yusuf ibn Matruh (d. 884), a close friend of the deceased, stood up for him and represented him as a man who worshipped regularly and devotedly in the mosque. Ultimately the judge, impressed by this testimony but also fearful of Hashim's influence, contrived to secure the support of the amir for his decision: the amir ordered the proper division of Qumis's substantial inheritance.[60]

The story told by al-Khushani is one of political conniving. Qumis's career follows the common trajectory of a courtier who achieves his position by merit but is felled by the machinations of a rival. In this case the courtier's point of weakness was his religious status. As a Christian or a convert, Qumis was susceptible to identification as an outsider or even, in his death, as an impostor. Qumis's fall did not mark the end of Christians and Jews at court, where they often served as agents for their communities and as interpreters and translators in diplomatic contexts.[61] A number of bishops served as intermediaries and envoys in the negotiations between the Umayyad regime and the rebellious Banu Hafsun and with Christian rulers. The Jewish physician and community leader Hasday ibn Shaprut became famous for his diplomatic skills during the reign of the caliph 'Abd al-Rahman III al-Nasir li-Din Allah and for his role in negotiating peace with Ramiro II, king of Leon. However, we can see how someone like Qumis

---

60. Al-Khushani, *Kitab al-qudat bi Qurtuba*, Arabic, 130–134; Spanish, 159–164. If Qumis died a Muslim, his estate belonged to his heirs according to Islamic law. Perhaps up to one-third of Qumis's wealth could pass into the hands of Christian kindred (bequests cannot exceed one-third of an estate). In response to a question posed by 'Isa ibn Dinar, and in an opinion transmitted by Sahnun, Ibn al-Qasim said that he saw no objection if a Muslim made bequests to his close relations such as parents or siblings who were Christian or Jewish; see Ibn Rushd, *Bayan*, 12:477. If Qumis did not have any Muslim heirs, the rest of his estate would devolve to the treasury, but it seems likely he did, given Hashim's determination to wrest away the inheritance.

61. Two of the martyrs of the 850s, Isaac and Argimirus, served the Umayyad regime in some capacity before they retired to the monastic life; it is not known why they left their positions. Abbot Samson of the monastery of Pinna Mellaria translated letters from the amir to the Frankish king in the early 860s until he was accused of trying to pass military secrets through his translations. Once he lost favor in court and suffered accusations of heresy, he retired from public life and wrote his *Apologeticus* (864), in which he defends himself against heresy and attacks his enemies. His attacks, which clearly express his bitterness and should be taken with a dose of salt, suggest close collaboration between the church and the regime and the integration of church officials into court life. His attacks center on his enemy Hostegesis, bishop of Malaga, whom he accuses of getting drunk with the amir's sons and other courtiers and of spending misappropriated funds on gifts for them. Hostegesis's father (who purportedly converted to Islam to avoid prosecution for stealing from the Christian community) and uncle (who was deposed from the bishopric of Granada) also had positions at court, as did another relative by marriage. Samson accuses two other Christian courtiers, a father and son, of sexual debauchery with eunuchs and concubines. See Coope, *Martyrs of Cordoba*, 57–59.

would be vulnerable in a context in which influence depended in part on one's ability to command a personal network of alliances.

Conversion formularies suggest that by the tenth century conversion had become a regular and regulated public act. Although conversion fell within the qadi's jurisdiction, the formularies indicate that other functionaries in this period could authorize conversion documents: the chief of police (*sāhib al-shurṭa*), the prefect of the city (*sāhib al-madīna*), the market inspector (*al-muhtasib*), and the chief of public complaints (*sāhib al-radd*). The formularies treat the legal transition from one category (Christian, Jew) to another (Muslim) as relatively straightforward. A signed, dated, and witnessed document of conversion belonged to the convert as evidence of his or her change in legal status. This document attested that the convert affirmed that he or she was of sound mind and adopted Islam voluntarily. It also recorded the completion of a few basic ritual requirements. First, the convert had recited the *shahāda* or testimony of the faith and, if converting from Christianity, had testified that Jesus was a messenger of God; if converting from Judaism, that Moses and Ezra were messengers of God. Converts of all faiths had to affirm that Islam abrogated all other religions. Second, the document attested that the convert had performed lustration or ablution and prayer and had undertaken to fulfill the prescriptions of Islam, including ablution, prayer, *zakāt* (payment of the legal alms tax), the fast of Ramadan, and pilgrimage to Mecca (for those able to undertake it). The signature confirmed that the signer understood and accepted everything formally stated in the text.[62]

A new Muslim might Arabicize his name or take an Islamic first name. Ibn al-ʿAttar comments that when he prepares a conversion document and the name of the father of the convert is not familiar or is one of the more cumbersome or distasteful names of the ʿajam, he may write so-and-so (*fulān*) son of the servant of God (ibn ʿAbd Allah), effectively ascribing a new name to him. He notes that he renders the convert's father as "servant of God" because there is truth to it since all (Christians and Jews as well as Muslims) are servants of God. He observes that assigning a name like al-Islami is

---

62. Ibn al-ʿAttar, *Kitab al-watha'iq wa-l-sijillat*, ed. P. Chalmeta and F. Corriente (Madrid: Academia Matritense del Notariado, Instituto Hispano-Arabe de Cultura, 1983), 405–417. For description and discussion of these formularies, see Pedro Chalmeta, "Le passage à l'Islam dans al-Andalus au xe siècle," in *Actas del XII Congreso de la Union Européenne d'Arabisants et d'Islamisants (Málaga 1984)* (Madrid: Union Européene d'Arabisants et d'Islamisants, 1986), 161–183; Shatzmiller, "Marriage, Family, and the Faith." Another conversion formulary may be found in al-Jaziri's (d. 1189) collection *al-Maqsad al-mahmud fi talhis al-ʿuqud*, ed. Asunción Ferreras (Madrid: Consejo Superior de Investigaciones Científicas, 1998), 424–427.

also correct because the convert's *nisba* (ascription of origin or lineage) is Islam.[63]

In the formularies circumcision is not specified as a requirement for conversion, but according to Ibn Ashhab (as recorded by Ibn Abi Zayd), a conversion to Islam is not complete until the convert has been circumcised.[64] Ibn al-Qasim identifies conversion with circumcision when he confirms the obligation to circumcise male and female slaves and introduce them to Islam if they are not People of the Book, for example, if they are Berbers or Majus, Zanj, Sudan, and Saqaliba.[65] Circumcision is obligatory (*sunna wājiba*) for Muslim men and approved of as a noble deed (*makruma*) for women in the Maliki sources on the basis of a hadith of the Prophet.[66] Jurists knew that Jews were ritually circumcised and consciously sought to differentiate the Islamic practice from the Jewish: Malik opined that Muslims should not circumcise on the seventh [*sic*] day because this is what Jews do. He recommended that circumcision coincide with the requirement of prayer, between the ages of seven and ten.[67]

The act of conversion required minimal doctrinal education but did call for recognition of fundamental doctrinal differences between Islam and Christianity or Judaism. As the conversion formularies indicate, the

---

63. Ibn al-ʿAttar, *Kitab al-watha'iq*, 406. Perhaps Ibn al-ʿAttar's comments express the conventional practice in al-Andalus. There were differences of opinion about whether assigning a convert the name Ibn ʿAbd Allah was appropriate practice. Al-ʿUtbi records Malik's disapproval (from Sahnun in a transmission from Ashhab and Ibn Nafi) when he was asked about a man named Ishaq whose father was a Christian and who identified himself as Ishaq ibn ʿAbd Allah. Ibn Rushd explains in his commentary that it is not disapproved of if a convert takes a proper Muslim name when he converts, but what is disapproved of, as in this case, is the ambiguity involved in referring to himself as "Ibn ʿAbd Allah"—the listener is likely be misled into thinking that he is the son of a Muslim. See Ibn Rushd, *Bayan*, 14:488.

64. Al-Qayrawani, *Nawadir wa-ziyadat*, 4:337.

65. Ibn Rushd, *Bayan*, 2:162–163.

66. Al-Qayrawani, *Nawadir wa-ziyadat*, 4:336. On female circumcision, see Jonathan P. Berkey, "Circumcision Circumscribed: Female Excision and Cultural Accommodation in the Medieval Near East," *International Journal of Middle East Studies* 28 (1996): 19–38.

67. Al-Qayrawani, *Nawadir wa-ziyadat*, 4:338. Antiassimilationist Christian sources suggest that Christians were under pressure to circumcise in order to remain at court in al-Andalus. Jessica A. Coope suggests that Christian courtiers may have undergone the procedure and remained Christian (although she acknowledges that what it meant to be a Christian was a matter of controversy). See Coope, "Religious and Cultural Conversion to Islam in Ninth-Century Umayyad Cordoba," *Journal of World History* 4 (1993): 56–57. Ibn Habib mentions that Christians sometimes circumcised in a completely different context having to do with the proper burial of an unknown corpse (Ibn Rushd, *Bayan* 2:289). A question posed to Malik and transmitted by Ibn Nafiʿ, Ashhab, and Sahnun describes a Christian who circumcised his son (Ibn Rushd, *Bayan* 4:354). Do these references to circumcising Christians provide examples of transculturation, or do they indicate technical or initial steps toward conversion?

convert had to acknowledge both Muhammad's status as God's Messenger and the Qur'anic position on Jesus or Moses and Ezra. Although this minimal requirement was perhaps an insurmountable obstacle for some, it may have eased the way for others ready to consider conversion because it allowed the convert to continue to respect or revere Jesus and Moses.[68] Whether a person could convert to Islam or claim to be a Muslim and at the same time fail to perform the religious obligations was a matter for casuistic debate.[69] The sources record a few juridical problems that suggest some of the ritual difficulties confronted by the convert. For example, Yahya ibn Yahya reports Ibn al-Qasim's view that the ignorant convert from the ahl al-dhimma who performs the wrong number of *rukūʿ* (bowings; s.*rakaʿa*) for sunset prayer should repeat his prayers once he knows what he has done wrong.[70] Sahnun, Ibn Mawwaz, and Ibn Habib discuss in their books (as excerpted and commented on by Ibn Rushd) whether one should pray behind someone who has not memorized the Qur'an or has memorized the Qur'an but mispronounces the Arabic.[71]

The formal act of conversion often represented "a first step in a long trajectory of transformation" that took place over time and within a context of relationships.[72] An exception, of course, was a deathbed conversion, considered legally valid as the following mas'ala indicates. A question posed by the Andalusi jurist ʿIsa ibn Dinar (d. 827) to Malik's student Ibn al-Qasim about the proper burial of a deathbed convert provides a telling example of how family relationships embraced conversion. As related by ʿIsa, the son-in-law of a Christian woman told her: "adopt Islam so that we can [ritually] purify you and pray over you [when you die]." She agreed, ordered

---

68. Coope suggests, citing Eulogius's *Liber apologeticus martyrum* (12), that "many Christians believed that Islam and Christianity were not fundamentally all that different. They argued that both Muslims and Christians 'worship God and the law' and that Islam, like Christianity, is 'a cult of the true God'" (Coope, "Religious and Cultural Conversion to Islam," 59). See Aldana García, *Obras completas de San Eulogio*, 197.

69. Yasin Dutton writes, "From the earliest period until now there has been discussion as to whether it [acceptance of God as Lord and Muhammad as final prophet and Messenger] should also be accompanied by the correct outward practices detailed by Islamic law that form part and parcel of the practice of Islam." See Dutton, "Conversion to Islam: The Qur'anic Paradigm," in *Religious Conversion: Contemporary Practices and Controversies*, ed. Christopher Lamb and M. Darrol Bryant (London: Cassell, 1999), 151–165 (quotation, 154).

70. Ibn Rushd, *Bayan*, 2:75.

71. Ibn Rushd, *Bayan*, 1:448–450

72. Lewis R. Rambo and Charles E. Farkadian describe a heuristic model of seven stages of conversion in "Converting: Stages of Religious Change," in Lamb and Bryant, *Religious Conversion*, 23–34 (quotation, 32).

that her clothes be washed in preparation (a convert should pray in clothes cleansed of any impurities),[73] and asked, "What should I say?" She was instructed to say, "I testify that there is no god but God and that Muhammad is his servant and messenger and that Jesus son of Mary is the spirit of God and his word" (see Qur'an 4:171). She said this and died. Despite her conversion, she was buried in the cemetery of the Christians. Ibn al-Qasim said that the body should be exhumed and ritually washed and prayed over unless the corpse had already begun to decay.[74]

Inscriptions from extant grave markers dating to the mid-ninth century identify the deceased as Muslim with the formula that he (or she) testified that there is no god but God and that Muhammad is the messenger of God. In two instances the markers indicate that the concubine of the amir al-Hakam I, named Khatira, and the *umm walad* (concubine mother of a child) of the amir Muhammad, named Badi', died in the faith.[75] The epitaph of a woman who died on the 15th day of Ramadan in the year 328 AH (June 25, 940) presents a fuller statement of belief. The inscription, which is damaged, presumably began with her name and with the shahada; this portion is not intact. The extant text begins with a Qur'anic verse (9:33): "It is he who has sent his messenger with guidance and the religion of truth, to [cause it to] prevail over all [other] religion, even though the polytheists [*al-mushrikūn*] may detest (it)." The term *al-mushrikūn* (*shirk* literally means associating something other than God with God) here refers to the idolatry of the pre-Islamic Arabs, but the choice of quotation may also be intended to refer to the Christians (who were sometimes disparaged as mushrikun).[76]

---

73. See Ibn Rushd, *Bayan*, 1:186, for discussion of the cleanliness of a Christian convert's clothes for his first prayer.

74. Ibn Rushd, *Bayan*, 2:255–256. Another mas'ala about proper burial and legal-religious identity considers the case of a young captive from Rum (Byzantium) who died before his owner had a chance to instruct him in Islam: Should his body be prepared and buried according to the rites of Islam? Ibn al-Qasim's opinion was that if he did not convert, he should not be prayed over as a Muslim. Ibn Rushd's commentary includes other views (including opinions about whether or in what circumstances a young slave from the People of the Book can be compelled to adopt Islam). Ibn Dinar's opinion is that he should be buried according to Muslim rites because his master was a Muslim (and intended to convert him to Islam); Ibn Habib's view is that the child should not be buried as a Muslim if his master did not dress him as a Muslim and introduce him to the legal requirements of Islam; Sahnun's opinion is that he should not be buried as a Muslim because he was not subject to the laws of Islam before understanding the obligations of Islam and being responsible for them—which comes at puberty (Ibn Rushd, *Bayan* 2:213–215).

75. Évariste Lévi-Provençal, *Inscriptions arabes d'Espagne* (Leiden: E. J. Brill; Paris: E. Larose, 1931), 2–3.

76. Ibn al-'Attar's conversion formulary for a Christian woman who converts to Islam links her attestation of the shahada to this Qur'anic verse (9:33), followed by her testimony that Jesus son of

The inscription continues, articulating a relevant point of differentiation between Islam and the unbelief of the Arabs of the "Age of Ignorance": "[she also testifies that] paradise is true and the resurrection is true and that 'the Hour will come: there can be no doubt about it or about (the fact) that God will raise up all who are in the graves'" (Qur'an 22:7).[77]

The change in legal status to Muslim, however easy to achieve, was irrevocable. Three closely related fatwas examine the conversion and apostasy of minors, testing the prohibition of apostasy at the margins—at the physical boundary between childhood and adulthood, when a Muslim became legally accountable. 'Ubayd Allah ibn Yahya (d. 910) addressed the problem of conversion and apostasy in a case submitted to him by a qadi who asked how he should treat a young man (ghulām) who came to him and converted to Islam (the qadi had the conversion witnessed and documented). A few days later the young man said that he wanted to return to Christianity. 'Ubayd Allah responded that since it appeared that the youth had not yet reached puberty, the qadi should threaten him and imprison him for a few days in an effort to change his mind. If he refused to return to Islam, "he would not be the first to be seduced by Satan," and he should be left to face God's wrath. The qadi also consulted Ibn Lubaba, who concurred. Ibn Sahl, who recorded and discussed this fatwa (and the one to follow) in al-Ahkam al-kubra, disapproved of 'Ubayd Allah's response and provided excerpts from the masā'il (legal questions and opinions; s. mas'ala) he considered relevant (citing Sahnun, Ibn al-Qasim, Ibn Habib, Ashhab, al-Mughira, and Ibn Sahnun). His commentary challenges the fatwa indirectly by opening up a discourse that could support an alternative interpretation.[78]

Mary is a servant of God and a messenger, God's word and spirit sent to Mary; Ibn al-'Attar, *Kitab al-watha'iq*, 415–416.

77. Lévi-Provençal, *Inscriptions*, 4–5. Extant inscriptions from al-Andalus in the tenth century often cite verse 5 of sura 35: "O People! Certainly the promise of God is true. Let not then this present life deceive you, nor let the Chief Deceiver deceive you about God." See Lévi-Provençal, *Inscriptions*, 64, 89, 96, 105. Leor Halevi observes that verses 9:33 and 22:7 were "two of the most favored verses in ninth-century Egyptian epitaphs," but in the tenth century other verses became more common (at least in the extant record) in Egypt. See Leor Halevi, *Muhammad's Grave: Death Rites and the Making of Islamic Society* (New York: Columbia University Press, 2007), 25–26.

78. Ibn Sahl in Khallaf, *Ahl al-dhimma*, 43–46. The text does not provide clear guidance, but it may be significant that Ibn Sahl does provide a contrary opinion to that of 'Ubayd Allah: al-Mughira would have the young apostate killed if he persisted in his apostasy after maturity, noting that if a Muslim born to Muslim parents apostasized before attaining maturity and persisted afterward, he would be executed. Many of the opinions Ibn Sahl cites have to do with the inheritance of converts and apostates who die before attaining maturity (a related problem of legal identity).

A fatwa issued by Ibn Lubaba (839–926) tries to clarify the limits of minors' legal accountability and affirms the importance of the convert's (and apostate's) consciousness of his adoption and renunciation of Islam. The case also provides another perspective on conversion as part of family dynamics. In this case a boy who had not yet attained physical maturity (*ṣabiyy lam yablagh*) came to the qadi with the intention tᵣ convert, and the qadi placed him under the care of a Muslim sponsor. The parents of the boy visited him regularly and tempted him to return to their faith. When the father informed the qadi that the youth (*ghulām*) had indeed done so, the qadi consulted Ibn Lubaba for his opinion. The jurisconsult replied that if the boy had reached the age of reason (*qad ʿaqala*), for example, if he were ten years old, then the qadi should pressure him not to apostasize. If the boy remained determined to return to his previous faith, he should be sent back to his parents. The punishment of death did not apply to him. The matter of the death penalty was not pressing unless (or until?) the boy attained maturity.[79]

A male minor became legally responsible as an adult when he reached what the jurists considered to be physical maturity. This was distinct from the age when a boy was expected to assume his religious obligations and was recognized to have an awareness of his religion (according to a hadith cited in ʿUtbi's *Mustakhraja*, a child should start praying at age seven and be punished for not doing so at age ten).[80] Thus in Ibn Lubaba's view, if the boy was at least ten, he was old enough to know (*qad ʿaqala*) what he was doing when he chose to become Muslim, but if he was not yet physically mature (*lam yablagh*), he was not old enough to be punished by death for apostasy. The age of consciousness was particularly relevant in determining the religion and legal status of children of converts.

The case presented to Ibn Lubaba describes the qadi's concern to place the boy in a Muslim household, presumably to provide instruction for the convert and protect him against apostasy. Another case, presented to Ibn Zarb (d. 991) later in the century, specifically raises this issue. An eight-year-

---

79. Ibn Sahl in Khallaf, *Ahl al-dhimma*, 46–47; it is possible the fatwas of Ibn Lubaba and ʿUbayd Allah addressed the same case. On this fatwa, see also David J. Wasserstein, "A *Fatwa* on Conversion in Islamic Spain," in *Studies in Muslim-Jewish Relations*, vol. 1, ed. Ronald L. Nettler (Chur, Switzerland: Harwood Academic Publishers, 1993), 177–188. For a discussion of similar cases in the Ottoman context, see Eyal Ginio, "Childhood, Mental Capacity and Conversion to Islam in the Ottoman State," *Byzantine and Modern Greek Studies* 25 (2005): 90–119, esp. 101–113.

80. Cited in al-Qayrawani, *Nawadir wa-ziyadat*, 1:268.

old Jewish boy converted to Islam.[81] The question was whether he should be allowed to remain with his parents. The jurist replied that it was best not to remove him from his parents. When he reached puberty, he should be asked to profess his Islam. If he refused, he should be beaten and exhorted to do so, but not killed (in contrast to the opinion of Ibn Kinana).[82] Ibn Zarb privileged the parents' legal right of guardianship over an interest in confirming the convert in his faith by removing him from his family. A legal factor that is not explicitly mentioned but may have been at issue was whether a boy of eight (younger than ten) had adequate consciousness of his conversion.

The discussion of age as a legal boundary in cases of conversion and apostasy tested legal limits and had foundation in experience. The variations of opinion among jurists offered room for discretion, and the evidence of the fatwas suggests that jurists in Cordoba were ready to apply force to bring young men back to the fold but did not immediately impose the death penalty if they resisted. The martyrologies show judges struggling similarly with females accused of apostasy. Eulogius's account of Flora's martyrdom describes a girl's deepening faith and dedication to Christianity constrained by and coming into conflict with the boundaries prescribed by Islamic law for children of interfaith marriages. The way Eulogius describes how the Muslims in the story related to Flora is of course expressive of his sense of profound injustice and outrage, and his account is dedicated to her sanctity. Nonetheless, the narrative presents another instance of a Muslim judge dealing with matters of legal identity and accountability. Flora's self-defense tested limits: Should a person who is Muslim by birth be punished for apostasy if she has never known Islam? If so, how should she be punished?

Jurists had considered the problem of Muslims being raised as non-Muslims before the martyrdoms. Al-'Utbi records a report from the transmission of Muhammad ibn Khalid: Ibn al-Qasim was asked about the children born to a Muslim man and his Christian wife who were raised as Christian by their mother and refused Islam when they reached maturity. He replied that they should be coerced into Islam but not killed. Ibn Rushd provides a rationale in his commentary that reflects the legal experience of a later generation but helps clarify the issues at stake. In his opinion, the

81. Mercedes García-Arenal observes that there is scarce documentation of Jewish conversion to Islam in al-Andalus, but that conversion formularies and fatwas like this one suggest it did occur; see "Jewish Converts to Islam in the Muslim West," *Israel Oriental Studies* 17 (1997): 227–238.

82. Al-Wansharisi, *Mi'yar*, 2:354.

mother raised her children to be Christians before they reached physical maturity, and so they could not be killed for refusing Islam (as apostates). He cites the words of the Prophet referring to the natural faith or *fiṭra* of the newborn (understood to be a sort of essential Islam) and the way babies acquire formal religion: "Every child is born in the condition of fitra, and his parents make him Jewish or Christian." According to Ibn Rushd, there was no disagreement among jurists that if the mother had not raised the children as Christians, they would be Muslims (because their father was Muslim), and they would be killed for apostasy if they rejected Islam after attaining maturity (*bulūgh*), because there was no disagreement that the child followed the father in religion.[83]

Flora's Muslim father died, it seems, when she was an infant or young child, and she was raised by her Christian mother. She lived as a secret Christian (Eulogius records that her piety and commitment were remarkable for one so young) out of fear of discovery by her older Muslim brother, who may have been responsible for overseeing her upbringing (according to Islamic law, she should have been raised as a Muslim). At a certain point, however, she and a sister ran away (without telling their mother) to live openly as Christians among Christians. Her brother, learning of this, may have forced their (or at least Flora's) return by putting pressure on the church and the convent community and by having a number of priests arrested. Once Flora returned home, her brother tried to persuade her to repent and return to Islam with both blandishments and beatings, to no avail. Finally, he brought her before the qadi. The brother and Flora described her situation to the qadi differently, in ways that spoke directly to the question of when Flora became Christian and whether she should be accountable for her apostasy. The brother claimed that both of them had been raised to practice Islam, but that she had been turned away from her faith by the Christians and seduced into believing that Christ was God. Flora denied her brother's statement and claimed that she had never known Islam (raising questions about her apostasy). She asserted that she had been raised a Christian

83. Ibn Rushd, *Bayan*, 16:438–439. Al-ʿUtbi also records Ibn al-Qasim's discussion of the circumstances of a daughter conceived by a Christian man (who died before her birth) and borne by a Christian woman (who converted after her birth). She was given a Muslim name and raised by Muslim siblings and then died. In this case he considers the child to be Muslim (she should be buried in the Muslim graveyard, and her siblings and her mother should inherit from her, not her Christian relatives on her father's side). This he sees as analogous to the situation when a Muslim purchases a child captive and converts her to Islam, gives her a Muslim name, and raises her in the faith. Ibn Rushd again discusses *fiṭra* or the concept of natural religion in his commentary, as he does in the example referred to above (Ibn Rushd, *Bayan*, 14:331–333).

since her infancy and that she had promised herself as a bride to Christ. The qadi ordered that Flora be beaten and returned to her brother, whom he charged with instructing her in Islam. He warned that if she continued to reject Islam, she should be brought back before him. Flora deferred this eventuality by fleeing one night, having recovered from her beating, to seek refuge among Christians. Sometime later, while staying with her sister, she met Eulogius; six years later (in November 851) Flora became a martyr.[84]

The contrast between religion of birth (legal status) and religion of practice (upbringing) in the case of child converts/apostates is at the heart of the story of Leocritia, who, as noted earlier, had Muslim parents but was secretly baptized and instructed by a Christian nun who was a relative. Albar's account of her conversion conveys a sequential process from receiving the faith and retaining it in her heart to deeper commitment when "she came to years of wisdom and attained the lights of knowledge." This description of a child's awareness of her religion echoes the understanding of the Muslim jurists that religion becomes established over time with cognitive development. The response of Leocritia's parents when she made her Christian identity known follows the recommendations of the fatwas: the young child should be urged to return to Islam and, if necessary, beaten. Ultimately she, like Flora, faced death for her defiant refusal to "return" to Islam.[85]

How the conversion of a father affected the children of the convert and questions about the religious identity of a child whose father was Muslim but who was brought up as a Christian or a Jew were Islamic juridical concerns that are also manifest in the martyrologies. The case of the child whose Muslim father converts (apostasizes from Islam) was also a matter of interest in the ninth century; the martyrologies provide evidence for this circumstance in the story of the secret Christians Aurelius and Sabigotho, who were both charged with apostasy (both had Muslim fathers) and were the parents of two children. Jurists' consideration of the problem offers an approach to the question of children's legal-religious identity and age from another angle. The situation, from the juridical perspective, depended on whether the father apostasized before the child was born, when he or she was young, or after he or she reached maturity, and on whether and when the child knew that the father was originally a Muslim. The Andalusi jurist ʿAbd al-Malik ibn Hassan (d. 846) reports

---

84. See Aldana García, *Obras completas de San Eulogio*, 126–129. The Muslim relatives of Aurelius, who was raised by a Christian aunt, intervened before his adolescence to make sure he received a proper Islamic education (133).

85. Sage, *Paul Albar of Cordoba*, 202–210

Ibn al-Qasim's view that if a father apostasizes before his children are mature (he identifies physical maturity with nocturnal emission for boys and with menstruation for girls), the children should be coerced into Islam but not killed; the same treatment would apply if they were born after his apostasy and knew of or discovered his apostasy. If they grew up as Christian and learned of their father's apostasy only after they had become men and women, they should be left alone in their religion.[86]

Ibn al-'Attar's tenth-century conversion formularies may have established or confirmed an emergent norm that seven was the critical age for the determination of the legal-religious identity of children of converts. He wrote in his commentary on the conversion formulary of a Jewish man converting to Islam that the convert's children (male and female) under the age of seven become Muslim, and that if a child reverts to his or her previous religion at puberty, then he or she should be compelled to be Muslim and killed if he or she does not repent. He observed a difference of opinion among jurists over whether the penalty of death applied to a child whose father converted when he or she was under seven if the child was not properly introduced to Islam before attaining maturity (recall Flora's self-defense).[87]

A case presented to the jurist Abu Ibrahim Ishaq ibn Ibrahim (d. 965) for his opinion provides another example of identity confusion due to the conversion to Islam of the father and the circumstances of the household after his death. This case dates perhaps as much as a century after the cases described in the martyrologies and to a time close to the composition of Ibn al-'Attar's notarial handbook.[88] The qadi's inquiry and the jurist's opinion exemplify how complications of legal interpretation persisted even if basic principles were established by this time. The situation presented to the Cordoban jurisconsult was as follows: A Christian woman was brought before the qadi on the grounds that her father was a Muslim. When he died, she remained with her Christian mother until she married a Christian and had a child. Some twenty years passed. When the qadi interrogated her, she informed him that her father was a Christian who converted to Islam while he was away serving in the guard (hasham). At the time of his conversion, she was cognizant of her religion (*wa hiyya ta'qilu dīnahā*) and remained a Christian, and when her father died, she stayed on with her mother. The

---

86. Ibn Rushd, *Bayan*, 16:439–440.

87. Ibn al-'Attar, *Kitab al-watha'iq*, 411.

88. Al-Wansharisi, *Mi'yar*, 2:347–348.

neighbors said that they had heard that the father had converted to Islam and that the daughter had not yet reached maturity (*bulūgh*) when he died. The questions posed to the jurist were procedural: Who should confirm the woman's claim that her father was a Christian who converted to Islam? Was it the responsibility of the *muhtasib* to take up her case?[89] Was the testimony of the witnesses valid, especially given the time that had passed?

Ishaq ibn Ibrahim responded in his fatwa that the woman's statement established that her father was a Muslim and that she was a Christian. To avoid penalty, she needed to provide credible testimony (from a legitimate witness) (*bayyinat 'adl*) establishing her claims about the circumstances of her father's conversion. If she could not do so, then she should be treated like other apostate daughters of Muslims who are invited, and if necessary coerced, to return to Islam or suffer the penalty of death. The jurist suggested that there should be no rush to proceed along those lines, however, given that the evidence of the case was problematic: the testimony of the neighbors was hearsay. The statement of the Christian woman affirming that her father was a Muslim corroborated part of their testimony and was basis enough, in the jurist's view, to determine that she was legally a Muslim (and hence an apostate) unless or until she provided evidence to support her claims; the jurist seemed inclined to give her that opportunity.

Ishaq ibn Ibrahim wrote in his fatwa that he considered the case to be distinctive from the mas'ala about a man who converts to Islam and has a child approaching maturity or the mas'ala about someone who converts and has small children who remain in their religion and refuse to accept Islam when they reach maturity because of the nature of the evidence. His opinion did not hinge on the woman's age when her father converted or on her religious upbringing because the only "fact" of the case he accepted was what was undisputed: the father was a Muslim, the daughter was a Christian. The text is interesting as an example of legal reasoning in practice and also as evidence of social life. The fatwa describes a specific example of individual conversion: in this case the father's conversion is associated with his enrollment in the hasham and seems to have been peripheral to his family's daily experience. It is not clear how much the neighbors or the defendant knew about law regarding conversion and apostasy. The qadi wrote in his inquiry to the jurist that the neighbors had not come forward sooner out of ignorance; the woman may have simply stated the facts of her life, and

---

89. The *muhtasib* was the official market inspector and censor (typically identified as *sāhib al-sūq* in al-Andalus); the term may also denote an individual who takes it on himself to redress an apparent offense.

the focus on her age at the time of her father's conversion and her awareness of her religion may have resulted from the qadi's interrogation, or she may have known the importance of key factors and terms. The motivations of the neighbors to testify against the woman when they did are intriguing to consider: What may have changed in her personal circumstances or in the neighborhood? Was the charge against this woman part of a trend of accusations or a unique case? These questions, unfortunately, cannot be answered.

This chapter describes al-Andalus as a society in transition in the ninth and tenth centuries. The period characterized as crisis (*fitna*) by the regime and its chroniclers until 'Abd al-Rahman III reasserted the rule of his dynasty and restored the unity of the political community was a period of anxiety and creativity for Muslim religious authorities. The determination of the fuqaha' and judges to protect Islam from corruption made them suspicious of close contact with non-Muslims and the demographic, cultural, and social developments that attended and facilitated increased communication, interaction, and personal interdependence in the ninth and early tenth centuries. The spread of Arabic, spoken and written, in their view, for example, provided a means for the possible corruption of the faith of believers and the interpolation of alien ideas and practices. The instruction of "outsiders" in the pure language of the revelation threatened its besmirching. Their concerns informed an ambivalent attitude toward conversion, even if conversion affirmed the truth of Islam and expanded the community of believers. Mixed marriages and mixed families boded the corruption of the faith of children and future generations, even if interfaith marriage was sanctioned by the Qur'an and instrumental in the expansion of the community. If they did not like what was happening, jurists and judges nonetheless rallied to respond to the boundary testing of their times and parsed the implications of social circumstances for competing or overlapping legal principles. The legal discourse and judicial practice of the period provided (transmutative) structure in a context of change. Religious authorities may thus have disapproved of friendly relations between Muslims and non-Muslims, criticized interfaith marriage, and considered converts and their families and descendants as a social group to be potentially destabilizing, but their commitment to addressing legal problems arising from conversion and the fact of mixed families inspired them to determine authoritative guidelines for all manner of relationships and situations, as we will see in the next chapter, and allowed for the accommodation of practices of which they disapproved.

CHAPTER 3

Between Enemies and Friends

> An ascetic buried in the cemetery of the poor visited the jurisconsult Ibn Waddah in his dreams after Ibn Waddah failed to visit his grave. When the jurist expressed surprise that the dead man was aware of his regular visits and his greetings and invocations, the ascetic informed him that on that very day Ibn Waddah's son had sat on his grave with a Jew discussing matters which were nothing but unbelief (*kufr*).

The father in the story related in this chapter's epigraph, Ibn Waddah, was actively involved in protecting his community from innovation and heresy.[1] He compiled a collection of hadiths of the Prophet and reports from the early community of Muslims in his *Kitab al-bida'*, the earliest extant Andalusi treatise dedicated to the subject of innovations. He and other Maghribi and Andalusi *fuqahā'* (jurists) were concerned about the corruption of the faith by the insinuation of ideas and practices that deviated from the Qur'an and the sunna of the Prophet and the upright ancestors, as interpreted by Malik and his disciples and by the religious authorities dedicated to upholding their teachings.[2] In the continuation of the story, Ibn Waddah questions his son about his graveside meeting and learns that he and his interlocutor talked about "God, the Qur'an, and other things." Fierro suggests that the identification of the man in the cemetery as a Jew should not be taken at face

---

1. Maribel Fierro quotes and translates the full version of this story from Ibn al-Kharrat's (d. 1186) *Kitab al-ʿaqiba* (Leiden ms. Or. 955, ff. 152a–152b) in "Religious Beliefs and Practices in al-Andalus in the Third/Ninth Century," *Rivista degli studi orientali* 66 (1992): 21–22. The question whether the dead hear the living was itself a matter of discussion among jurists.

2. Fierro suggests that Malikis of North Africa and al-Andalus were particularly concerned with *bidʿa* (innovation in matters of religion), as evident in the number of writers who addressed the subject, and that they had a reputation for being hard on the *ahl al-bidʿa* (people of innovation—innovators); see Maribel Fierro, "The Treatises against Innovations (*Kutub al-bidaʿ*)," *Der Islam* 69 (1992): 210.

value—the term "Jew" may have been used as a way to disparage a Muslim of dubious conviction, someone the son claimed had faith in rational disputation (*kalām*).[3] Whether or not we are to understand that the son is being led astray by a Jew, the story identifies wayward belief (and disputation) with "the Jew."

Although the story may reflect a specific concern about kalam among Andalusi Maliki *'ulamāʾ* (religious scholars) in this period, the image of the Muslim and the Jew meeting clandestinely in the graveyard evokes general suspicions about cross-confessional intimacy. In the view of those who were anxious about deviation from the true path, engaged communication and interaction with Christians and Jews posed a serious danger. From this perspective, Christians and Jews had long ago deviated from the truth revealed to them by their prophets, and their very presence among Muslims served as a source of corruption. Numerous censures of innovations related to ritual practice cited by Maliki authorities such as Ibn Waddah (and later al-Turtushi) are attributed to imitation of Jews and Christians, such as embellishing mosques, visiting and praying in places associated with the Prophet's life and mission, raising hands and voice during invocation in prayer, and not working on Friday (comparable to the Sabbath).[4] Al-Wansharisi reports that the corrupt practice of blowing the horn of the Jews (shofar) at sunset to mark the end of the daily fast during Ramadan (as Jews marked the end of the fast of Yom Kippur) originated in al-Andalus.[5]

The corruption of the faith was understood to have eschatological significance as a patent sign of the End Times. The corruption of the faith, of course, had numerous descriptions and qualities. Specific manifestations of corruption could be identified in various contexts as a way of criticizing contemporary society. Ibn Habib provides us with a description of corruption that illustrates the formidable attraction of Christianity and Judaism: At the end of time the Muslim community will suffer misfortunes and fall into decline while the other religious communities flourish, such that some Muslims will become Jews and others Christians.[6] Ibn Waddah warns,

---

3. Fierro, "Religious Beliefs and Practices," 22.

4. Fierro, "Treatises against Innovations," 204–246. Ibn Waddah, *Kitab al-bidaʿ*, ed. Maribel Fierro (Madrid: Consejo Superior de Investigaciones Científicas, 1998); al-Turtushi, *Kitab al-hawadith wa-l-bidaʿ: El libro de las novedades y las innovaciones*, ed. Maribel Fierro (Madrid: Consejo Superior de Investigaciones Científicas, 1993).

5. Al-Wansharisi, *Al-Miʿyar al-muʿrib wa-l-jamiʿ al-mughrib* (Rabat: Dar al-Gharb al-Islami, 1981–1983), 2:466.

6. Ibn Habib, *Taʾrikh*, ed. Jorge Aguadé (Madrid: Consejo Superior de Investigaciones Científicas, 1991), 155.

"They say the temptations will come with the People of the Book and they will be due to them. And they say God will send a red wind from the East and that the people will flee to the mosques and to the 'ulama' but will find them [the 'ulama'] changed into apes and swine." He also cites a prediction that the Muslims will inevitably adopt the customs of the communities that preceded Islam.[7]

The expectation of the corruption of the faith in time did not diminish the legal-religious authorities' commitment to defend against it, and this commitment informed juridical perspectives on intercommunal relations. Fuqaha', however, were bound to consider a number of competing principles in the elaboration of their opinions about particular instances of inter-communal interaction, and they had to balance their interest in maintaining boundaries between communities and the realities of these boundaries being crossed, if not trampled. Interfaith marriage and conversion, after all, brought Muslims into intimate contact with Christians and Jews.

The fuqaha' of the ninth and tenth centuries sought to construct the parameters of Muslim-*dhimmī* ("protected person") relations at a time when dhimmis were not only neighbors but also relatives. They recognized that the legal identity of a Muslim was not exclusively an identity of opposition to non-Muslims; a Muslim was also, in legally significant terms, a son, father, brother, husband, daughter, mother, sister, or wife; a master, patron, client, or slave. He or she had a number of legally relevant social identities. Fuqaha' did not establish that one identity (Muslim) absolutely precluded another (son) when significant relationships involved dhimmis. Instead, they struggled to define boundaries that accommodated personal obligations.

Fuqaha' defined Muslim identity by the delineation of fundamental proscriptions and prescriptions and the articulation of distinctive religious practices, but in the domain of social practice the real work was in the details. The fuqaha' discussed the legal implications of a variety of social contingencies involving relations between Muslims and dhimmis and participated in the definition of an idealized way of speaking and interacting with others that contributed to a sense of Muslim habitus, that there was a Muslim way of being. The apparent accommodation of the legal obligations and social needs of mixed families in a transitional society may have been practical and perhaps encouraged conversion. The effort to elaborate a Muslim habitus,

---

7. Ibn Waddah, *Kitab al-bida'*, 11.3, 41. Uri Rubin argues that "the punitive metamorphosis" of Muslim heretics and sinners into apes and pigs in eschatological traditions represents the idea of their assimilation of Jewish and Christian ways. See his article "Apes, Pigs, and the Islamic Identity," *Israel Oriental Studies* 17 (1997): 89–105.

however, also reflected the complex social circumstances of converts and their children and perhaps added to the difficulties of assimilation. A convert to Islam would have to learn more than rudimentary Arabic and the basic requirements of the faith to be socially integrated as Muslim in certain contexts, and perhaps only his or her offspring would become properly inculcated with an appropriate understanding of how to present the Muslim self in relation to others of various statuses and contexts and perhaps transcend the social station of their parents.[8] At the same time, the converted Muslims and their descendants, as members of an increasingly differentiated society, themselves contributed to the elaboration of plural Muslim ways of being in a dynamic process.

This chapter will review a number of exemplary legal problems that address close contact between Muslims and Christians or Muslims and Jews, in a variety of roles to demonstrate how the refinement of boundaries accommodated close interpersonal relationships. The Muslim husband, father, son, sibling, patron, and neighbor and the dhimmi wife, mother, parent, child, sibling, client, and neighbor figure in a number of legal-juridical questions that test principles and take the measure of social conventions, such as those of filial responsibility and neighborliness. Legal questions having to do with each of these personas demonstrate some of the legal and social complications associated with interfaith marriage and conversion, and questions having to do with etiquette and manners reveal more of the strategies, devices, and language the fuqaha' employed to establish and affirm ideal boundaries between communities (and suggest how these boundaries were tested). In the period of social transformation the opinions of legal-religious scholars described and acknowledged graduated positions for the dhimmi between enemy and friend and accommodated, often through casuistic exception making, intimacy between Muslims and Christians and Jews.

As we have seen, the Qur'an allows marriage with Christian and Jewish women according to certain conditions, as articulated in Qur'an 5:5: "(Lawful to you in marriage) are (not only) chaste women who are believers, but chaste women among the People of the Book, revealed before your time— when you give them their due dowers, and desire chastity, not lewdness, nor secret intrigues." Although interfaith marriage was permissible for Muslim

---

8. As Erving Goffman writes in *The Presentation of Self in Everyday Life* (New York: Doubleday, 1959), "A status, a position, a social place is not a material thing to be possessed and then displayed; it is a pattern of appropriate conduct, coherent, embellished, and well articulated. Performed with ease or clumsiness, awareness or not, guilt or good faith, it is nonetheless something that must be enacted and portrayed, something that must be realized" (75).

men, marriage to a woman from outside the community challenged, if it did not threaten, the solidarity of the community and its dedication to the mission of the Prophet. This is exemplified in the story about the assassination of one of the early governors of al-Andalus who was accused of acting like a "king" and introducing innovations to the rulership. At the center of the story is the corrupting role of his noble Christian wife, who urges him to wear a crown, as the Visigothic kings had done, against his better judgment. In another version, at the wife's instigation the governor ensures that all who enter his presence are forced to bow before him by having the entrance to his reception room constructed low. Ultimately, members of the military leadership conspire against the governor and justify his assassination on grounds of apostasy.[9]

Men of religion expressed disapproval of interfaith marriage most often in regard to domestic life because of concern about the corrupting influences of the dhimmi wife and mother who was free to practice her own faith and perhaps remained emotionally attached to her confessional community.[10] The evidence of the Christian martyrs would seem to affirm their fears by demonstrating how Christian mothers and Christian relatives might well expose Muslim children to un-Islamic beliefs and practices, especially if the Muslim father were absent. The reader may recall that Flora had a Christian mother and a Muslim father; her father died when she was young, and she was raised as a Christian. Aurelius had a Muslim (convert) father and a Christian mother; when he was orphaned, he was raised as a Christian by a paternal aunt and had the opportunity to seek instruction from priests (when he reached adolescence, his Muslim relatives insisted that he study Arabic and Islam). Nunilo and Alodia purportedly had a Muslim father and a Christian mother and were raised as Christians. When their father died and their mother married another Muslim, the sisters were sent to live with a Christian aunt. Aurea's father was a Muslim from Seville, and her mother a Christian; for more than thirty years she lived as a nun in the convent in Cuteclara with her mother, without knowledge of her Muslim relatives. Sabigotho's parents were both Muslim, but when her father died (in her infancy), her mother married a Christian who converted both mother and daughter. Leocritia had been born to Muslim parents but was baptized

9. *Akhbar majmuʿa fi fath al-Andalus*, ed. and trans. Emilio Lafuente y Alcantara (Madrid: Real Academia de la Historia, 1867), Arabic, 20; Spanish, 31–32; Ibn ʿAbd al-Hakam, *Ibn ʿAbd al-Hakem's History of the Conquest of Spain*, trans. John Harris Jones (Gottingen: W. F. Kaestner, 1850), 27.

10. See Ibn Rushd, *al-Bayan wa-l-tahsil wa-l-sharh wa-l-taujih wa-l-taʿlil fi masaʾil al-Mustakhraja*, ed. Muhammad Hajji (Beirut: Dar al-Gharb al-Islami, 1984–1987), 2:349.

in secret by a female Christian relative and nun (the fact that she had a Christian relative suggests that at least one of her parents was a convert). The father of Maria and Walabonsus was responsible for ensuring their Christian education. He was a Christian landowner who married a Muslim (an illegal marriage) who subsequently converted to Christianity. When their mother died, the father sent Walabonsus to study in the monastery of St. Felix and Maria to the convent in Cuteclara.[11]

Stories like that of the governor and his Christian wife suggest that Muslims married into prominent Christian families in the immediate post-conquest era, and the evidence of the martyrologies suggests that mixed marriages took place across the social spectrum in the ninth century; many cases of interfaith marriage in this period and into the tenth century were also a consequence of conversion rather than of arrangement. Whatever the circumstances, mixed marriages could create complicated legal situations.

A *mas'ala* (legal question; pl. *masā'il*) addressing the final resting place of a child of a mixed marriage highlights the tension between a legal concern for categorical distinctions (Muslim, Christian) and the social reality of the family as a unit consisting of individuals with social (and legal) relationships to one another. In chapter 2 I referred to a mas'ala having to do with a deathbed convert who was (wrongly) buried in a Christian cemetery; both that mas'ala and this one have to do with the religious and communal identity of individuals who were related to Muslims by strong kinship bonds but were also legally liminal figures. The assignment of the appropriate burial place reflects a determination to categorize individuals who are on the margins and to separate them physically and symbolically. Even so, the discussion allows for extenuating circumstances.

The situation is as follows: A Muslim man had a Christian wife who gave birth to their child. While the man was away, the child died, and his mother buried him among the people of her religion (presumably in a Christian cemetery). The same day or the next, the man learned of the situation. Should the body be exhumed and moved? Al-ʿUtbi records Muhammad ibn Khalid's report of Ibn al-Qasim's response that he had no objection to the exhumation of the body and its transfer to a Muslim cemetery if there was no fear that the body had decayed; otherwise, the body should not be moved. Ibn Rushd remarks in his commentary that ʿIsa ibn Dinar's report is

---

11. María Jesús Aldana García, *Obras completas de San Eulogio: Introducción, traducción, y notas* (Córdoba: Servicio de Publicaciones, Universidad de Córdoba, 1998), 121–122, 126–132, 134.

clearer and more accurate: if the body has not decayed, it is objectionable to leave the body in place.[12]

One can understand why a mother might seek to bury her child among her own people. She could even have a legal argument: if a Muslim father died or divorced the Christian mother of his child while the child was young, the mother had claims to legal custody. In death, however, according to the opinions just cited, the child's legal and formal religious status determined that he should be buried with fellow Muslims. The mas'ala conjures up parents divided over this determination, the mother seeking to bury her child in the Christian cemetery, perhaps alongside members of her own family, the returning father dismayed and hoping to rebury him in the Muslim cemetery among his own people.

Ibn al-Qasim's primary concern is the integrity of the body: he would leave the body undisturbed rather than jeopardize its condition. Ibn Rushd's commentary draws attention to two slightly different perspectives on the possibility that the Muslim child might rest eternally in the Christian cemetery. In Ibn Khalid's rendition of Ibn al-Qasim's opinion, there is no objection to moving the body (assuming no decay), which implies that there is no opprobrium to leaving the child in place. Ibn al-Rushd prefers Ibn Dinar's report, which he considers a clearer statement of Ibn al-Qasim's position: it is objectionable not to move him (assuming no decay). A variation in wording makes segregation in death an imperative. Elsewhere Ibn Rushd expresses the imperative in emotional terms: the unbelievers are tortured in their graves, and this would cause a Muslim buried among them to suffer.[13]

The mas'ala has symbolic significance: the deceased child is recognized, implicitly, as Muslim, and the Muslim body (cadaver) has its proper place (in the Muslim burial grounds). The equivocation expressed by Ibn al-Qasim's concern for the integrity of the deceased's body (perhaps superseding his concern for where the body is laid to rest) and by the variations in the transmissions of Muhammad ibn Khalid and 'Isa ibn Dinar is firmly resolved by Ibn Rushd in his assertion of what is most correct. The contrast between the ninth-century transmissions and the eleventh-century perspective conveys the intervening development of a more systematic legal system and perhaps firmer conventions about burial practices.

The question of the guardianship of the young children of a Muslim father and a Christian mother after the death of the mother demonstrates

12. Ibn Rushd, *Bayan*, 2:283.

13. Ibn Rushd, *Bayan*, 2:256.

how early authorities of the developing Maliki *madhhab* or "school" of law handled competing legal principles and sometimes disagreed over which principle to privilege. In this case the question is whether the interest in keeping the children within the faith overrides legal convention in custody cases. Ibn al-Qasim and Ashhab would award custody to the Muslim father, but Sahnun argued that custody devolves to the mother's mother, as in any other case involving young children. The Andalusi jurists Muhammad ibn Lubaba, Ayyub ibn Sulayman (d. 913), and Muhammad ibn Walid (d. 921) subsequently upheld Sahnun's opinion.[14]

In another question of custody (recorded by al-ʿUtbi), ʿIsa ibn Dinar asked Ibn al-Qasim about a Muslim man who divorces his Christian wife. Does he take the children? Or if the Muslim father dies, does his family have custody? Ibn al-Qasim replies that the mother has the greater claim to custody after divorce as long as she does not marry again; if a Muslim father dies, then the Christian mother of his children has custody. The question follows: What if the divorced mother does remarry? ʿIsa asks, what if the mother remarries and she has a sister, a Muslim or a Christian, who wants to take the children? Does the sister have greater claim to them than the father? Ibn al-Qasim gives priority to the father over the maternal aunt if the mother marries or dies. But ʿIsa reports that he asked Sahnun his opinion of the situation of the divorced Christian mother who remarries, and Sahnun responded that yes, the Christian grandmother or aunt has a greater right to the children than their father.[15] The difference of opinion here, as elsewhere, gives a *qāḍī* (judge) called on to adjudicate such matters room to maneuver. If the consensus among Andalusi jurists was that the Christian grandmother or aunt gained custody of young children if their mother remarried, then that would guide his judgment.

Conversion complicated personal and legal relationships. As noted previously, conversion could affect the legal status of a marriage and the legal status of children. Maliki jurists determined that the religious status of children followed that of the father, but if the father were a Christian or Jew who converted to Islam, his children would not necessarily share his faith. According to Ibn al-ʿAttar's conversion formularies, as we have seen, if children were younger than age seven when their father converted, they

---

14. Ibn Sahl in M. ʿAbd al-Wahhab Khallaf, *Watha'iq fi ahkam qada' ahl al-dhimma fi al-Andalus* (Cairo: al-Markaz al-ʿArabi al-Dawli li-l-Iʿlam, 1980), 86 (hereafter cited as Khallaf, *Ahl al-dhimma*).

15. Ibn Rushd discusses the semantics of the differences of opinion recorded here and notes that prevailing opinion favors custody by the mother's relatives. See Ibn Rushd, *Bayan*, 5:413–415. See also Sahnun, *al-Mudawwana al-kubra l-il-imam Malik* (Beirut: Dar Sadir, 1997), 2:359.

became Muslim; otherwise they remained in the faith (and legal community) in which they were born.[16] In certain circumstances of conversion, then, a family might legally include a Muslim father and a dhimmi wife, some Muslim children, and some dhimmi children.

A convert to Islam commonly had dhimmi parents, siblings, and other relatives to whom he or she had emotional attachments. The stories of the martyrs include accounts of parents, brothers, and other relatives taking desperate measures to bring their Christian or apostate kin to Islam. The ninth-century compendia include a number of opinions having to do with the legal responsibilities of such relationships, and some of these recur in fatwas. For example, questions arise: Can a Muslim arrange the marriage of his Christian sister or daughter? If a Muslim's Christian father dies, can he perform the burial rites for him? Can a Muslim walk his mother to church? Can he share food with her on holidays? The questions posed express the individual's sense of moral obligation, and the responses acknowledge those obligations implicitly in their deliberation and variety. Taken as a whole, the range of opinion generally militates against a categorical break in relationships and responsibilities.

Many legal questions arise that address the circumstances of a shared environment and imply a shared commitment to civility and neighborliness. How should a Muslim respond to the friendly overtures of a Jewish neighbor? May a Muslim exchange gifts with a Christian neighbor? Should a Muslim offer condolences to a dhimmi neighbor? May Muslims share food sacrificed for the holidays with dhimmi neighbors or eat the food they have prepared for their holidays? What if a Christian blesses individual Muslims? These questions express concerns about communal solidarity and the problem of how the dhimmi neighbor fits into one's circle. The responses reflect an effort to define decorum between Muslims and dhimmis that is distinct from the code of civility among Muslims.

Hovering behind some of the questions of how Muslims should relate to and interact with dhimmis is the problem of ritual purity and food taboos, and so I will address this subject before returning to the juridical discussion of these questions.[17] Systems of purity and food taboos define boundaries

---

16. Al-Jaziri's (d. 1189) conversion formulary notes that according to Ibn Wahb, the young children also become Muslim if the mother converts but the father does not; al-Jaziri, *al-Maqsad al-mahmud fi talhis al-ʿuqud*, ed. Asunción Ferreras (Madrid: Consejo Superior de Investigaciones Científicas, 1998), 425.

17. I have explored some aspects of the development of Maliki purity law in this regard in Janina M. Safran, "Rules of Purity and Confessional Boundaries: Maliki Debates about the Pollution of the

between insiders and outsiders and are of particular concern in plural societies, perhaps notably in periods of communal formation and communal insecurity and perhaps also in contexts of common symbolic idiom and cross-cultural engagement. Marion Holmes Katz observes in her study of the emergence of Sunni laws of ritual purity that "the function of the [Islamic] law of purity in defining the boundaries of the community may be most prominent in minority and sectarian communities (for instance, among the Muslims in China, and among the Shi'ites), but it is always available; it is always *one of* the meanings of the law."[18]

Muslims must be in a state of ritual purity, achieved through ablution or lustration with water (or sand in certain circumstances) before undertaking any ritual activity, such as the five daily prayers, and this is one set of ritual and symbolic activities that sets them apart from non-Muslims. A. Kevin Reinhart provides a synthetic construction of the Islamic system of purity as it more generally came to be worked out among jurists of the different Sunni madhhabs. The system of purity determines that certain bodily "happenings" or "events" (*aḥdāth*) and acts require appropriate ritual purification before ritual activity may be performed. For example, urination, defecation, flatulence, touching the genitals, and touching a person of the opposite sex with desire require ablution (*wuḍū'*); intercourse, menstruation, and parturition require lustration (*ghusl*). Some substances are considered to be defiling impurities (*najas* and *najāsa*) and may affect the water used for wudu' and ghusl; these substances must be washed off clothing or one's person before ritual activity and include wine, swine, blood, urine, vomit, pus, and carrion.[19] The

---

Christian," *History of Religions* 42 (2003): 197–212. On the neglect by modern scholarship of the subject of Islamic rituals generally and of Islamic purity laws and rituals more specifically, see Ze'ev Maghen, "Much Ado about *Wuḍū'*," *Der Islam* 76 (1999): 205–252. On food prohibitions in Islam, see Michael Cook, "Early Islamic Dietary Law," *Jerusalem Studies in Arabic and Islam* 7 (1986): 217–277.

18. Marion Holmes Katz, *Body of Text: The Emergence of the Sunni Law of Ritual Purity* (Albany: State University of New York Press, 2002), 205 (her emphasis). Muslims, Christians, and Jews in Cordoba were aware of significant symbolic points of difference in their practices of ritual purity and in their observance of food taboos. Katz discusses the relevance of interconfessional contact in her introduction and the possibility that each confessional system was "a dialectical form of a broader language of purity that all contemporary inhabitants of the region [the Near East] probably understood to some extent" (8). Rahel Wasserfall discusses how Moroccan Jewish women (settled in Israel) construed their observance of ritual purification after menstruation as definitively Jewish; the practice distinguished them from "Arabs" or Muslims. See her essay "Menstruation and Identity. The Meaning of *Niddah* for Moroccan Women Immigrants to Israel," in *People of the Body: Jews and Judaism from an Embodied Perspective*, ed. Howard Eilberg-Schwartz (Albany: State University of New York Press, 1992), 309–327.

19. A. Kevin Reinhart takes up Mary Douglas's idea that purity practices form part of a symbolic system and defines the Islamic system in general terms in "Impurity/No Danger," *History of Reli-*

person who is in a state of ritual impurity requiring ablution is *muḥdath* (affected) or, if requiring lustration, *junub* (precluded). The state of ritual impurity is temporary in the sense that it is a condition that happens to a person and can be changed; a person in a state of ritual impurity is not "contagious" and does not contaminate others. However, the question does arise in Maliki texts in our period: Is "the Christian" najas, that is, equivalent to something impure and defiling? The question is striking because in our understanding of the developed Sunni system of purity, "'defiling' refers to things, never to persons."[20] The basic contours of the system may still have been uncertain in the first and second centuries of Islam, as Katz argues; underlying the general principles of the rules of purity Reinhart describes is a history of juridical engagement with differences of approach, opinion, and interpretation across and within madhhabs. Changes of interest and consensus are also apparent over time; for example, none of the four predominant Sunni schools of law require wudu' after the consumption of

---

gions 30 (1990): 1–24. His work is tremendously useful in its distillation of the definitive features of Islamic purity law and stimulating in its conception of the logic of the system as the rededication of the body to obedience to the will after involuntary or unavoidable bodily acts that cause violations of the boundaries of the body and reflect loss of control. Brannon Wheeler, "Touching the Penis in Islamic Law," *History of Religions* 44 (2004): 89–119, observes that all the human acts that require ablution or lustration have to do with eating, bodily functions, and sex. He invites us to consider, on the basis of his textual analysis, the symbolic opposition of purity and impurity in terms of the opposition of existence in Eden and humanity's fallen state. Ritual preclusion (a state of impurity) may be considered the natural state of men and women, characteristic of their living in the world, as opposed to the state of perpetual purity Adam and Eve enjoyed in Eden. As he describes, all the activities that require ablution and lustration are natural occurrences necessary to, and functions of, human existence. Fallen humanity can enter "a temporary and artificial state of purity for specific ritual activities" through the ritual performance of ablution and lustration (100). Marion H. Katz investigates what Muslim scholars have had to say about the meaning of *wuḍū'* and observes that although many jurists asserted that purity rituals were acts of worship beyond human understanding, others invested them with significance. She identifies, across genres and over centuries, "a consistent repertory of themes—the fall of Adam, the moral agency exercised through the individual limbs, the generation of the resurrection body, and the construction of spatial hierarchies. . . . Most fundamentally, scholars regarded *wuḍū'* as a response to the problem of sin." However, in contrast to Wheeler, she argues, "While there is a clearly recognizable repertoire of oppositions that recur in connection with *wuḍū'*, there is no consistent overall structure underlying the system." She suggests, "Rather than seeking a single interpretive rubric that will serve as a key for the understanding of *wuḍū'*, it may be more appropriate to examine the multiple schemas and associations that are inculcated through its performance." See Katz, "The Study of Islamic Ritual and the Meaning of *Wuḍū'*," *Der Islam* 82 (2005): 106–145 (quotations, 133, 137).]

20. See Reinhart, "Impurity/No Danger," 7 and n. 15. Ze'ev Maghen treats the subject of the contamination of one person by another in "Close Encounters: Some Preliminary Observations on the Transmission of Impurity in Early Sunni Jurisprudence," *Islamic Law and Society* 6 (1999): 348–392. He asserts that "despite initial appearances, Sunni Islam has in fact constructed what may be the only religious purity code extant which *does not recognize—let alone emphasize—the category of ceremonially contaminating or contagious human beings*" (350; Maghen's emphasis).

cooked food, and this is not a topic of interest in legal compendia of the medieval period, but Katz reveals that "at a certain point in the past the question of cooked food was the focus of a lively point of contention."[21] The defilement of the Christian is another focus of attention that has since faded away from Sunni discussions of purity law, but when it was a focus, it spoke to, and had implications for, concerns about boundaries as much as it belonged to debates about the elaboration of purity laws.

Katz observes that all the Qur'anic verses enjoining purity practices occur in suras that deal with the definition of the Muslim community and the clarification of its boundaries. Although ninth-century Maliki jurists do not cite the verse, the question of the defilement of the Christian (given the explicit use of the term *najas* in relation to people) probably derives from a specific Qur'anic verse (9:28): "O you who believe! Truly the polytheists [*mushrikūn*; s. *mushrik*] are unclean [najas]; so let them not, after this year of theirs, approach the Sacred Mosque [in Mecca]." Considering this verse in its Qur'anic context, Katz sees a clear identification of the mushrikun with Christians and Jews, arguing that "the dominant theme of the passage as a whole is the Muslim community's accession to the covenantal status forfeited by the Jews and the Christians, and the importance of observing the legal obligations sealing this privileged relationship with God."[22] As Qur'an commentaries articulate, the verse was subject to interpretation: Does the term *mushrikūn* refer exclusively to the unbelieving pagan Arabs of Muhammad's time, or does it include, more broadly, People of the Book? Are they to be excluded from the Sacred Mosque in Mecca only, or from the sacred precinct (*al-ḥarām*), the Hijaz, or all of Arabia? From all mosques? What does it mean to say that people are najas? Are they unclean (defiled and defiling) in their body and being, like other things that are najas? Are they unclean because they do not perform the rites of purification, or does their unbelief make them unclean (are they morally impure)? The Andalusi Qur'an exegete al-Qurtubi (d. 1273), after preliminary discussion of the verse, takes the position that all non-Muslims are barred from entering any mosque because they are in a state of temporary ritual impurity requiring lustration (precluded like the junub) and do not know or follow the rules of purification.[23] In the ninth century the issue of whether and how "the

---

21. Katz, *Body of Text*, 103; see chap. 3 (101–144).

22. Katz, *Body of Text*, 50; see chap. 1 (29–58).

23. Muhammad ibn Ahmad al-Qurtubi, *al-Jamiʿ li-ahkam al-Qur'an*, ed. ʿAbd al-Razzaq al-Mahdi (Beirut: Dar al-Kutub al-Arabi, 2001), 8:94–97.

Christian" was najas was a subject of debate that circled around the interpretation of Malik's sometimes differing opinions. The opinions and discussion do not fully differentiate and sometimes merge different strands of thought about whether the Christian (like or unlike the mushrik) is impure and defiling (najas), in a state of ritual impurity (junub), or is morally impure (as a consequence of his unbelief), and what this means for the Muslim who has contact with him.[24] Over time the idea that a non-Muslim could be defiled and defiling in his or her person gave way to a more specific interest in whether and how individuals who had contact with defiled and defiling things might transmit that defilement and impinge on the ritual purity of Muslims. The trend of interpretation, following practice, moved away from using purity laws to assert barriers to contact between Muslims and non-Muslims.[25]

Many of the opinions about the pollution of "the Christian" in the ninth century have to do with the water used for ritual ablutions and lustration. For example, Sahnun reports from Ibn al-Qasim that Malik said, "Do not perform ablution with the *su'r* [water rinsed from the mouth] of the Christian, or with what he puts his hand into." Ibn Habib adds that the Muslim should also refrain from using water from the Christian's house or his vessels (except under duress) and use sand rather than water from a communal trough. Acting on the basis of this opinion would preclude the sharing of water in certain contexts and might well develop into the establishment of distinct facilities. However, although Ibn Habib forbade performing ablution

---

24. Katz, *Body of Text*, 150, also observes that "in the earliest period of the development of the Islamic law of ritual purity there seems to have been a certain ambiguity and interchangeability in the use of the concepts of *janāba* (the state of sexual pollution experienced by human beings) and *najāsa* (the status of substantive impurity)." There are some suggestive parallels in Jonathan Klawans, "Notions of Gentile Impurity in Ancient Judaism," *Association for Jewish Studies Review* 20 (1995): 285–312, which examines the history of how biblical law and rabbinic law treat whether (and how) Gentiles are impure and the implications for Jews and their interactions with Gentiles.

25. Katz proposes that the belief that non-Muslims were "substantively impure" was a secondary development in the law of ritual purity, inspired or supported by a new understanding of Qur'an 9:28 that emerged around the time of the Umayyad caliph ʿUmar ibn ʿAbd al-Aziz (r. 717–720). She observes that Sunni scholars came to reject the idea in the classical and postclassical period, along with the idea that women and corpses could also be substantively impure (a view that jurists saw was inconsistent with practices such as women's performance of ablutions and the washing of corpses before burial). She cites al-Shafiʿi's statement that no living human is ever substantively impure as emblematic of the classical Sunni position. See Katz, *Body of Text*, chap. 4 (145–206). Questions about whether Christians (and others) might pollute and whether the things they handled or made might be polluted, however, continued to surface in later centuries; see Leor Halevi, "Christian Impurity versus Economic Necessity: A Fifteenth-Century Fatwa on European Paper," *Speculum* 83 (2008): 917–945, for an elucidating discussion of a particular fatwa in its legal and social contexts.

with water used by a Christian, he did not require the repetition of prayer, which lessens the impact of his opinion. Legal-religious authorities also noted variations in the record of Malik's opinion: in *al-Mudawwana* he is cited for the opinion referred to above, but in *al-ʿUtbiyya* (al-ʿUtbi's *Mustakhraja*) he is recorded both as having no objection and as expressing disapproval of using the su'r of the Christian. Sahnun's opinion is that even if one believes that the Christian drinks wine or eats pork, there is no objection to the overflow of his su'r in case of need or otherwise.

We see in the variations among the opinions attributed to Malik and among those of the ninth-century jurists fragments of an early stage in the Maliki development of the system of purity. Ibn Rushd al-Jadd provides rational order to these opinions in his commentary on *al-ʿUtbiyya*. He identifies the essence of the problem as twofold: the uncertainty about the impurity or purity of the hands or the mouth of the Christian, and the question whether water (in any quantity) is polluted by najasa (in any quantity) if it does not change its color, smell, or taste. In his view, if the najasa of the Christian's hands or mouth is established, then it is reprehensible (*makrūh*) to use water he touched or his su'r, out of deference to the differences of opinion about the effects of najasa on water.[26] Ibn Rushd's twelfth-century opinion legitimizes the sharing of water and expresses the direction of Maliki juridical thinking in the centuries that intervened between Ibn Habib and himself. Ibn Rushd reduced a sense of danger about pollution through shared water to a specific case—if it the impurity of the Christian's hand or mouth is certain (presumably if he is seen eating, drinking or handling najasa)—and in his expression of dislike, rather than prohibition, he accommodated uncertainty about the circumstances of the specific case.

We can see a triangulation among developing juridical consensus about the purity of water, the practicalities of sharing water, and an interest in social segregation in three fatwas dating to the late eleventh and early twelfth centuries (notably in different political and social contexts from ninth- and tenth-century al-Andalus). These fatwas show Maliki jurists arguing against the questioners' implicit interest in exclusion and segregation in contexts where Muslims and dhimmis shared water, upholding the principle of the purity of water (in wells and rivers). Ibn al-Hajj (d. 1135), the qadi of Cordoba, argued that a Muslim who buys a house and later discovers that he must share a well with a Jewish or Christian neighbor cannot claim "defect" and have the sale annulled on these grounds because (according to Qur'an 5:5)

---

26. Ibn Rushd, *Bayan*, 1:33–36.

God permits Muslims to eat the food of Christians and Jews. When the Qayrawani jurist al-Lakhmi (d. 1085) was asked about Muslims and Jews sharing water from a river that ran through a town, he replied that the water was not polluted by the Jews any more than it was polluted by the activities of the Muslims themselves (such as bathing or washing clothes). Abu al-Qasim al-Suyuri (d. 1067) of Qayrawan was asked to address the case of neighbors who refused to draw water from a common well used by a Jew who drank wine and seemed to have been an aggravation to them (the neighbors may have been seeking to force the Jew to move). The jurist made suggestions to mitigate the disturbances (the Jew should not consume wine in public, and if he did not stop, he could be compelled to move—but not to sell his house), but he did not see any justification for not sharing the well.[27]

The opinions of jurists of the ninth century regarding the "pollution" of the Christian may be read as part of a discourse generated out of their contextually specific anxiety about communal identity and differentiation, which had roots extending back to Malik's day. Thus when Maghribi and Andalusi jurists concerned about intercommunal interaction and how to address interfaith marriage consulted Malik's opinions, they found disapproval expressed in terms of concern for ritual (and moral) purity and food taboos.[28] Sahnun asked Ibn al-Qasim about Malik's view of marriage with women of the *ahl al-dhimma* (people of the [pact of] protection), and he replied that Malik disapproved of it but did not forbid it. He disapproved because the dhimmi wife eats pork and drinks wine, and the Muslim husband kisses her (and this is in her mouth) and has intercourse with her. When she has children, she nourishes them according to her religion; she feeds them food that is forbidden and gives them wine to drink.[29] The focus on the wife's potential for pollution and her association with the violation of food taboos

27. Al-Wansharisi, *Mi'yar*, 5:208; 8:433–434, 437. See also Matthias Lehmann, "Islamic Legal Consultation and the Jewish-Muslim 'Convivencia,'" *Jewish Studies Quarterly* 6 (1999): 41–43.

28. Malik reportedly accommodated other forms of social contact with non-Muslims despite concerns for purity (citations are not always consistent). An interesting example comes from an epistle Malik ibn Anas sent to the Abbasid caliph Harun al-Rashid and his wazir Yahya ibn Khalid al-Barmaki. Here Malik cites Ibn Mas'ud's opinion that there is no objection (on the basis of purity) to shaking hands with a Christian or a Jew or to performing prayer in their houses (the reader may recall the discussion of prayer in churches). See *Risalat imam ahl al-Madina fi-l-sunan, al-mawa'iz, wa-l-adab ila Amir al-Mu'minin Harun al-Rashid wa-ila Yahya ibn Khalid al-Barmaki* (Cairo: Al-Matba'a wa-l-Maktaba al-Muhammadiyya, 1893), 24. Malik reportedly did not object to Muslims wearing clothes worn or made by Christians (used clothes should be washed), although we have seen that prayer in Christian cloth was subject to discussion; see Halevi's discussion, "Christian Impurity versus Economic Necessity," 931–933.

29. Sahnun, *Mudawwana* 2:306.

presents her in a visceral way as an outsider in her own home, even in the intimacy of her husband's embrace. It should be recalled, however, that intimate relations between Muslim men and women always required purification, and that the common condition of temporary "impurity" or ritual preclusion in Islam was regularly redressed through the performance of ritual ablution and lustration.[30] We may see here an intermingling of concern for the Muslim husband's and children's moral purity with concerns about ritual purity. The mother nourishes her children in two ways, by feeding them food permitted in her religion and by raising them—perhaps according to the beliefs of her religion. The association of the ahl al-dhimma with wine and pork, in this instance and in others, may also have been a form of stigmatization derived from, but also somewhat independent of, concerns about ritual purity and food taboos. In practice, a dhimmi wife might agree to (or be required to) perform lustration after menstruation and to refrain from bringing wine and pork into the home and from consuming forbidden foods.[31]

A similar association of concern about food taboos (and the nourishment of children) and the impulse toward social distance is expressed in Malik's disapproval of a Christian or Jewish nursemaid for a Muslim child on the grounds that she may consume wine or pork.[32] He did not object to a

---

30. Ze'ev Maghen demonstrates how piety and passion "coexist rather comfortably in classical Islam" in *Virtues of the Flesh—Passion and Purity in Early Islamic Jurisprudence* (Leiden: E. J. Brill, 2005), 111. He argues that ablutions provide a way to pass between two modes of love, love of God and love of a spouse; through ablutions the two loves are compatible—the Muslim has a "portal" to transition from the sensual, bodily, human domain to the domain of the spiritual, incorporeal, divine, through which he passes many times a day (32). Maghen points out that although the Zahiri Ibn Hazm (interpreting Qur'an 9:28 literally) considered all non-Muslims to be najas, he did not see this as an obstacle to marriage with women of the People of the Book; the Muslim husband should have intercourse with his wife and then cleanse himself appropriately (68–69).

31. Manuela Marín points out that the existence of a notarial formulary for the marriage of a Muslim man and a Christian or Jewish woman (al-kitābiyya; woman of the Book) in al-Jaziri's (d. 1189) collection suggests that such marriages took place at some point. She notes that the contract requires the woman to agree to undertake the Islamic acts of ritual purity after menstruation and childbirth and to abstain from all the foods prohibited for Muslims. See Manuela Marín, *Mujeres en al-Andalus* (Madrid: Consejo Superior de Investigaciones Científicas, 2000), 143–144; al-Jaziri, *Maqsad mahmud*, 48. Al-'Utbi records Malik's opinion (from Sahnun from Ashhab and Ibn Nafi') that a Muslim husband may not compel his Christian wife to perform ritual purification. Ibn Rushd observes in his exegesis that Sahnun records a different opinion in *Mudawwana*; the husband may compel his Christian wife to perform lustration after menstruation on the basis of the view that intercourse with her requires her ritual purification. Ibn Rushd relates the issue to the question whether the non-Muslim wife is married according to (with the understanding that she will follow) the prescriptions of Islam. See Ibn Rushd, *Bayan*, 1:121–124.

32. Sahnun, *Mudawwana*, 2:415. For a general overview of Islamic legal views on breastfeeding, see Avner Giladi, *Infants, Parents and Wet Nurses: Medieval Islamic Views on Breastfeeding and Their Social*

Muslim woman nursing a Christian child, but he did disapprove of her going and staying in their houses (as a matter of modesty and concern for her
moral purity).[33]

Jurists discussed the sharing of food more broadly as an act of social conviviality. Their opinions express unease with cross-confessional conviviality
that was in tension with their commitment to Qur'an 5:5: "The food of the
People of the Book is lawful unto you" (the same verse permits marriage
between Muslim men and chaste women of the People of the Book). As
Ibn Abi Zayd al-Qayrawani's treatment of the subject in al-Nawadir wa-
l-ziyadat conveys, the jurists of the period interpreted Qur'an 5:5 variously.
He reports that Malik disapproved of, but did not forbid, the meat slaughtered by Christians for their churches or to Jesus or Gabriel. He clarifies the
point that in contrast, what is slaughtered to idols is forbidden according to
Qur'an 5:3.[34] Malik is cited more than once in a number of sources for his
general disapproval of meat slaughtered by People of the Book and for his
concerns about the food they prepare and the vessels in which they prepare
it.[35] His opinions express concern for ritual slaughter and food taboos, as
well as for social distance. According to Ibn Abi Zayd al-Qayrawani, Malik
disapproved of receiving food Christians distributed on behalf of their
dead because it contributed to the aggrandizement of their polytheism
(shirk). Ibn al-Qasim echoed him in this, disapproving of gift exchanges on
Christian holidays because it contributed to the aggrandizement of the Christians' shirk and kufr.[36] Malik's disapproval of Muslims eating food Christians slaughtered for their festivals and churches is recorded in al-Mudawwana,

---

Implications (Leiden: E. J. Brill, 1999), 68–114. Giladi argues that in fact, Muslims often employed
dhimmi nurses. He writes, "The picture that arises . . . for large areas of the Muslim world is that
seeking help from non-Muslim nurses was common where communities of Jews, Christians, and
adherents of other faiths lived side by side with Muslims . . . particularly among the higher urban
strata where the traditional way the extended family functioned was no longer strictly adhered to.
The hypothesis that jurists in the Eastern parts of the Muslim world were more often called upon
to sanction the services of infidel wet nurses, whereas in Spain, with its communities of Jews and
Christians, the practice was more easily accepted, deserves further examination" (111).

33. Ibn Rushd, Bayan, 5:154.

34. Sura 5:3 reads: "Forbidden to you (for food) are: dead meat, blood, the flesh of swine, and that
on which has been invoked the name of other than God; that which has been killed by strangling,
or by a violent blow, or by a headlong fall, or by being gored to death; that which has been (partly)
eaten by a wild animal; unless you are able to slaughter it (in due form); that which is sacrificed on
stone (altars); (forbidden) also is the division (of meat) by raffling with arrows: that is impiety."

35. Ibn Rushd, Bayan, 3:303, 378; al-Qayrawani, al-Nawadir wa-l-ziyadat, ed. 'Abd al-Fattah Muhammad al-Hulw, et al. (Beirut: Dar al-Gharb al-Islami, 1999), 4:365–369.

36. Al-Qayrawani, Nawadir wa-ziyadat, 4:368–369.

al-Mustakhraja (al-ʿUtbiyya), and *al-Nawadir wa-l-ziyadat*. Ibn al-Qasim shared this disapproval, but Ibn Wahb and ʿIsa ibn Dinar opined that there was no objection, and Ashhab asserted that the food was permissible according to the Qurʾan (5:5). Sahnun differentiated between food slaughtered for holidays, of which he disapproved, and food People of the Book slaughtered for themselves, which was not objectionable.[37] Sharing food on holidays and special occasions and exchanges of gifts, of course, promote feelings of solidarity. It is probably for this reason that Malik also disapproved of Muslims sharing the meat they slaughtered for festivals with dhimmi neighbors; Sahnun reports that he heard from Ibn al-Qasim that Malik had no objection but then later said that there was no good in it.[38] The range of opinions about Muslims and dhimmis sharing food could accommodate close contact (of course, Jews had their own food laws and taboos) or preclude commensuality, allowing scope for common practice and changes in conventions.

The shared participation of Muslims and dhimmis in festival celebrations was common throughout the Islamic world. It attracted occasional critical comments and warnings from members of the political and religious sectors but also, more often than not, was passively accepted. The popular appeal of holidays in al-Andalus promoted an experience of social bonds rooted in a common ground that boundary makers found troubling but that persisted despite their denunciations. Juridical sources suggest intercommunal gift exchanges and commensuality and perhaps common participation in celebrations of holidays that overlapped for Muslims and Christians, such as the births of Jesus and John the Baptist (both are identified as prophets in the Qurʾan) and holidays that perhaps involved native (pre-Christian and pre-Islamic) traditions (for example, the equinoxes and the summer and winter solstices).

Yahya ibn Yahya determined in a fatwa that it was not permissible for Muslims to exchange gifts with Christians or Muslims on Christmas (al-Milad) or accept invitations or in any way participate in the holiday. He said that he had consulted with Ibn Kinana about the practice in al-Andalus, and Ibn Kinana had repudiated it (disapproved of it). Yahya concluded that Muslims should treat the day as they would any other, and he warned, reciting a hadith of the Prophet referring to the Persians and their holidays, that whoever imitates the ʿajam (foreigners) in their celebrations of "their

---

37. Ibn Rushd, *Bayan*, 3:378, 272; al-Qayrawani, *Nawadir wa-ziyadat*, 4:365.

38. Ibn Rushd, *Bayan*, 3:343–344, 345.

Nayrūz" (new year) and "their *Mahrajān*" (festival) will be gathered with them on the Day of Reckoning.[39]

The holiday of *al-ʿAnṣara*, or the birthday of St. John (Yahya ibn Zakariyya), commemorated on June 24, may have been marked, at least by some, in ways reminiscent of pre-Islamic and pre-Christian rituals associated with the summer solstice. Yahya condemned its celebration and declared impermissible various activities associated with the holiday, such as the parading of horses. His criticisms center in particular on the activities of women, for example, the way they decorated their homes, took cloth out at night to collect the dew, and neglected their work on this day. He declared that on this day women should not bathe in water (unless it was to purify themselves) and should not make stuffed cabbage leaves and vegetables, presumably the traditional food of the occasion.[40] In the tenth century Ibn Lubaba echoed this view, declaring the day of al-ʿAnsara to be an error in religion and custom.[41]

Questions regarding Muslim celebration of or participation in Christian holidays recur often enough to suggest that this was an issue of genuine concern to Andalusi jurists. Ibn Waddah asked the North African scholar Abu Zakariyya Yahya ibn Sulayman (d. 852) about a prayer leader who received gifts from children on Christian holidays (with the response that the imam should no longer serve as imam). Ibn Waddah, in turn, advised a petitioner to return any gifts he received for the first of January. Ibn Waddah also consulted with Sahnun about eating food prepared by Christians for holidays like al-Milad, Mahrajan, and Nayruz, and he confirmed his disapproval.[42] When Ibn Waddah was asked about the Andalusi practice of commemorating another holiday (difficult to identify), he condemned it in the harshest terms, citing the Qur'an: "Do not follow the way of the deviants," and "Do not follow the way of those who do not know."[43]

39. Al-Wansharisi, *Miʿyar*, 11:150–151. The opinion of Yahya ibn Yahya, probably expressed in a fatwa, is quoted by a later jurist, Abu Asbagh ʿIsa ibn Muhammad al-Tamili, in his fatwa issued in response to a question about celebrating the new year on the eve of January 1. Yahya's opinion, as reported by al-Tamili, continues with the condemnation of the celebration of al-ʿAnsara. Malik disapproved of sharing the food Christians slaughtered for their holidays or distributed at funerals; al-Qayrawani records Malik's disapproval of joining in boat rides on their holidays. See al-Qayrawani, *Nawazil wa-ziyadat*, 4:365–369 (366 in particular).

40. Al-Wansharisi, *Miʿyar*, 11:151–152.

41. Al-Wansharisi, *Miʿyar*, 11:92.

42. Fernando de la Granja, "Fiestas cristianas en al-Andalus," *Al-Andalus* 34 (1969): Arabic, 25, 26; Spanish, 41, 43; *Al-Andalus* 35 (1970): 138–140; see also 133–138, 141–142.

43. Al-Wansharisi, *Miʿyar*, 11:293. One of the Qur'anic phrases comes from Moses' instruction to Aaron (7:142).

Jurists invoked other specific Qur'anic verses to define legal and social limits between Muslims and their dhimmi parents, siblings, children, and neighbors. For example, when Malik was asked whether a Muslim convert from Christianity could arrange the marriage of his Christian sister, he said no (if she was from among the *ahl al-jizya,* the people who pay the poll tax) and cited a line of Qur'an 8:72: "You owe no duty of protection to them" (*mā lakum min walāyatihim min shay'in*).[44] The full verse addresses the significance of the *hijra,* the emigration of Muhammad's followers from Mecca to Medina, and the requirement of hijra for all believers who want to be part of the community of mutual protection: "Those who believed, and adopted exile [hijra], and fought for the faith with their property and their persons, in the cause of God, as well as those who gave (them) asylum and aid—these are (all) friends and protectors of one another. As to those who believed but came not into exile; you owe no duty of protection to them until they come into exile." Malik's quotation implies that the dhimmi convert has made his own hijra and has separated himself from his former community. The Muslim brother owes no personal "duty of protection" or legal obligation to his sister.

The question is posed more generally in a mas'ala transmitted by 'Isa ibn Dinar, who recorded a response that affirms the separation of legal communities. Can a Muslim arrange the marriage of a Christian woman? Ibn al-Qasim replies categorically that a Muslim cannot arrange the marriage of a Christian woman, whether she is a sister, daughter, or *mawlā* (client—a manumitted slave), and whether to a Christian or to a Muslim. In response to the question, if she takes the matter to the Muslim authorities (*al-sulṭān*), can they arrange a marriage? Ibn al-Qasim replies that she should be directed to her own people.[45] On another occasion, however, Ibn al-Qasim concedes that a Muslim can contract the marriage of his Christian daughter to a Muslim, but if the marriage is to a Christian, then the father has no duty of protection for her (*laysa li-abīhā min walāyatihā shay'un*) according to the words of God: "You owe no duty of protection to them."[46]

---

44. Ibn Rushd, *Bayan,* 4:293. Ibn al-Qasim expands on and conditions Malik's view, stating that if the brother and sister were freed slaves and the brother converted but the sister remained a Christian, he could arrange her marriage. See also Sahnun, *Mudauwana,* 2:176. On guardianship and the legal capacity of women in Maliki law see Cristina de la Puente, "Juridical Sources for the Study of Women: Limitations of the Female's Capacity to Act According to Maliki Law," in *Writing the Feminine: Women in Arab Sources,* ed. by Manuela Marín and Randi Deguilhem (London: I. B. Taurus, 2002), 95–110.

45. Ibn Rushd, *Bayan,* 4:481.

46. Ibn Rushd, *Bayan,* 5:66.

Although marriage between Muslim men and Christian (and Jewish) women was licit, it involved bridging two legal systems, and the constraints attending marriage arrangements may have made them difficult to achieve, depending on the temper of the times. Asbagh reports that Ibn al-Qasim affirmed that a Christian could contract the marriage of his Christian daughter, sister, or ward to a Muslim.[47] When Asbagh asked him his opinion if the ward wanted to marry a Muslim and the guardian refused, he replied that the matter should be referred to rulings of their religion and their judges.[48]

The probing questions of fuqaha' concerned about confusion in circumstances of crossed boundaries also raise the possibilities of deception: What if a Muslim man marries a Christian or Jewish woman under false pretenses, having told her that he is of her religion? What if a Muslim man marries a Christian woman but does not know that she is Christian? Al-'Utbi and Ibn Abi Zayd al-Qayrawani both record Malik's opinion that if a Muslim man deceived his new wife about his religion, then she had the right to dissolve the marriage. A Muslim man who unwittingly married a Christian woman had no argument against the validity of the marriage unless he stipulated that her being Muslim was a condition of the marriage or unless it was known that when he married her he thought that she was Muslim from her words or appearance (because she spoke and looked like a Muslim).[49]

Ties of walā' (patronage-clientage) obtained between masters and freed slaves, creating an association of near kinship. In many instances conversion of a slave preceded manumission; this was commonly true for the military slaves and palace eunuchs and favorites in the ninth and tenth centuries and historically true for mawālī of the Umayyad dynasty. However, Christian and Jewish slaves were not required to convert and might attain their freedom in various ways, including manumission, redemption, or as a legal consequence of their status as mothers of their masters' children (the mother

---

47. The formulary in al-Jaziri's collection for a marriage between a Muslim and a woman of the People of the Book indicates that the woman's walī (legal guardian or legal representative with authority to conclude the marriage contract such as her father or brother) gives her in marriage; in the absence of a wali, the notary should charge the bishop to serve as such (Maqsad al-maqsud, 47–48).

48. Ibn Rushd, Bayan, 5:80–81.

49. Ibn Rushd, Bayan, 4:459. Ibn Rushd notes in his commentary that Malik is recorded elsewhere as stating that the marriage between the Muslim and the deceived woman is sound, and that Rabi'a's opinion is that she does not have the right to choose because Islam is not a defect (thus the analogy to a purchase of defective merchandise does not apply). Ibn Rushd explains that the opinion that the woman has a choice to reject the marriage recognizes that she intended his religion to be a condition of the marriage. She has the right of refusal, like a man who buys a slave girl thinking that she is Christian in order to marry her to his Christian slave, or because he has forsworn owning Muslim (female) slaves, and then finds out that she is Muslim. See also al-Qayrawani, Nawadir wa-ziyadat 4:527.

acquired the distinctive status of *umm walad*).[50] This created an ambiguous situation—the relationship between master and freed slave was defined by wala', but the relationship between a Muslim and a dhimmi would seem to preclude bonds of mutual obligation. A case presented to Abu Salih Ayyub ibn Sulayman (d. 914) illustrates the challenge of denying wala' between Muslims and dhimmis, and in this case the Cordoban jurist seems to treat wala' as a potential or dormant relationship. A female Christian captive was purchased by a Muslim man. She bore her master children before he died. The questions posed are these: Is she a free woman (the presumption here would be that the master acknowledged the children as his, and she was an umm walad)? If she seeks to reside in Dar al-Harb (the Domain of War), can she go, or must she be prevented from doing so? If she dies with money, who inherits from her, the people of her religion, her children, or the children of her master's brother if her children are no longer alive? The mufti replied that the woman was indeed free but that she should not leave and settle in Dar al-Harb because her wala' went to the heirs of her master, and if she should become Muslim, they would receive her inheritance.[51]

Malik and Ibn al-Qasim used Qur'an 8:72 to assert the separation of the Muslim convert from his or her natal community and to preclude involvement in its affairs in another context. When Malik was asked about offering condolences to a Muslim whose unbelieving (*kāfir*) father had died, he replied that it did not please him, according to God's words: "You owe no

---

50. Jurists did consider whether a child taken captive could be compelled to adopt Islam. Al-ʿUtbi presents a report by the Andalusi Muhammad ibn Khalid that Ibn al-Qasim's view was that he could not be compelled to adopt Islam if he was of the People of the Book and already aware of (ʿaqala) his religion. Ibn al-Rushd identifies six different opinions about this, including categorical yes and categorical no, as well as consideration of whether the captive had his parents (both or just the father) with him when taken captive (and whether the parents were retained by the same owner); see Ibn Rushd, *Bayan*, 2:213–215.

51. Al-Wansharisi, *Miʿyar*, 9:235. A cluster of opinions in the masaʾil literature centers on the assignment of wala' in various circumstances. For example, Sahnun asks: If a Christian and a Muslim share a Muslim slave (presumably converted) and manumit him together, who has the wala' of the Christian's "portion" since the Christian cannot be patron to the Muslim freedman (and cannot inherit from him)? Ibn al-Qasim replies that it goes to the community of Muslims as a whole (*Mudawwana*, 3:364). Elsewhere he states his opinion that if a Christian owns a slave who becomes Muslim and frees him or her, the wala' of the freed person goes to the Muslims as a community. If the former master converts, the wala' reverts to him in the case of the umm walad and the slave who contracted his manumission (*Mudawwana*, 3:352–353). Al-Qayrawani records Malik's opinion about the reverse situation: the wala' of a Christian who is manumitted by a Muslim goes to that Muslim. The Muslim patron cannot inherit from his Christian client by manumission, however. Al-Qayrawani includes a variety of opinions about what should become of the Christian's heritable goods. The main question is whether they go to the treasury of the Muslims or to his Christian heirs (*Nawadir wa-ziyadat*, 13:257–258; see also 260).

duty of protection to them until they come into exile." The message was that the Muslim's relationship with his father had been severed by conversion. Neither could inherit from the other.[52]

In fact, jurists often reconciled this principle with conventions of filial and familial responsibility. Legal opinions about the funerary rites of a Muslim's non-Muslim parent exemplify how casuistry allowed for accommodation. In principle, burial rituals, like other religious rituals, excluded the participation of members of other confessions. Addressing concerns about filial responsibility, Malik reportedly observed in this connection that the son's bonds to his father ended with his death. However, Malik made an exception: a Muslim should not wash the body of his unbelieving father or follow the funeral procession or bury him except out of fear that the body would be neglected.[53] This exception invites elaboration; as the statement suggests, laying a body to rest involved a series of ritual actions.

Ibn Abi Zayd al-Qayrawani's chapter "On the Attendance of the Muslim at the Funeral of the Unbeliever or the Procession or the Interment and the Attendance of the Unbeliever [at the Funeral] of the Muslim" illustrates how the discussion of this issue in detail (on the basis of the exception) enlarged the scope for adaptation and accommodation.[54] We see distinctions made between private and public ritual actions, as well as different considerations if a non-Muslim father was faced with the death of his Muslim son. The chapter presents Ibn Habib's opinion in conjunction with, and in elaboration of, the opinions of the Meccan ʿAta, as well as Malik. We begin with Ibn Habib's generalization: "A Muslim does not carry the bier of an unbeliever or walk alongside it or stand at his grave, and an unbeliever does not carry the bier of a Muslim, but there is no objection if the unbeliever goes to the grave and lays the body in the ground and throws dirt on top of it."[55] Ibn Habib articulates a difference in status and dignity between Muslims and unbelievers in terms of the appearance of members of either community at the public ritual of the procession to the grave and interment. He

---

52. Ibn Rushd, *Bayan*, 2:211–213; al-Qayrawani, *Nawadir wa-ziyadat*, 1:662.

53. Ibn Rushd, *Bayan*, 2:218; al-Qayrawani, *Nawadir wa-ziyadat*, 1:612; Sahnun, *Mudauwana*, 1:187.

54. For a case of unbelievers attending funerals of believers, see the report that Christians and Jews attended the funeral of ʿUbayd Allah ibn Yahya in 910 in ʿIyad ibn Musa, *Tartib al-Madarik wa-taqrib al-masalik li-maʿarifat aʿlam madhhab Malik* (Rabat: Wizarat al-Awqaf wa-al-Shuʾun al-Islamiyya, 1965–1983), 4:423.

55. Jurists recognized that non-Muslims might also have personal reasons for attending the funerals of Muslims. Al-Qayrawani records that although Ashhab and Ibn al-Qasim asserted that the unbelieving father should not undertake the burial of his son, Ashhab said that the father was not forbidden from escorting him to the grave or blessing him; al-Qayrawani, *Nawadir wa-ziyadat*, 1:612.

goes on to the more specific subject of the burial of a non-Muslim relative: "If a Muslim loses someone for whom he is responsible, for example, his mother, father, or brother, who is an unbeliever, there is no objection to his attending to the body and preparing it and shrouding it until it is taken out. Then the body of the deceased should be handed to the people of his religion." Ibn Habib's opinion here balances the Muslim's responsibility to an individual with concern for the public and communal nature of the procession and burial. He is ready, however, to allow the Muslim to proceed out the door: "If he fears the body will be neglected, then he may lead it to the grave at a remove from those who carry the bier." Ibn Habib affirms his position (and reinforces his qualification) with reference to the sunna of the Prophet: "It is narrated that the Prophet permitted this if he [the Muslim] goes in front of the procession."[56]

Ibn Abi Zayd follows Ibn Habib's opinion with a report that 'Ata (d. 734 or 735) said that if a Muslim's Christian mother dies, he should shroud her and accompany her to the grave site but keep himself apart (he also notes that Ibn Habib said that this separation applies whether he is walking or riding). He then cites Malik's opinion that there is no objection to taking care of all the Christian mother's funerary affairs and then turning her over to her people. The Muslim should not accompany her to the grave except out of fear of neglect. In that case he should lead her body to the grave and bury her.[57] The juxtaposition of opinions here suggests how Ibn Habib developed his position and also prompts us to observe that the difference in gender was not substantively relevant here.

Death rituals are intrinsic to communal identity. As Leor Halevi demonstrates in his book on funerary practices in early Islamic society, Muslim jurists "endeavored to enact a ritual that would signal the divergence of their religious community from others."[58] The ninth- and tenth-century elaborators of the Maliki legal tradition, drawing on the authoritative opinions of Malik and others, defended burial rites as rituals of demarcation but at the same time acknowledged exceptions that allowed individual Muslims to

---

56. Al-Qayrawani, *Nawadir wa-ziyadat,* 1:663; see also Ibn Rushd, *Bayan,* 2:218.

57. Al-Qayrawani, *Nawadir wa-ziyadat,* 1:664.

58. Leor Halevi, *Muhammad's Grave: Death Rites and the Making of Islamic Society* (New York: Columbia University Press, 2007), 159. For a sense of how the opinions cited and expressed by the proponents of the developing Maliki tradition coincided with, and were informed by, opinions about funerary practices as they developed elsewhere and in other developing Islamic legal traditions, see *Muhammad's Grave,* especially 68–69, 155–160. Interestingly, 'Ata is cited by other sources for the opinion that Muslims should not wash or shroud the corpses of non-Muslims even if they are kin (69).

participate in the transition of a loved one from life to death or at least ensure that a parent or child or other person of significant blood relationship
received a proper burial. Distance and dignity were upheld in symbolic details: if a Muslim must attend the burial of a non-Muslim, he must not carry
the bier, he should lead rather than follow the procession to the burial site,
and he should keep himself apart.[59]

The preclusion of Muslims (converts) inheriting from dhimmis and
dhimmis inheriting from Muslims could be obviated in part through bequests.
According to the opinion of Ibn al-Qasim as reported by Sahnun and 'Isa
ibn Dinar and recorded in al-'Utbiyya, a Muslim may make bequests to close
relatives who are Christians or Jews, for example, to parents and siblings.
In fact, Ibn al-Qasim expressed his approval of this (although Malik
disapproved).[60] The testator, of course, had to be careful to conform to the
rules for bequests to ensure that his or her will was carried out.[61] Casuistry
allowed for the inheritance of dhimmis in other instances where the religious identity of the deceased at the time of death was uncertain or disputed,
for example, if a man died leaving a Muslim daughter and a Christian sister,
each of whom claimed that he died in her faith, or if a man died leaving a
Muslim son and a Christian daughter who contested his religious (and legal)
identity at death. In these situations all parties received some satisfaction.[62]

Opinions about whether it was permissible for a Muslim to walk his
blind mother to church allowed for a similar mitigation of the principle of
social distance. Ibn Rushd points out that some sources cite Malik as having
no objection, but others cite his disapproval. Al-'Utbi reports Ibn Wahb's
opinion that there is no objection to a son walking his mother to church as
long as he does not enter the church or give his mother anything that will
benefit the church.[63]

---

59. The reader will note that opinions referring to the *kāfir* or unbeliever are reformulated in the
discourse to refer to dhimmis (the Christian mother or father). In this way the identity of the Muslim in relation to the "other" is recontextualized to suit the circumstances of a society with a large
dhimmi (especially Christian) population.

60. Ibn Rushd, *Bayan*, 12:474. Sahnun records Malik's opinion that it is not permissible for Muslims
to make bequests for dhimmis in *al-Mudawwana* (6:18), although Malik did not object to a dhimmi
making a bequest to a Muslim as long as he was not leaving wine or pork or owed his *jizya* (poll tax)
payment. Malik was asked whether Christians and Jews could benefit from a bequest dedicated to
travelers; he replied that such a bequest (like those for the poor and miserable) was intended for the
Muslims only (*Bayan*, 13:38).

61. Ibn Rushd, *Bayan*, 13:334.

62. Ibn Rushd, *Bayan*, 14:291–292.

63. Ibn Rushd, *Bayan*, 4:205–206; 16:441.

The Qur'an was also invoked to establish social distance between Muslims and dhimmi neighbors. Sahnun reports from Ashhab that Malik disapproved of exchanging gifts with a Christian neighbor, citing Qur'an 60:1: "O you who believe! Take not my enemies and yours as friends (or protectors)—offering them (your) love, even though they have rejected the truth that has come to you, and have (on the contrary) driven out the Messenger and yourselves (from your homes), (simply) because you believe in God your Lord! If you have come out to strive in my way and to seek my good pleasure, (take them not as friends), holding secret converse of love (and friendship) with them: for I know full well all that you conceal and all that you reveal. And any of you that does this has strayed from the straight path."[64]

The response may be different when the situation is not reciprocal. Sahnun cites Ashhab and Ibn Nafi''s transmission of Malik's opinion that there is no objection to a Christian blessing Muslims (or a Muslim) in his prayers if he intends honor in this. Ibn Rushd finds it incumbent to add that there is no offense if the Christian is blessing his (Muslim) relatives and neighbors, but he should not do it if it leads Muslims to be drawn into friendship with unbelievers. He cites Qur'an 58:22: "You will not find any people who believe in God and the Last Day, loving those who resist God and His Messenger, even though they were their fathers or their sons, or their brothers, or their kindred."[65]

Legal-juridical opinions about verbal exchanges with dhimmi neighbors convey the powerful pull of social reciprocity and acknowledge conventions of neighborliness. Ibn Rushd, in his extended and impassioned critique of Malik's opinion that one should not offer condolences to a Muslim for the death of his unbelieving father, observes that this was a matter of comforting one's fellow Muslim. Does anyone doubt that the Prophet was comforted for the death of his uncle Abu Talib? Ibn Rushd notes that Malik would allow such comfort for an unbelieving neighbor upon the death of his unbelieving father, according to what may be described as the protection or claims of neighborliness (li-dhimāmi l-jiwāri). The words used to express condolences in these situations were, of course, weighed. According to Malik, one should say in this instance: "I heard of what befell your father. May God unite him with the preeminent in his religion and the best in his community [milla]." Sahnun said that a Muslim could console the unbeliever, and Ibn Sahnun said that a Muslim could console his dhimmi neighbor, by

64. Ibn Rushd, Bayan, 18:421.

65. Ibn Rushd, Bayan, 4:354.

saying, "May God recompense you for your loss and bless your father with the best of what he rewards someone from his religion."[66]

Generations of proponents of the Maliki madhhab recognized the symbolic power of language and worked consciously to define certain parameters of a "linguistic habitus"—to use Pierre Bourdieu's term—or linguistic "sense of place" in their consideration of verbal formulas. As Bourdieu explains, "Linguistic 'sense of place' governs the degree of constraint which a given field [context] will bring to bear on the production of discourse, imposing silence or a hypercontrolled language on some people while allowing others the liberties of a language that is securely established. This means that competence, which is acquired in a social context, and through practice, is inseparable from the practical mastery of situations in which this usage of language is *socially acceptable*."[67] The knowledge and appropriate contextual use of verbal formulas differentiated those who were adept in their mastery of the official language from those who were not. This mastery must have been an important social marker among speakers of Arabic in al-Andalus during the period of transculturation and conversion.[68]

Formulaic verbal responses to certain cues, such as sneezing, and formulaic interactions with other Muslims on certain occasions reflexively acknowledge the community's relationship to God and express communal identity and solidarity. In this connection, Ibn Abi Zayd al-Qayrawani's *Nawadir wa-ziyadat* provides examples of condolences expressed by the Prophet and others as models for Muslims to follow when addressing the circumstances of death and records God's injunction to say "To God

---

66. Ibn Rushd, *Bayan*, 2:211–213; see also al-Qayrawani, *Nawadir wa-ziyadat*, 1:660–663 for opinions about consoling the unbeliever or the dhimmi. Emile Tyan defines *jiwār* as a pre-Islamic Arab form of contract "by which an individual belonging to one group puts himself under the protection of an individual of another group and resides near him." See Tyan, *Institutions du droit public musulman. Tome premier: Le califat* (Paris: Recueil Sirey, 1954), 60 and 60–67 for discussion of the qualities that distinguish jiwar from other kinds of bonds. See also Milka Levy-Rubin, *Non-Muslims in the Early Islamic Empire: From Surrender to Coexistence* (Cambridge: Cambridge University Press, 2011), 32–34 for discussion of the term as a form of protection with pre-Islamic origins, as a Qur'anic term, and its early usage in the Islamic era.

67. Pierre Bourdieu, *Language and Symbolic Power*, trans. Gino Raymond and Matthew Adamson (Cambridge, MA: Harvard University Press, 1991), 82 (emphasis in original).

68. Jessica Coope infers from the writings of Eulogius and Paul Albar that Christians in ninth-century Cordoba had become adept at passing for Muslims (or had become acculturated). She refers to the example of the Christian merchant John who was beaten for taking Muhammad's name in vain and swearing Islamic oaths about his merchandise. See Coope, "Religious and Cultural Conversion to Islam in Ninth-Century Umayyad Cordoba," *Journal of World History* 4 (1993): 58.

we belong and to him is our return" (Qur'an 2:156) when faced with calamity.[69]

Proper greetings and forms of verbal exchange informed interactions between individuals of various statuses in a range of contexts in Islamic society. Thus it is not surprising to find fuqaha' addressing the subject of the proper way to exchange greetings with dhimmis.[70] Malik's *Muwatta'* includes a section on greetings where we find, in addition to two references to dhimmis, a sprinkling of reports about the etiquette of greeting exchanges. The section opens with a report that the Prophet said that when a rider meets a walker, he should be the first to greet; when one of a group of people gives a greeting, that is sufficient for all. We learn that Ibn 'Abbas and 'Abd Allah ibn 'Umar disapproved of elaborate greetings that extended beyond the conventional "Peace be upon you and the mercy of God and His blessing." Yahya ibn Yahya reports Malik's disapproval of greeting a young woman and his lack of objection to greeting an old woman, but generally the text presents reports that emphasize the importance of greeting for male sociability. 'Abd Allah ibn Umar is cited as saying, "We go out in the morning only for the sake of the greeting. We greet whomever we meet."[71]

Opinions about greetings between Muslims and dhimmis articulate a kind of linguistic code that differentiates community insiders from outsiders. Al-'Utbi records from Ashhab that when Malik was asked about greeting the ahl al-dhimma and responding to their greetings, he said not to. Circumstances, however, could make it difficult to avoid exchanging greetings with dhimmis. The Qayrawani jurist al-Qabisi (d. 1013) was presented with the following situation: A man has a Jewish neighbor who grew up among Muslims. They exchange favors, and when they meet they exchange news and smile. The question is: When Jews greet you, how should you respond? Al-Qabisi's fatwa conveys the ideal state of relations between Muslims and dhimmis and tries to draw the fine line between friendship and neighborliness: "It is best not to mix with people who are not of your religion. You can render a service to a neighbor from the ahl al-dhimma

---

69. Al-Qayrawani, *Nawadir wa-ziyadat*, 1:160–163.

70. Mark R. Cohen discusses greetings and other aspects of sociability between Muslims and Jews in "Sociability and the Concept of *Galut* in Jewish-Muslim Relations in the Middle Ages," in *Judaism and Islam: Boundaries, Communication, and Interaction; Essays in Honor of William M. Brinner*, ed. Benjamin H. Hary, John L. Hayes, and Fred Astren (Leiden: E. J. Brill, 2000), 37–51. He relies primarily on a fourteenth-century text on rules about dhimmis by the Hanbali Ibn Qayyim al-Jawziyya.

71. Malik ibn Anas, *Al-Muwatta' of Imam Malik ibn Anas: The First Formulation of Islamic Law*, trans. Aisha Abdurrahman Bewley (London: Kegan Paul, 1989), 404–405.

and speak politely with him, without undue deference. If he greets you, saying, 'Peace be upon you,' you should say, 'And on you,' without adding anything. You do not need news of his household. Conduct yourself as one must with a neighbor, but with a certain reserve."[72]

Ibn Rushd elaborates on Malik's opposition to exchanging greetings with dhimmis and provides the opinion with the authority of the Qur'an and hadith.[73] His citations and interpretations demonstrate how greetings establish social identity and assert hierarchy and provide insight into how the exchanges of greetings may express or deflect aggression in the guise of politeness. He begins by explaining that wishing peace on someone, the conventional way of greeting a Muslim, was the equivalent of asking God to grant him or her long life (tahiyya) and was a form of honor or deference (ikrām) exclusive to Muslims. He cites the Qur'an (24:61), "Greet one another [fa-sallimū ʿalā anfusikum] with a greeting from God [tahiyyatan min ʿindi llāhi], one that is blessed and good." He follows with a report transmitted from Abu ʿAbd al-Rahman al-Juhani, who said that he heard the Prophet say: "I am riding tomorrow to some Jews. Do not initiate greetings, and if they greet you (saying 'Peace be upon you'), then say, 'And upon you.'" The proper response to greetings offered by dhimmis, Ibn Rushd explains, is to shorten the reply to "And upon you," as expressed by the Prophet, and not to reply as one would to Muslims.

If a mistake is made, Ibn Rushd cites Malik's opinion that a Muslim who greets a Jew or a Christian should not withdraw the greeting.[74] In his elaboration we see that the Muslim does not have to acknowledge the difference in their identities even though he failed to do so in the exchange. He does not have to say something like, "I made a mistake in greeting you, so do not think that I intended to greet you as I would a Muslim. I know that you are not a Muslim." Ibn Rushd recognizes that taking back or apologizing for the greeting will profoundly affect the interaction and cause the "withdrawal" of the dhimmi's happiness or goodwill.

The exchange of words between individuals when they first encounter each other is highly significant and bounded by convention. Subverting the code may be a form of aggression, and mistakes in language may be taken as such, depending on the context of the interaction. Ibn Rushd cites the

---

72. Al-Wansharisi, Miʿyar, 11:300–301.

73. Ibn Rushd, Bayan, 18:196–198; the interpretation of Qur'an 24:61 is from, The Qur'an, trans. Alan Jones, published by E.J.W. Gibb Memorial Trust (Exeter: Short Run Press, 2007).

74. Malik ibn Anas, Muwatta', 404.

Prophet's instruction that if a Jew greets you and says, "Poison be upon you" (*al-samm ʿalayka*), say "Upon you." Ibn Rushd explains that omitting the "and" in one's reply is essential (thus one deflects the curse; otherwise one brings down "poison" on both one's interlocutor and oneself). He cites the Prophet's wife ʿAʾisha as relating the Prophet's instruction in context. She recalls that some Jews came before the Prophet and said *al-samm ʿalaykum*, and the Prophet said, ʿalaykum. ʿAʾisha, in turn, said, "Poison be upon you and God's curse and wrath, o you brethren of apes and swine!" The Prophet admonished her, urging forbearance. When she protested, "Did you hear what they said?" he replied, "And did you not hear what I answered them?" The Prophet's response to the Jews is both politic and artful, deflecting the insult (intentional or not) back on them without disrupting the interaction.[75]

What does it mean when Christians writing in Arabic (even those writing polemics against Islam) adopt Islamic idiomatic expressions, such as the invocation "in the name of God, the merciful and the compassionate"? Christian writers who were self-consciously aware of their Christian identity assimilated Arabic-Islamic literary conventions to such a degree that they were unselfconscious in their apparent "Islamicization." In this example a marker of confessional identity no longer works as such in and of itself. In the push-pull to assert identity and power in culturally relevant terms, something new is created.

The possibility raised in questions about valid and invalid marriages—that a Muslim man might unwittingly marry a Christian woman because she speaks like a Muslim and looks like a Muslim—conjures up a society in which individuals of different confessional communities increasingly spoke (and sometimes wrote) the same language and where subtleties of pronunciation, vocabulary, usage, context, and self-presentation might have become increasingly significant for those intent on the expression and discernment of social identity and status. "Speaking the same language" in al-Andalus could thus mean more than sharing a common argot—fluency meant familiarity with customary modes of expression and knowledge of how to employ them to express identity and delimit or subvert boundaries.

---

75. Current sociolinguistic theory argues for the significance of the context of the ongoing verbal interaction and for the role of the participants in the evaluation of polite or impolite behavior. See Richard J. Watts, *Politeness* (Cambridge: Cambridge University Press, 2003). ʿAʾisha and the Prophet respond to the situation she describes differently, perhaps because of their personalities and relationship, the way each interprets the Jews' speech (intended insult or not), and the relative investment of each in the interaction. The Prophet asserts his authority in the situation and demonstrates the value of forbearance to his community.

When jurists address conventions of verbal exchange between Muslims and non-Muslims, we see their participation, on some level, in the development of a Muslim habitus in a context where distinctions of culture were uncertain and, in their view, required refinement to identify Muslims as Muslims. This was part of their engagement in the definition of relations between Muslims and dhimmis in a context where relationships between individuals across a theoretical divide were in reality often quite close, and, at the same time, where identities were not fixed. Instead of securing a definite border between Muslim and non-Muslim, jurists found themselves in the middle of a borderland. They adapted their methods and objectives in an effort to manage change in an increasingly diverse and differentiated society. Their focus on the limits of individual relationships may be viewed as a process of defining boundaries within the larger society of Muslims and dhimmis that was both exclusive and inclusive, responsive to social and cultural differentiation and contributing to it.

Political and social changes in the ninth and early tenth centuries and the tensions and eruptions of violence associated with them stimulated the process of the development of Islamic (Maliki) law in al-Andalus as a process of boundary making. The discussion of this chapter thus far has centered on how jurists approached and defined boundaries between Muslims and dhimmis in their practical concern with personal relationships and social roles. Jurists accommodated social realities in their discussion of contingencies and acknowledgment of differences of opinion and interpretation. The jurists' attention in most of the examples was attracted by and directed toward circumstances of Muslim individuals who were connected in some way with dhimmis. The dhimmis were incidental to the discourse. However, dhimmis occasionally also entered the purview of jurists and judges as plaintiffs (as well as defendants) in Islamic courts. In the next section of this chapter I suggest that the dynamic interaction of social change and legal-juridical discourse gradually generated an increasingly stable legal system, and turn to examples of dhimmis using Islamic law for their own interests. Finally, a look at the evolution of the "rules of the market" as a subset of law and as a distinctive genre of legal writing provides suggestive evidence of the institutionalization of legal practice. These two indexes of the formalization of the legal system provide contrasting perspectives on the stabilization of patterns of intercommunal interactions and on the limits of integration: the participation of dhimmis in the legal system suggests a system that is predictable and a collaborative adaptation of interests; the "rules" of the market inspector, in contrast, are dedicated to the imposition of Islamic law, and dhimmis appear in the pages of manuals, especially in later texts, as subject to restriction and constraint and as objects of Islamic domination.

As the exercise of law became more routine and formalized, the legal questions concerning Muslims and dhimmis became more procedural. Formalization took place as an outcome of judicial practice, the systematization of legal interpretation, and the expansion of Umayyad administration. The process involved elaboration of a notarial system, record keeping, and a ramified legal-judicial institutional system including, for example, the officer of complaints, the market inspector, and to some degree the chief of police and the city prefect (ṣāḥib al-madīna). Over time the forms and contexts of social interaction among individuals of different confessional communities become more routinized.

The routinization of Islamic law and cooperative relationships across communities is evident in al-Andalus when dhimmis and Muslims formed partnerships and when dhimmis familiar with Islamic law used the law and the Islamic courts to protect their interests. In most cases Muslims, Christians, and Jews sought justice in the courts of their own communities, but dhimmis could find themselves brought before the qadi by a Muslim plaintiff or could seek redress in an Islamic court in a complaint against a Muslim. A number of fatwas describe Christians writing to the amir ('Abd Allah) seeking justice and his referral of matters to the qadi and the shūrā (council of jurisconsults).[76] In a section of al-Nawadir wa-l-ziyadat dedicated to the conduct and practice of justice (adab al-qaḍā'), Ibn Abi Zayd presents opinions of Malik and his disciples, as recorded in the writings of ninth-century jurists, that pertain to dhimmis in Muslim courts. These address basic questions, for example, where the qadi should hold his sessions, what to do if a Muslim plaintiff or defendant refused to come before the qadi in the presence of a dhimmi, and what to do if a disputant did not know Arabic (who would interpret and translate?).[77] Fatwas from the late ninth and tenth centuries offer examples of some of the challenges of handling cases involving dhimmis: texts needed to be translated, proxies (wukalā'; s wakīl) for the dhimmis needed to be appointed, and oaths had to be adjusted (in one case two Christian defendants swore their oaths in the name of the one God in their church).[78]

Evidence indicates that in the tenth century dhimmi plaintiffs sought to bring complaints against coreligionists to an Islamic court when they

---

76. Ibn Sahl in Khallaf, *Ahl al-dhimma*, 58–60, 82–83.

77. Ibn Abi Zayd, *Nawadir wa-ziyadat*, 8:20–21, 44, 61.

78. Ibn Sahl in Khallaf, *Ahl al-dhimma*, 57.

thought it was to their advantage. A dhimmi who sought adjudication in an Islamic court must have had confidence in his (or her) ability to negotiate the system and must have sustained reasonable hope that his interests would be served.[79] Arguably, as the legal and judicial system became more extensive, more formal, and more document based, it also became more accessible to dhimmis who knew how to negotiate the system.

Two fatwas (perhaps related) from the turn of the tenth century describe a Jew being brought to an Islamic court by a young man who claimed to be Muslim but could well have been a Jewish slave seeking freedom from his Jewish owner through manipulation of Islamic law. In the first fatwa, jurists of the shura of the qadi Ahmad ibn Ziyad considered a case in which a young man challenged a Jew's claim that he was his slave on three grounds: (1) the young man claimed to be a freeman born to free parents in Toledo; (2) he claimed that he was a Muslim with Muslim parents and that the Jew had forced him into Judaism; and (3) he claimed that the Jew had beaten him and locked him up when he sought to leave his service. The first two claims would preclude his being a slave owned by a dhimmi (he claimed that he was a Muslim hired to work for the Jew), and the claim of mistreatment (which was demonstrated by marks on his back) demanded attention whether he were a freeman or a slave. The opinions presented in the fatwa, however, do not address the specific issue of the legal status of the young man. The Jew claimed that the slave was a Jew he had purchased from another Jew from Toledo four years earlier, and he produced a document to support his claims. However, the document was in Hebrew, and the judge's delegate (amīn) responsible for investigating the claims of both parties decided to retain the young man under his own protection while the matter was investigated. The man escaped from the amin's house, and the Jew demanded compensation for the value of the slave. The question addressed by the jurists Ibn Walid, Ibn Lubaba, 'Ubayd Allah ibn Yahya, Ahmad ibn Yahya, Ibn Ghalib, Yayha ibn 'Abd al-Aziz, Ayyub ibn Sulayman, and Sa'd ibn Mu'adh was whether the amin owed compensation (in fact, the slave reappeared in the qadi's court). In other words, the original case generated a second case. Another fatwa that perhaps addresses the original case or one

---

79. Gideon Libson, *Jewish and Islamic Law: A Comparative Study of Custom during the Geonic Period*, (Cambridge, MA: Harvard University Press, 2003), 101–103, reports much discussion in the Jewish responsa of the geonic period concerning Jews seeking legal validation of deeds and pursuing litigation in Muslim courts. In his view, "One of the main channels of contact through which Islamic law could influence Jewish law, whether directly or indirectly, was through Jews having recourse to the Muslim courts" (101).

very similar takes up the claims of a young man that he was a freeman, the son of free parents, who entered the service of a Jew and converted to Islam; the Jew would not let him leave his service. The Jew claimed that he had bought the slave from a Jew from Toledo four years earlier. The jurists Ibn Lubaba, Ibn Ghalib, and Ibn Walid were of the opinion that if the young man could not provide evidence to support his claim (as plaintiff), and the Jew swore an oath that the man was his slave, then the qadi should order the sale of the slave and pay the price to the Jew.[80]

A sampling of fatwas provides further evidence of Jews seeking recourse to Muslim courts.[81] In one case a Jewish defendant sought judgment in a Muslim court because he had a document in Arabic with exonerating evidence from Muslim witnesses. Ibn al-ʿAttar (d. 1009) offered the opinion that if the accused produced a document that proved his innocence unequivocally, and his Muslim witnesses were sound, then the accusers must let him seek judgment in the court of the Muslims.[82] In another case a Jewish man sought justice from the qadi in a legal problem with a Jewish woman because he claimed that the Jewish judges were biased against him (they were enemies of his father). He had supporting documents in Arabic from the qadi and Muslim witnesses, and she had Jewish witnesses. The jurisconsults of tenth-century Cordoba who were consulted in this case had various opinions about the circumstances in which Jews might seek adjudication in matters of "money and legal claims" from an Islamic court, and their opinions together addressed the following issues: the identity of the witnesses (must both the defendant and the plaintiff have Muslim witnesses?), the agreement of both parties to seek Islamic justice as a qualification, and the substance of the case—was the matter a subject of Islamic but not Jewish law? Their views offered a range of possibilities for the presiding judge. Ibn Zarb's opinion focused most specifically on the case at hand: if the Jew had the testimony of Muslims establishing that the Jewish judges or witnesses against him were indeed biased against him, then their judgment could not apply (and he could pursue his defense with Muslim witnesses in an Islamic court); if

---

80. Ibn Sahl in Khallaf, *Ahl al-dhimma*, 47–56. Ibn Sahl disapproves of the opinion of the jurists in the second example and remarks that the claims of both parties about the nature of their relationship should have been more fully investigated.

81. See Lehmann, "Islamic Legal Consultation and the Jewish-Muslim 'Convivencia,'" 50–53, on the two cases of Jews seeking adjudication in the Islamic court.

82. Al-Wansharisi, *Miʿyar*, 10:56.

he did not have such evidence, the woman could pursue her claim against him with the Jewish judges.[83]

Cases involving dhimmis brought to an Islamic court typically required the evidence of Muslim witnesses. The securing of testimony may have been pro forma in many instances, but in one interesting example a Muslim was able and willing to attest to a Christian's good character. According to a tenth-century fatwa, a Christian man identified by a witness as a bad character was seen walking with a Muslim woman who subsequently disappeared. Her brother accused him of kidnapping. Another witness, however, testified to the Christian's noble character and integrity. He affirmed that the Christian's interactions and social relations with Muslims were good and that he was not known to mix with, or be involved with, immoral people. The qadi had the Christian imprisoned pending consultation and the jurists Ibn Harith and Ibn Zarb recommended that the statements of the witnesses be reexamined and the accused remain in custody in the meantime.[84]

Two fatwas having to do with pious endowments (s. *hubs* or *hubus*, pl. *ahbās*) made by Jews develop the impression that Jews were adept at pursuing their interests within the framework of Islamic law and with the support of Islamic courts.[85] They date to the period of the *tā'ifa* (party) rulers (after the collapse of Umayyad rule in the early eleventh century and before the arrival of the Almoravids in the late eleventh century) and demonstrate how the individuals cited adapted to the Islamic legal system and were able to manipulate it to ensure their interests (in this case, the transfer of property to their descendants). Although the endowments under discussion were structured to serve family interests, they ultimately evolved into endowments for the welfare of Muslims. In the first example, in which the plaintiff's claims were upheld, Ibn Sahl was asked about a Jew who designated some property as a hubs for his daughter and her progeny (*'alā ibnatihi wa-'alā 'uqbihā*) that would support the poor Muslims after her line died out. At some point a man of status and power forced the Jew to sell half the hubs to him. The jurist opined that the sale must be voided and the property returned to the

---

83. Al-Wansharisi, *Mi'yar*, 10:128–131. See also Sahnun, *Mudawwana*, 4:400, 5:368–369, and al-Qayrawani, *Nawadir wa-ziyadat*, 8:238, on circumstances when a Muslim judge may preside over a dispute between dhimmis; and Sahnun, *Mudawwana*, 5:154, 156–157, and al-Qayrawani, *Nawadir wa-ziyadat*, 8:424–426, on the testimony of dhimmis.

84. Al-Wansharisi, *Mi'yar*, 2:346–347.

85. On the subject of pious endowments in al-Andalus, see Alejandro García Sanjuán, *Hasta que Dios herede la tierra: Los bienes habices en al-Andalus (siglos x–xv)* (Huelva: Universidad de Huelva, 2002); on the fatwas under examination here see 101–102; see also Lehmann, "Islamic Legal Consultation and the Jewish-Muslim 'Convivencia,'" 48–50.

endowment on the grounds that a forced sale was invalid, but he also cited an opinion that the sale and purchase of ahbas were invalid for Muslims and an opinion that they were invalid for both Muslims and People of the Book.[86] In the second example, Abu 'Umar ibn al-Qattan was asked whether a hubs established by a Jew for the benefit of the mosque of Cordoba was legal. He replied that it was not and cited the Prophet's statement, recorded in al-Mudawwana: "We do not ask for help from the *mushrik*."[87] The possibility (apparently realized in the first case) that a Jew might establish an endowment following Islamic conventions and for the benefit of the Muslims proved problematic for judges and jurists—was it up to the Muslim judge to uphold a Jew's endowment? Did the same rules apply? Was the creation of a hubs by a Jew meaningful, given God's words: "He who aspires to a religion other than Islam, nought will be received of him and he will be among the losers in the afterlife"?[88]

Another case dealt more specifically with the equivalence of endowments established by Muslims and by dhimmis and the jurisdiction of an Islamic court. The Cordoban jurist Ibn 'Attab (d. 1069) issued his opinion that the two endowments were in fact fundamentally different. His opinion was directed to the following situation: A Muslim had purchased some gardens from two Jewish men quite some time ago. Eventually, he established this property as a hubs for the benefit of his children and ultimately for the support of learning, the ransoming of prisoners, and the manumission of slaves. The hubs had been established for thirteen years when a Jew appeared claiming that the land his two uncles had sold to the Muslim had actually been a hubs established for his benefit. He had a document, written in Arabic, establishing the hubs and sought to claim it. Ibn 'Attab, however, dismissed his claim because he considered that the sale to the Muslim was valid. With some elaboration he asserted that dhimmis have the right to break their deeds of endowments and sell their properties, while Muslims do not; he also established that it was not up to the qadi to protect and preside over the endowments of dhimmis.[89]

In matters of business between Muslims and dhimmis, fuqaha' often cited Malik's disapproval of hires, partnerships in commenda-type (*qirāḍ*) contracts (limited contracts between investors who put up capital and agents who contributed labor and got a partial share of the profits of the trade or

---

86. Al-Wansharisi, *Mi'yar*, 7:59–60.

87. Al-Wansharisi, *Mi'yar*, 7:65–66.

88. Al-Wansharisi, *Mi'yar*, 7:65–66.

89. Al-Wansharisi, *Mi'yar*, 7:438–439; Ibn Sahl in Khallaf, *Ahl al-dhimma*, 65–69.

enterprise described in the contract) or other partnerships (sharing sheep), and forms of indemnification between Muslims and dhimmis.[90] In one example Malik is cited for his disapproval of a Muslim working for a Christian, whether it was to guard his olive trees, plow his fields, or build something for him.[91] However, jurists also cited more accommodating opinions. Sahnun asked Ibn al-Qasim his opinion about leasing land from a Christian, and he replied that Malik disapproved, but he also offered his view that there was no objection if the Christian's property did not have vines used to make wine.[92] Ibn Abi Zayd al-Qayrawani records Malik's disapproval of qirad contracts with Christians, but also Ibn Wahb's statement that there was no objection.[93] As in other instances of legal discourse we have discussed, differences of opinion accommodated social practice.

Tenth-century jurists in Cordoba confirmed the validity of a qirad contract between a Muslim and a dhimmi in their response to a case where a Muslim claimed that he had sold some cloth to a Jew and had not received its price, while the Jew claimed that he had been acting as the Muslim's agent, had sold the cloth, and had returned the sale price minus his commission. In the jurists' view, an agreement like this must be upheld if the agent swore to the truth of his statement. The case suggests that Muslims and dhimmis did participate in business contracts together in tenth-century al-Andalus even if they more commonly formed partnerships with their coreligionists.[94] Although one might expect the Jewish agent accused of theft to be vulnerable before an Islamic court, in fact the jurists upheld his claims.[95] The ruling in favor of the Jew in this case suggests a legal environment conducive to commerce and reinforces the point that Islamic law (the contract) and the Islamic legal system could be used by well-informed dhimmis to pursue and protect their interests in ways that were routine and predictable.

The market, of course, was a significant field of social interaction and came under the jurisdiction of the ṣāḥib or walī al-sūq (official of the market),

---

90. See, for example, Ibn Rushd, Bayan, 3:278.

91. Sahnun, Mudawwana, 4:433.

92. Sahnun, Mudawwana, 5:557. See Ibn Sahl in Khallaf, Ahl al-dhimma, 56–57, for the case of a perfumer who leased land from Christians.

93. Al-Qayrawani, Nawadir wa-ziyadat, 7:294.

94. See Olivia Remie Constable, Trade and Traders in Muslim Spain (Cambridge: Cambridge University Press, 1994), 57–70; also S. D. Goitein, A Mediterranean Society: The Jewish Communities of the Arab World as Portrayed in the Documents of the Cairo Geniza, vol. 2, The Community (Berkeley: University of California Press, 1971), 292–298.

95. Al-Wansharisi, Miʿyar, 6:227–228 and 10:452 (it is not clear whether the same case is under discussion); Ibn Sahl in Khallaf, Ahl al-dhimma, 73–77.

later also referred to as the *muḥtasib*.[96] This official had various responsibilities; among them, he monitored the weights and measures and ensured fair trade, kept the streets clear, and undertook the prevention of any actions deemed reprehensible. Jurists considered the market to be a place of moral danger or doubt. A pious man would do well to avoid the market if possible. In the masa'il literature and in fatwas, jurists considered many aspects of commerce and the trades, and their opinions became, at least in part or in early iterations, the basis of *ḥisba* manuals (guidelines for the market inspector) designed to guide the regulation of the market and define the purview of the sahib al-suq. Development of the genre of hisba manuals grew out of the elaboration of law and the related multiplication of legal institutions. Hisba manuals delineate restrictions that read as more rigid and binding than the legal-juridical sources on which they were originally based and are perhaps misleading as evidence for legal practice and social life for that reason; they are, however, highly suggestive as evidence of the will to impose structure and reinforce boundaries among communities.

An early text of "Rules of the Market" by Yahya ibn ʿUmar al-Kinani (828–901) is preserved in al-Wansharisi's fatwa collection.[97] Hisba manuals attributed to Andalusis and Maghribis of later periods, including those of Ahmad ibn ʿAbd Allah ibn ʿAbd al-Raʾuf (perhaps of Cordoba in the tenth century), Muhammad ibn Ahmad ibn ʿAbdun (of Seville), who wrote in the twelfth century, Abu ʿAbd Allah Muhammad ibn Abi Ahmad al-Saqati (of Malaga), who probably wrote in the early thirteenth century, and ʿUmar al-Jarsifi of the late thirteenth century, are extant and have been published. Although the earlier texts retain some of the qualities of the masa'il literature, the later texts are more comprehensive, and subjects of discussion appear as instructions or "rules" rather than as matters of juridical debate.

Al-Kinani grew up in Cordoba and settled in Qayrawan after traveling to the Hijaz, Egypt, and Iraq. He was a student of Ibn Habib and Sahnun, among others. The extant portion of his text deals with a variety of subjects pertaining to the market. He refers to dhimmis in only one instance, but the question he addresses speaks directly to the problem of the impostor. In response to a question about how to handle a Jew who imitates Muslims in dress and does not wear a distinguishing belt or sash, he asserts that the Jew

96. See Pedro Chalmeta Gendrón, *El "Señor del Zoco" en España: Edades Media y Moderna, contribución al estudio de la historia del mercado* (Madrid: Instituto Hispano-Arabe de Cultura, 1973).

97. Al-Wansharisi, *Miʿyar*, 6:406–422; Arabic edition also by M. A. Makki, "Nass jadid fi-l-hisba," *Revista del Instituto de Estudios Islámicos en Madrid* 4 (1956): 59–151; Spanish translation, Emilio García Gómez, "Unas 'Ordenanzas del zoco' del siglo ix," *Al-Andalus* 22 (1957): 253–316.

should be punished with lashes and imprisonment. To serve as a warning, he should also be paraded in the places where Christians and Jews gather. Al-Kinani reports that his contemporary, the Maliki jurist and twice qadi of Qayrawan 'Abd Allah ibn Ahmad ibn Abi Talib (d. 888), had written instructions to one of the judges that the identifying belts of Jews and Christians be wide and clearly visible and had declared the punishment for a first-time offense to be twenty lashes and some period of confinement.[98]

Ahmad ibn 'Abd Allah ibn 'Abd al-Ra'uf's treatise on the manners and mores of the hisba and the muhtasib is a relatively early example of the genre and depends heavily on Ibn Habib's *Wadiha*. It begins with matters of ritual and religious obligation (prayer, funerals, the fast, the *zakāt* or legal alms), includes matters of marriage and pious endowments, and then addresses sales and the trades, one business at a time. Ibn 'Abd al-Ra'uf discusses Muslims' interactions with Jews and Christians primarily in the section on butchers. We read that Malik disapproved of Muslims purchasing meat from dhimmi butchers and that 'Umar ibn al-Khattab ordered that dhimmi butchers be expelled from the market. Ibn Habib said that he had no objection to dhimmis having their butchery in the market if it was off on one side and the dhimmis were prohibited from selling to Muslims. Ibn 'Abd al-Ra'uf instructs that Muslims should not buy meat slaughtered by dhimmis and are prohibited from buying meat that the Jews themselves do not eat, like all meat the Jews consider unkosher.[99] He cites Ibn Habib regarding the disapproval of eating meat slaughtered by Christians for the church or in the name of the Messiah or the cross or anything of that sort (although the meat is not absolutely prohibited because of the Qur'anic verse (5:5) permitting the food of the People of the Book). As for meat slaughtered by Christians for their holidays or other occasions, such as funerals, it is best to avoid eating it so as not to encourage their idolatry (shirk).[100]

---

98. Al-Wansharisi, *Mi'yar*, 6:69, 421; García Gómez, "Unas 'Ordenanzas del zoco,'" 292.

99. The meat the Jews do not eat is proscribed because it is not "the food of those to whom the Book was given," which is permitted for Muslims in the Qur'an (5:5). Ibn Lubaba (d. 926) expresses a different position in a fatwa in which he excoriates the judgment of someone who deemed nonkosher meat forbidden to the Muslims. He observes that Ibn al-Qasim disapproved of nonkosher meat and of buying from Jewish and Christian butchers but considers Ibn Wahb's opinion permitting it to be better supported. See al-Wansharisi, *Mi'yar*, 5:250. This opinion suggests that Jewish butchers may have regularly sold cuts of meat forbidden to them to Muslims. Al-'Utbi records that when Malik was asked about buying from a Jewish butcher in al-Andalus during the winter when meat was scarce, he said that he personally would not do so (Ibn Rushd, *Bayan*, 3:303).

100. "Risalat Ahmad ibn 'Abd Allah ibn 'Abd al-Ra'uf fi adab al-hisba wa-l-muhtasib," in Évariste Lévi-Provençal, *Documents arabes inédits sur la vie sociale et économique en occident musulman au Moyen Age (Trois traités hispaniques de ḥisba)* (Cairo: Institut Français d'Archéologie Orientale, 1955), 94–95.

The fact that Christians and Jews drank wine and Muslims were prohibited from doing so meant that the sale of wine came under the scrutiny of the market inspector. Ibn ʿAbd al-Raʾuf states that if a Muslim buys wine from a Christian, the wine cask should be destroyed; the Christian may keep any payment he receives, but if he has not yet received payment, he will take the loss; the price of the wine should go toward the benefit of poor Muslims. Both buyer and seller should be punished. If a Muslim destroys the wine of a Christian (in other circumstances), he should be punished, but Malik expressed varying opinions about whether the Christian should be compensated.[101]

Ibn ʿAbd al-Raʾuf's text clearly draws on the masaʾil literature in its discussion of meat and wine. His inclusion of more than one opinion about buying meat from dhimmis gives his strictures a certain ambiguity. The later hisba manuals, to the extent that they discuss interactions with dhimmis, express a different mode and spirit of engagement with Christians and Jews. Of the three dating to the post-Umayyad period, al-Saqati does not mention dhimmis except to say, in a long exposition of the frauds practiced by slave traders (including false claims that slave girls had recently been imported from the frontier), that slave boys and girls should not be sold to Christians and Jews lest they adopt their religion.[102] The writings of Ibn ʿAbdun and al-Jarsifi may reflect changing developments in the history of Muslim-dhimmi relations and express their personal biases. Although not much is known about the authors apart from what they reveal themselves, the texts are products of political, social, and demographic contexts quite different from ninth- and tenth-century al-Andalus. The texts express a

---

Ibn ʿAbd al-Raʾuf sanctions eating cheese made by Christians, 101 (rennet made cheese an issue). See also Ibn Rushd, *Bayan*, 3:272, 378; al-Qayrawani, *Nawadir wa-ziyadat*, 4:365–369.

101. "Risalat Ahmad ibn ʿAbd Allah ibn ʿAbd al-Raʾuf," 95.

102. Al-Saqati, *Un manuel hispanique de ḥisba: Traité d'Abu ʿAbd Allah Muhammad b. Abi Muhammad As-Sakati de Malaga*, Arabic text published by G. S. Colin and E. Lévi-Provençal (Paris: Librairie Ernest Leroux, 1931); Spanish translation by Pedro Chalmeta Gendrón, "'El kitab fi adab al-hisba' (Libro del buen gobierno del zoco) de al-Saqati," *Al-Andalus* 32 (1967): 125–162, 359–398; 33 (1968): 143–195, 367–434. Colin and Lévi-Provençal date the text to the early twelfth century; Chalmeta argues for the first quarter of the thirteenth century. Al-Saqati dedicates his text to the discussion of all the frauds and tricks perpetrated by venders, traders, and artisans on hapless customers, and he offers his experienced counsel to the officer of the hisba. He provides compelling details about aspects of production and sale as evidence of all the muhtasib needs to know to govern the market properly. His text cites the Qurʾan, the words of the Prophet, and the example of the companions and is enlivened by anecdotes from Malaga and from elsewhere, such as Baghdad, Kufa, Granada, and Cordoba, lines of verse, and personal observations. The focus on tricks and ruses and al-Saqati's engaging style give the text what Chalmeta calls a "picaresque" literary quality.

particular interest in stiffening barriers between communities and asserting Muslim predominance; they may be intimations of a renewed objectifica- tion of "the other" in some circles that was perhaps conditioned by the end of the conversion period, according to Bulliet's model, and stimulated by political crises, gains and losses on the military frontier, and the ideology and circumstances of Almoravid rule in Ibn 'Abdun's case.[103] In the period when Ibn 'Abdun presumably lived and wrote, riots broke out in Cordoba and the Jewish quarter burned (1135), and hostility toward and suspicions of the Christian population informed the transfer of Christians to North Africa in 1126.[104] However, we should acknowledge that the generic quality of the texts obscures the complexities of the social interactions they address; their admonitions intriguingly suggest that modes of social interaction and social convention prevailed that did not conform to a social hierarchy de- fined strictly in terms of religious community, and that intercommunal in- tellectual exchange was taking place. The representations of these two texts by authors about whom we know little need to be considered in relation to other texts and more fully in historical context if they are to be used more than suggestively.[105] Ibn 'Abdun's text and the tone he takes regarding dhimmis, for example, contrast with the magisterial work of Ibn Rushd, his near contemporary, suggesting multivalent attitudes among fuqaha' and other Muslim writers in the twelfth century (I will revisit this subject in chapter 4).[106]

---

103. Maribel Fierro, "A Muslim Land without Jews or Christians: Almohad Policies Regarding the 'Protected People,'" in *Christlicher Norden—muslimischer Süden*, ed. Matthias M. Tischler and Alexan- der Fidora (Münster: Aschendorff Verlag, 2011), 232, argues that "the process by which Muslims had become a majority seems to have gone hand in hand with a hardening of the 'dhimmi' situation" and makes the striking point that this is when al-Turtushi (d. 1126), writing in Alexandria, recorded the well-known version of the "Pact of 'Umar" with its "absolute and unqualified" prohibitions.

104. See Vincent Lagardère, "Communautés mozarabes et pouvoir Almoravide en 519H/1125 en Andalus," *Studia Islamica* 67 (1988): 99–119, for a discussion of the expulsion of Christians from Seville, Cordoba, and Granada in 1126 because of their support for Alfonso I of Aragon, "the Bat- tler"; he associates Ibn 'Abdun's strictures on the Christians with this context.

105. Norman Roth, *Jews, Visigoths, and Muslims in Medieval Spain: Cooperation and Conflict* (Leiden: E. J. Brill, 1994), 113–116, observes that the few extant Jewish sources present a mixed account of the experience of Jews in the Almoravid period, and he believes that very little changed. He warns of reading too much into Ibn 'Abdun's treatise: "Thus we must not allow ourselves to be misled by such widely-publicized sources as the twelfth-century market regulations of Seville, written by Mu- hammad ibn 'Abdun, which undoubtedly are more a reflection of the 'ideal' situation sought by a fanatical jurist than the actual situation in Seville, where in any case the Jews still represented a very substantial and influential part of the population" (114).

106. Ross Brann's analysis of representations of Jews in Arabic literary texts demonstrates ambiva- lence in the way Andalusi Muslim writers thought of and imagined Jews in the eleventh and twelfth

Ibn ʿAbdun directs his manual to the organization of society and the promulgation of regulations to protect the welfare of Muslims. He instructs that Muslims should not serve Christians and Jews in demeaning jobs such as rubbing them down (in the baths?), taking out the garbage, cleaning lavatories, and acting as grooms for their riding beasts (rather, dhimmis should serve Muslims in these functions). Muslim women must be prohibited from entering churches because the priests are sinful and practice adultery and sodomy. The muhtasib should also prevent Christian women from doing so except on holidays and Sundays because they eat, drink, and fornicate with the priests. Ibn ʿAbdun seems particularly interested in the corruption of priests. He calls for a ruling allowing priests to marry (as in the East) as a solution to their dissolute interactions with women (wherever you find one priest, he observes, you find two or three women with him). He also calls for the circumcision of priests and observes that although they claim to follow the practice of Jesus and celebrate the day of his circumcision, they themselves neglect the practice.[107]

Ibn ʿAbdun promotes the separation of Muslims from Christians and Jews. In addition to precautions about who slaughters meat for Muslims and about the sale of clothes formerly belonging to Christians and Jews, he forcefully denounces any signs of acculturation and fraternization, disparaging Christians and Jews in the process. As he puts it, Jews and Christians must not be allowed to dress in the manner of notable men, jurists, or men of good reputation. They should not be greeted with "Peace be upon you" because (in his words) Satan has mastery over them; they have forgotten God; they are the partisans of Satan and are doomed. They need to wear a recognizable sign that marks their disgrace.[108] Ibn ʿAbdun admonishes that Jews and Christians should not be sold books of learning (ʿilm) unless the books concern their own law, because they translate these books and attribute them to their people and their bishops, even though they are the works of Muslims. He also recommends that Jewish or Christian physicians not attend to Muslims.[109]

Al-Jarsifi, for his part, delivers a summary of the proper relationship between Muslims and dhimmis in a paragraph that echoes Ibn ʿAbdun's

---

centuries. See Brann, *Power in the Portrayal: Representations of Jews and Muslims in Eleventh- and Twelfth-Century Islamic Spain* (Princeton, NJ: Princeton University Press, 2002).

107. "Risalat Ibn ʿAbdun fi-l-qadaʾ wa-l-hisba," in Lévi-Provençal, *Documents arabes inédits*, 48–49; French translation by E. Lévi-Provençal in Ibn ʿAbdun, *Séville musulmane au début du xiie siècle: Le traité d'Ibn ʿAbdun sur la vie urbaine et les corps de métiers* (Paris: G. P. Maisonneuve, 1947), 108–109.

108. "Risalat Ibn ʿAbdun," 49, 50, 51; Ibn ʿAbdun, *Séville musulmane*, 110, 112, 114.

109. "Risalat Ibn ʿAbdun," 57; Ibn ʿAbdun, *Séville musulmane*, 128.

concern to protect the status and dignity of Muslims. The muhtasib "must prevent dhimmis from overlooking Muslims in their homes and spying on them; likewise from displaying wine and pork in Muslim markets; from riding horses with saddles, and in a livery proper to Muslims or savouring of arrogance. He should affix to them a badge to distinguish them from Muslims, such as the *shakla* for men and the *juljul*-bell for women. [The muhtasib] should also prevent Muslims from performing on their behalf whatever brings disgrace and humiliation upon themselves, such as throwing out the sweepings, bringing in the implements of wine-drinking, looking after pigs, and so on, for therein is implied the ascendancy of heathenism over Islam. Whoever does such things must be chastised."[110]

The rules Ibn 'Abdun and al-Jarsifi laid out and perhaps strived to enforce suggest that relations between Muslims and dhimmis were not to their liking—it may be that all (or some) of the things they decried were in fact in practice. They express irritation about perceived dhimmi arrogance and Muslim humiliation and a determination to reverse the situation. They wrote in periods of military insecurity and political instability, when, as often as not, Muslims were humiliated on the battlefield and Muslim cities were vulnerable to attack. Ibn 'Abdun (and al-Jarsifi after him) may have inflected his text with personal animus toward dhimmis and expressed concerns about the state of Muslim-dhimmi relations that reflected a more general anxiety and in so doing promoted his authority in a time of practical insecurity. The market inspector's role as morals police and his charge to keep order in the marketplace governed a perspective on dhimmis as a distinct category from Muslims, and hisba manuals of this late period present rules in a way that dispenses with contingency, exception, and difference of opinion and asserts social hierarchy.[111] Pragmatic relations between Muslims and dhimmis persisted (with disruptions and disturbances) where Muslims, Christians, and Jews continued to live together even if, with the waning of conversion, the intimacy of mixed families no longer obtained as it had in the ninth and tenth centuries.

110. G. M. Wickens, "Al-Jarsifi on the *Ḥisba*," *Islamic Quarterly* 3 (1956): 181; "Risalat 'Umar ibn 'Uthman ibn al-'Abbas al-Jarsifi fi-l-hisba," in Lévi-Provençal, *Documents arabes inédits*, 122; see J. Derek Latham, "Observations on the Text and Translation of al-Jarsifi's Treatise on 'Hisba'," *Journal of Semitic Studies* 5 (1960), 124–143 for a close critical reading of Wicken's translation.

111. Thami El Azemmouri, "Les *Nawazil* d'Ibn Sahl: Section relative a l'*ihtisab*," *Hespéris Tamuda* 14 (1973): 18–21, notes the contrast between a collection of fatwas (like Ibn Sahl's) having to do with hisba matters and the genre of hisba manuals.

CHAPTER 4

Borders and Boundaries

> 'Isa ibn Dinar asked Ibn al-Qasim about how to treat a Muslim who went to the land of polytheism [arḍ al-shirk] and became a Christian. He fought against Muslims and took booty from them. Later he was taken captive by the Muslims and (in these circumstances) he pronounced the shahāda (the testament of the faith) and returned to Islam.

The central question in the mas'ala (legal question; pl. masā'il) of the epigraph is one of legal status (legal implications follow) complicated by the crossing of legal jurisdictions: Is the individual in this case to be treated as an apostate, a ḥarbī (an individual from the Domain of War) or a Muslim?[1] The boundaries jurists discussed and defined to differentiate Muslims from Christians and Jews in al-Andalus could be complicated by the political and military "border" between Muslim and Christian territory. This "border" was imagined and was not a demarcated and mutually recognized, regulated, and controlled territorial limit. I use the term "border" in quotation marks to characterize the conception of Dar al-Islam (the Domain of Islam) and Dar al-Harb (the Domain of War) as distinct territories subject to different systems of law, although neither the Christians nor the Muslims on either side of the "border" used such a term in this period.[2] The definition of Dar al-Harb as a territory derived fundamentally from the political

---

1. Ibn Rushd (al-Jadd), *Al-Bayan wa-l-tahsil wa-l-sharh wa-l-tawjih wa-l-ta'lil fi masa'il al-Mustakhraja*, ed. Muhammad Hajji (Beirut: Dar al-Gharb al-Islami, 1984–1987), 2:600–601 (the question in the epigraph), 601–602 (the response and Ibn Rushd's commentary).

2. Benita Sampedro Vizcaya and Simon Doubleday, introduction to *Border Interrogations: Questioning Spanish Frontiers*, ed. Benita Sampedro Vizcaya and Simon Doubleday (New York: Berghahn Books, 2008), 4.

allegiance or orientation of its inhabitants, that is, whether they recognized the sovereignty or suzerainty of the legitimate Muslim ruler. The harbi was someone who had not recognized and submitted to Islamic rule (as subject or, as the jurists conceded, as tributary); in the eyes of the jurist the harbi, the Muslim, the *dhimmī* ("protected person"), and the tributary were legally distinct. The limits of Dar al-Islam and Dar al-Harb, however, were historically (rather than conceptually) indistinct, and the region between competing kingdoms was a borderland accessible to and inhabited by Muslims, Christians, and Jews. Loyalties and allegiances were variable, and identity was not easily fixed. ʿIsa ibn Dinar's question quoted in the epigraph links crossing an understood border between Dar al-Islam and Dar al-Harb (between a place where the laws of Islam applied and a place where they did not apply) and crossing the boundary of religious identity between Muslim and Christian, recognizing that they were not the same and seeking clarification. Legal and jurisdictional questions having to do with this "border" as the jurists construed it give us another perspective on the boundaries between communities.

Questions about crossing "borders" bring into focus the special status of dhimmis in particular and their relationship to the Muslims they lived among and the regime they lived under. In this regard, the concept of the *ahl al-dhimma* (people of the [pact of] protection) as a legal category was tested on a case-by-case basis. Jurists were prompted in multiple contexts to differentiate between Christians who were enemies and Christians who were dhimmis and to elaborate on the transition from one legal status (enemy) to another (protected person). The concept of the ahl al-dhimma as a community within and of Dar al-Islam emerges from the discourse. Jurists acknowledged the role dhimmis shared in the defense of Islam and their vulnerability as coreligionists of the enemies of Islam. The impact of the political-military and ideological border on the attitudes and interactions of Muslims, Christians, and Jews was complicated historically, but this book offers the following insight: the proximity of Dar al-Harb and the porous and indefinite quality of the borderland between Dar al-Harb and Dar al-Islam drew attention to the legal meanings of *dhimma* or protection and in the ninth and tenth centuries sharpened the juridical perspective that dhimmis were part of a shared political community and that the ruler had a commitment to their protection. The perspective on the meaning of dhimma could change, however, as circumstances on the "border" changed. The dhimmi, whom I have characterized as "between enemy and friend," complicated the difference between "us" and "them," as did the circumstances of life in the borderlands.

The boundary between the lands under Muslim rule and the lands under Christian rule in the ninth and tenth centuries is often represented in modern times as a line on a map delineated by the Duero River and the Pyrenees Mountains or following the Duero and Ebro rivers.[3] The line across the Iberian Peninsula represents, or rather asserts, a divide that has an immediate rhetorical impact. The delineation of a border between the domains of Islam and the domains of Christendom is a way of structuring the past that identifies religion with land and identity; the further demarcation of borders between individual Christian kingdoms privileges the state and perhaps overemphasizes its military and administrative organization. It might be useful to envision territorial sovereignty in this period more concentrically, radiating out of specific centers of power, and to bear in mind that sometimes sovereignty was more theoretical than real.

The borderland territories are described by the Arabic chronicles as *thughūr* (s. *thaghr*) marches (literally, front teeth), a term used to refer to the Umayyad borderland with Byzantium in the East. The term commonly characterized a different administrative status than the districts (*kuwar*) centered on the major cities of Muslim settlement and economy in the southern and eastern regions of the peninsula.[4] In the ninth and tenth centuries the borderlands were a place for raids, and control of fortresses might pass back and forth between Muslims and Christians according to the successes of military adventures and campaigns. The Arabic geographies and chronicles refer to the thughur broadly, and in the tenth-century accounts some geographic (and perhaps administrative) distinctions emerge, but the terms are imprecise. Texts refer to three frontier zones in the tenth century as the upper, middle, and lower marches, but the middle and lower (western) thu-

---

3. Thomas F. Glick, *Islamic and Christian Spain in the Early Middle Ages* (Princeton, NJ: Princeton University Press, 1979), 58–59, observes that Arab geographers describe a mountain chain to mark an idealized topographical border between Christian and Muslim territory where none existed. The mountain chain extended from somewhere between Barcelona and Tarragona southward toward Tortosa and then westward to the Atlantic between the mouths of the Duero and Tajo rivers.

4. On the definition of *thaghr* and its usage in Andalusi sources, see Eduardo Manzano Moreno, *La frontera de al-Andalus en época de los Omeyas* (Madrid: Consejo Superior de Investigaciones Científicas, 1991), 23–69. Jacinto Bosch Vilá observes that the information about the thughur provided by the Arabic chronicles, geographies, and biographical dictionaries is sketchy and sometimes contradictory; Jacinto Bosch Vilá, "Algunas consideraciónes sobre al-tagr en al-Andalus y la division politico-administrativa de la España musulmana," in *Etudes d'orientalisme dédiées à la mémoire d'E. Lévi-Provençal* (Paris: Maisonneuve et Larose, 1962) 2:23–33; trans. Michael Kennedy, "Considerations with Respect to 'Al-Thaghr in al-Andalus' and the Political-Administrative Division of Muslim Spain," in *The Formation of al-Andalus*, vol. 1, *History and Society*, ed. Manuela Marín (Aldershot: Ashgate Variorum, 1998), 377–387.

ghur are not always differentiated, and sometimes the easternmost part of the upper march is referred to as the eastern thaghr. The upper march comprised the territory around the farthest towns under Islamic jurisdiction in the northeast, centered on Zaragoza and the Ebro River valley, including Tudela, Huesca, Lerida, and Balaguer; the middle march was centered on Toledo (and after 946) Medinaceli and included a line of fortresses along the Tajo River; the lower (western) march included the open plains around Merida, situated on the Guadiana. The Duero River valley has sometimes been described as a no-man's land between the Christian kingdom of Asturias and the Umayyad amirate of al-Andalus in the eighth and ninth centuries, a deserted region that was gradually repopulated by Christians from the north in the tenth and eleventh centuries. Evidence of personal and place names in the region, however, has supported a reevaluation, and historians now believe that the Duero River valley included continuous Christian settlements and new Christian and Muslim settlements. These settlements were commingled and associated in some way with castles on both sides of the river. The settlements in this region may not have fallen into any clearly defined administrative category or structure until the tenth century.[5] The legal texts do not contribute one way or another to this argument, but it is worth observing that in some masa'il Muslim and Christian fortresses seem quite close to each other, but in others the terrain between Muslim and Christian settlement is described as *mafāza* (desert or deserted).[6]

The discussion of the legal texts regarding dhimmis and harbis in the borderland must be situated in historical context, so a brief military and political history of the borderland region follows. The circumstances of the borderland informed the questions jurists addressed, and when this chapter turns to discussion of the masa'il, the reader will recognize how the legal sources provide a perspective on warfare that differs from the characterization of events in the chronicles, the rhetoric of official pronouncements, and poetic encomiums. In the ninth and tenth centuries the borderland was a place of pragmatic alliances and uncertain loyalties. The occasional rupture of political ties between border lords and the Umayyad ruler generated

5. Claudio Sánchez Albornoz is credited with the thesis of the no-man's land. Thomas F. Glick summarizes the revisionary arguments in *From Muslim Fortress to Christian Castle: Social and Cultural Change in Medieval Spain* (Manchester: Manchester University Press, 1995), 113–114; see also Eduardo Manzano Moreno, "The Creation of a Medieval Frontier: Islam and Christianity in the Iberian Peninsula, Eighth to Eleventh Centuries," in *Frontiers in Question: Eurasian Borderlands, 700–1700*, ed. Daniel Power and Naomi Standen (New York: St. Martin's Press, 1999), 32–54.

6. See Ibn Rushd, *Bayan*, 3:20 and 3:59, for reference to the mafaza between the settlements of the Muslims and their enemies.

questions about the legal status of Muslims and dhimmis residing in the domains of a border lord turned rebel similar to questions related to the rebellion of the Banu Hafsun. Political instability contributed to uncertainty about the "border" between Dar al-Islam and Dar al-Harb and complicated questions about legal identity for jurists in their categorization of people who lived in the region and in their resolution of legal questions. By the middle of the tenth century the border lords were brought more closely under Umayyad rule. By this time the border region had become more settled, and cross-border interaction intensified. Legal questions about crossing "borders" for trade and diplomacy discussed in the ninth century became increasingly pertinent in the tenth.

The Umayyads in Cordoba exerted limited control over the borderlands and relied on border lords to defend and administer the farthermost fortresses, towns, and communities, for the most part accepting their practical autonomy and dynastic claims. In the upper march the Banu Qasi (descendants of Casius) were a dominant military and political presence of indigenous origin dating back to the eighth century who, upon conversion, more or less acknowledged Umayyad suzerainty in exchange for their continued dominion. Notably, the Banu Qasi had kinship and political ties to the Arista dynasty of Navarre and exemplify the flexibility of political and religious identity on the frontier at the time. In the middle of the ninth century the Umayyad amir Muhammad sent the Tujibis of Arab origin to the upper march to counter the independence of the Banu Qasi, with the result that the two clans fought each other as well as other Muslim and Christian rivals into the next century. The borderlands offered opportunities for *muwalladūn* (indigenous converts and their descendants; s. *muwallad*) such as the Banu Qasi (largely based in Tudela), the Banu ʿAmrus and Banu Sabrit in Huesca in the upper march, and Ibn Marwan al-Jilliqi, who established dynastic lordship in the lower march in Merida and the region around Badajoz in the first decades of the ninth century. Berbers also achieved dynastic ambitions, such as the Banu Dhi'l-Nun, who established dominion in the mountains around Santaver in the upper march, and the Banu Tajit in Coria and Egitania (and at the end of the century, Merida).[7] At times the border lords broke

---

7. When al-Hakam I appointed ʿAmrus "the Muwallad" from Huesca as governor of Toledo in an effort to bring the city more tightly under his control, he announced in a public letter his choice of "a man from your people and progeny." The amir's intentions were not to rule by persuasion, however. He first ordered the construction of a citadel and then the massacre of most of the notables of the city. Ibn al-Qutiyya, *Taʾrikh iftitah al-Andalus (Historia de la conquista de España de Abenalcotía el Cordobés)*, ed. and trans. (into Spanish) Julián Ribera (Madrid: Revista Archivos, 1926), Arabic, 46; Spanish, 36–37; English translation, David James, *Early Islamic Spain: The "History" of Ibn al-Qutiya*

with Cordoba and initiated or supported rebellions against the Umayyad regime, sometimes involving Christian allies. Umayyad rulers were thus occasionally forced to send armies to bring rebellious borderland regions back under their jurisdiction. Not infrequently, border lords who submitted and agreed to swear loyalty, pay tribute, and participate in military campaigns against the regime's enemies (and not seek alliances with them) were formally invested and restored as semi-independent lords. Occasionally the ruler replaced a habitually insubordinate lord with one of his own officials, but as often as not, dynastic lordship would be reestablished. In the second quarter of the ninth century, for example, ʿAbd al-Rahman II was able to establish his own governors in Merida, Toledo, and Zaragoza and assert direct control, but rebellion broke out shortly after his death in Toledo and Merida, and in the upper march local lords contended with the Banu Qasi for dominance. Toledo, in particular, became notorious in the chronicles of ʿAbd al-Rahman III's reign for its long history of regular outbreaks of rebellion until the caliph finally brought the city into submission in 932 after defeating the Leonese army sent to relieve his siege.

In the process of consolidating his reign as amir, ʿAbd al-Rahman III undertook refortification of abandoned fortresses and towns, sent his commanders on campaigns to the north, and went on campaign himself. These campaigns had as much to do with bringing the borderlands in line as with attacking Christian positions; while the amir was on campaign in 920 and 924, he confirmed, replaced, and subordinated border lords. After his triumph over Bobastro and declaration of the caliphate, ʿAbd al-Rahman III ordered representatives of the major borderland dynasties to come to Cordoba to demonstrate their loyalty, commit to payment of tribute, and secure their investiture. Allegiances to Cordoba were not so easily secured, however. The history of ʿAbd al-Rahman III's involvement with the border lords of the upper march after this act of obeisance is illustrative.[8] When the (now) caliph led the campaign of Osma against the Christians in 934 and the Tujibi lord of Zaragoza, Muhammad ibn Hashim, and the lords of Huesca (Fortun ibn Muhammad) and Barbastro (ʿAmrus ibn Muhammad) of the Banu Sabrit refused to join him, he had to take action against them. The

(London: Routledge, 2009), 86–88; Ibn Hayyan, *Crónica de los emires Alhakam I y ʿAbdarrahman II entre los años 796 y 847 [Muqtabis II-1]*, trans. Mahmud ʿAli Makki and Federico Corriente from the manuscript (Zaragoza: Instituto de Estudios Islámicos y del Oriente Próximo, 2001), 30–35, 38–39, 40, 48–50, 87, 93–94, 124, 291.

8. See Manzano Moreno, *Frontera de al-Andalus*, 346–370, and Maribel Fierro, *ʿAbd al-Rahman III: The First Cordoban Caliph* (Oxford: Oneworld Publications, 2005), 48–52, 60–68.

submission of Muhammad ibn Hashim al-Tujibi to the caliph's authority did not last long, and so the following year the caliph returned with his army to lay siege to Zaragoza. The siege continued after the caliph himself returned to Cordoba, but within months rebellion spread across the upper march, including border lords hitherto demonstrably loyal to the caliph, such as the Tujibis of Calatayud and Daroca, and extended into the middle march.[9] The caliph again led his armies to the north. He left one commander, Durri, to secure the middle march, sent Najda to Santaren and Ahmad ibn Muhammad ibn Ilyas to Huesca and Barbastro, and personally led the campaign against Zaragoza. The terms of Muhammad ibn Hashim's surrender required him to stay in Cordoba for thirty days and demonstrate his obedience. He could return to Zaragoza as governor for life, with the right to name his successor, if he agreed to pay tribute, send specified hostages to Cordoba (to ensure his compliance with the agreement), fight in support of the caliph when called on to do so, and not support the caliph's enemies. The oath of submission according to these terms was sworn in the mosque of Zaragoza in the presence of the caliph and many witnesses on November 21, 937.[10]

The caliph did not have the power to uproot entrenched interests in the borderlands or enforce his authority and jurisdiction from Cordoba. His ability to command, let alone control, the border lords was clearly limited, but he did eventually manage to prevent them from threatening his rule, and for the most part they promoted and defended the interests of the regime as they promoted and defended their own. After Muhammad ibn Hashim was taken captive in the battle of Simancas, 'Abd al-Rahman III worked to liberate him in his protracted negotiations with the Leonese king Ramiro II (r. 931–951). Muhammad ibn Hashim had by then become one of the caliph's trusted governors and commanders and proved his continued loyalty when he was eventually released. The battle of Simancas in August 939 turned out to be the last battle the caliph participated in personally. Ibn Hayyan attributes the significant rout of the army and the humiliating loss

---

9. Manzano Moreno, *Frontera de al-Andalus*, 355–357, surmises that the rebellion may have had to do with the appearance of an "anticaliph" who was none other than Ahmad ibn Ishaq al-Qurayshi, the commander left in charge of the siege of Zaragoza.

10. Ibn Hayyan records the text of the aman (the terms of Muhammad ibn Hashim's submission and 'Abd al-Rahman III's guarantee of safety) and describes Ibn Hashim's processional arrival in Cordoba and formal investiture as governor-commander of Zaragoza in *al-Muqtabis [V] de Ibn Hayyan*, ed. P. Chalmeta, F. Corriente, and M. Subh (Madrid: Instituto Hispano-Arabe de Cultura, 1979), (Arabic) 404–407, 423–425; Spanish translation, *Crónica del califa Abdarrahman III an-Nasir entre los años 912 y 942 (al-Muqtabis V)*, trans. María Jesús Viguera and Federico Corriente (Zaragoza: Instituto Hispano-Arabe de Cultura, 1981), 303–305, 316–317.

of the caliph's Qur'an and coat of mail to betrayal by the lord of Huesca, Fortun ibn Muhammad, and other commanders who broke ranks; the caliph's punishment was swift, harsh, and exemplary.[11] The historian provides a testimonial report that Fortun was sent to Cordoba, where he was quickly displayed above the palace gate with his tongue cut out, but alive, according to caliphal orders. When the caliph returned to the city, he paused before the crucified figure and insulted and cursed him. After Fortun managed to spit blood and saliva at him, the caliph ordered his execution, and he was pierced by lances. A few days later the caliph ordered the prefect of the city (ṣāḥib al-madīna) to pull ten of the best horsemen from the ranks of the troops under review. He ordered them crucified and declared their cowardice before all who were assembled, deaf to the many cries for mercy.[12]

Campaigning in Dar al-Harb was not ultimately directed to territorial expansion. In the ninth century preoccupations of the Umayyad amirs and limitations of manpower precluded a focused and persistent program of conquest, even if it was important for the regime to show the flag. Sporadic campaigns took place during the reigns of the amirs Hisham I, al-Hakam I, 'Abd al-Rahman II, and Muhammad. By the turn of the ninth century the Christian kingdom of Asturias had emerged in the northwest. Rebellion in the borderlands against Umayyad rule and a power struggle between the amir al-Hakam and two of his uncles provided an opportunity for the Franks to advance on Gerona and Barcelona and make those cities the basis of the Carolingian march. Muslim-controlled Tudela, Huesca, Lerida, and Tortosa came to mark the boundary between the Franks and the Muslims.[13] The Basques occupied Pamplona at the turn of the century as well, and this city became the center of the incipient kingdom of Navarre, formed with

11. 'Abd al-Rahman III had removed Fortun ibn Muhammad from the governorship of Huesca when he refused to participate in the campaign of Osma but restored him after suppressing the rebellion of the upper march in 937. Fortun and his brother 'Amrus of the Banu Sabrit were sons of Muhammad al-Tawil and Sancha of Aragon.

12. Ibn Hayyan provides a few versions of the events surrounding the battle of Simancas (Al-Khandaq) in his history and distinctively emphasizes the treachery of Fortun ibn Muhammad ibn Tawil. He also mentions that his own grandfather was among those who lost their lives in the battle (*Muqtabis [V]*, Arabic, 432–447; Spanish, 323–336). Another account, related in *Akhbar majmu'a a fi fath al-Andalus*, ed. and trans. Emilio Lafuente y Alcantara (Madrid: Real Academia de la Historia, 1867), presents a conspiracy among the prominent soldiers against the commander Najda, who is described in disparaging terms as an example of the base or depraved men 'Abd al-Rahman III came to appoint (a criticism of his designation of a freed slave soldier as commander); Arabic, 155–156; Spanish, 135. For an analysis, see Pedro Chalmeta Gendrón, "Simancas y Alhandega," *Hispania* 36 (1976): 359–444.

13. On the development of this frontier from the Christian side, see A. R. Lewis, "Cataluña como frontera militar (870–1050)," *Anuario de Estudios Medievales* 5 (1968): 15–29.

Banu Qasi support against the expansionary interests of the Asturians and the Franks. During the *fitna* (civil war) of the middle of the ninth century, Alfonso III (r. 866–910), king of Asturias took the opportunity to expand eastward into the plains and to launch raids against the Muslims from fortified Zamora on the Duero. His conquest of Braga and Oporto, to the west, would become the basis for the county of Portugal, and of Burgos, to the east, for that of Castile. After his death and the accession of his heirs, the city of Leon became the seat of the Kingdom of Leon.

Shortly after ʿAbd al-Rahman III came to the throne, "the tyrant" (*al-ṭāghiya*) Ordoño II of Asturias-Leon (r. 914–925) launched a devastating attack on the city of Evora, reportedly killing seven hundred men and taking four thousand women and children captive.[14] The "enemy of God" Sancho of Navarre also tested the new ruler's authority, attacking Tudela and taking its governor (one of the Banu Qasi) captive.[15] ʿAbd al-Rahman III's military capabilities were stretched by his program to bring insurgent al-Andalus back under Umayyad control, but he sent one of his generals north in a show of force in the summer of 916 (his first campaign in enemy territory); the army traversed the land of the enemies and "brought fear into their hearts after a long period of security."[16] Thus began renewed attention to the borderlands after the hiatus caused by the fitna, and a more engaged contest for power against the Christians to the north. The following year the same commander, Ibn Abi ʿAbda, led a raid into al-Qilaʿ (the area that was to become the county of Castile) and besieged the fortress of Castro Muros (San Esteban de Gormaz); this time the Muslims were overcome, and Ibn Abi ʿAbda died a "martyr." The following year (918) Sancho led a campaign in the upper march to Tudela and across the Ebro into the valley of Tarazona, attacking the fortress of Valtierra. In 919 ʿAbd al-Rahman III sent a campaign that, as accounts record, successfully avenged the fallen Muslims and inspired terror in the hearts of the enemy, reaping abundant booty and captives. Ordoño II, hoping to take advantage of ʿAbd al-Rahman III's preoccupation with defeating the last of the Banu Hafsun in Bobastro, prepared to campaign in the autumn of 919 but was deterred when the amir sent an army to the middle march. ʿAbd al-Rahman, thus provoked to fight Ordoño in person, called for a general mobilization to fight the "enemies of God." He mustered widespread enthusiasm by ap-

---

14. Ibn Hayyan, *Muqtabis [V]*, Arabic, 93–95; Spanish, 81–83.

15. Ibn Hayyan, *Muqtabis [V]*, Arabic, 124–125; Spanish, 103–104.

16. Ibn Hayyan, *Muqtabis [V]*, Arabic, 167; Spanish, 104–105

pealing to the population from the *minbar* or pulpit of the Great Mosque of Cordoba on a number of Fridays. The great army assembled in April 920 and departed a month later for Guadalajara, from where it crossed into enemy territory. The Muslims ruined crops and fields and destroyed fortresses, churches, and monasteries. They faced off against Sancho's army, which fled into the mountains, and in the confrontation with Ordoño's and Sancho's combined forces, the Muslims prevailed. The fleeing Christians took refuge in the fortress of Muez, which the Muslims took by force, reportedly killing more than five hundred of the fugitives in the amir's presence. At the end of the successful campaign the amir distributed gifts, including horses and robes of honor, to the men of the march and sent the heads of the infidels on pikes back to Cordoba.[17] After the campaign of Pamplona in 924, 'Abd al-Rahman III did not personally lead another campaign to the upper march until the campaign of Osma against Ramiro II in 934, and again in 939 (his last campaign). Nonetheless, the pattern of raid and counterraid persisted, with occasional raids by land and sea against the Franks, a pattern punctuated by periods of quiet secured by truce (as with Toda, regent of Pamplona, in 934, the count of Barcelona in 940, and Ramiro II of Leon in 935 and again in 941).

Generally speaking, the stakes of warfare became greater in the tenth century, when the armies and ambitions of the Christian kingdoms became stronger and bolder, and the Umayyad caliphate invested its great wealth in asserting its dominion both in al-Andalus and across the Straits of Gibraltar. Warfare against the enemy was sometimes defensive, but it was also important politically and ideologically. At the same time, diplomacy became even more essential and increasingly common in practice.

In the prevailing circumstances of the tenth century, even if a fortress or town was taken, it usually could not be garrisoned or secured; at best its fortifications could be dismantled. Successful raids yielded booty and captives, devastated the crops and stores of Christian settlements, and may have checked Christian expansion. When successful campaigns against the Christians took place, they supported Umayyad claims to legitimacy: every regime-organized raiding campaign was an occasion to display the ruler's defense of the faithful and commitment to jihad against the unbelievers (*al-kafara*), the polytheists (*al-mushrikūn*), and the "enemies of God," identified more particularly, as well, as Basques, Galicians (and later Leonese), and Franks.

---

17. Ibn Hayyan, *Muqtabis* [V], Arabic, 135–136, 145–147, 155–168; Spanish, 110–111, 117–118, 125–133.

'Abd al-Rahman III presented campaigning in the north as the enactment of his "command of the faithful." He characterized his raids against the Christians in terms of the opposition of the truth of Islam to unbelief and in terms of his righteous rule against tyranny (although the rhetoric of his reign focused at least as much on his uniting the Muslims and protecting their faith from the corruption of internal enemies and from Fatimid Shi'i "deviance"). He had news of successes against the unbelievers and the mushrikun read in the Great Mosque; the departing and returning armies demonstrated his power, authority, and commitment to jihad; and the heads of the fallen enemies and captives were presented to the public as trophies.

'Abd al-Rahman III's successor, al-Hakam (II) al-Mustansir Billah (r. 961–976), maintained Umayyad dominance of the peninsula with a strong presence in the borderlands, developing Medinaceli as a base in the middle march for his commander Ghalib ibn 'Abd al-Rahman. Al-Hakam II may not have led any campaigns himself, but like his father, he relied on the border lords and his commanders (especially Ghalib, a freedman client of 'Abd al-Rahman III) to keep the region secure. Instead of making appearances on the field of battle, he received visiting delegations at court in ceremonies of lavish display and strict protocol and projected his power and authority in the orchestrated departures and arrivals of the army. The trophies of his commanders' successes that were paraded through the streets of Cordoba included shackled prisoners and heads on pikes.[18]

Muhammad ibn Abi 'Amir (the future al-Mansur) revived personal leadership of the ṣā'ifa (the annual campaign). He began his military career at the outset of the reign of the young caliph Hisham (II) al-Mu'ayyad. Ibn Abi 'Amir used jihad against the Christians to great effect, consolidating and expanding his personal power with each success in the field; as his reputation grew, he exploited every opportunity to eliminate his rivals, one by one, until he ruled unchallenged from 981 to 1002 in the name of the caliph. As champion of jihad, under the banners of the Umayyads, he promoted popular support for his rule, secured Berber recruits in North Africa, achieved recognition and loyalty among the military commanders and

---

18. The evidence for al-Hakam II's reign is more limited than for that of his predecessor, 'Abd al-Rahman III. Manzano Moreno is skeptical about the report of the thirteenth-century historian Ibn 'Idhari that al-Hakam II went on campaign to the north after completing his expansion and renovation of the Great Mosque of Cordoba or against San Esteban in 963 because of the lack of any detail or discussion, and he points out that the Cordoban scholar Ibn Hazm asserts that the caliph never went on campaign after assuming his title (*Frontera de al-Andalus*, 370–380).

border lords, and inspired the admiration of chroniclers.[19] Ibn Hayyan reports that Ibn Abi ʿAmir campaigned against the Christians (al-Rum) all the days of his life, trampling their land and seizing their goods until they feared him as they feared fate.[20] A list of Ibn Abi ʿAmir's campaigns (totaling fifty-six) provided by a fifteenth-century text succinctly conveys the rigor of his commitment to warfare and the extent of his reach.[21] Among his more spectacular exploits were the sack of Barcelona (985) and the devastation of Santiago de Compostela (997).

Questions about boundaries between Muslims and non-Muslims at the "border" between Dar al-Islam and Dar al-Harb appear in the portion of juridical texts dedicated to matters of warfare under the rubric of jihad and have a long history. In the section of al-Nawadir wa-l-ziyadat dedicated to jihad, Ibn Abi Zayd al-Qayrawani (d. 996) gives a sort of historical survey of juridical opinion identified with Malik (d. 795) and his Egyptian and Medinese disciples, notably Ibn al-Qasim (d. 806), Ibn Wahb (d. 812), Ashhab (d. 820), and Ibn al-Majishun (d. 829), and their students and the next generation of students who all became Maliki authorities, notably Yahya ibn Yahya (d. 839), Asbagh ibn al-Faraj (d. 840), Ibn Habib (d. 853), Sahnun (d. 854), al-ʿUtbi (d. 869), Ibn Sahnun (d. 871), and Ibn al-Mawwaz (d.895). The practice and experience of warfare extends back to the foundational history of Islam, and the juridical discussion of pertinent issues shows accretions over time and encompasses a variety of contexts. Jurists of the ninth and tenth centuries of the emerging Maliki madhhab (school of law) took some interest in looking back to early models; we find scattered references to the days of the Prophet and the early battles against the mushrikun, the

---

19. On the idealization of al-Mansur's character, see Cristina de la Puente, "La caracterización de Almanzor: Entre la epopeya y la historia," in Estudios onomástico-biográficos de al-Andalus, vol. 8, ed. Maria Luisa Avila and Manuela Marín (Madrid: Consejo Superior de Investigaciones Científicas, 1997), 367–402.

20. Luis Molina discusses and presents an excerpt from a text of unknown authorship titled Dhikr bilad al-Andalus that he dates between the end of the fourteenth century and the fall of Granada at the end of the fifteenth century; the remarks by Ibn Hayyan are from this text. See Luis Molina, "Las campañas de Almanzor a la luz de un nuevo texto," Al-Qantara 2 (1981): 209–263 (remarks by Ibn Hayyan, 222); and Molina, "Las campañas de Almanzor: Nuevos datos," Al-Qantara 3 (1982): 467–472.

21. Dhikr bilad al-Andalus, in Molina, "Campañas de Almanzor a la luz de un nuevo texto," 222–229 and 230–237 (Spanish). The eleventh-century geography by Ahmad ibn ʿUmar al-ʿUdhri, Tarsiʿ al-akhbar wa-tanwiʿ al-athar wa-l-bustan fi ghara'ib al-buldan wa-l-masalik ila jamiʿ al-mamalik, ed. ʿAbd al-ʿAziz al-Ahwani (Madrid: Instituto de Estudios Islámicos, 1965), 74–81, provides a chronology of Ibn Abi ʿAmir's first twenty-five campaigns. For a Spanish translation of this part of al-ʿUdhri's text and analysis, see J. M. Ruiz Asencio, "Campañas de Almanzor contra el reino de León (981–986)," Anuario de Estudios Medievales 5 (1968): 31–64.

campaigns against the break-away Arab tribes known as the wars against apostasy (*ridda*) after the prophet Muhammad's death, the Islamic conquests, and, more frequently, warfare on the frontier with Byzantium. Points of interest for them included divisions of the spoils of war, the treatment of defeated enemies (combatants and noncombatants), the exchange of emissaries, and the terms of truces, among other matters. Ibn Abi Zayd al-Qayrawani provides a perspective on truces, for example, that enlarges our understanding of the juridical context for truce making in al-Andalus. The Andalusi jurist Yahya ibn Yahya upheld the practice of truces (Umayyad rulers made truces), but al-Qayrawani cites the Egyptian Ibn al-Mawwaz's book for a general disapproval of truces, with specific examples drawn from the early 'Abbasid period. According to Ibn al-Mawwaz, when the Byzantine emperor offered one hundred thousand dinars a year for a truce to 'Abd Allah ibn Harun (son of Harun al-Rashid), the '*ulama*' (religious scholars) counseled against acceptance, arguing that people would abandon what was then a thriving region and leave the thughur vulnerable; the '*ulama*' had also opposed the truce proposed between the emperor and the caliph al-Mahdi. Ibn al-Mawwaz asserts, speaking to a problem of classification and underlining the need for definition, that *jizya* (poll tax) should be accepted only from those subject to Islamic *ḥukm* (rule or legal jurisdiction) and Muslim *sulṭān* (authority). Ibn Mawwaz's statement is situated in the larger textual discussion of Ibn Abi Zayd al-Qayrawani's compilation, where opinions also encompassed conditions when a truce might be acceptable; discourse about these matters contributed to a consensus supporting a practice (already in evidence) of arranging truces.

The question of how to handle spies evolved juridically because it too became a matter of practical concern. Ibn Wahb reported that when Malik was asked about a Muslim spying on behalf of an enemy against Islam, he indicated that he had no basis for an opinion and suggested that the imam (the ruler) should exercise his judgment. Al-Qayrawani's chapter on spies gives us an idea of how the jurists elaborated from there. Ibn Sahnun reported that his father explained that the handling of a spy in the land of Islam depended on whether the spy was a harbi who entered with *amān* (people traveling into Dar al-Islam from outside needed a document of safe-conduct; *amān* means "security" and refers to the ruler's formal grant of security) or without, a dhimmi, or a Muslim. The life of the harbi spy caught without aman might be spared if he converted (he would become a slave). If he entered with aman, as a merchant might, then his fate would be in the hands of the ruler: he might be killed, or he might be spared and granted a new aman. A dhimmi spy or a Muslim spy should be killed

(Sahnun observed, however, that some jurists said that the Muslim might be flogged and imprisoned as exemplary punishment and then banished from the borderlands). As Ibn Sahnun's report describes, on the authority of his father, the legal identity of the offender had a part in the determination of his fate; jurists might also consider the nature of the offense and whether it was a first offense.[22]

Sahnun's reported discussion of the fate of the harbi spy who had aman describes a situation worthy of consideration: harbis sometimes crossed into Dar al-Islam with aman in order to settle down and stay. In Sahnun's opinion, such an individual, if caught as a spy, lost the protection of the aman and would have to be treated as a dhimmi in the same circumstances: he should be killed, but his heirs would inherit. Ibn Abi Zayd al-Qayrawani's text provides some further evidence of the phenomenon of Christians crossing the "border" to live in Dar al-Islam. The harbi seeking aman in order to settle in Dar al-Islam may even have had a specific designation. An opinion of Asbagh's reported by Ibn Habib refers to a woman seeking to enter the land of Islam to marry and remain as a *jāniha* (fem.; masc. *jānih*: someone who "turns"). The term was perhaps historically and contextually specific (in the way *muwallad* was) and represents a social differentiation with debatable legal significance for the jurists of the ninth century who considered whether and how a harbi who traveled to Dar al-Islam for a limited purpose might be legally different from a harbi who immigrated. The term also conveys an interest in marking the difference between a non-Muslim immigrant and a dhimmi, although jurists seemed to determine, at least in the given example, that the janiha was not legally different from a dhimmi despite the different circumstances of her coming under the protection of Islam.[23]

Al-'Utbi's *Mustakhraja* may be deployed usefully to highlight the interests of the Andalusi jurists in defining boundaries in the borderlands, given the cacophony of opinions in Ibn Abi Zayd al-Qayrawani's *Nawadir wa-ziyadat*. Al-'Utbi's text provides a number of masa'il dealing with issues of "border" and boundary crossing, illustrates some of the complicated legal scenarios that could arise, and suggests prevailing views in al-Andalus. Questions about

---

22. Al-Qayrawani, *al-Nawadir wa-l-ziyadat*, ed. 'Abd al-Fattah Muhammad al-Hulw, et al. (Beirut: Dar al-Gharb al-Islami, 1999), 3:352–354. Sahnun's example of a Muslim spy writes to the enemy of the Muslims' weaknesses. Spies played a number of roles, including acting as guides into Muslim territory; Ordoño II, for example, employed such guides, and when he suspected that two of them undermined his campaign in the Guadiana valley, he had them decapitated (Ibn Hayyan, *Muqtabis* [V], Arabic, 120–123; Spanish, 100–102).

23. Al-Qayrawani, *Nawadir wa-ziyadat*, 3:154–155.

specific situations and practices addressed larger issues, such as the difference between aman and dhimma, the connection between crossing borders and conversion or apostasy, and the application of principles of Islamic law across "borders." A number of questions having to do with interactions between Muslims and dhimmis specific to the borderlands contributed to the legal elaboration of the relationship between Muslim and dhimmi in ways that asserted boundaries but also allowed for accommodation of practice.

Negotiations for truces were conducted by intermediaries, often identified in the chronicles as Jewish and Christian. The Jewish courtier Hasday ibn Shaprut played an important role in concluding a truce between ʿAbd al-Rahman III and the count of Barcelona and other Frankish lords interested in the security of their merchants, and in the conclusion of the truce with Ramiro II. Ibn Shaprut, who was a physician, also became involved in negotiations with Toda of Navarre that resulted in his treating her grandson Sancho, "the Fat," for obesity in Cordoba and the caliph's participation in restoring him to the throne of Leon in 960.[24] Jewish envoys (Bernat and Baruch) are mentioned as agents on behalf of the Franks and Leonese as well. Christian envoys also passed between courts; the chronicles sometimes identify them by name and title. Envoys from the Umayyad side are often identified as religious leaders (bishops). Envoys from the Christian side—for example, from Ramiro II—sometimes had Arabic names and may have been Christian emigrants from al-Andalus, former Muslims, or Muslims employed by the king.[25] The Umayyad regime's use of Jewish and Christian envoys may have been a matter of employing men with appropriate language skills and cultural acuity, but it may also have reflected deference to jurists' aversion to putting Muslims under the jurisdiction of "unbelievers."

People traveling into Dar al-Islam from outside needed a document of safe-conduct, or their personal safety and belongings were at risk. A question for jurists was whether the aman had to be respected for envoys who

---

24. See David J. Wasserstein, "The Muslims and the Golden Age of the Jews," *Israel Oriental Studies* 17 (1997): 184–186.

25. Ibn Hayyan, *Muqtabis [V]*, Arabic, 465; Spanish, 349; a delegation to ʿAbd al-Rahman III from Ramiro II in late 940/early 941 included associates (*aṣḥāb*) of the "tyrant" Ramiro, such as ʿAbd Allah ibn ʿUmar, Asad al-ʿAbbadi, Saʿid ibn ʿUbayda al-ʿAbbadi, and Ghitar, as well as the regular messengers from Ramiro to Cordoba involved in negotiating the peace, Musa ibn Rakaysh and Aghlab ibn Muzahir. On Arabic names in Leon, see Richard Hitchcock, *Mozarabs in Medieval and Early Modern Spain* (Aldershot: Ashgate, 2008), 53–68; Victoria Aguilar, "Onomástica de origen árabe en el reino de León (siglo x)," *Al-Qantara* 15 (1994): 351–363; and Victoria Aguilar Sebastián and Fernando Rodríguez Mediano, "Antroponomia de origen árabe en la documentación (siglos VIII–XIII)," in *El reino de León en la Alta Edad Media*, vol. 6 (Madrid: Caja España de Inversiones, Caja de Ahorros y Monte de Piedad y Archivo Histórico Diocesano de León, 1994), 497–633.

were renegades. Yahya ibn Yahya asked Ibn Qasim about aman in a situation where a man sent by the enemies to the Muslims with a gift turned out to be a Muslim who had emigrated and apostasized. The question was: Should he be asked to repent and return to Islam (and presumably made to stay if he did repent or be killed as an apostate if he did not), or should he be allowed to return to the land of the enemy? Ibn al-Qasim upheld the protection of the safe-conduct and allowed for the man to return to the land of the enemy.[26] Sahnun addressed a different situation in which the Christian envoy wanted to become Muslim and stay in Dar al-Islam. He reported what Malik said (according to Ibn al-Qasim) about some members of a Byzantine delegation to the caliph (in the East) who became Muslim and whose fellow delegates wanted to force them to return with them; in Malik's view the Christian delegates had the right to take the converts with them to their country. Ibn al-Qasim, Sahnun reported, invoked the example of the Prophet and Abu Jandal (who converted to Islam against the wishes of his father and was obliged to return with him after the treaty of Hudaybiyya was concluded). Two issues arise in the discussion presented by Ibn Rushd: the legitimacy of the conversion of the Christian envoy in these circumstances and the completion of the mission. Ibn Rushd observes that Ibn Habib said that the conversion was accepted unless prior conditions had been made (precluding the conversion of envoys). Ibn Rushd supports the argument attributed to Malik that a converted envoy should go back to complete the mission with a hadith he considers more appropriate than the reference to Abu Jandal. In this hadith Abu Rafi', a messenger from the unbelieving Quraysh to the prophet Muhammad, reported that when he met the Prophet, he was filled with love of Islam and refused to go back to the Quraysh. The Prophet, however, told him that he was not one to break an agreement or hold up a correspondence. He sent the messenger back but invited him to return if what he felt in his heart persisted.[27]

Yahya ibn Yahya raised another question that probed the protections granted visiting embassies. In this example an envoy seeking a truce arrived from the land of the enemy, and the delegation included a fugitive slave. Ibn al-Qasim's view was that the master of the slave did not have the right to seize him; he was protected by the 'ahd (pact or treaty) of the envoys and could return to the land of the enemy. Ibn Rushd explains that Ibn al-Qasim's position was the same whether the slave was a Muslim or not, and that

26. Ibn Rushd, *Bayan*, 3:31; see also al-Qayrawani, *Nawadir wa-ziyadat*, 3:136.

27. Ibn Rushd, *Bayan*, 3:45–46; al-Qayrawani, *Nawadir wa-ziyadat*, 3:148.

generally, people who entered Dar al-Islam under protection, like merchants, did not have to sell their Muslim slaves (Christians and Jews living within Dar al-Islam were not allowed to own Muslim slaves) or relinquish any captives who came with them. Ibn Habib, however, disagreed with Ibn al-Qasim and believed that the rules that applied to dhimmis should apply to travelers from enemy territory with aman: they should have to sell their Muslim slaves and ransom their prisoners.[28] The similarities and differences between the protections (and limits) of aman and dhimma were tested by juridical discussions of these and other such specific questions. Ibn Habib's opinion in this case, contrary to Ibn al-Qasim's, argued that the harbi traveling with aman for a specific purpose should not be entirely exempted from Islamic law, and that the limits to his protection were analogous to the limits imposed on the dhimmi. The variations of opinions in these matters reflect an uncertainty about law in the borderlands and across "borders," and particular decisions were likely made expediently.

Individuals appear in the chronicles acting as spies and guides for the enemy, as mercenary soldiers in military service to the enemy, as political allies of the enemy, and as refugees among them and are condemned as renegades. Such individuals appear in the legal texts especially when they cross into Islamic jurisdiction. Their actions against the Muslims and their (possible) apostasy from Islam became legal concerns. For example, Yahya ibn Yahya asked Ibn al-Qasim about a man who stayed behind in Barcelona after the Muslims withdrew from the city. He raided and terrorized the Muslims, killed them and took captives, and seized their money and property. Yahya queried whether the man's blood could be shed and his possessions taken, and if he were taken captive, whether he could be enslaved. Ibn al-Qasim considered the marauder to be comparable to a Muslim combatant or rebel within the lands of Islam; he should be judged by the ruler in those terms (he would not be enslaved, and his money and property would not be considered booty). If he were forced to fight against the Muslims out of fear for his life, then he would not be subject to punishment at all.[29] According to this opinion, the marauder remained a Muslim (thus he could not be enslaved, nor could his belongings or women and children be treated as booty) even if he were in violation of the law and no longer lived in Dar al-Islam.

28. Ibn Rushd, *Bayan*, 3:24–25. See also Sahnun ibn Sa'id, *al-Mudawwana al-kubra l-il-imam Malik* (Beirut: Dar Sadir, 1997), 2:18–19; and al-Qayrawani, *Nawadir wa-ziyadat*, 3:144–153, for extensive discussion of related subjects.

29. Ibn Rushd, *Bayan*, 3:41–43; al-Qayrawani, *Nawadir wa-ziyadat*, 3:352; al-Wansharisi, *al-Mi'yar al-mu'rib wa-l-jami' al-mughrib* (Rabat: Dar al-Gharb al-Islami, 1981–1983), 2:129–130.

The jurist likened the marauder to the rebel inside the domains of Islam, an opinion that suggests that the "border" here was not legally significant.

The history of the border lords and of the fluctuations in their allegiance to the ruler finds reflection in the juridical texts. Rebel lords incorporated Christians from enemy territory into their strongholds and their armies, but what was the legal status of the security offered to such individuals by a governor who was in rebellion against the legitimate ruler? Yahya ibn Yahya asked Ibn al-Qasim whether the rebel was in fact bound by his aman (imagine that his relationship to the Christians in his entourage changed); Ibn al-Qasim asserted that as a Muslim, he was still bound by his contracted agreement guaranteeing them security (he could not shed their blood or take their children and property). The lord could, however, tell the Christians that he was going to revoke the aman and send them back to their original lands (and they would become ahl al-ḥarb—people of [the Domain of] War again). When Ibn al-Qasim was asked whether they could stay if they offered to pay the jizya in exchange for the right to do so, he replied that he would not like for them to be sent back in these circumstances.[30]

A number of questions pertain to Christians fighting against Christians across the divide between Dar al-Islam and Dar al-Harb. Jurists addressed different forms of commitment between Muslims and non-Muslims, and sometimes the terminology elides differences between Muslims and Christians within the boundaries of Dar al-Islam and Muslims and Christians across "borders." For example, the Christians and Jews who lived in Dar al-Islam under Muslim rule were commonly referred to as ahl al-dhimma, people of the [pact of] protection, and they paid an annual poll tax (jizya). Enemies in Dar al-Harb who had a truce (hudna) with the Muslims were protected from attack, and jurists like Yahya ibn Yahya might refer to them as ahl dhimmatinā, people of our protection (a term close to but not the same as ahl al-dhimma); they paid an annual tribute referred to as jizya, the same term used for the poll tax paid by dhimmis as a condition of their protection.[31] The terminological confusion reflects a conceptual problem requiring differentiation. The assemblage of issues and juridical opinions as a whole work toward that end and bring into focus the distinctive status of the ahl al-dhimma.

---

30. Ibn Rushd, *Bayan*, 3:10–11. Another question tests the limits of aman granting: What if a man from a raiding party is captured by enemy forces, the Muslims pursue them, and the enemy asks their captive to grant them aman? When the Muslim horsemen catch up to them, must they respect the aman? See *Bayan*, 3:74.

31. Ibn Rushd, *Bayan*, 3:25; al-Qayrawani, *Nawadir wa-ziyadat*, 3:345.

Yahya ibn Yahya asked Ibn al-Qasim a series of questions about different circumstances in which the relationship between Muslims and dhimmis required clarification because of the existence of the "border." First, he asked about a band of Christian dhimmis in the Muslim thaghr who raided enemy territory on their own, without Muslims, in order to gain booty. Were they subject to paying the fifth (khums), the portion of the booty that goes to the ruler? Ibn al-Qasim's reply was not direct: he disliked the ruler permitting them to raid. When prompted (why do you disapprove if they are not raiding with our armies?), Ibn al-Qasim cited the Prophet's refusal to ask for help from the mushrikun and equated the dhimmis' raids with helping the Muslims. Yahya persisted in his line of questioning until he got a direct answer from Ibn al-Qasim: if it happens (that dhimmis raid in enemy territory), they do not owe the khums.[32] Yahya developed the scenario: What if a Muslim arbiter (ḥakam) divides the booty among them? Does he do it according to the custom of Islam? Ibn al-Qasim replied: Yes, if they designate him and agree to him, let him divide the spoils among them according to Islam. If they do not choose the Muslim hakam, they should have their bishops—the people of their religion—apportion things according to their own custom. This exchange conveys a tension between an ideal, that Muslims do not seek the help of non-Muslims, and the reality, that Christians did fight against Christians and otherwise supported the Muslims against their enemies. Ibn Rushd's commentary suggests how principle might be adapted to exigencies when we compare his report of Malik's opinion with his report of an opinion of Ibn Habib's. Malik's position was that it was not permissible for the ruler to ask unbelievers for help to fight against unbelievers or to permit them to raid unbelievers (independently or alongside Muslims) because they deemed things permissible in raiding that the Muslims did not. Ibn Habib's opinion was situationally specific; in his view it was permissible for the ruler to strengthen his forces with the men and weapons of someone with whom he had a treaty in order to fight an enemy among the ahl al-harb with whom he did not have a treaty.[33]

---

32. In another set of questions Ibn al-Qasim makes a distinction between thieving and raiding: a Muslim and a slave or a Muslim and a Christian who steal together should divide their spoils; the Muslim freeman and Muslim slave would be subject to payment of the khums, but the Christian thief would not. Muslims should not, however, seek the support of slaves or Christians in their armies (Ibn Rushd, Bayan 3:15–18).

33. Ibn Rushd, Bayan, 3:5–7, 85; see also Sahnun, Mudawwana, 2:40–41. Sahnun presents Ibn al-Qasim's opinion that Muslims should not seek the help of mushrikun or fight with them, with the exception of servants and sailors, to whom he had no objection.

The security of dhimmis in the borderlands could be vulnerable when their identity as subjects of the Muslim ruler was blurred by their crossing into recognized enemy territory or in the event of their falling into the hands of the enemies. Yahya ibn Yahya asked Ibn al-Qasim about some dhimmis who fled into the land of the enemies one night. Muslim horsemen caught them in Dar al-Harb and divided them up as booty. The dhimmis claimed that they had fled into Dar al-Harb out of fear of oppression and of being sold; they lived near an Arab tribe that harassed and abused the *ahl al-jizya* (people of the jizya) in the area. The answer to the question hinged on the truth of the dhimmis' statement because if they had joined the enemy in other circumstances, they would have been in violation of their pact of protection and could be killed or captured and sold as a consequence. If their fear of oppression (from someone known for oppression) were true, the dhimmis would be allowed to return to their previous status and pay the jizya if their security could be assured; if their security could not be assured, they would be allowed to go where they chose in the land of the enemy.[34]

In the middle of a raid, dhimmis could find themselves in a difficult situation. What if, Yahya asked, the enemy swoops down on a group of dhimmis living in the vicinity of a Muslim city, and they flee and surrender to the enemy (whose forces include a Muslim leader)? The immediate question was whether they would now be subject to captivity by Muslims should the opportunity arise; that is, would their status have changed from dhimmis to harbis? Ibn al-Qasim replied that if the dhimmis fled to the enemy because they feared mistreatment among the Muslims, then nothing of theirs— blood, women, or belongings—would be permitted to the Muslims. If, however, they fled Dar al-Islam without any Muslim aggression against them and were subsequently attacked by Muslims in the land of the enemy, then their blood, women, and property would be permitted to the Muslims. Yahya's question has a follow-up: What if the dhimmis were attacked while they were with the Muslim who led the enemy against the *ahl al-Islam* (people of [the Domain of] Islam), and they said that they were not leaving for the land of the enemy but were moving within the Dar al-Islam and had not (knowingly) joined the enemy but rather had approached the Muslim commander? Ibn al-Qasim did not think that their blood or belongings were "permitted" as long as they were in the Dar al-Islam with this kind of

---

34. Ibn Rushd, *Bayan*, 3:11–12; al-Qayrawani, *Nawadir wa-ziyadat*, 3:344, 469–470.

excuse. (Ibn Rushd observes that if it were not for this excuse, joining the enemy forces would be the same as transferring to the land of the enemy).[35]

A city or a fortress could fall into Muslim hands when it was abandoned (sometimes temporarily and expediently) by its inhabitants and defenders (for example, 'Abd al-Rahman III found Pamplona deserted on his campaign in 924), or it could surrender according to terms or be taken by force; in the last circumstance the combatants were subject to being killed or taken captive, the women and children became captives, and the property was booty. When Muslim cities and fortresses fell into Christian hands, the conquerors had to decide what to do about the Christians and Jews who had been living under Muslim rule who might be among the captives. Yahya ibn Yahya raised a question about some dhimmis (Christians and Jews) who remained in a city that had belonged to the Muslims but was conquered by the enemy. The Muslims in a nearby fortress complained that these (former) dhimmis were spying for the enemy, and when Muslims attacked the captured city, some of the Christian dhimmis joined the enemy in their counterattack. If the Muslims captured any of these dhimmis, they claimed that they had been forced to fight and had feared that they would be killed if they did not. It was not known whether their claims of coercion were true and whether they really feared death. Yahya's question was whether it would be permissible for these dhimmis to be killed if it were known that they pursued the Muslims, or on account of the accusations of the people in the neighboring fortress. Ibn al-Qasim opined that if it were known that a specific dhimmi had killed a Muslim, then he could be killed. If he were simply seen in pursuit of the Muslims or involved in plundering, it would not be permitted to kill him were he to be taken captive, but he should be imprisoned. This mas'ala suggests that even though the dhimmis were now living under Christian rule, they still had some claim to the protection of the Muslims; in the legal discourse they are still referred to as ahl al-dhimma. Ibn al-Qasim seemed to respect some aspect of their claim to dhimmi status in his response. Ibn Rushd, however, argues that the ahl al-dhimma in this case were acting as combatants at war against the Muslims and should be treated as such unless they had proof that they were being coerced.[36]

Al-'Utbi's *Mustakhraja* also records questions and answers exchanged between Sahnun and Ibn al-Qasim pertaining to matters of jurisdiction between Dar al-Islam and Dar al-Harb. Some of these masa'il refer to

---

35. Ibn Rushd, *Bayan*, 3:18–19; al-Qayrawani, *Nawadir wa-ziyadat*, 3:344–345.

36. Ibn Rushd, *Bayan*, 3:19–20, al-Qayrawani, *Nawadir wa-ziyadat*, 3:345.

relations with the Byzantine Empire (Rum) and the Byzantine-Islamic borderlands, whereas others are more specifically identified with al-Andalus; the inclusion of the former in al-'Utbi's compilation suggests that they were taken to be analogous to the latter by Andalusi jurists. The following situation is not located geographically and has a hypothetical quality, exploring a further dimension of how changing circumstances in the "border" region might generate changes in identity and legal status. Sahnun reports Ibn al-Qasim's opinion about a fortress of Muslims who apostasized from Islam (one might speculate about the circumstances of this kind of mass conversion), fought against Muslims, and were killed. The question is whether their children could be taken captive and their property treated as booty (in other words, whether it would be appropriate to treat the combatants of this fortress as harbis) or whether, as Ibn al-Qasim asserted, their children should be safe from captivity and their property should revert to the treasury (whether they should be treated as apostates). Complicating matters (and perhaps suggesting what is at the heart of this question), Sahnun reports that Ashhab equated the ahl al-Islam and the ahl al-dhimma in this regard, positing that apostates, like dhimmis, cannot be enslaved, the children cannot be taken captive, and their property cannot be appropriated. Ibn Rushd's commentary contrasts Ashhab's view with a report of Asbagh's opinion that apostates who fight against the Muslims, like ahl al-dhimma who fight against the Muslims, thereby lose their claims to protection; they may be killed, their women and children may be taken captive, and their possessions may be divided as booty. Ibn Rushd supports the interpretation of Ibn al-Qasim (the apostates should be treated as apostates) and indicates why the analogy between apostates and dhimmis, made by both Ashhab and Asbagh with different conclusions, is problematic: the situation of dhimmis who fight against the Muslims is different from that of the apostates because by fighting they forfeit their protection; the important point is that the original status of apostates is that of free persons, but the freedom of dhimmis is contingent on their pact of protection.[37] According to this clarification, the

---

37. Ibn Rushd, *Bayan*, 3:57–59; see also al-Qayrawani, *Nawadir wa-ziyadat*, 3:343, 348–350. As al-Qayrawani records, Ibn Habib objected to Asbagh's opinion on the basis of the analogy of apostates to dhimmis who break their pact (as described above). He explained his view after describing how the first two caliphs of Islam handled the *ahl al-ridda* (apostates). Abu Bakr treated the Arabs who broke away from the community after the Prophet's death as people who violated a pact: he killed the warriors and took the women and children captive (they were divided up with the booty). 'Umar, however, considered them to be apostates and returned the women and children (who had become slaves) to their clans, treating them as children of apostates. This, in Ibn Habib's view, was the appropriate way to treat apostates who fought against the Muslims.

family and property of a Muslim who became Christian and fought against the Muslims would be protected, but the property and family of a dhimmi who did so could be legally subject to the rules of war.

Sahnun reports Ibn al-Qasim's response to another situation, this time located more specifically in the context of al-Andalus, where the status of dhimmis who crossed between territories became an issue. Sahnun asked about a boat captured at sea coming from the lands of the Franks or elsewhere in the lands of polytheism. Jews on the boat claimed that they were under the protection of the ruler of al-Andalus and paid the jizya to him. Ibn al-Qasim indicated that without documentary evidence supporting the claim, the Jews should be considered *fay'* (gains acquired from the enemy without fighting and thus the property of the treasury). The scene becomes more vivid with Sahnun's next question: What if it were verified that they were dhimmis of the ruler of al-Andalus, and they claimed that those who seized them took their possessions? Ibn al-Qasim replied that if the men who were accused of seizing the Jews' property were honest, upright, and trustworthy, no oath would be required of them; if they were not trustworthy, they should be made to swear the truth.[38] One can imagine the Jews seeking restitution for their goods sometime after their ship was boarded and brought to shore and wonder how well they fared. Leaving and returning to Dar al-Islam could be hazardous. Protected status had to be recognized and upheld in practice (and not only by jurists).[39]

As documents and letters from the treasure trove of the Cairo Geniza attest and the work of the scholars who have studied them demonstrates, Jews developed extensive trading networks across the Mediterranean. Jewish merchants may have played an important role in whatever trade was undertaken between al-Andalus and the Christian north; evidence also suggests that Christian merchants came to al-Andalus with aman to trade. Most Andalusi Muslim merchants traded exclusively within Dar al-Islam, but a few may have specialized in trade across the "border."[40] Juridical opinion

---

38. Ibn Rushd, *Bayan*, 3:62–63.

39. Ibn al-Qasim was asked about the security of the money of someone from enemy territory who comes to the land of Islam with aman (presumably to conduct trade). What becomes of the money he deposited with a Muslim if he is taken captive (or killed) after he has returned to his homeland? Ibn al-Qasim's reply is that as a captive, his money is forfeit (the money of a slave belongs to the master and in this case is part of the booty). If he is killed in battle (not as a captive) or dies in his own land, the money should be returned to his heirs by virtue of the aman (Ibn Rushd, *Bayan*, 3:26–27; see also Sahnun, *Mudauwana*, 2:24).

40. See Olivia R. Constable, *Trade and Traders in Muslim Spain* (Cambridge: Cambridge University Press, 1994), 38–51.

discouraged Muslims from traveling in Dar al-Harb, but this did not necessarily preclude the practice. Ibn Habib, for example, reported that Malik did not allow for Muslims to enter Dar al-Harb as merchants or otherwise. He considered it incumbent on the ruler to be vigilant in preventing this because a Muslim in Dar al-Harb would be subject to the laws of the unbelievers. According to Sahnun, Malik said that he "did not like" Muslims to travel to the "land of polytheism" (ard al-shirk) to trade (in other words, he did not forbid it). It is clear that Muslims sometimes did travel in Dar al-Harb with or without a grant of security for official purposes (and perhaps otherwise). One purpose might be for the redemption of captives.[41]

The permeability of the "border" created situations where Christians from enemy territory crossed into Dar al-Islam without securing a formal aman. These instances could be mundane and domestic and suggest a practical disregard for the concept of a "border" when personal relationships were involved. Yahya ibn Yahya asked, for example, about an "infidel" ('ilj) from the land of the enemy who entered Dar al-Islam without an agreement and was found among his relatives. He claimed that he wanted to become one of the ahl al-jizya and stay in the land of the Muslims, or he said he had just come to visit his relatives. In response Ibn al-Qasim asserted that the ruler (imam) could not enslave and sell such a person, and that the man who caught him among his relatives would not have any claim to him. The ruler could choose to let him settle if he paid the jizya; if the infidel refused to pay the jizya, the ruler should send him back with aman (his blood could not be shed, and he could not be enslaved). In the example presented by Yahya, then, the ruler would either allow the Christian to settle in exchange for the jizya or give the Christian visitor the grant of aman he had not previously obtained so he could return to his home territory.[42]

In this case the claims of the Christian visitor were not called into question because he was found among his relatives. In other situations the claims of the outsider found in Dar al-Islam or approaching Dar al-Islam without documentation might be at greater risk, although in the following question such travelers were also given the benefit of the doubt. Yahya asked about a situation where some infidels from the enemy traveled to Dar al-Islam without a pact and were seized in Dar al-Islam or in the deserted territory (mafaza) between the Muslims and the enemy, headed toward Dar al-Islam. They did

41. Al-Qayrawani, Nawadir wa-ziyadat, 3:383; Ibn Rushd, Bayan, 4:170–171; Sahnun, Mudawwana, 2:16–18.

42. Ibn Rushd, Bayan, 3:26–27.

not appear to be ready for combat or to be looking to launch an attack. They claimed that they wanted to live in the land of Islam as free men, but without paying the jizya. What should the ruler do about them? Ibn al-Qasim replied that the imam might not sell or kill them, but he should impose payment of the jizya on them. If they were asked to pay the jizya and agreed, he must settle them; if they refused, he should return them to a place that was safe for them (they were not subject to predation).[43]

Jurists, in addressing questions pertaining to the "border" as a legal boundary, thus tested the definition of categories of such people as people under the protection of dhimma and people under the protection of aman, emigrants and longtime settled dhimmis, and ahl al-dhimma rebels and apostate rebels. The "border" brought the legal status of individuals on the margins into question and hence brought categories into focus. Juridical discourse both affirmed categorical distinctions and accommodated many kinds of contingent circumstances because jurists dealt not only with categories but also with relationships. Not surprisingly, the validity of marriages across borders and the status of slaves and children became subjects of interest in the discourse of Andalusi and Maghribi jurists. Two examples of masa'il about the legal validity of a marriage are suggestive. In the first, a Muslim man returned from Dar al-Harb with a harbi woman he said was his wife (he gave his wife the ṣadāq, the dower required in an Islamic marriage); in the second, a Muslim went to Dar al-Harb, became a Christian there, and married a Christian; after some years he returned to Islam, she converted, and they came to settle in the land of the Muslims. According to Sahnun, the marriage would be valid in the first instance but not in the second (because of the man's apostasy); Ibn Habib, however, would consider the second marriage valid.[44]

Masa'il about the status of slaves and children who crossed the "border" also challenged jurists to consider the legal significance of movement from one legal domain to another for legal categories and legal relationships. For example, jurists agreed that if a free Muslim was taken captive by the enemy and escaped to Dar al-Islam, he would be a free man, as before, but a Muslim slave who was taken captive and escaped still belonged to his master. A more complicated situation required more deliberation. A Muslim who escaped from the land of the enemy had a slave with him who claimed that he was (originally) a free Muslim who had been taken captive as a boy. Upon

43. Ibn Rushd, *Bayan*, 3:20–22; see also 3:71.

44. Ibn Rushd, *Bayan*, 3:142; al-Wansharisi, *Miʿyar*, 3:250.

examination, the slave proved fluent in Arabic and was able to describe where he lived and the clan he belonged to. Formal witnesses *('udūl)* from this clan confirmed his story in part: a boy had been taken captive, but they were not certain that he was the one. Ibn al-Qasim informed Yahya that the person in question should remain in the man's possession until or unless he (the slave) could secure legal testimony from Muslim witnesses supporting his claim and his identity.[45]

The status of Christian slaves from the land of the enemy who came to Dar al-Islam depended on circumstances; in many instances they might be recognized as free. For example, when a Muslim claimed that the infidel he brought with him from the land of the enemy was someone he had taken captive or a slave he had bought and the infidel, contradicting him, claimed that he had come to Dar al-Islam of his own free will in the company of the Muslim, Ibn al-Qasim accepted the statement of the infidel (unless the Muslim could provide legal testimony proving his claims). In another example Sahnun asked Ibn al-Qasim about two Christian men who arrived in Dar al-Islam, and each one claimed the other as his slave. Ibn al-Qasim rejected the claims of both (unless they were supported by evidence) and considered both to be free. Sahnun asked another series of questions of Ashhab (recorded by al-'Utbi) that tackled the intersection of slave status and aman (touched on earlier). Ashhab opined that if a harbi slave came to the land of the Muslims without his master (in flight? as his agent?) and converted or remained an infidel but secured aman, his master would have no claims to him even if he subsequently arrived in Dar al-Islam. If the master was already present in Dar al-Islam, however, the situation would be different: if a harbi sought aman, came to Dar al-Islam, and converted or remained in his religion, and a slave of his followed, the slave still belonged to his master. If the slave converted to Islam but the master did not, he should be sold.[46]

Muslims ransomed fellow Muslims (according to Malik they were required to do so), and the masa'il also provide evidence of Christians ransoming fellow Christians. In this context additional challenging questions might be posed about border crossings and legal status, for example, of slave mothers and children. Al-'Utbi records that Ibn al-Qasim was asked about

45. Ibn Rushd, *Bayan,* 3:23.

46. Ibn Rushd, *Bayan,* 3:51–52, 52–54. Sahnun posed the question to Ibn al-Qasim whether slaves who converted to Islam in Dar al-Harb were no longer the property of their masters; Ibn al-Qasim replied that he never heard Malik give an opinion about this, but that in his view their status as property would not change unless they came to Dar al-Islam, and then it would (Sahnun, *Mudawwana,* 2:22–23); see also al-Qayrawani, *Nawadir wa-ziyadat,* 3:283–284.

the following situation: A Muslim bought a woman who had been captured in the borderlands, and she became pregnant by him. Her family arrived to ransom her; should her owner accept the ransom? Ibn al-Qasim said no but agreed that her owner could manumit her and accept the ransom after her womb had recovered from his semen (after a waiting period) even if she had given birth to his child. Her slave status here was the obstacle to exchange for ransom (as an *umm walad*, mother of her master's child, she could not be sold). Ibn Rushd asserts in no uncertain terms in his commentary that if she were pregnant, she should not be ransomed (while pregnant) because the child born in the land of war would become Christian.[47]

Two questions Yahya ibn Yahya posed to Ibn al-Qasim addressed the connection between place of birth and identity. The first reads as follows: If someone was born in Dar al-Islam to Muslim parents and was taken captive as a child (with his parents or without them) and became Christian, should he be asked to repent and return to Islam (presumably if he were later taken captive and brought back to Dar al-Islam)? Ibn al-Qasim's response treats such an individual as someone who apostasized before the age of legal responsibility; he replied that the individual should not be killed, but he should be subject to beatings, intimidation, and roughness, if necessary, to bring him back to Islam. Ibn al-Qasim added that as someone who was born free in Dar al-Islam to free Muslims, he should not be enslaved (he should not be treated as booty by his captors). Ibn al-Qasim's response to Yahya's second question about the treatment of an individual born to Muslims (captives) in the domain of polytheism who became Christian (leaving the religion of his parents) was different. If this individual was captured, he should be treated like any other captive from the land of the enemy. If the imam granted him life, he would be part of the collective booty of the Muslims who captured him.

Ibn Rushd's discussion focuses the issues and reveals differences of opinion among the early authorities. He explains that Ibn al-Qasim's opinion expresses an understanding that a person is subject to the law (*hukm*) of the place where he lives. The person born in Dar al-Harb to Muslim parents is subject to the law of Dar al-Harb, not to the laws of Islam (the individual in the second case would thus not be considered an apostate). The opposing view is that children born to Muslims (or a Muslim father) are Muslim even if they are born in Dar al-Harb. He also points out that the status of the

---

47. Ibn Rushd, *Bayan*, 3:91–92; the questioner, as al-ʿUtbi records, was Abu Zayd ibn al-Ghamr. Ibn al-Qasim disapproved of a Muslim having intercourse with his wife or slave in captivity for fear that he would have children in the land of war (*Bayan*, 3:35).

Muslim child raised in Dar al-Harb depends, in the view of some, on whether his father was (or parents were) with him in Dar al-Harb; according to some, if he was too young to know his religion and was raised in "unbelief," he may legally be treated as booty (as a harbi) if he were captured and would not be compelled to return to Islam.[48]

The issue of identity, territory, and paternity (and, explicitly, maternity) came up in other questions about the status of the children of free Muslim or dhimmi women who were born in captivity (the mothers having become pregnant during captivity) who were subsequently restored to Dar al-Islam when they were swept up in a Muslim raid. The status of the mothers in these circumstances was not in dispute: a Muslim woman would be restored to her free status, and a dhimmi would resume her status as dhimmi. The status of the children (young and older), however, was at issue—were they free, or would they belong to the treasury (as fay')? Ibn Habib strongly disagreed with Ibn al-Qasim's opinion that older children (those who had attained puberty) of both a Muslim woman and a dhimmi woman were fay' (identified as Christian captives). He was especially loath to see the offspring of a free Muslim, albeit a freeborn Muslim woman (the paternity of the children is not indicated but is implicitly Christian) lose his status because of captivity; he identified impregnation under captivity with coercion when he asked: What of the child born to a Muslim woman who was raped by a Christian in the land of Islam—would that child not be Muslim? If she were raped by a slave, would not the child be free?[49]

Although law (hukm) was different in Dar al-Harb and Dar al-Islam, and the legal status of an individual changed from one domain to another as defined by the law of the land, masa'il about the legal identity of liminal types conjure up a more complicated situation and test this boundary between two legal systems. Dhimmis who found themselves in Dar al-Harb because of circumstance (perhaps in the fog of battle, perhaps because they were taken captive in a raid), slaves who were taken captive or were fugitives, and Muslims who became Christians in Dar al-Harb and reverted to Islam

---

48. Ibn Rushd, *Bayan*, 3:31–34. Ana Fernández Félix discusses these two perspectives on identity and the concept of *fiṭra* (the original identity of a newborn is Muslim, and the parents make the infant a Christian or a Jew or introduce him/her to another faith) in her chapter, "Children on the Frontiers of Islam," in *Conversions islamiques: Identités religieuses en Islam Mediterranéen/Islamic Conversions: Religious Identities in Mediterranean Islam* (Paris: Maisonneuve et Larose, 2001), 61–72. The implications of fitra were subject to discussion and debate when it came to application.

49. Al-Qayrawani, *Nawadir wa-ziyadat*, 3:281–282. The children of a slave woman taken captive and then recovered by the Muslims belong to her master, according to Ibn al-Qasim; Ashhab says that they are fay'.

would likely find their legal identity unchanged when they returned to Dar al-Islam. Children born to Muslim parents (or only a Muslim mother) in Dar al-Harb who crossed back into Dar al-Islam, however, tested the limits of the "border" with the limits of legal-religious identity by birth, paternity, and upbringing (age is an issue in this context). Jurists like Ibn Habib were willing to consider captivity as an extenuating circumstance when they were considering the legal-religious identity of a child born to a Muslim woman in Dar al-Harb.

The masa'il collected in chapters on jihad in the ninth- and tenth-century juridical texts define a border between Dar al-Islam and Dar al-Harb that is more jurisdictional than ideological. Jurists established authority over the "border" through their elaboration of its significance in matters of legal status and legal rights and, in the process, affirmed their authority over identity and relationships. The judges of the borderlands and the jurists they consulted defended the "border" by patrolling the boundaries of Islam. In the process, they reinforced the ruler's (and their own) commitment to the 'ahd al-dhimma; as we have seen, many of the masa'il assert the integrity of dhimmi status across the "border" and affirm the difference between a harbi and a dhimmi; at the same time, they acknowledge that the status of the harbi can change with aman or with settlement and payment of the jizya.

The collections of masa'il present a diffuse perspective on jihad. Ibn Rushd's *Muqaddamat mumahhadat* is described as a commentary on the subjects raised and addressed in Sahnun's *Mudawwana*; the chapter on jihad is essentially an early twelfth-century treatise on jihad that brings together commentary on the Qur'anic revelations about jihad and the material covered in many of the masa'il to provide a coherent definition of legitimate warfare. In this representation the practice of jihad as divine obligation (*fard*) is contingent and subject to interpretation.[50] The text allows us to see how the masa'il and the practice and experience of warfare in the thughur informed a juridical conceptualization of jihad.[51]

Ibn Rushd's commentary on al-'Utbi's *Mustakhraja*, as we have seen, reflects his efforts to systematize legal opinion. His commentary typically

---

50. Ibn Rushd (al-Jadd), *al-Muqaddamat al-mumahhadat li-bayan ma iqtadathu rusum al-Mudawwana min al-ahkam al-shar'iyat wa-l-tahsilat al-muhkamat li-ummahat masā'iliha al-mushkilat*, ed. Zakariyya 'Amirat (Beirut: Dar al-Kutub al-'Ilmiyya, 2002), 1:171–191.

51. Jurists within the Maliki madhhab and across different madhhabs structured their discussions of jihad variously, with different emphases on themes and sources. David Cook discusses the Andalusis Ibn Hazm (d. 1064) and Ibn al-'Arabi (d. 1148/1149) in *Understanding Jihad* (Berkeley: University of California Press, 2005), 57–63.

evaluates the opinion expressed in a particular mas'ala in *al-Mustakhraja* by referring to and assessing different juridical opinions; he sometimes introduces supporting or contradicting evidence and analogies drawn from the Qur'an or the sunna of the Prophet and the early community. Ibn Rushd's assessment of legal opinions and his conclusions indicating what he considered most correct were part of a process of shaping and guiding the Maliki madhhab of al-Andalus and the Maghrib. Ibn Rushd's interpretive methods and orientation (*dhahab*) are more fully on display in *al-Muqaddamat al-mumahhadat*.

Each chapter of *al-Muqaddamat* is devoted to a subject of *fiqh* (jurisprudence) and is divided into subheadings. The chapter on jihad has six: the definition of jihad; booty; on what the mushrikun take from the Muslims; *ribāṭ* (defense of the borderlands); captives; and jizya. Each heading begins with a lexicographical definition followed by exegesis of relevant Qur'anic verses. The identification and discussion of significant issues are integrated with and follow the exegesis and include discussion of juridical points of difference (*ikhtilāfāt*). Ibn Rushd directs the discussion so that his survey and summation of opinions culminate in his own interpretation.

The definition of jihad begins with the fundamentals: j-h-d at root means "to exert oneself," and exerting oneself (striving) in the cause (way) of God and the promotion of his word is the path to the Garden: "And strive you in his cause as you ought to strive" (Qur'an 22:78).[52] Ibn Rushd identifies four types of jihad: jihad of the heart (exerting control over one's base emotions and desires); jihad of the tongue and of the hand (both efforts to restrain others from doing wrong); and jihad of the sword (fighting the unbelievers over religion and in the cause of God until they accept Islam or pay the jizya and are humbled). The discussion of the chapter, like the content of the masa'il, focuses on jihad of the sword. He begins with praise for its merits as "the best of works" and the promise of the Garden for those who die fighting in the cause of God: "O you who believe! Shall I lead you to a bargain that will save you from a grievous penalty? That you believe in God and his messenger, and that you strive (your utmost) in the cause of God, with your property and your persons: that will be best for you, if you but knew! He will forgive you your sins and admit you to gardens beneath which rivers flow, and to beautiful mansions in gardens of eternity: that is indeed the supreme achievement. And another (favor will he bestow),

---

52. Ibn Rushd, *Muqaddamat mumahhadat*; the first section of the chapter on jihad corresponds to 1:171–179.

which you do love—help from God and a speedy victory. So give the glad tidings to the believers" (Qur'an 61:10–13).

Ibn Rushd presents the evolution of jihad in the Prophet's lifetime through Qur'anic exegesis, starting with the first ten years of Muhammad's mission when he was in Mecca and did not have permission to fight (Qur'an 15:94, 5:13, 2:256). When Muhammad emigrated to Medina, God granted him and the believers permission to fight against those who fought them: "To those against whom war is made, permission is given (to fight), because they are wronged—and verily, God is most powerful for their aid" (Qur'an 22:39; 2:191 and 4:90 are also cited). The Muslims fought only under these defensive conditions for eight years until the revelation of the "sword verse": "Fight those who believe not in God nor the Last Day, nor hold that forbidden which has been forbidden by God and his messenger, nor acknowledge the religion of truth, from among the People of the Book until they pay the jizya with willing submission and feel themselves subdued" (9:29). Ibn Rushd explains developments in the terms and qualifications of this warfare with further exegesis, including a shift from the requirement that all the Muslims fight together to a division of the community into warriors and those who "devote themselves to study of religion" (9:122) and the understanding that the obligation to fight does not apply to every individual Muslim.[53] This is further elaborated in the discussion of the six requisites of a fighter: that he be a Muslim, a male, free, of age, sound of mind, and sound of body (this includes having enough wherewithal to meet his basic needs). Proper conduct of jihad requires proper intention, so the warrior should fight to raise the word of God and strive for the reward of God.

Ibn Rushd's exegesis of the obligation of jihad informs and supports his observation that jihad in his day was an obligation that fell only on the qualified and was satisfied for the community as a whole by those who undertook it. This included guarding the far reaches of Muslim habitation (*aṭrāf al-muslimīn*) and shoring up the thughur. If Muslims were protecting the border region, there was no need for other Muslims to participate in jihad unless the enemy invaded. (The discussion goes on to consider at some length flight from the enemy and when it might be permissible for

---

53. Vincent Lagardère argues that after the battle of Zallaqa in 1086 a new conception of jihad as an obligation for all Muslims emerged in al-Andalus and the Maghrib; see *Les Almoravides: Le djihad andalou (1106–1143)* (Paris: Harmattan, 1998), 163–188. The interest in persuading Muslims to take up arms in circumstances of danger and the ways and means of mobilization do not necessarily require a reconception of jihad. Ibn Rushd, who supported the substitution of jihad for pilgrimage for Andalusis and Maghribis in this period of insecurity, does not present jihad as a universal obligation in this treatise.

Muslims to do so: If the number of the enemy is double that of the Muslims? If they are better armed and equipped?) The section on ribat reflects the view that defense of the borderlands is an aspect of jihad—the act of defending the region is called *ribāṭ*, Ibn Rushd explains, because it "ties together" (r-b-t) the openings of the thughur. The words of the Prophet highlight the merits of this defense: "The ribat of one night in the cause of God is better than a thousand nights of standing and days of fasting without break-fast." (Forty days is the recommended minimum for ribat.) The text establishes that sometimes sparing the blood of the Muslims is as important as, or more important than, shedding the blood of the enemies. Ibn Rushd, in fact, asserts that it is not correct to say that either protection of the Muslims or fighting in the land of the enemy is absolutely (in all circumstances) better. As a (possible) qualification, Ibn Habib is quoted for his remark that someone living in the borderlands with his family and children is not a *murābiṭ* (participant in ribat) because ribat requires one to leave one's home and security; ribat is choosing to abide in a place of fear.[54]

Booty, of course, was a benefit of successful jihad and thus the object of considerable juridical attention. Ibn Rushd uses Qur'anic verses to differentiate between *ghanīma* (booty taken in warfare) and *fay'* (gains acquired from the enemy without fighting).[55] Discussion centers on how the spoils are divided in agreement with statements in the Qur'an, such as the following: "And know that out of all the booty that you may acquire (in war), a fifth share is assigned to God—and to the Messenger, and to near relatives, orphans, the needy, and the wayfarer" (Qur'an 8:41). Ibn Rushd provides various views of how the fifth (*khums*) should be distributed and on what the fifth may be assessed. One of the tricky questions (with ramifications) was how to treat the land itself: the Prophet took the khums from the land of Khaybar (an oasis north of Medina inhabited by Jews) and divided the land; on the other hand, 'Umar ibn al-Khattab (the second caliph) left the lands conquered beyond the Arabian Peninsula in the possession of their inhabitants in exchange for the jizya (the imposition of a land tax [*kharāj*] was another matter).[56]

---

54. Ibn Rushd, *Muqaddamat mumahhadat*, 1:183–184.

55. On *ghanīma*, see sura 8:41; on *fay'*, see sura 59:6, 7; Ibn Rushd, *Muqaddamat mumahhadat*, 1:179–181.

56. Jurists struggled to reconcile these two precedents (and the practice of leaving the ahl al-jizya in control of their lands). For example, it can be argued, as Ibn Rushd reports, that the Prophet divided the land of Khaybar because God promised it to the people who pledged allegiance to Muhammad (in anticipation of war with the Meccans before the conclusion of the treaty of Hudaybiyya) in the

The subject of "what the mushrikun acquire from the Muslims" is a structured discussion of many of the same masa'il we have discussed about the status and rights of people and property crossing borders back and forth, for example, the envoy with aman who arrives with a Muslim slave in his entourage, or the Muslim child taken captive who becomes Christian and is then recovered by the Muslims in a raid. Ibn Rushd explains that there are thirty-six masa'il or legal questions that attend this subject, and he represents them as the multiplication of six categories of things that the enemy gains from the Muslims and six situations. He outlines and describes the categories ("things") under consideration: freeborn Muslims, freeborn dhimmis, the money and belongings (including slaves) of Muslims and dhimmis, mothers and children of the Muslims, slaves who have permission to trade, and slaves who have contracts for their manumission; and the six situations: the "thing" is sold, brought with aman, taken as booty, converts to Islam, is among the enemy when the enemy accepts a truce (*hudna*), or is among the enemy when the enemy seeks terms of surrender and agrees to pay the jizya.[57] Ibn Rushd's interest here is in the captivity of Muslims, dhimmis, and slaves and their legal status or identity when they cross back into Dar al-Islam, depending on how they come back under Islamic legal jurisdiction. His structuring of the subject in terms of categories and contingencies acknowledges the "border" as a boundary tester. The organization of the discussion expresses control over a multiplicity of complex situations, but it also asserts the principle of contingency.

Ibn Rushd summarizes the Maliki position on how Muslims should handle captives as a matter of the imam or ruler's discretion. He can choose to kill the captive, enslave him, give him aman and let him go, take ransom for him, or give him dhimma and impose the jizya on him. In Ibn Rushd's view, all the relevant Qur'anic verses support this view (8:57, 47:4, 8:67). The imam should make his decision on the basis of the welfare of the Muslims, so he may choose to kill the captive known for his horsemanship and bravery or for harassing the Muslims, or he may ransom him for a great deal

---

following verse: "Allah has permitted you many gains that you shall acquire and he has given you these beforehand and he has restrained the hands of men from you" (sura 48:20). Some thus say that the division of the oasis was a specific event and not a precedent for future division of conquered land. Ibn Rushd, *Muqaddamat mumahhadat*, 1:180–181. The matter was complicated by variations in accounts of the conquest and division of Khaybar, the Prophet's subsequent decision to allow the Banu Khaybar to remain to cultivate the palms, and 'Umar's later expulsion of the Banu Khaybar from the oasis. See al-Baladhuri's history of the conquest of Khaybar in *The Origins of the Islamic State*, trans. Philip Khuri Hitti (New York: Columbia University Press, 1914), 1:42–49.

57. Ibn Rushd, *Muqaddamat mumahhadat*, 1:182–183.

of money (a range of options for the fate of different sorts of captives are offered). Ibn Rushd presents some differences of opinion about the interpretation of the relevant verses; some argue that Qur'an 8:57 abrogates the other two and that the captive should be killed in every case; some say that 47:4 abrogates 8:57 and that the captive should be let go or ransomed in every case. Ibn Rushd considers these far-fetched and points to the example of the Prophet, who both killed and kept captives; his actions clarify what is in the Qur'an (and the view that the imam has discretion).[58]

Ibn Rushd's discussion of the jizya defines the ahl al-dhimma and distinguishes them from other unbelievers. The jizya is taken in exchange for safety and security of persons and property and the right to remain in "unbelief." Ibn Rushd clarifies that there are two forms of jizya: the jizya collected by agreement with the unbelievers and the jizya that may be imposed on those who are conquered or captured by force. The main questions under discussion include how much the jizya should be in both circumstances (is there a minimum or maximum?), how it should be assessed (on individuals, on the collective, or on land?), and when (at the start of the year or when the Muslims pay their *zakāt* [legal alms] at the end of the year?). The *jizya ṣulḥiyya* (the conciliatory or peacefully agreed-on jizya) is set by the terms of the *ṣulḥ* or surrender treaty (for Ibn Rushd, the default payment should be four dinars if the terms are unclear). Ibn Rushd says that in his view, if the ahl al-harb offer what 'Umar accepted from those he defeated by force (*ahl al-'anwa*) and are ready to pay it "out of hand" and submit (according to Qur'an 9:29), then the imam has no choice but to accept ('Umar imposed a jizya of four dinars).[59] He notes that Malik, following the example of 'Umar, considered the jizya on the ahl al-'anwa to be four dinars or its equivalent of forty dirhams. The jizya does not apply to children, women, and slaves. Notably (in light of the previous discussion of harbis who sought to settle in Dar al-Islam), Ibn Rushd observes that Malik assigned the jizya of the ahl al-'anwa to any harbi seeking aman in order become a dhimmi.

The definition of the jizya as a poll tax on free dhimmi men emerged out of a discourse about whether the jizya should be imposed on individuals, the

---

58. Ibn Rushd, *Muqaddamat mumahhadat*, 1:184–186.

59. Malik set the jizya for the ahl al-'anwa at four dinars or forty dirhams, following 'Umar's precedent. However, 'Umar also imposed three days of lodging and food for the Muslims on the dhimmis, and Malik did not consider this part of the jizya but in excess of it. (Al-Shafi'i set a minimum of one dinar and no maximum for the ahl al-'anwa; Abu Hanifa would offer a sliding scale for men of different means.) Ibn Rushd, *Muqaddamat mumahhadat*, 1:187; Ibn Rushd, *Bayan* 4:189–191.

collective, or land and a related discourse about whether those subject to payment of the jizya owned the land they lived on and cultivated. Regarding the latter issue, Ibn Rushd presents as predominant the view that jizya payers did own their land and could transfer it through sale and inheritance to others. The discussion of when the jizya should be paid (Malik did not stipulate) leads Ibn Rushd to the analogy of the Muslims' payment of zakat at the end of the year and his preference for this date. He says that even though the jizya is a form of humiliation, while the zakat is a form of purification, because the dhimmis live in security, confirmed in their own religion and moving freely among the Muslims, what is required of them (payment) is (in some way comparable to) what is required of the Muslims (and so payment at the end of the year for the Muslims can support the argument for payment at the end of the year for dhimmis).[60]

Although Ibn Rushd lived and wrote later than the time frame of this book, his legal writings and opinions illuminate trends unfolding in the centuries before his death that have been the subject of our attention. His work exemplifies how Maliki jurisprudence engaged with methods of legal reasoning promoted by the partisans of *usul al-fiqh* (the sources of jurisprudence). These "sources" are primarily the Qur'an and hadith as well as analogy and consensus; the reader has seen evidence of how the chapter on jihad in *al-Muqaddimat* is particularly grounded in both Qur'anic exegesis and the Maliki masa'il literature; it refers to the example (and statements) of the Prophet as well as the opinion of Malik, and uses analogy when there is no evident position in the sources. Ibn Rushd's work also embodies the trend in legal writing toward synthesis and direction. He presents an understanding of jihad that is streamlined in such a way as to provide a practical guide for Maliki judges and jurists.[61]

---

60. Ibn Rushd, *Muqaddamat mumahhadat*, 1:186–191 (section on jizya). Ibn Rushd also makes the analogy to rent, which is paid at the end of the year, and the land tax, which is paid after the harvest. The last section of the chapter is about what peoples may be granted the jizya.

61. It is interesting to compare Ibn Rushd al-Jadd's chapter on jihad with that of his grandson, Ibn Rushd al-Hafid. The grandson (d. 1198) was also a jurist and a qadi (of Seville), as well as a physician and philosopher (he is better known in the west as Averroës). His discussion of jihad in *Bidayat al-mujtahid wa-nihayat al-muqtasid* reproduces some of the discussion of the earlier work but is more general in content; he outlines what "the jurists" agree on or disagree about, often without specific identification. He is not concerned directly with the masa'il, and as a corollary, the ahl al-dhimma do not appear as a matter of interest until the end, when the subject of jizya leads to the question whether they are liable to a duty on goods that they trade. See Ibn Rushd (al-Hafid), *The Distinguished Jurist's Primer*, trans. Imran Ahsan Khan Nyazee (Reading, England: Garnet, 2000), 1:454–487. On the Almohad context and character of *Bidayat al-mujtahid*, see Maribel Fierro, "The Legal Policies of the Almohad Caliphs and Ibn Rushd's *Bidayat al-mujtahid*," *Journal of Islamic Studies* 10 (1999): 226–248.

Ibn Rushd's perspective on jihad is informed by and is part of the boundary-making process described throughout this book. Particularly intriguing is how Ibn Rushd expresses a practical and politically flexible understanding of the obligation of jihad that emphasizes contingency and the discretion of the ruler, especially when his work is considered more specifically in the historical context of al-Andalus in the late eleventh and early twelfth centuries. The historical contextualization demonstrates how Ibn Rushd's assertion of the importance of the imam's discretion was put into practice. Ibn Rushd and contemporary jurists offered legal opinions that accommodated political and practical circumstances and were nuanced rather than belligerent toward Christians who tested the limits of their protection, even in a context of jihad. The following discussion further advances the idea that the commitment of jurists (and rulers) to the principles of the ʿahd al-dhimma (pact of protection) mediated conceptions of and interactions with "the enemy."

In Ibn Rushd's lifetime (1058–1126) Alfonso VI of Leon-Castile expanded his domains far south of the Duero River (notably by taking Toledo in 1085), and the Almoravids crossed the Straits of Gibraltar to check his ambitions at the behest of the petty rulers of al-Andalus. In 1090 the Almoravid amir Yusuf ibn Tashufin determined to assert dominion over al-Andalus and secured control over Muslim Granada and Malaga and then Cordoba, Seville, Jaen, Almeria, Denia, and Murcia. The struggle for Valencia (featuring "the Cid" Rodrigo de Bivar) lasted for five years until 1102, when Alfonso VI decided that he could not hold the city and departed with its Christian population; by the end of the decade Zaragoza too came under Almoravid control and the rule of the Commander of the Muslims in Marrakesh. However, the "border" between Muslim- and Christian-controlled territories did not stabilize with the defeats of the armies of Alfonso VI (or the king's death without a male heir) and the consolidation of Almoravid rule. Alfonso I of Aragon, "the Battler," wrested control of Zaragoza away from the Almoravids in 1118 and began campaigning aggressively in al-Andalus. Ibn Rushd thus served as qadi of Cordoba and prayer leader (1117–1121) in a period of external threat and related internal unrest. In 1119 or 1120 the population of Cordoba rebelled against its governor, Abu Bakr Yahya ibn Rawad. Violence broke out between the city's inhabitants and the Berber garrison, reportedly over an incident of sexual misconduct on the occasion of the feast of the Sacrifice; when the governor failed to punish the perpetrator and turned on the protestors, they attacked the qaṣr (palace) and put him to flight. The Almoravid ruler ʿAli ibn Yusuf ibn Tashufin led an army of Berbers from North Africa to besiege the city in the spring of 1121, and the city finally came to terms. Historical accounts indicate the involvement of the legal-religious authorities (probably including Ibn Rushd) in the negotiations between the angry population and the governor and then with 'Ali ibn Yusuf.

A fatwa that Ibn Rushd gave in response to questions posed by Ali's brother Tamim ibn Yusuf ibn Tashufin, the Almoravid resident commander of al-Andalus from 1107 to 1126, demonstrates the jurist's application of legal principles he commented on in *al-Bayan* and distilled in *al-Muqaddamat*. In essence, Christian merchants from Toledo came to Cordoba to trade in a time of truce. Some Cordobans claimed that they recognized among the items for sale things that had been taken from them by a raiding party they were certain had come from Toledo, in a raid that also had taken Muslim captives. How should the matter of the goods be handled? If, as the Cordobans claimed, the merchants were holding captives back in Toledo that they had taken during the truce, did the Cordobans have the right to hold the merchants hostage until the captives were returned? Ibn Rushd replied that if the Toledans raided in Muslim territory and seized Muslim goods and took Muslims captive, the protection they were granted by the truce would not apply because the truce granted them the right to enter Muslim lands to trade, not to raid, seize goods, and take captives. He further replied that if the merchants were kept as hostages until the return of the captives and the goods and this came to pass, then the truce would endure; if they refused these terms, then the truce would be broken, a state of war would apply, the merchants would become captives, and their belongings would become fay'. Any of the belongings that were confirmed to belong to individuals before the raid would be returned to them.[62]

Ibn Rushd is identified with the Almoravid ruler's decision to expel some of the Christians of Cordoba, Seville, and Granada in 1126 after Alfonso the Battler's campaign in 1125 (or rather to deport them—fatwas speak to the resettlement of Christians from Granada and Seville in the Maghrib).[63] Alfonso defeated the Almoravid army at Aransol, near Cordoba, on March 9, 1126, and by the end of the month Ibn Rushd set out for Marrakesh to explain to the Commander of the Muslims, 'Ali ibn Yusuf ibn Tashufin, what

---

62. Al-Wansharisi, *Mi'yar*, 9:598–599.

63. See Vincent Lagardère, "Communautés mozarabes et pouvoir Almoravide en 519 H/1125 en Andalus," *Studia Islamica* 67 (1988): 99–119; and Delfina Serrano, "Dos fetuas sobre la expulsión de mozárabes al Magreb en 1126," *Anaquel de Estudios Árabes* 2 (1991): 163–182. Lagardère has written extensively on the Almoravids and refers to these events in a number of contexts. See Lagardère, *Almoravides*, for a history of Almoravid rule in al-Andalus.

was happening on the peninsula. He was well received by the Almoravid ruler, and as they discussed in a number of meetings what prompted him to come, the amir took his counsel to heart. Shortly after Ibn Rushd returned from this trip, he took to bed with the illness that brought about his demise.[64]

The historian Ibn ʿIdhari provides more details (probably drawing on an account by Ibn al-Sayrafi that is no longer extant).[65] He reports that Ibn Rushd informed the amir of the treachery and deceit of the pact-protected Christians (referred to as *al-muʿāhidūn* or the pact-protected), explaining what they brought about with their secret appeal to Alfonso and how this action broke the ʿahd and violated the terms of the dhimma (Ibn ʿIdhari reports elsewhere the communications between the Christians of Granada and Alfonso and describes how Christians rushed to join forces with Alfonso when he began his passage southward).[66] According to the historian, the amir paid close attention to Ibn Rushd and decided to expel the rebellious Christians from the strategically important towns and regions in which they lived and transfer them across the straits as the least punishment obligatory for their treachery. In the course of their conversation, the jurist advised the amir to construct a wall around Marrakesh, and the amir undertook this immediately and ordered that the walls of the cities of al-Andalus be inspected (and attended to). This order was fulfilled after the dismissal of the governor of Cordoba and Granada and his replacement by two amirs, one for each region.[67]

The Almoravid rulers regularly sought the counsel of Maliki *fuqahāʾ* (jurists) and commonly relied on the qadis of al-Andalus as local authorities

64. Al-Nubahi, *Kitab al-marqaba al-ʿulya*, ed. E. Lévi-Provençal (Cairo: Scribe Egyptien, 1948), 98–99.

65. Ibn ʿIdhari, *al-Bayan al-mughrib* (portion having to do with Almoravid rule), published by Ambrosio Huici-Miranda, "Un fragmento inédito de Ibn ʿIdari sobre los Almoravides," *Hesperis Tamuda* 2 (1961): 85–87 (henceforth "Fragment inédito"). *Al-Hulal al-mawshiyya* (author unknown) provides a similar account, observing that Ibn Rushd gave the amir a fatwa authorizing the expulsion. See *al-Hulal mawshiyya*, ed. I. S. Allouche (Rabat: Institute des Hautes Études Marocaines, 1936), 75, 79–81; Spanish translation and edition by Ambrosio Huici Miranda, *al-Hulal al-mawshiyya: Crónica árabe de las dinastías Almorávide, Almohade y Benimerín* (Tetuan: Editora Marroqui, 1952), 108, 115–116. For further discussion and the text of a letter issued by ʿAli ibn Tashufin referring to the actions he will undertake in response to his meeting with, and on the advice of, the *faqīh mushāwar* (jurisconsult) Ibn Rushd, see Mahmud Makki, "Wathaʾiq taʾrikhiyya jadida ʿan ʿasr al-murabitin," *Revista del Instituto de Estudios Islámicos en Madrid* 7–8 (1959–1960): 123–127 (letter, 167).

66. See Ibn ʿIdhari, "Fragmento inédito," 83–84; *Hulal mawshiyya*, Arabic, 75–77; Spanish, 109–111.

67. Ibn al-Athir, *Annales du Maghreb et de l'Espagne*, trans. Emile Fagnan (Algiers: Typographie Adolphe Jourdan, 1901), 525–526; unabridged facsimile reproduction published by Adamant Media (Chestnut Hill, MA) in 2006 as an Elibron Classics Replica Edition. *Hulal mawshiyya*, Arabic, 70–71; Spanish, 103–104.

and intermediaries.[68] Shortly after the expulsion of the Christians in 1126, ʿAli ibn Yusuf sought fatwas from the qadi of Granada, Ibn Ward, and other Andalusi fuqaha' about the sale of the Christians' property in al-Andalus and the status of their churches and monasteries and the pious endowments that supported them (more specifically, the inquiry concerned the property of the Christians from Seville who had been relocated to Meknes).[69] Ibn Ward's fatwa is preserved in al-Wansharisi's collection.[70] He affirms, with some elaboration of the practicalities involved, that the Christians can arrange for the sale of their private property. Considering whether the relocated Christians have the right to build new churches and monasteries, he demurs and proposes that they fulfill their religious obligations in their homes, without display. As for their churches and monasteries in al-Andalus, the *aḥbās* (pious endowments) of dhimmis are not inviolate (unlike those of Muslims), and unless the founders of particular endowments come forward, the property and income of the ahbas properly devolve to the treasury of the Muslims. Ibn Ward also considered questions posed by the amir's son, Abu Bakr ibn ʿAli ibn Yusuf ibn Tashufin, governor of Seville, about the status of protected Christians from Seville who fled to enemy territory and were then recovered, and about the status of the Christians who had converted to Islam in Seville before the expulsion. In Ibn Ward's view, summarized here, those who fled and then were recaptured and did not resist the Muslim captors and had not joined up with the enemy forces or had a good excuse for their actions (and thereby did not violate the terms of their protection) were nonetheless in the same category as their coreligionists who were expelled and should be expelled accordingly. His position is not based on whether these Christians violated the terms of their protection but

---

68. See Rachid El Hour, "The Andalusian Qadi in the Almoravid Period: Political and Judicial Authority," *Studia Islamica* 90 (2000): 67–83; Vincent Lagardère, "La haute judicature à l'epoque Almoravide en al-Andalus," *Al-Qantara* 7 (1986): 135–228. The reported burning of copies of al-Ghazali's *Ihya ʿulum al-din* in 1107 should not be equated with the narrow-mindedness of the Almoravid amir (ʿAli ibn Yusuf ibn Tashufin) or the Andalusi legal-juridical authorities without further investigation. See Delfina Serrano, "Why Did the Scholars of al-Andalus Distrust al-Ghazali? Ibn Rushd al-Jadd's *Fatwa* on *Awliya' Allah*," *Der Islam* 83 (2006): 137–156. See also Lagardère, *Almoravides*, 189–244.

69. Serrano discusses this fatwa and one by the qadi ʿIyad of Granada (d. 1148–1149) on the income of a pious endowment that had once been a church but had since become a mosque (after the deportation of the Granadan Christians in 1126) and provides translations of both fatwas in "Dos Fetuas"; see also Muhammad ibn ʿIyad, *Madhahib al-hukkam fi nawazil al-ahkam (La actuación de los jueces en los procesos judiciales)*, trans. Delfina Serrano (Madrid: Consejo Superior de Investigaciones Científicas, 1998), 359–361. See also Lagardère, "Commonautés mozarabes," 112–113.

70. Al-Wansharisi, *Miʿyar*, 8:56–64.

reflects respect for the general order of expulsion. As for the converts, Ibn Ward considered their conversions valid even if they were inspired by fear of expulsion. He gave the governor discretion in this case: he could still expel the converts if he deemed that they might cause harm to the Muslims.

In an opinion permitting the deported Christians to build churches in their new places of residence (differing from Ibn Ward's position), Ibn al-Hajj, appointed qadi of Cordoba not long after the death of Ibn Rushd and a contemporary of Ibn Ward, explains that the amir expelled Christians (*naṣārā*) who were protected by the ʿahd (*muʿāhidūn*) as a precaution to protect the Muslims and as an act compelled by fear.[71] He asserts that they had the same rights according to the ʿahd al-dhimma (also referred to as ʿaqd al-dhimma) that they had had before and that because the Commander of the Muslims moved them for the reasons he did, each contingent had the right to build one place of worship (they were prohibited from beating clappers). Notably, Ibn al-Hajj does not ascribe the relocation of the Christians to their treachery or their violation of the pact of protection, but to the amir's decision based on his concern for the welfare of the Muslims.

The text of Ibn Rushd's fatwa is lost.[72] His reported assertion that the Christians of Seville and elsewhere had violated the terms of their protection by aiding and participating in Alfonso's campaign is consonant with the masa'il discussed previously in this chapter (and extracted from his *Bayan*). But what was the justification for deportation? The fatwas of Ibn Ward and Ibn al-Hajj addressing some of the legal problems arising from the expulsion and relocation suggest that Ibn Rushd's fatwa was not entirely authoritative. If the Christians violated the terms of their protection, why were they allowed to sell their property in al-Andalus and live as protected people in Meknes and elsewhere in the Maghrib? Ibn Ward may have considered the ruler's edict sufficient in itself. Ibn al-Hajj, interestingly enough, provides a different argument altogether. In any case the ruler's exercise of his discretion is paramount. Perhaps Ibn Rushd developed his argument from the point of the violation of the ʿahd al-dhimma along these lines: having

---

71. Ibn al-Hajj's opinion is recorded in al-Wansharisi, *Miʿyar*, 2:215, in a fifteenth-century fatwa about the status of synagogues in Touat (referred to earlier). It should be noted that Vincent Lagardère identifies the Ibn al-Hajj referred to in the fatwa as the twelfth-century qadi of Cordoba (d. 1135), but John O. Hunwick identifies him as Ibn al-Hajj al-Fasi (d. 1336). See Vincent Lagardère, *Histoire et societé en occident musulmane au Moyen Age* (Madrid: Casa de Velázquez, 1995), 65–66; and John O. Hunwick, "The Rights of *Dhimmi*s to Maintain a Place of Worship: A Fifteenth-Century *Fatwa* from Tlemçen," *Al-Qantara* 12 (1991): 141.

72. See al-Wansharisi, *Miʿyar*, 2:151, for a brief reference to Ibn Rushd's fatwa calling for expulsion of the Christians.

lost their right to protection, the Christians who supported Alfonso the Battler devolved to the status of captives, and their fate was up to the ruler to decide. As Ibn Rushd outlined in *al-Muqaddamat*, they might be killed, given aman and freed, ransomed, enslaved, or granted dhimma and have the jizya imposed on them. Once the Christians were relocated from Seville, for example, to Meknes, the jizya was imposed on them, and they formally became dhimmis again.

Questions about the "border" were often of immediate importance to Ibn Rushd and his colleagues. Despite the sometimes threatening situation (as Alfonso's armies swept through the countryside toward Granada and engaged the Muslims in battle not far from Cordoba) and moments of political upheaval, Ibn Rushd remained committed to the principles of legal protection on paper and in practice, a commitment grounded in and expounded in terms of the principles of the madhhab to which he committed his life.

The Almoravids presented themselves as leaders of jihad, and their successes in warfare against the Christian kingdoms in Iberia were central to their authority as long as they managed to sustain them. The Almoravid leadership of jihad was supported by and may also have been tempered by (depending on circumstances) the Maliki fuqaha' of al-Andalus. Certainly, the Almoravids' treatment of Christians as dhimmis and harbis came under the influence of the Andalusi fuqaha'.

As we have seen, jurists considering legal questions regarding "border" crossings common in life in the borderlands habitually acknowledged the protected status of dhimmis. The concepts of the 'ahd al-dhimma as a social contract and the ahl al-dhimma as a legal category were integral to jurists' understanding of the political order, Islam, and the rights and obligations of Muslims. Jurists viewed the ahl al-harb as a legally significant category as well. They were the enemy, and their persons and property were fair game for Muslim warriors, but the aman granted by the imam to an individual or the hudna arranged with an enemy ruler were contracts to be respected on the authority of the imam. Also significantly, an individual harbi could change legal categories: he or she could become a captive (and a female could become an umm walad should she bear a Muslim child), a dhimmi, or a Muslim. The legal categories important to jurists differentiated individuals and groups along lines that differed from the confessional categories of Muslim, Christian, and Jew, and these boundaries were tested distinctively in the presence of the "border." Viewed through the legal lens, the "enemy" had a legal status and in some cases legal claims on Muslims inasmuch as they had contractual relationships with Muslims.

Conclusion

The title of this book, *Defining Boundaries in al-Andalus*, refers to the idea of definitive boundaries between Muslims and Christians and Jews—an idea rooted in the Qur'anic history of humankind and the sunna of the Prophet, embodied in Islamic law, and expressed in signs and acts integral to Islamic culture. The title also, more essentially, refers to the process of defining boundaries, boundaries that were mutable and negotiated at the margins of what distinguished "us" from "them" in a recursive engagement with social and cultural change. The focus of the book on law as a boundary-making mechanism offers a circumscribed view of a process of differentiation of the Muslim community from the communities of Christians and Jews who lived under the same ruler in a common physical environment and social space, and of a mode of engagement. In principle, Islamic law applied only to Muslims; in practice, the law extended to *dhimmīs* ("protected persons") in Dar al-Islam and even *ḥarbīs* (individuals from the Domain of War) to the extent that Muslims interacted with and had relationships with them. In ninth- and tenth-century al-Andalus Muslims interacted with dhimmis in a variety of social contexts: official, transactional, and personal.

The structure of Umayyad rule is the first context for investigating legal boundary making. Relationships among individual rulers, judges, and jurists—the politics of the *shūrā* (council of jurisconsults)—informed legal opinions and decisions. The biographies of the *fuqahā'* (jurists) personify how legal opinions and decisions were made discursively. A close-up view of some of the rivalries among fuqaha' in the middle of the ninth century and of the ways by which consensus was achieved provides insight into an early stage in the emergence of the Maliki *madhhab*, or school of law, in al-Andalus. In the late ninth century and the tenth century jurists who were descendants and students of those prominent in the middle of the ninth century developed the madhhab further. Some fuqaha' in this period (and later) proved more interested than others in assimilating hadith transmissions and principles of criticism and interpretation associated with *uṣūl al-fiqh* (the sources of jurisprudence) with a rationalizing approach to the *ra'y* (legal opinion) of Malik.

Unfortunately, it is difficult to locate specific legal opinions in specific political and social contexts. With rare exceptions, one is forced to look for correspondences between opinions and circumstances, and this is especially true for the opinions in the *masā'il* (legal questions and opinions; s. *mas'ala*). Nonetheless, correspondences between opinions having to do with inter-faith marriage and conversion and the evidence of the martyrologies, for example, are compelling and a basis for grounding legal casuistry in social life. Chapter 2, "Society in Transition," is dedicated to developing these correspondences and to the portrayal of a society undergoing dramatic so-cial differentiation and cultural transformation. Chapter 3, "Between Enemies and Friends," discusses how fuqaha' negotiated the nexus between social roles and legal obligations between Muslims and dhimmis and demonstrates how casuistry allowed for accommodation. The discussion of the "border" in Chapter 4 provides another view of dhimmis. Dhimmis were within the bounds of the political community defined by the ruler and, in contrast to harbis, were protected by Islamic law. Jurists' commitment to the concept of *dhimma* (protection) is thrown into relief in this context. Investigation of the distinction between dhimmi and harbi as another tested and negotiated boundary underscores the importance of historical context for understand-ing the legal status of dhimmis.

Evidence discussed in all the chapters and the cumulative analysis of boundary making allow us to develop an understanding of the legal status of Christians and Jews in al-Andalus from the perspective of ninth- and tenth-century Maliki fuqaha'. Jurists addressed the subject on three levels: consti-tutional, categorical, and associational. The constitutional understanding of legal status was the most abstract: the imagined social contract of the *'ahd al-dhimma* or "pact of protection" defined the legal relationship between the ruler and his non-Muslim subjects and allowed for the practice of day-to-day intercommunal living. The definition of the category of *ahl al-dhimma* (people of the [pact of] protection) constituted the meaningful legal bound-ary. Jurists determined that laws did not apply uniformly to all individuals and constructed legal categories to structure interpretation and practice. Rules of inheritance, for example, based on Qur'anic principles, applied dif-ferently to men and women. Men and women, slaves and freemen, children and adults, the mentally impaired, and the physically disabled were subject to the law in different ways. Juridical opinion assumed categorical differ-ences between Muslims and dhimmis. In some instances jurists directly af-firmed categorical boundaries with assertions of rights and privileges exclusive to Muslims; in other instances they did so through the assignment of liminal persons into proper categories. Jurists most often engaged with dhimmis and negotiated the categorical boundaries in legal opinions that involved relationships between Muslims and dhimmis. This level of interpretation, most closely related to practice, is often missing from the conception of legal status in modern scholarship. Understanding the legal status of dhimmis in terms of constitution and category alone can lead to a static and ahistorical view of Islamic law and society. The focus on boundary making on the level of relationships reminds us to think of the constitutional and categorical definitions as flexible and contested in everyday practice.

This book discusses two political crises that provoked explicit attention to the constitutional 'ahd al-dhimma: the Christian martyrdoms that took place in Cordoba in the 850s and the "crossing over" of dhimmis from Granada, Cordoba, and Seville to support Alfonso I in his campaigns against the Muslims in 1125. One can discern in the accounts of the Christian martyrs that the imagination of a social contract between the ruler and the Christian community informed how events were understood by those involved and can infer that the unfolding of events prompted specific legal opinions guiding the ruler in his responses, as he and those he consulted interpreted the social contract according to exigent circumstances. The amir 'Abd al-Rahman II supported the judge of Cordoba's ruling of blasphemy in the case of the first voluntary martyr, Isaac, and the blasphemer was executed. Isaac was an individual who had crossed the bounds of acceptable speech. Had Isaac been a Muslim blasphemer, he would have been subject to the penalty of death, but the grounds for executing a Christian for blasphemy were not the same since he was not directly subject to Islamic law and as a dhimmi was allowed to hold his own beliefs. Contemporary juridical opinion likely determined that this instance of explicit, public blasphemy by a Christian was a violation of the "pact of protection" particular to the individual, who was punished for his crime. When a number of other Christians followed Isaac's example, the official perspective shifted from the individual case to addressing a problem of Christian leadership and communal discipline. The amir Muhammad's collective punishment of the Christian community of Cordoba suggests that he may have felt that the Christian community as a whole no longer warranted or was at risk of losing the protection he accorded it. He responded to the continued provocation of the martyrs as a challenge to his authority and may well have understood it to be within his rights to put all to death for violation of the terms of protection as he understood them even if, ultimately, he did not.

The apparent "treason" of dhimmis from Granada, Cordoba, and Seville in communicating with Alfonso I and joining forces with him in 1125 prompted a political crisis for the Almoravid ruler ʿAli ibn Yusuf ibn Tashu-fin. The imagined social contract between dhimmis and the Muslim ruler was fundamentally a contract of submission in exchange for protection, and refusal to submit abrogated the contract. A number of masaʾil discuss a variety of circumstances in which dhimmis might forfeit their right to protection, including (not surprisingly) joining enemy forces (not under compulsion or out of fear but with full cognition of doing so). A jurist like Ibn Rushd would seemingly have no compunction in declaring the "treasonous" dhimmis to be in violation of the "pact," thereby forfeiting their protection. The problem arises in how to treat the offenders. This was a political as well as a legal problem, and the decision to deport at least some of the Christians was at the discretion of the ruler. Ibn Rushd may have accorded the ruler such discretion by treating this as an instance in which the ruler determined the status of captives. Ibn al-Hajj, in contrast, viewed the ruler's decision to deport the Christians as an instance of his exercise of discretion for the benefit of the Muslims rather than as a consequence of the violation of the pact of protection. The deportation of Christians from al-Andalus raised constitutional questions about the status of dhimmis.

Pattern treaties are models for the "constitutional" conditions of protection of dhimmis who submit to the rule of Islam by treaty. The situation of any particular model in its legal context and its relation to practice can be difficult to determine and cannot be assumed. It is interesting to note that the text of the "Pact of ʿUmar" in its fullest version, which reads as a series of dictates packaged as a petition (perhaps in a chancery), does not mention blasphemy or aiding and abetting the enemy as violations of the dhimma, but both actions were interpreted as such in al-Andalus in the ninth and the twelfth centuries. Al-Shafiʿi's pattern treaty, on the other hand, more clearly and comprehensively a juridical construct, does specify that a dhimmi who speaks improperly about Muhammad, the book of God, or his religion nullifies his right to protection, as does a dhimmi who fights with those who wage war against the Muslims or shows them the weak spots of the Muslims or shelters their spies.[1] But how directly relevant is the pattern treaty in al-Shafiʿis late eighth- or early ninth-century *Kitab al-umm* to the legal opinions and judgments of Maliki fuqahaʾ and judges, and to the decisions of the rul-

---

1. Al-Shafiʿi, *Kitab al-umm*, ed. Mahmud Matraji (Beirut: Dar al-Kutub al-ʿIlmiyya, 1993), 4:280–284.

ers in Cordoba? The text is embedded in al-Shafiʿi's extended juridical discussion of matters pertaining to the *jizya* (poll tax) and is a product of his developing method of interpretation of the sources of law. Al-Shafiʿi's writings were beginning to be introduced in al-Andalus in the mid-ninth century, but the judgments made in the cases of the Christian martyrs of Cordoba were rooted in another juridical tradition. Ninth-century Andalusi jurists who followed the opinions of Malik and his disciples discussed blasphemy (and apostasy) in casuistic detail and had their stock of opinions to draw on. Similarly, when the Christians of Granada, Cordoba, and Seville joined those who waged war against the Muslims, Maliki jurists drew on a legal discourse rooted in the masa'il, and the ruler made a political decision.

The eleventh-century jurist Ibn Sahl's presentation of a fatwa dating to the late ninth or early tenth century about whether to destroy a synagogue in Cordoba makes no reference to what would seem to be the relevant passage in the "Pact of ʿUmar": "We shall not build, in our cities or in their environs, any new monastery or church or convent or hermitage, nor shall we repair any of them that fall to ruin."[2] The Cordoban jurists ʿUbayd Allah ibn Yahya, Muhammad ibn Lubaba, Ibn Ghalib, Ibn Walid, Saʿd ibn Muʿadh, Yahya ibn ʿAbd al-ʿAziz, Ayyub ibn Sulayman, and Saʿid ibn Khamir apparently had no difficulty in determining that the synagogue should be destroyed, given sound testimony to its being a new (postconquest) construction (after hearing the position of the Jewish community). In their view, the laws (*al-sharāʾiʿ*) of Islam did not allow the ahl al-dhimma to build new churches or synagogues in Muslim towns or in their midst. Ibn Sahl, who preserved the fatwa in *al-Ahkam al-kubra*, grounds the jurists' opinion in the masa'il, drawing on Ibn Habib's *Wadiha* and Sahnun's *Mudawwana*, and in doing so reveals a discourse that he considered relevant for the instruction of later generations (and that may have informed the jurists' position).[3] The excerpted masa'il (also excerpted in al-Qayrawani's *Nawadir wa-ziyadat*) speak to the importance of the original context of surrender (by treaty or by force) and, in the case of surrender by treaty, whether the treaty stipulated the right to use and maintain houses of worship to begin

---

2. This is from the version of the "Pact of ʿUmar" in al-Wansharisi, *al-Miʿyar al-muʿrib wa-l-jamiʿ al-mughrib* (Rabat: Dar al-Gharb al-Islami, 1981–1983), 2:237–238. The passage differs slightly in al-Turtushi's *Siraj al-muluk* (Cairo: Bulaq, 1872), 229.

3. Ibn Sahl in M. ʿAbd al-Wahhab Khallaf, *Watha'iq fi ahkam qada' ahl al-dhimma fi al-Andalus* (Cairo: al-Markaz al-ʿArabi al-Dawli li-l-Iʿlam, 1980), 77–80; al-Wansharisi demonstrates how debates about dhimmi houses of worship continued (*Miʿyar*, 2:214–253); al-Qayrawani, *al-Nawadir wa-l-ziyadat*, ed. ʿAbd al-Fattah Muhammad al-Hulw, et al. (Beirut: Dar al-Gharb al-Islami, 1999), 3:376.

with. Ibn Sahl cites Malik's student Ibn al-Majishun (d. 829) extensively: although Ibn al-Majishun allowed that the ahl al-dhimma could build churches (and keep wine and pigs) in areas remote from Muslim settlement and acknowledged that their treaties of surrender could stipulate the right to repair their houses of worship where they lived among Muslims, he did not concede that a treaty could allow for new construction in areas of Muslim settlement. In his view, if the imam granted dhimmis such a right, he did so out of ignorance (he referred to the Prophet's statement enjoining Muslims "not to raise up Judaism and Christianity" as an interdiction of the construction of houses of worship). Conceptually, dhimmis' rights emanated from the imam, but Ibn Majishun here asserted limits to the ruler's authority. The constitution of the ʿahd al-dhimma was, in fact, a matter of contest and negotiation among the ruler, the fuqahaʾ, and the dhimmis themselves, as evidenced by the foundation of new churches and monasteries in the mountains around Cordoba (outside the areas of Muslim settlement) in the early ninth century.

Islamic law is constructed around legal categories, and the corpus of Islamic legal writing includes texts explicitly dedicated to categorical definitions and boundaries, among them pattern treaties and *ḥisba* manuals (guidelines for the market inspector). Jurists in the ninth and tenth centuries both assumed and tested the legal boundaries between Muslims and dhimmis. Even basic assumptions about categorical distinctions, for example, that a Christian cannot lead Muslims in prayer, might be tested: recall the masaʾil about impostors participating in or leading prayer and the fatwa about the prayer leader during Ramadan who turned out to have been a Christian.[4] If the interpretation of law depended on legal categories, then the assignment of individuals to their proper categories was fundamentally important. The assignment of liminal figures to their proper categories was a kind of patrolling of boundaries. A number of masaʾil having to do with the legal-religious identity (and legal status) of particular individuals have appeared in the course of this book. The masʾala about a house collapsing over a Muslim and a Jew and the undeterminable identity of the corpses is similar to the problem of identifying corpses on a battlefield.[5] In both cases superficial qualities, such as clothing, hair, and circumcision, were not determining (in

---

4. Ibn Rushd (al-Jadd), *al-Bayan wa-l-tahsil wa-l-sharh wa-l-tawjih wa-l-taʾlil fi masaʾil al-Mustakhraja*, ed. Muhammad Hajji (Beirut: Dar al-Gharb al-Islami, 1984–1987), 16:426; al-Qayrawani, *Nawadir wa-ziyadat*, 1:290; al-Wansharisi, *Miʿyar*, 1:156.

5. Ibn Rushd, *Bayan*, 2:284, 289.

the second example, Ibn Habib observed that sometimes Christians were circumcised). These masa'il concerned proper burial practices: a Muslim should receive proper burial rites. Two other masa'il discussed in these pages specifically addressed whether liminal individuals (a deathbed convert and the child of a mixed marriage) had been buried in the proper place or should be exhumed and reburied.[6] 'Isa ibn Dinar, Ibn Habib, and Sahnun considered the proper burial rites and burial place of a Christian slave owned by a Muslim who died before the age of reason, with differences of opinion centering on whether and how deeply the slave had been introduced to Islam.[7] Another mas'ala treated the question of a child (deceased) whose legal-religious identity tested a number of boundaries: she had been conceived by two Christians; her father had died before she was born; and sometime after her birth her mother had converted, and she had been raised as a Muslim. Where should such a child be buried, and according to which burial rites? What should be determining here, the fact that her father was a Christian or her Muslim upbringing?[8] In this mas'ala, as in the previous one, age was one factor among others complicating the assignment of category. We have also seen age as a factor in determining the legal-religious identity of converts and apostates and their children. All these questions pertaining to category, of course, affirm the importance of categories. Casuistry tested limits because social life tested limits.

The shift of legal opinion away from treating non-Muslims as physically impure as a category presents a striking example of accommodation to practice. All the ninth-century discourse about whether and how "the Christian" might be impure and polluting and about the use of common water sources for practical and ritual purposes resolved into basic positions as jurists and judges made practical decisions and favored opinions within the discourse that supported them. Resolutions included, in one example, the position that non-Muslims should not enter mosques (on the basis of Qur'an 9:28) and, in another, that there was no objection to sharing water with dhimmi neighbors. This is not to say that questions did not continue to come up or that the idea of the non-Muslim as *najas* (something impure and defiling) was not persistent. For example, the shura of the judge Ibn Ziyad agreed that the *'ajam* ("foreigners"; in this context, the non-Muslims) should not

---

6. Ibn Rushd, *Bayan*, 2:255–256, 283.

7. Ibn Rushd, *Bayan*, 2: 213–215.

8. Ibn Rushd, *Bayan*, 14:331–333.

cut through Maqbarat Mut'a with their funeral processions, remarking in their fatwa that given that Muslims were forbidden from walking over the tombs of Muslims, it could not but be forbidden to impure unbelievers.[9]

In the bulk of the masa'il literature, dhimmis appear in questions and opinions that have to do with Muslims' legal concerns in an associational context. The legally significant relationships and interactions between Muslims and dhimmis played a role in how legal discourse interpreted the status of dhimmis as distinct from Muslims. I have described a tension in the masa'il literature between an interest on the part of jurists to maintain separation between Muslims and dhimmis and a commitment to uphold principles that allowed for interaction, most notably Qur'anic verses that allowed for the sharing of food and for the marriage of Muslim men and Christian and Jewish women. Sahnun's report of Malik ibn Anas's disapproval of marriage between a Muslim and a dhimmi because the dhimmi wife eats pork and drinks wine and the Muslim husband kisses her and has intercourse with her comes to mind.[10] Although this opinion invokes food taboos in the cause of keeping Muslim men and dhimmi women apart, Malik did not forbid interfaith marriage because of Qur'an 5:5: "(Lawful to you in marriage) are (not only) chaste women who are believers but chaste women among the People of the Book." The gap between prohibition and disapproval accommodated practice.

Interfaith marriage and conversion generated social differentiation and the multiplication of close and legally complicated relationships between individual Muslims and individual dhimmis. Such relationships intensified legal discourse about a range of related topics, and differences of opinion accommodated many of these relationships. The importance of social practice in the shaping of legal opinion is evident in masa'il in which jurists invoked Qur'anic verses of separation but, through the casuistry of exception making, accommodated close social relationships.

The reader may recall the recurrence of a phrase from Qur'an 8:72, "You owe no duty of protection to them," in legal discourse about the arrangement of marriages in mixed families, the offering of condolences to non-Muslims, and funerary practices in mixed families. Al-'Utbi reported from Sahnun from Ibn al-Qasim that when Malik was asked whether a Muslim convert from Christianity could arrange the marriage of his dhimmi sister,

9. Ibn Sahl in Khallaf, *Watha'iq fi ahkam qada' ahl al-dhimma*, 81–82.

10. Sahnun, *al-Mudawwana al-kubra l-il-imam Malik* (Beirut: Dar Sadir, 1997), 2:306.

he demurred, citing Qur'an 8:72.[11] 'Isa ibn Dinar asked Ibn al-Qasim the question as a general proposition and received a categorical reply: a Muslim cannot arrange the marriage of a Christian woman, whether she is a sister, daughter, or *mawlā* (client), and whether to a Christian or to a Muslim.[12] In another opinion, however, Ibn al-Qasim conceded that a Muslim could contract the marriage of his Christian daughter to a Muslim. He invoked the Qur'anic phrase "You owe no duty of protection to them" to support his opinion that a father could not arrange his daughter's marriage to a Christian.[13] Ibn al-Qasim's opinion suggests that despite the Qur'anic principle, there were possibilities for interpretation.

According to Ibn al-Qasim as transmitted by al-'Utbi, when Malik was asked about offering condolences to a Muslim whose unbelieving (*kāfir*) father had died, he replied that it did not please him, according to God's words: "You owe no duty of protection to them until they come into exile." Malik evidently asserted in this way that a Muslim's emotional relationship with his father (or other non-Muslim relatives) should be considered severed by conversion.[14] As discussed in chapter 3, jurists addressed a number of questions having to do with close family relationships that tested this perspective. Legal opinions about the funerary rites of a Muslim's non-Muslim parent exemplify how casuistry allowed for accommodation. In principle, Muslims did not participate in burial rituals of members of other confessions. However, as relayed by Ibn al-Qasim, Malik made an exception: a Muslim should not wash the body of his unbelieving father or follow the funeral procession or bury him except out of fear that the body would be neglected.[15] Elsewhere Malik is cited for the view that a Muslim may assume responsibility for the preparation of the body of his Christian mother for burial and then turn her over to the Christians for interment. He conceded that a Muslim would be permitted to lead the procession to the grave and bury her if he feared neglect.[16] Ibn Habib developed the position more fully (and with greater accommodating effect): "If a Muslim loses someone for whom he is responsible, for example, his mother, father, or brother,

---

11. Ibn Rushd, *Bayan*, 4:293; Ibn al-Qasim expands on and conditions Malik's view, stating that if the brother and sister were freed slaves and the brother converted but the sister remained a Christian, he could arrange her marriage. See also Sahnun, *Mudawwana*, 2:176.

12. Ibn Rushd, *Bayan*, 4:481.

13. Ibn Rushd, *Bayan*, 5:66.

14. Ibn Rushd, *Bayan*, 2:211–213; al-Qayrawani, *Nawadir wa-ziyadat*, 1:662.

15. Ibn Rushd, *Bayan* 2:218; al-Qayrawani, *Nawadir wa-ziyadat*, 1:612; Sahnun, *Mudawwana*, 1:187.

16. Al-Qayrawani, *Nawadir wa-ziyadat*, 1:664.

who is an unbeliever, there is no objection to his attending to the body and preparing it and shrouding it until it is taken out. Then the body of the deceased should be handed to the people of his religion. *If he fears* the body will be neglected, then he may lead it to the grave at a remove from those who carry the bier."[17] In these and other examples of jurists taking into account the legal implications of interpersonal relationships between Muslims and dhimmis, one sees the "legal status" of dhimmis being negotiated by Muslims on a microlevel.

The ninth-century masa'il evoke a time of social differentiation and cultural transformation and an effort on the part of jurists to control change and protect the integrity of Islam and the Muslim community through attention to boundaries. The casuistry of legal opinions and the discourse (personal and textual) among fuqaha' about Muslims in relation to dhimmis tested legal principles in ways that were socially meaningful. Extant fatwas, discussed throughout this book, indicate that Andalusi jurists in the late ninth and tenth centuries addressed legal problems arising from social situations similar to those apparent in the masa'il. Fatwas that 'Isa ibn Sahl culled from the archives of the qadi of Cordoba that date to the turn of the century and the judgeship of Ahmad ibn Muhammad ibn Ziyad address subjects such as the custody of young children of an interfaith marriage, the conversion and apostasy of children and adolescents, the slave of a dhimmi who converted to Islam, the slave owned by a dhimmi who claimed to have been born free to free Muslim parents, the blasphemy of a Christian, the captive from Dar al-Harb who had children by her master and sought to leave Dar al-Islam after his death, and the fate of a synagogue in Cordoba. Later in the tenth century Ishaq ibn Ibrahim was asked his opinion about a Christian woman whom the neighbors claimed had a Muslim father. Ibn al-'Attar, on one occasion, and Asbagh ibn Sa'id, Ibn Harith al-Khushani, Ibn Maysur, and Ibn Zarb, on another, consulted on cases involving Jews seeking justice in an Islamic court. Ibn Zarb revisited the question of a child's conversion in another fatwa having to do with an eight-year-old Jewish boy.

One can read in the tenth-century legal opinions engagement in discourse with earlier opinions. In some instances the reader recognizes continuity between a mas'ala or a cluster of masa'il and a later fatwa. Yet each case had its peculiarities. In some instances the qadi sought counsel about procedure (for example, if the evidence was problematic), as well as about

---

17. Al-Qayrawani, *Nawadir wa-ziyadat*, 1:663; see also Ibn Rushd, *Bayan*, 2:218.

judgment. Jurists sometimes remarked on different aspects of a case or referred to different opinions from the masa'il (and an occasional Qur'anic verse or hadith) to support their own. In Ibn Sahl's pointed opinion, individual jurists sometimes failed to consult the appropriate masa'il or interpret them properly, and his collection, *al-Ahkam al-kubra*, was an effort to provide instruction.

Political order, a stable system of justice, and the development of law in al-Andalus were all achieved, to some extent and in different ways, by rulers, judges, and jurists addressing Muslim-dhimmi relations and legal boundaries between Muslims and dhimmis. One might generalize that by the end of the caliphal period in al-Andalus, political security, the multiplication of legal-judicial offices, continuity of legal personnel through lineages of scholarship (including kinship lines), and the ramified elaboration of legal opinion provided a stable framework for Muslim-dhimmi relations. At the same time, the challenges of social differentiation and cultural change associated with conversion may have attenuated, and the social category of *muwalladun* became less significant (the term, used to identify indigenous Muslims, dropped out of use) as other social (ethnic) categories became more meaningful.[18] However, the political vicissitudes of the long history of al-Andalus that followed the collapse of Umayyad rule, and the warfare that punctuated that history, posed different and varied challenges for rulers, judges, and jurists and for Muslims, Christians, and Jews.

---

18. Wasserstein describes how the civil war of 1009–1031 was played out among three ethnic groups: the (neo-)Berbers, the Slavs, and the Andalusis. The Andalusi Muslims, by this period and in this context, had a common identity. See David J. Wasserstein, *The Rise and Fall of the Party-Kings* (Princeton, NJ: Princeton University Press, 1985), 55–81.

BIBLIOGRAPHY

Primary Sources*

*Authors are listed by the names by which they are most commonly referred

Akhbar majmu'a fi fath al-Andalus. Edited and translated by Emilio Lafuente y
    Alcantara. Madrid: Real Academia de la Historia, 1867.

Albar, Paul. *Vita Eulogii.* In *Paul Albar of Cordoba: Studies on His Life and Writings,*
    translated by Carleton M. Sage, 190–214. Washington, DC: Catholic
    University of America Press, 1943.

al-Baladhuri. *The Origins of the Islamic State.* Translated by Philip Khuri Hitti. New
    York : Columbia University Press, 1914.

*Le calendrier de Cordoue publié par R. Dozy, nouvelle edition accompagnée d'une traduction
    française annotée par Charles Pellat.* Leiden: E. J. Brill, 1961.

Crónica anónima de 'Abd al-Rahman III al-Nasir. Edited and translated by E.
    Lévi-Provençal and E. García Gómez. Madrid: Consejo Superior de
    Investigaciones Científicas, 1950.

al-Dabbi. *Bughyat al-multamis fi ta'rikh rijal ahl al-Andalus.* Edited by F. Codera and
    J. Ribera. Bibliotheca Arabico-Hispana, 3. Madrid: Josephum de Rojas, 1885.

Eulogius. *Memoriale sanctorum, Liber apologeticus martyrum,* and *Documentum
    martyriale.* In *Obras completas de San Eulogio: Introducción, traducción, y notas,*
    Spanish translation by María Jesús Aldana García. Córdoba: Servicio de
    Publicaciones, Universidad de Córdoba, 1998.

Al-Hulal al-mawshiyya. Edited by I. S. Allouche. Rabat: Institute des Hautes Études
    Marocaines, 1936. Spanish translation and edition by Ambrosio Huici
    Miranda. *al-Hulal al-mawshiyya: Crónica árabe de las dinastías Almorávide,
    Almohade y Benimerín.* Tetuan: Editora Marroquí, 1952.

Ibn 'Abd al-Hakam. *Ibn 'Abd al-Hakem's History of the Conquest of Spain.* Translated
    by John Harris Jones. Göttingen: W. F. Kaestner, 1850.

Ibn 'Abdun. *Séville musulmane au début du xiie siécle: Le traité d'Ibn 'Abdun sur la vie
    urbaine et les corps de métiers.* Translated by E. Lévi-Provençal. Paris: G. P.
    Maisonneuve, 1947.

Ibn al-Athir. *Annales du Maghreb et de l'Espagne.* Translated by Emile Fagnan.
    Algiers: Typographie Adolphe Jourdan, 1901. Reprint as an Elibron Classics
    Replica Edition, Chestnut Hill, MA: Adamant Media, 2006.

Ibn al-'Attar. *Kitab al-watha'iq wa-l-sijillat.* Edited by P. Chalmeta and F. Corriente.
    Madrid: Academia Matritense del Notariado, Instituto Hispano-Árabe de
    Cultura, 1983.

Ibn Bashkuwal. *Kitab al-sila*, 2 vols. Cairo: al-Dar al-Misriyya li-l-Ta'lif wa-l-Tarjama, 1966.

Ibn al-Faradi. *Ta'rikh 'ulama' al-Andalus*, 2 vols. Edited by Bashar 'Awad Ma'rouf. Tunis: Dar al-Gharb al-Islami, 2008.

Ibn Habib. *Ta'rikh*. Edited by Jorge Aguadé. Madrid: Consejo Superior de Investigaciones Científicas, 1991.

Ibn Hayyan. *Muqtabis II-1*. Facsimile produced by Joaquín Vallvé Bermejo. Madrid: Real Academia de la Historia, 1999. Spanish translation, *Crónica de los emires al-Hakam I y 'Abd Ar-Rahman II (al-Muqtabis II-I)*. Translated by Mahmud 'Ali Makki and Federico Corriente. Zaragoza: Instituto de Estudios Islámicos y del Oriente Próximo, 2001.

——. *al-Muqtabis III: Chronique du règne du calife Umaiyade 'Abd Allah á Cordoue*. Edited by Melchor M. Antuña. Paris: Paul Geuthner, 1937.

——. *al-Muqtabis [V] de Ibn Hayyan*. Edited by P. Chalmeta, F. Corriente, and M. Subh. Madrid: Instituto Hispano-Árabe de Cultura, 1979. Spanish translation, *Crónica del califa Abdarrahman III an-Nasir entre los años 912 y 942 (al-Muqtabis V)*. Translated by María Jesús Viguera and Federico Corriente. Zaragoza: Instituto Hispano-Árabe de Cultura, 1981.

——. *al-Muqtabis fi akhbar balad al-Andalus (Muqtabis VII)*. Edited by A. A. Hajji. Beirut: Dar al-Thaqafa, 1965. Spanish translation, *Anales palatinos del califa de Córdoba al-Hakam II por 'Isa ibn Ahmad al-Razi*. Translated by Emilio García Gómez. Madrid: Sociedad de Estudios y Publicaciones, 1967.

——. *al-Muqtabis min anba ahl al-Andalus (II-2)*. Edited by Mahmud 'Ali. Makki. Cairo: Matabi' al-Ahram al-Tijariyya, 1971.

Ibn Hazm. *Jamharat ansab al-'arab*. Edited by E. Lévi-Provençal. Cairo: Dar al-Ma'arif, 1948.

Ibn 'Idhari. *al-Bayan al-mughrib* (portion having to do with Almoravid rule). Published by Ambrosio Huici-Miranda. "Un fragmento inédito de Ibn 'Idari sobre los Almoravides." *Hespéris Tamuda* 2 (1961): 43–112.

——. *al-Bayan al-mughrib fi akhbar al-Andalus wa-l-Maghrib*, 2 vols. Edited by E. Lévi Provençal and G. S. Colin. Leiden: Brill, 1948–1951. French translation, *Histoire de l'Afrique et de l'Espagne intitulée al-Bayano l-Mogrib*, 2 vols. Translated by E. Fagnan. Algiers: Imprimerie Orientale P. Fontana, 1901–1904.

Ibn 'Iyad, Muhammad. *Madhahib al-hukkam fi nawazil al-ahkam (La actuación de los jueces en los procesos judiciales)*. Spanish translation by Delfina Serrano. Madrid: Consejo Superior de Investigaciones Científicas, 1998.

Ibn Khaldun. *The Muqaddimah*, 2 vols. Translated by Franz Rosenthal. London: Routledge and Kegan Paul, 1986.

Ibn al-Qutiyya. *Ta'rikh iftitah al-Andalus (Historia de la conquista de España de Abenalcotía el Cordobés)*. Edited and translated into Spanish by Julián Ribera. Madrid: Revista Archivos, 1926. English translation, David James. *Early Islamic Spain: The "History" of Ibn al-Qutiya*. London: Routledge, 2009.

Ibn Rushd (al-Hafid). *The Distinguished Jurist's Primer*, 2 vols. Translated by Imran Ahsan Khan Nyazee. Reading, England: Garnet, 2000.

Ibn Rushd (al-Jadd). *al-Bayan wa-l-tahsil wa-l-sharh wa-l-tawjih wa-l-ta'lil fi masa'il al-Mustakhraja*, 20 vols. Edited by Muhammad Hajji. Beirut: Dar al-Gharb al-Islami, 1984–1987.

———. *al-Muqaddamat al-mumahhadat li-bayan ma iqtadathu rusum al-Mudawwana min al-ahkam al-shar*ʿ*iyyat wa-l-tahsilat al-muhkamat li-ummahat masa'iliha al-mushkilat*, 2 vols. Edited by Zakariyya ʿAmirat. Beirut: Dar al-Kutub al-ʿIlmiyya, 2002.

Ibn Sahl. *al-Ahkam al-kubra*. Excerpted and edited by Thami El-Azemmouri. "Les *Nawāzil* d'Ibn Sahl: Section relative a l'*ihtisab*." *Hespéris Tamuda* 14 (1973): 7–107. Also excerpted and edited by M. ʿAbd al-Wahhab Khallaf in a number of publications: *Watha'iq fi ahkam al-qada' al-jina'i fi al-Andalus*. Cairo: al-Markaz al-ʿArabi al-Dawli li-l-Iʿlam, 1980. *Watha'iq fi ahkam qada' ahl al-dhimma fi al-Andalus*. Cairo: al-Markaz al-ʿArabi al-Dawli li-l-Iʿlam, 1980. *Thalath watha'iq fi muharabat al-ahwa' wa-l-bidaʿ fi al-Andalus*. Cairo: al-Markaz al-ʿArabi al-Dawli li-l-Iʿlam, 1981. *Watha'iq fi shu'un al-ʿumran fi al-Andalus*. Cairo: al-Markaz al-ʿArabi al-Dawli li-l-Iʿlam, 1982. *Watha'iq fi al-tibb al-islami wa wazifatihi fi muʿawanat al-Qada' fi al-Andalus*. Cairo: al-Markaz al-ʿArabi al-Dawli li-l-Iʿlam, 1982. *Tisʿa watha'iq fi shu'un al-hisba ʿala al-masajid fi al-Andalus*. Kuwait: Jamiʿat al-Kuwait, 1984. *Watha'iq fi shu'un al-hisba fi al-Andalus*. Cairo: al-Markaz al-ʿArabi al-Dawli li-l-Iʿlam, 1985. Rashid ibn Hamid al-Nuʿaymi edited the *Ahkam al-kubra* in its entirety: "An Edition of Diwan al-Ahkam al-Kubra by ʿIsa b. Sahl (d. 486 AH/1093 AD). PhD diss., St. Andrews University, 1978.

Ibn Waddah. *Kitab al-bidaʿ*. Edited by Maribel Fierro. Madrid: Consejo Superior de Investigaciones Científicas, 1998.

ʿIyad ibn Musa (al-Qadi ʿIyad). *al-Shifa bi taʿrif huquq al-mustafa*, 2 vols. Edited by ʿAli Muhammad al-Bajawi. Cairo: ʿIsa al-Babi al-Halabi, 1977. English translation, *Muhammad Messenger of Allah ("Ash-Shifa" of Qadi ʿIyad)*. Translated by Aisha Abdarrahman Bewley. Inverness, Scotland: Madinah Press, 2006.

———. *Tartib al-madarik wa-taqrib al-masalik li-maʿarifat aʿlam madhhab Malik*, 8 vols. Rabat: Wizarat al-Awqaf wa-al-Shu'un al-Islamiyya, 1965–1983.

al-Jaziri. *al-Maqsad al-mahmud fi talhis al-ʿuqud*. Edited by Asunción Ferreras. Madrid: Consejo Superior de Investigaciones Científicas, 1998.

al-Khushani. *Akhbar al-fuqaha' wa-l-muhaddathin*. Edited by M. Luisa Ávila and Luis Molina. Madrid: Consejo Superior de Investigaciones Científicas, 1992.

———. *Kitab al-qudat bi-Qurtuba (Historia de los jueces de Cordoba)*. Edited and translated into Spanish by Julián Ribera. Madrid: Maestre, 1914.

Malik ibn Anas. *al-Muwatta of Imam Malik ibn Anas: The First Formulation of Islamic Law*. Translated by Aisha Abdurrahman Bewley. London: Kegan Paul, 1989.

———. *Risalat imam ahl al-Madina fi-l-sunan, al-mawaʿiz, wa-l-adab ila Amir al-Mu'minin Harun al-Rashid wa-ila Yahya ibn Khalid al-Barmaki*. Cairo: Al-Matbaʿa wa-l-Maktaba al-Muhammadiyya, 1893.

al-Maqqari. *Nafh al-tib min ghusn al-Andalus al-ratib*, 8 vols. Edited by Ihsan ʿAbbas. Beirut: Dar Sadir, 1968.

al-Nubahi. *Kitab al-marqaba al-ʿulya*. Edited by E. Lévi-Provençal. Cairo: Scribe Egyptien, 1948.

Al-Qayrawani, Ibn Abi Zayd. *al-Nawadir wa-l-ziyadat*, 15 vols. Edited by ʿAbd al-Fattah Muhammad al-Hulw, Muhammad Hajji, Muhammad ʿAbd al-Aziz al-Dabbagh, Muhammad ibn Amin Bu Khabzah, Ahmad al-Khatabi, and ʿAbd Allah al-Murabit al-Targhi. Beirut: Dar al-Gharb al-Islami, 1999.

———. *La Risala; ou, Epître sur les éléments du dogme et de la loi de l'Islam selon le rite Malikite*. Arabic text with French translation by Leon Bercher. Algiers: Editions Populaires de l'Armée, 1968.

Al-Qurtubi, Muhammad ibn Ahmad. *al-Jamiʿ li-ahkam al-Qur'an*, 20 vols. Edited by ʿAbd al-Razzaq al-Mahdi. Beirut: Dar al-Kutub al-Arabi, 2001.

Sahnun ibn Saʿid. *al-Mudawwana al-kubra l-il-imam Malik*, 6 vols. Beirut: Dar Sadir, 1997.

Al-Saqati. *Un manuel hispanique de hisba: Traité d'Abu ʿAbd Allah Muhammad b. Abi Muhammad As-Sakati de Malaga*. Edited by G. S. Colin and E. Lévi-Provençal. Paris: Librairie Ernest Leroux, 1931. Spanish translation by Pedro Chalmeta Gedrón. "'El kitab fi adab al-hisba' (Libro del Buen Gobierno del Zoco) de al-Saqati." *Al-Andalus* 32 (1967): 125–162, 359–398; 33 (1968): 143–195, 367–434.

Al-Shafi'i. *Kitab al-umm*, 8 vols. Edited by Mahmud Matraji. Beirut: Dar al-Kutub al-ʿIlmiyya, 1993.

"The Treaty of Tudmir (713)." Translated by Olivia Remie Constable in *Medieval Iberia: Readings from Christian, Muslim, and Jewish Sources*, 37–38. Edited by Olivia Remie Constable. Philadelphia: University of Pennsylvania Press, 1997.

al-Tulaytuli. *al-Muqniʿ fi ʿilm al-shurut (Formulario notaria)*. Edited by Francisco Javier Aguirre Sádaba. Madrid: Consejo Superior de Investigaciones Científicas, 1994.

al-Turtushi. *Kitab al-hawadith wa-l-bidaʿ: El libro de las novedades y las innovaciones*. Edited by Maribel Fierro. Madrid: Consejo Superior de Investigaciones Científicas, 1993.

———. *Siraj al-muluk*. Cairo: Bulaq, 1872.

Al-ʿUdhri. *Tarsiʿ al-akhbar wa-tanwiʿ al-athar wa-l-bustan fi ghara'ib al-buldan wa-l-masalik ila jamiʿ al-mamalik*. Edited by ʿAbd al-ʿAziz al-Ahwani. Madrid: Instituto de Estudios Islamicos, 1965.

Al-Wansharisi. *al-Miʿyar al-muʿrib wa-l-jamiʿ al-mughrib*. Rabat: Dar al-Gharb al-Islami, 1981–1983.

Scholarship

Acién Almansa, Manuel. *Entre el feudalismo y el Islam: ʿUmar ibn Hafsun en los historiadores, en las fuentes y en la historia*. Jaen: Universidad de Jaen, 1994.

Acién Almansa, Manuel, and Antonio Vallejo Triano. "Urbanismo y estado islamico: De Corduba a Qurtuba-Madinat al-Zahra'." In *Genèse de la ville islamique en al-Andalus et au Maghrib occidental*, edited by Patrice Cressier and Mercedes García-Arenal, 107–136. Madrid: Casa de Velázquez, 1998.

Aguilar, Victoria. "Onomástica de origen árabe en el reino de León (siglo x)." *Al-Qantara* 15 (1994): 351–363.

Aguilar Sebastián, Victoria, and Fernando Rodríguez Mediano. "Antroponomia de origen arabe en la documentación (siglos viii–xiii)." In *El reino de León en la Alta Edad Media*, 6:497–633. Madrid: Caja España de Inversiones, Caja de Ahorros y Monte de Piedad y Archivo Histórico Diocesano de León, 1994.

Aillet, Cyrille. *Les mozarabes: Christianisme, islamisation et arabisation en péninsule ibérique (IX–XII siècle).* Madrid: Casa de Velázquez, 2010.

Alfonso, Esperanza. "La construcción de la identidad judía en al-Andalus en la Edad Media." *El Olivo* 23 (1999): 5–24.

———. "Los límites del saber: Reacción de intelectuales judíos a la cultura de procedencia islámica." In *Judíos y musulmanes en al-Andalus y el Maghreb*, edited by Maribel Fierro, 59–84. Madrid: Casa de Velázquez, 2002.

Altschul, Nadia R. "The Future of Postcolonial Approaches to Medieval Iberian Studies." *Journal of Medieval Iberian Studies* 1 (2007): 5–17.

———. "Postcolonialism and the Study of the Middle Ages." *History Compass* 6 (2008): 588–606.

Ángeles Gallego, María. "The Impact of Arabic Diglossia among the Muslims, Jews, and Christians of al-Andalus." In *A Comparative History of Literatures in the Iberian Peninsula*, edited by Fernando Cabo Aseguinolaza, Anxo Abuín Gonzalez, and César Domínguez, 351–365. Amsterdam: John Benjamins, 2007.

Arce Sainz, Fernando. "Arquitectura y rebelión: Construcción de iglesias durante la revuelta de ʿUmar ibn Hafsun." *Al-Qantara* 22 (2001): 121–145.

Arjona Castro, Antonio. "Urbanismo de la Córdoba califal." *Revista del Instituto Egipcio de Estudios Islámicos en Madrid* 29 (1997): 73–86.

Ávila, María Luisa. "Nuevos datos sobre la biografía de Baqi b. Majlad." *Al-Qantara* 6 (1985): 321–367.

Balibar, Etienne. *Politics and the Other Scene.* Translated by Christine Jones, James Swenson, and Chris Turner. London: Verso, 2002.

Barth, Fredrik, ed. *Ethnic Groups and Boundaries: The Social Organization of Cultural Difference.* Boston: Little, Brown and Company, 1969.

Berkey, Jonathan P. "Circumcision Circumscribed: Female Excision and Cultural Accommodation in the Medieval Near East." *International Journal of Middle East Studies* 28 (1996): 19–38.

Bhabha, Homi. *The Location of Culture.* London: Routledge, 1994.

Bosch Vilá, Jacinto. "Algunas consideraciónes sobre al-Tagr en al-Andalus y la division politico-adminstrativa de la España Musulmana." In *Etudes d'orientalisme dédiées à la mémoire d'E. Lévi-Provençal*, 23–33. Paris: Maisonneuve et Larose, 1962. Translated by Michael Kennedy. "Considerations with Respect to 'Al-Thaghr in al-Andalus' and the Political-Administrative Division of Muslim Spain." In *The Formation of al-Andalus*, vol. 1, *History and Society*, edited by Manuela Marín, 377–387. Aldershot: Ashgate Variorum, 1998.

Bourdieu, Pierre. *Language and Symbolic Power.* Translated by Gino Raymond and Matthew Adamson. Cambridge, MA: Harvard University Press, 1991.

Brann, Ross. "The Arabized Jews." In *The Literature of al-Andalus*, edited by Maria Rosa Menocal, Raymond P. Scheindlin, and Michael Sells, 435–454. Cambridge: Cambridge University Press, 2000.

———. *Power in the Portrayal: Representations of Jews and Muslims in Eleventh- and Twelfth-Century Islamic Spain*. Princeton, NJ: Princeton University Press, 2002.

———. "Reflexiones sobre el árabe y la identidad literaria de los judíos de al-Andalus." In *Judíos y musulmanes en al-Andalus y el Magreb: Contactos intelectuales*, edited by Maribel Fierro, 13–28. Madrid: Casa de Velázquez, 2002.

Bulliet, Richard W. "Conversion Stories in Early Islam." In *Conversion and Continuity: Indigenous Christian Communities in Islamic Lands, Eighth to Eighteenth Centuries*, edited by Michael Gervers and Ramzi Jibran Bikhazi, 123–133. Toronto: Pontifical Institute of Medieval Studies, 1990.

———. *Conversion to Islam in the Medieval Period*. Cambridge, MA: Harvard University Press, 1979.

———. *Cotton, Climate, and Camels in Early Iran*. New York: Columbia University Press, 2009.

Burman, Thomas E. *Religious Polemic and the Intellectual History of the Mozarabs, c. 1050–1200*. Leiden: E. J. Brill, 1994.

Calder, Norman. *Studies in Early Muslim Jurisprudence*. Oxford: Oxford University Press, 1993.

Catlos, Brian A. *The Victors and the Vanquished: Christians and Muslims of Catalonia and Aragon, 1050–1300*. Cambridge: Cambridge University Press, 2004.

Chalmeta, Pedro. "Le passage à l'Islam dans al-Andalus au xe siècle." In *Actas del XII Congreso de la Union Européene d'Arabisants et d'Islamisants (Málaga 1984)*, 161–183. Madrid: Union Européene d'Arabisants et d'Islamisants, 1986.

———. *El "Señor del Zoco" en España: Edades Media y Moderna, contribución al estudio de la historia del mercado*. Madrid: Instituto Hispano-Árabe de Cultura, 1973.

———. "Simancas y Alhandega." *Hispania* 36 (1976): 359–444.

Christys, Ann. *Christians in al-Andalus (711–1000)*. Richmond, Surrey: Curzon Press, 2002.

Cohen, Anthony P. "Of Symbols and Boundaries; or, Does Ertie's Greatcoat Hold the Key?" In *Symbolising Boundaries: Identity and Diversity in British Cultures*, edited by Anthony P. Cohen, 1–19. Manchester: Manchester University Press, 1986.

Cohen, Jeffrey Jerome, ed. *The Postcolonial Middle Ages*. New York: St. Martin's Press, 2000.

Cohen, Mark R. "Sociability and the Concept of *Galut* in Jewish-Muslim Relations in the Middle Ages." In *Judaism and Islam: Boundaries, Communication, and Interaction; Essays in Honor of William M. Brinner*, edited by Benjamin H. Hary, John L. Hayes, and Fred Astren, 37–51. Leiden: E. J. Brill, 2000.

———. *Under Crescent and Cross*. Princeton, NJ: Princeton University Press, 1995.

———. "What Was the Pact of ʿUmar?" *Jerusalem Studies in Arabic and Islam* 23 (1999): 100–133.

Coleman, David. *Creating Christian Granada: Society and Religious Culture in an Old-World Frontier City, 1492–1600*. Ithaca, NY: Cornell University Press, 2003.

Constable, Olivia R. *Trade and Traders in Muslim Spain*. Cambridge: Cambridge University Press, 1994.

Cook, David. *Understanding Jihad*. Berkeley: University of California Press, 2005.

Cook, Michael. "Early Islamic Dietary Law." *Jerusalem Studies in Arabic and Islam* 7 (1986): 217–277.

Coope, Jessica A. *The Martyrs of Cordoba: Community and Family Conflict in an Age of Mass Conversion*. Lincoln: University of Nebraska Press, 1995.

————."Religious and Cultural Conversion to Islam in Ninth-Century Umayyad Cordoba." *Journal of World History* 4 (1993): 47–68.

Crone, Patricia. *God's Rule: Government and Islam*. New York: Columbia University Press, 2004.

Crone, Patricia, and Martin Hinds. *God's Caliph: Religious Authority in the First Centuries of Islam*. Cambridge: Cambridge University Press, 1986.

Cruz Hernández, M. "La persecución anti-Masarri durante el reinado de ʿAbd al-Rahman III al-Nasir li-Din Allah, según Ibn Hayyan." *Al-Qantara* 2 (1981): 51–67.

Dachraoui, Farhat. "Tentative d'infiltration S[h]iʿite en Espagne musulmane sous le régne de al-Hakam II." *Al-Andalus* 23 (1958): 97–106.

Daga Portillo, Rocío. "Aproximación a la obra *al-Aḥkām al-kubrā* del cadi ʿIsa ibn Sahl." *Miscelanea de estudios árabes y hebraicas* 36 (1987): 237–249.

————. "Crítica y política en los *Aḥkām al-kubrā* de Ibn Sahl," *Boletin de la Asociacion Española de Orientalistas* 28 (1992): 159–165.

Dunlop, D. M. "Hafs ibn Albar—The Last of the Goths?" *Journal of the Royal Asiatic Society* (1954): 137–151.

————. "Sobre Hafs ibn Albar al-Quti al-Qurtubi." *Al-Andalus* 20 (1955): 211–213.

Dutton, Yassin. "Conversion to Islam: The Qur'anic Paradigm." In *Religious Conversion: Contemporary Practices and Controversies*, edited by Christopher Lamb and M. Darrol Bryant, 151–165. London: Cassell, 1999.

————. *The Origins of Islamic Law: The Qur'an, the Muwatta' and Madinan ʿAmal*. Richmond, Surrey: Curzon Press, 1999.

El Hour, Rachid. "The Andalusian Qadi in the Almoravid Period: Political and Judicial Authority." *Studia Islamica* 90 (2000): 67–83.

Epalza, Mikel de. "Falta de obispos y conversion al Islam de los cristianos de al-Andalus." *Al-Qantara* 15 (1994): 385–400.

————. "Mozarabs: An Emblematic Christian Minority." In *The Legacy of Muslim Spain*, edited by Salma Khadra Jayyusi, 1:154–160. Leiden: E. J. Brill, 1994.

Epalza, Mikel de, and Enrique Llogrebat. "Hubo mozárabes en tierras Valencianas?" *Revista de Estudios Alicantinos* 36 (1982): 7–31.

Fattal, Antoine. *Le statut légal des non-musulmans en pays d'Islam*. Beirut: Imprimerie Catholique, 1958.

Fernández Félix, Ana. "Children on the Frontiers of Islam." In *Conversions islamiques: Identités religieuses en Islam Mediterranéen/Islamic Conversions: Religious Identities in Mediterranean Islam*, 61–72. Paris: Maisonneuve et Larose, 2001.

——. *Cuestiones legales del Islam temprano: La ʿUtbiyya y el proceso de formación de la sociedad islámica Andalusi*. Madrid: Consejo Superior de Investigaciones Científicas, 2003.

Fierro, María Isabel (Maribel), and Manuela Marín. "La islamicización de las ciudades Andalusies a través de sus ʿulamas (s. ii/viii–comienzos s. iv/x). In *Genèse de la ville islamique en al-Andalus et au Maghreb occidental*, edited by Patrice Cressier and Mercedes García Arenal with Mohammed Meouak, 65–97. Madrid: Casa Velázquez, 1998.

Fierro, Maribel. *ʿAbd al-Rahman III: The First Cordoban Caliph*. Oxford: Oneworld Publications, 2005.

——. "El alfaqui beréber Yahya b. Yahya al-Laythi (m. 234/848), ʿel inteligente de al-Andalus.'" In *Estudios onomástico-biográficos de al-Andalus*, vol. 8, edited by María Luísa Ávila and Manuela Marín, 269–344. Madrid: Consejo Superior de Investigaciones Científicas, 1997.

——. "Árabes, beréberes, muladíes y *mawālī*: Algunas reflexiones sobre los datos de los diccionarios biográficos Andalusíes." In *Estudios onomástico-biográficos de al-Andalus*, vol. 7, edited by Manuela Marín and Helena de Felipe, 41–54. Madrid: Consejo Superior de Investigaciones Científicas, 1995.

——. "Cuatro preguntas en torno a Ibn Hafsun." *Al-Qantara* 16 (1995): 221–257. Translated by Michael Kennedy. "Four Questions in Connection with Ibn Hafsun." In *The Formation of al-Andalus*, edited by Manuela Marín, 1:291–328. Aldershot: Ashgate-Variorum, 1998.

——. "El derecho Maliki en al-Andalus: Ss. II/VIII–V/XI." *Al-Qantara* 12 (1991): 119–132.

——. "Heresy in al-Andalus." In *The Legacy of Muslim Spain*, edited by Salma Khadra Jayyusi, 2:895–908. Leiden: E. J. Brill, 1994.

——. *La heterodoxia en al-Andalus durante el periodo Omeya*. Madrid: Instituto Hispano-Árabe de Cultura, 1987.

——. "The Introduction of *Hadith* in al-Andalus (2nd/8th–3rd/9th centuries)." *Der Islam* 66 (1988): 68–93.

——. "The Legal Policies of the Almohad Caliphs and Ibn Rushd's *Bidayat al-Mujtahid*." *Journal of Islamic Studies* 10 (1999): 226–248.

——. "Los Malikies de al-Andalus y los dos arbitros." *Al-Qantara* 6 (1985): 79–102.

——. "*Mawālī* and *Muwalladūn* in al-Andalus (Second/Eighth–Fourth/Tenth Centuries)." In *Patronate and Patronage in Early and Classical Islam*, edited by Monique Bernards and John Nawas, 195–245. Leiden: E. J. Brill, 2005.

——. "Los *mawālī* de ʿAbd al-Rahman I." *Al-Qantara* 20 (1999): 65–97.

——. "A Muslim Land without Jews or Christians: Almohad Policies Regarding the 'Protected People.'" In *Christlicher Norden—muslimischer Süden*, edited by Matthias M. Tischler and Alexander Fidora, 231–247. Münster: Aschendorff Verlag, 2011.

——. "La politica religiosa de ʿAbd al-Rahman III." *Al-Qantara* 25 (2004): 119–156.

——. "Proto-Malikis, Malikis, and Reformed Malikis in al-Andalus." In *The Islamic School of Law: Evolution, Devolution, and Progress*, edited by Peri Bearman, Rudolph Peters, and Frank E. Vogel, 57–76. Cambridge, MA: Islamic Legal Studies Program of Harvard University, Harvard University Press, 2005.

———. "Religious Beliefs and Practices in al-Andalus in the Third/Ninth Century." *Rivista degli studi orientali* 66 (1992): 15–33.

———. "Religious Dissension in al-Andalus: Ways of Exclusion and Inclusion." *Al-Qantara* 22 (2001): 463–487.

———. "The Treatises against Innovations (*Kutub al-Bidaʿ*)." *Der Islam* 69 (1992): 202–246.

Fierro, Maribel Isabel. "Andalusian 'Fatawa' on Blasphemy." *Annales Islamologiques* 25 (1990): 103–117.

Fierro Bello, María Isabel. "Accusations of '*Zandaqa*' in al-Andalus." *Quaderni di Studi Arabi* 5–6 (1987–1988): 251–258.

Friedmann, Yohanan. *Tolerance and Coercion in Islam: Interfaith Relations in Muslim Tradition*. Cambridge: Cambridge University Press, 2003.

García-Arenal, Mercedes. "Jewish Converts to Islam in the Muslim West." *Israel Oriental Studies* 17 (1997): 227–238.

García Gómez, Emilio. "Unas 'Ordenanzas del Zoco' del Siglo IX." *Al-Andalus* 22 (1957): 253–316.

García Sanjuan, Alejandro. *Hasta que Dios herede la tierra: Los bienes habices en al-Andalus (siglos x–xv)*. Huelva: Universidad de Huelva, 2002.

Garen, Sally. "Santa Maria de Melque and Church Construction under Muslim Rule." *Journal of the Society of Architectural Historians* 51 (1992): 288–305.

Giddens, Anthony. *The Constitution of Society*. Berkeley: University of California Press, 1984.

Giladi, Avner. *Infants, Parents and Wet Nurses: Medieval Islamic Views on Breastfeeding and Their Social Implications*. Leiden: E. J. Brill, 1999.

Ginio, Eyal. "Childhood, Mental Capacity and Conversion to Islam in the Ottoman State." *Byzantine and Modern Greek Studies* 25 (2005): 90–119

Glick, Thomas F. *From Muslim Fortress to Christian Castle: Social and Cultural Change in Medieval Spain*. Manchester: University of Manchester Press, 1995.

———. *Islamic and Christian Spain in the Early Middle Ages*. Princeton, NJ: Princeton University Press, 1979.

Glick, Thomas F., and Oriol Pi-Sunyer. "Acculturation as an Explanatory Concept in Spanish History." *Comparative Studies in Society and History* 11 (1969): 136–154.

Goffman, Erving. *The Presentation of Self in Everyday Life*. New York: Doubleday, 1959.

Goitein, S. D. *A Mediterranean Society: The Jewish Communities of the Arab World as Portrayed in the Documents of the Cairo Geniza*, 6 vols. Berkeley: University of California Press, 1967–1988.

Granja, Fernando de la. "Fiestas cristianas en al-Andalus." *Al-Andalus* 34 (1969): 1–53; 35 (1970): 119–142.

Griffith, Sidney H. *The Church in the Shadow of the Mosque*. Princeton, NJ: Princeton University Press, 2008.

Guichard, Pierre. *al-Andalus: Estructura antropológica de una sociedad islámica en occidente*. Barcelona: Barral, 1976.

———. "Les mozarabes de Valence et d'al-Andalus entre le histoire et le mythe." *Revue de l'Occident musulman et de la Mediterranée* 40 (1985): 17–27.

———. "The Social History of Muslim Spain from the Conquest to the End of the Almohad Regime (Early 2nd/8th—Early 7th/13th Centuries)." In *The Legacy of Muslim Spain*, edited by Salma Khadra Jayyusi, 2:679–708. Leiden: E. J. Brill, 1994.

———. *Structures sociales "orientales" et "occidentales" dans l'Espagne musulmane.* Paris: Mouton et Co. and Ecole des Hautes Etudes en Sciences Sociales, 1977.

———. "Les villes d'al-Andalus et de l'occident musulman aux premiers siècles de leur histoire." In *Genèse de la ville islamique en al-Andalus et au Maghrib occidental*, edited by Patrice Cressier and Mercedes García-Arenal, 37–52. Madrid: Casa de Velázquez, 1998.

Gutiérrez Lloret, Sonia. "Ciudades y conquista: El fin de las *ciutatis* Visigodas y la génesis de las *mudun* islámicas del sureste de al-Andalus." In *Genèse de la ville islamique en al-Andalus et au Maghrib occidental*, edited by Patrice Cressier and Mercedes García-Arenal, 137–158. Madrid: Casa de Velázquez, 1998.

Halevi, Leor. "Christian Impurity versus Economic Necessity: A Fifteenth-Century Fatwa on European Paper." *Speculum* 83 (2008): 917–945.

———. *Muhammad's Grave: Death Rites and the Making of Islamic Society.* New York: Columbia University Press, 2007.

Hitchcock, Richard. *Mozarabs in Medieval and Early Modern Spain.* Aldershot: Ashgate, 2008.

Holsinger, Bruce. "Medieval Studies, Postcolonial Studies, and the Genealogies of Critique." *Speculum* 77 (2002): 1195–1227.

Hunwick, John O. "al-Maghili and the Jews of Tuwat: The Demise of a Community." *Studia Islamica* 61 (1985): 155–183.

———. "The Rights of *Dhimmīs* to Maintain a Place of Worship: A 15th Century *Fatwā* from Tlemçen." *Al-Qantara* 12 (1991): 133–155.

Idris, Hady-Roger. "Réflexions sur le Malikisme sous les Umayyades d'Espagne." In *Atti del 3 Congresso di Studi Arabi e Islamici (Ravello 1966)*, 397–414. Naples: Istituto Universitario Orientale, 1967. Translated by John Smedley. "Reflections on Malikism under the Umayyads of Spain." In *The Formation of al-Andalus*, edited by Maribel Fierro and Julio Samsó, 2:85–101. Aldershot: Ashgate-Variorum, 1998.

Ja'far, Muhammad Kamal Ibrahim. *Min qadaya-l-fikr al-Islami.* Cairo: Maktabat Dar al-'Ulum, 1978.

Johansen, Baber. "Casuistry: Between Legal Concept and Social Praxis." *Islamic Law and Society* 2 (1995): 135–156.

Kabir, Ananya Jahanara, and Deanne Williams, eds. *Postcolonial Approaches to the European Middle Ages.* Cambridge: Cambridge University Press, 2005.

Kassis, Hannah E. "Observations on the First Three Decades of the Almoravid Dynasty A.H. 450–480/1058–1088: A Numismatic Study," *Der Islam* 62 (1985): 311–325.

Katz, Marion Holmes. *Body of Text: The Emergence of the Sunni Law of Ritual Purity.* Albany: State University of New York Press, 2002.

———. "The Study of Islamic Ritual and the Meaning of *Wuḍū'*." *Der Islam* 82 (2005): 106–145.

Kennedy, Hugh. "From Antiquity to Islam in the Cities of al-Andalus and al-Mashriq." In *Genèse de la ville islamique en al-Andalus et au Maghrib occidental*, edited by Patrice Cressier and Mercedes García-Arenal, 53–64. Madrid: Casa de Velázquez, 1998.

———. *Muslim Spain and Portugal: A Political History of al-Andalus*. London: Longman, 1996.

Kister, M. J. "'Do Not Assimilate Yourselves . . .': La tashabbahu. . . ." *Jerusalem Studies in Arabic and Islam* 12 (1989): 321–371.

Klawans, Jonathan. "Notions of Gentile Impurity in Ancient Judaism." *Association for Jewish Studies Review* 20 (1995): 285–312.

Klein, Elka. *Jews, Christian Society, and Royal Power in Medieval Barcelona*. Ann Arbor: University of Michigan Press, 2006.

Koningsveld, P. Sj van. "Christian Arabic Literature from Medieval Spain: An Attempt at Periodization." In *Christian Apologetics during the Abbasid Period (750–1250)*, edited by Samir Khalil Samir and Jorgen S. Nielsen, 203–224. Leiden: E. J. Brill, 1994.

Kulikowski, Michael. *Late Roman Spain and Its Cities*. Baltimore: Johns Hopkins University Press, 2004.

Lagardère, Vincent. *Les Almoravides: Le djihad andalou (1106–1143)*. Paris: Harmattan, 1998.

———. "Communautés mozarabes et pouvoir Almoravide en 519 H/1125 en Andalus." *Studia Islamica* 67 (1988): 99–119.

———. "La haute judicature à l'epoque Almoravide en al-Andalus." *Al-Qantara* 7 (1986): 135–228.

———. *Histoire et societé en occident musulmane au Moyen Age*. Madrid: Casa de Velázquez, 1995.

Latham, Derek J. "Observations on the Text and Translation of al-Jarsifi's Treatise on 'Hisba'." *Journal of Semitic Studies* 5 (1960), 124–143.

Lehmann, Matthias. "Islamic Legal Consultation and the Jewish-Muslim 'Convivencia.'" *Jewish Studies Quarterly* 6 (1999): 25–54.

Lévi-Provençal, Évariste. *Documents arabes inédits sur la vie sociale et économique en occident musulman au Moyen Age (Trois traités hispaniques de hisba)*. Cairo: Institut Français d'Archéologie Orientale, 1955.

———. *L'Espagne musulmane au xe siècle*. 1932. New ed. Paris: Maisonneuve et Larose, 2002.

———. *Histoire de l'Espagne musulmane*, 3 vols. Paris: Maisonneuve, 1950.

———. *Inscriptions arabes d'Espagne*. Leiden: E. J. Brill; Paris: E. Larose, 1931.

Levy-Rubin, Milka. *Non-Muslims in the Early Islamic Empire: From Surrender to Coexistence*. Cambridge: Cambridge University Press, 2011.

Lewis, A. R. "Cataluña como frontera militar (870–1050)." *Anuario de Estudios Medievales* 5 (1968): 15–29.

Lewis, Bernard. *Islam: From the Prophet Muhammad to the Capture of Constantinople*. New York: Oxford University Press, 1987.

Libson, Gideon. "Halakhah and Law in the Period of the Geonim." In *History and Sources of Jewish Law*, edited by N. S. Hecht, B. S. Jackson, S. M. Passamaneck, D. Piatelli, and A. M. Rabello, 197–250. Oxford: Clarendon Press, 1996.

———. *Jewish and Islamic Law: A Comparative Study of Custom during the Geonic Period*. Cambridge, MA: Harvard University Press, 2003.

López-Morillas, Consuelo. "Language." In *The Literature of al-Andalus*, edited by Maria Rosa Menocal, Raymond P. Scheindlin, and Michael Sells, 33–59. Cambridge: Cambridge University Press, 2000.

Maghen, Ze'ev. "Close Encounters: Some Preliminary Observations on the Transmission of Impurity in Early Sunni Jurisprudence." *Islamic Law and Society* 6 (1999): 348–392.

———. "The Interaction between Islamic Law and Non-Muslims." *Islamic Law and Society* 10 (2003): 267–276.

———. "Much Ado about *Wuḍū'*." *Der Islam* 76 (1999): 205–252.

———. *Virtues of the Flesh—Passion and Purity in Early Islamic Jurisprudence*. Leiden: E. J. Brill, 2005.

Makki, M. A. "Nass jadid fi-l-hisba." *Revista del Instituto de Estudios Islámicos en Madrid* 4 (1956): 59–151.

———. "Watha'iq tarikhiyya jadida 'an 'asr al-Murabitin." *Revista del Instituto de Estudios Islámicos en Madrid* 7–8 (1959–1960): 109–198, 205–212.

Manzano Moreno, Eduardo. "La conquista de 711: Transformaciones y perviven-cias." In *Visigodas y Omeyas: Un debate entre la Antigüedad tardía y la alta Edad Media*, 401–414. Madrid: Consejo Superior de Investigaciones Científicas and Concorcio de la Ciudad Monumental de Mérida, 2000.

———. "The Creation of a Medieval Frontier: Islam and Christianity in the Iberian Peninsula, Eighth to Eleventh Centuries." In *Frontiers in Question: Eurasian Borderlands, 700–1700*, edited by Daniel Power and Naomi Standen, 32–54. New York: St. Martin's Press, 1999.

———. *La frontera de al-Andalus en época de los Omeyas*. Madrid: Consejo Superior de Investigaciones Científicas, 1991.

Marfil Ruiz, Pedro. "Córdoba de Teodosio a 'Abd al-Rahman III." In *Visigodas y Omeyas: Un debate entre la Antigüedad Tardía y la Alta Edad Media*, 117–141. Madrid: Consejo Superior de Investigaciones Científicas and Concorcio de la Ciudad Monumental de Mérida, 2000.

Marín, Manuela. "Los Banu Abi 'Isa: Una familia de 'ulama' Cordobeses." *Al-Qantara* 6 (1985): 291–320.

———. "Baqi b. Majlad y la introducción del hadit en al-Andalus." *Al-Qantara* 1 (1980): 165–208.

———. "Marriage and Sexuality in al-Andalus." In *Marriage and Sexuality in Medieval and Early Modern Iberia*, edited by Eukene Lacarra Lanz, 3–20. New York: Routledge, 2002.

———. "Nomina de sabios de al-Andalus (93–350/711–961)." *Estudios onomástico-biográficos de al-Andalus*, vol. 1, edited by Manuela Marín, 23–182. Madrid: Consejo Superior de Investigaciones Científicas, 1988.

———. "Parentesco simbólico y matrimonio entre los ulemas Andalusíes." *Al-Qantara* 16 (1995): 335–356.

———. "Šūrá et al-šūrá dans al-Andalus." *Studia Islamica* 62 (1985): 25–51.

Marín, Manuela, and Heather Ecker. "Archaeology, Arabic Sources and Christian Documents: From Muslim Fortress to Christian Castle; Social and Cultural Change in Medieval Spain." *British Journal of Middle Eastern Studies* 25 (1998): 335–348.

Mazzoli-Guintard, Christine. "Remarques sur le fonctionnement d'une capitale à double polarité: Madinat al-Zahra'–Cordoue." *Al-Qantara* 18 (1997): 43–64.

———. "L'urbanisation d'al-Andalus au xie siècle: Données chronologiques." In *Genèse de la ville islamique en al-Andalus et au Maghrib occidental*, edited by Patrice Cressier and Mercedes García-Arenal, 99–106. Madrid: Casa de Velázquez, 1998.

———. *Vivre à Cordoue au Moyen Age: Solidarité citadine en terre d'Islam aux xe–xie siècles*. Rennes: Presses Universitaires de Rennes, 2003.

Meouak, Mohamed. *Pouvoir souverain, administration centrale et élites politiques dans L'Espagne Umayyade (iie–ive/viii–xe siècles)*. Helsinki: Academia Scientiarum Fennica, 1999.

———. *Saqaliba, eunuques et esclaves à la conquête du pouvoir*. Helsinki: Academia Scientiarum Fennica, 2004.

Meyerson, Mark D. *The Muslims of Valencia in the Age of Fernando and Isabel: Between Coexistence and Crusade*. Berkeley: University of California Press, 1991.

Miller, H. D., and Hanna Kassis. "The Mozarabs." In *The Literature of al-Andalus*, edited by Maria Rosa Menocal, Raymond P. Scheindlin, and Michael Sells, 417–434. Cambridge: Cambridge University Press, 2000.

Miller, Kathryn A. *Guardians of Islam*. New York: Columbia University Press, 2008.

Millet-Gérard, Dominique. *Chrétiens mozarabes et culture islamique dans l'Espagne des viii–ix siècles*. Paris: Etudes Augustiniennes, 1984.

Molina, Luis. "Un árabe entre muladies: Muhammad b. ʿAbd al-Salam al-Jusani." *Estudios onomástico-biográficos de al-Andalus* 6, edited by Manuela Marín, 337–351. Madrid: Consejo Superior de Investigaciones Científicas, 1994. Translated by Michael Kennedy. "An Arab among Muwallads: Muhammad Ibn ʿAbd al-Salam al-Khushani." In *The Formation of al-Andalus*, edited by Manuela Marín, 1:115–128. Aldershot: Ashgate-Variorum, 1998.

———. "Las campañas de Almanzor a la luz de un nuevo texto." *Al-Qantara* 2 (1981): 209–263.

———. "Las campañas de Almanzor: Nuevos datos." *Al-Qantara* 3 (1982): 467–472.

———. "El estudio de familias de ulemas como fuente para la historia social de al-Andalus." In *Saber religioso y poder político en el Islam*, 161–173. Madrid: Agencia Española de Cooperación Internacional, 1994.

Monès, Hussein. "Le rôle des hommes de religion dans l'histoire de l'Espagne musulmane jusqu'a la fin du califat." *Studia Islamica* 20 (1964): 47–88. Translated by John Smedley. "The Role of Men of Religion in the History of Muslim Spain up to the End of the Caliphate." In *The Formation of al-Andalus*, edited by Maribel Fierro and Julio Samsó, 2:51–84. Aldershot: Ashgate-Variorum, 1998.

Morony, Michael G. "The Age of Conversions: A Reassessment." In *Conversion and Continuity: Indigenous Christian Communities in Islamic Lands, Eighth to Eighteenth Centuries*, edited by Michael Gervers and Ramzi Jibran Bikhazi, 135–150. Toronto: Pontifical Institute of Medieval Studies, 1990.

———. *Iraq after the Muslim Conquest*. Princeton, NJ: Princeton University Press, 1984.

Murillo, J. F., R. Hidalgo, J. R. Carrillo, A. Vallejo, and A. Ventura. "Cordoba: 300–1236 D.C.: Un milenio de transformaciones urbanas." In *Urbanism in Medieval Europe*, edited by Guy De Boe and Frans Verhaeghe, 47–60. Zellik: Scientific Institution of the Flemish Community, 1997.

Nirenberg, David. *Communities of Violence: Persecution of Minorities in the Middle Ages*. Princeton, NJ: Princeton University Press, 1996.

Noth, Albrecht. "Problems of Differentiation between Muslims and Non-Muslims: Re-reading the 'Ordinances of 'Umar' (al-Shurut al-'Umariyya)." In *Muslims and Others in Early Islamic Society*, edited by Robert Hoyland, 103–124. Aldershot: Ashgate, 2004.

Oliel, Jacob. *Les juifs au Sahara: Le Touat au Moyen Âge*. Paris: CNRS Editions, 1994.

Oliver Pérez, Dolores. "Sobre el significado de *mawlā* en la historia Omeya de al-Andalus." *Al-Qantara* 22 (2001): 321–344.

Penelas, Mayte. "Some Remarks on Conversion to Islam in al-Andalus." *Al-Qantara* 13 (2002): 193–200.

Puente, Cristina de la. "La caracterización de Almanzor: Entre la epopeya y la historia." In *Estudios onomástico-biográficos de al-Andalus*, vol. 8, edited by Maria Luisa Avila and Manuela Marín, 367–402. Madrid: Consejo Superior de Investigaciones Científicas, 1997.

———. "Juridical Sources for the Study of Women: Limitations of the Female's Capacity to Act According to Maliki Law." In *Writing the Feminine: Women in Arab Sources*, edited by Manuela Marín and Randi Deguilhem, 95–110. London: I. B. Taurus, 2002.

Rambo, Lewis R., and Charles E. Farkadian. "Converting: Stages of Religious Change." In *Religious Conversion: Contemporary Practices and Controversies*, edited by Christopher Lamb and M. Darrol Bryant, 23–34. London: Cassell, 1999.

Ray, Jonathan. *The Sephardic Frontier: The Reconquista and the Jewish Community in Medieval Iberia*. Ithaca, NY: Cornell University Press, 2006.

Reinhart, A. Kevin. "Impurity/No Danger." *History of Religions* 30 (1990): 1–24.

Renard, John. *Islam and the Heroic Image: Themes in Literature and the Visual Arts*. Macon, GA: Mercer University Press, 1999.

Rosen, Tova. "The Muwashshah." In *Literature of al-Andalus*, edited by Maria Rosa Menocal, Raymond P. Scheindlin, and Michael Sells, 165–189. Cambridge: Cambridge University Press, 2000.

Roth, Norman. *Jews, Visigoths, and Muslims in Medieval Spain: Cooperation and Conflict*. Leiden: E. J. Brill, 1994.

Rubin, Uri. "Apes, Pigs, and the Islamic Identity." *Israel Oriental Studies* 17 (1997): 89–105.

Ruggles, D. Fairchild. "Mothers of a Hybrid Dynasty: Race, Genealogy, and Acculturation in al-Andalus." *Journal of Medieval and Early Modern Studies* 34 (2004): 65–94.

Ruiz, Teofilo F. *From Heaven to Earth: The Reordering of Castilian Society, 1150–1350.* Princeton, NJ: Princeton University Press, 2004.

Ruiz Asencio, J. M. "Campañas de Almanzor contra el reino de León (981–986)." *Anuario de Estudios Medievales* 5 (1968): 31–64.

Rustow, Marina. *Heresy and the Politics of Community: The Jews of the Fatimid Caliphate.* Ithaca, NY: Cornell University Press, 2008.

Safran, Janina M. "The Command of the Faithful in al-Andalus: A Study in the Articulation of Caliphal Legitimacy." *International Journal of Middle East Studies* 30 (1998): 183–198.

———. "Identity and Differentiation in Ninth-Century al-Andalus." *Speculum* 76 (2001): 573–598.

———. "Rules of Purity and Confessional Boundaries: Maliki Debates about the Pollution of the Christian." *History of Religions* 42 (2003): 197–212.

———. *The Second Umayyad Caliphate.* Cambridge, MA: Harvard University Press, 2000.

Sage, Carleton M. *Paul Albar of Cordoba: Studies on His Life and Writings.* Washington, DC: Catholic University of America Press, 1943.

Sampedro Vizcaya, Benita, and Simon Doubleday, eds. *Border Interrogations: Questioning Spanish Frontiers.* New York: Berghahn Books, 2008.

Scales, Peter C. "Cordoba under the Umayyads, a 'Syrian' Garden City?" In *Urbanism in Medieval Europe*, edited by Guy De Boe and Frans Verhaeghe, 175–182. Zellik: Scientific Institution of the Flemish Community, 1997.

Scheindlin, Raymond P. *The Gazelle: Medieval Hebrew Poems on God, Israel, and the Soul.* 1991. Reprint, Oxford: Oxford University Press, 1999.

———. *Wine, Women, and Death: Medieval Hebrew Poems on the Good Life.* 1986. Reprint, Oxford: Oxford University Press, 1999.

Serrano, Delfina. "Dos fetuas sobre la expulsión de mozárabes al Magreb en 1126." *Anaquel de Estudios Árabes* 2 (1991): 163–182.

———. "Why Did the Scholars of al-Andalus Distrust al-Ghazali? Ibn Rushd al-Jadd's *Fatwa* on *Awliya' Allah.*" *Der Islam* 83 (2006): 137–156.

Shatzmiller, Maya. "Marriage, Family, and the Faith: Women's Conversion to Islam." *Journal of Family History* 21 (1996): 235–266.

Shochetman, Eliav. "Jewish Law in Spain and the Halakhic Activity of Its Scholars before 1300." In *An Introduction to the History and Sources of Jewish Law*, edited by N. S. Hecht, B. S. Jackson, S. M. Passamaneck, D. Piatelli, and A. M. Rabello, 271–298. Oxford: Clarendon Press, 1996.

Simonsohn, Uriel. *A Common Justice: The Legal Allegiances of Christians and Jews under Early Islam.* Philadelphia: University of Pennsylvania Press, 2011.

Stillman, Norman A. *The Jews of Arab Lands: A History and Sourcebook.* Philadelphia: Jewish Publication Society of America, 1979.

Tornero, Emilio. "Noticia sobre la publicación de obras inéditas de Ibn Masarra." *Al-Qantara* 14 (1993): 47–64.

Tritton, A. S. *The Caliphs and Their Non-Muslim Subjects: A Critical Study of the Covenant of Umar.* 1930. Reprint, London: Frank Cass, 1970.

Tyan, Emile. *Institutions du droit public musulman. Tome premier: Le califat.* Paris: Recueil Sirey, 1954.

Vallvé, Joaquín. "Nasr, el valido de ʿAbd al-Rahman II." *Al-Qantara* 6 (1985): 179–197.

Viguera, María J. "*Asluhu li'l-Maʿali*: On the Social Status of Andalusi Women." In *The Legacy of Muslim Spain*, edited by Salma Khadra Jayyusi, 2:709–724. Leiden: E. J. Brill, 1994.

Wasserfall, Rahel. "Menstruation and Identity: The Meaning of *Niddah* for Morrocan Women Immigrants to Israel." In *People of the Body: Jews and Judaism from an Embodied Perspective*, edited by Howard Eilberg-Schwartz, 309–327. Albany: State University of New York Press, 1992.

Wasserstein, David J. "An Arabic Version of Abot 1:3 from Umayyad Spain." *Arabica* 34 (1987): 370–374.

———. "Encore un fois ʿAbot' 1:3 dans l'Espagne Omeyyade." *Arabica* 38 (1991): 275–277.

———. "A *Fatwa* on Conversion in Islamic Spain." In *Studies in Muslim-Jewish Relations*, edited by Ronald L. Nettler, 1:177–188. Chur, Switzerland: Harwood Academic Publishers, 1993.

———. "Inventing Tradition and Constructing Identity: The Genealogy of ʿUmar ibn Hafsun between Christianity and Islam." *Al-Qantara* 23 (2002): 269–297.

———. "The Language Situation in al-Andalus." In *Studies on the Muwaššah and Kharja*, edited by A. Jones and R. Hitchcock, 1–15. Reading, England: Ithaca Press, 1991. Reprinted in *The Formation of al-Andalus*, edited by Maribel Fierro and Julio Samsó, 2:3–17. Aldershot: Ashgate-Variorum, 1998.

———. "The Library of al-Hakam II al-Mustansir and the Culture of Islamic Spain." *Manuscripts of the Middle East* 5 (1990–1991): 99–105.

———. "The Muslims and the Golden Age of the Jews in al-Andalus." *Israel Oriental Studies* 17 (1997): 179–196.

———. *The Rise and Fall of the Party-Kings.* Princeton, NJ: Princeton University Press, 1985.

Watts, Richard J. *Politeness.* Cambridge: Cambridge University Press, 2003.

Wheeler, Brannon. "Touching the Penis in Islamic Law." *History of Religions* 44 (2004): 89–119.

Wickens, G. M. "Al-Jarsifi on the *Hisba*." *Islamic Quarterly* 3 (1956): 176–187.

Wolf, Kenneth Baxter. *Christian Martyrs in Muslim Spain.* Cambridge: Cambridge University Press, 1988.

Zorgati, Ragnhild Johnsrud. "Beyond Boundaries: Islamic and Christian Legal Texts Dealing with Conversion and Mixed Marriages in Medieval Iberia." PhD diss., Faculty of Humanities, University of Oslo, 2007.

Index

borderlands, 168–69, 196, 210; *ahl al-dhimma* in, 169, 185–88, 203–8, 212–14; Christians fighting Christians in, 185; geography of, 170–71; historic context of, 171–79; Ibn Rushd's commentary on, 196–208; identity considerations in, 59, 169, 172–73, 194–96; jihad in, 33–34, 68, 179–88, 196–208, 212–14; jurisdiction in, 188–90; legal distinctions of, 168–69; pragmatic management of, 171–72; rebellions in, 172–74; safe-conduct (*amān*) in, 180, 182–84; slaves in, 192–94, 195n49; travelers and merchants in, 190–92

Bosch Vilá, Jacinto, 170n4

boundary making, 209–19; in administration of the marketplace, 155–56, 161–67; Christian martyrs' movement and, 91–99, 211; contextual reading of, 9, 18–25; corruption of the faith and, 125–28; emphasis on alterity in, 20; feasts and celebrations and, 87–90, 141–43; food and, 139–43; funerary rites and, 147–49; identity confusion and, 154–55, 214–15; in interfaith marriages, 105–6, 128–33, 139–40; intersection of legal opinion and everyday life in, 3, 22–23, 26–29, 155–56; legal context of, 5–6, 8–18, 144–47, 155–56; linguistic habitus and, 151–55; patron–clientage ties and, 145–46; purity practices and, 3, 133–43; in routine neighborly exchanges, 150–55; with servants and nursemaids, 140–41; social and cultural identity in, 17–24; symbolic terms of, 23; in territories under rebellion, 65–69; water purity and, 137–40. *See also* borderlands; social transformation

Bourdieu, Pierre: on habitus, 23, 151; on naming of social groups, 60–61

Brann, Ross, 102n40

Bulliet, Richard, 106–8, 165

Burgos, 176

burial rites, 29–30, 67n114, 115, 116n74, 130–31, 133, 137n25, 147–49, 215, 217–18

Cairo Geniza, 6–7, 11n19, 190

The Caliphs and Their Non-Muslim Subjects (Tritton), 12

Carolingians, 175, 176

Casius of Tudela, 110

Castile, 176

casuistry, 28–29, 48, 147, 149, 210, 215, 216, 217, 218

Christians, 210–11; alliances with *muwalladūn* of, 60; alliances with Umayyads of, 42–43; Almoravid expulsions of, 165n104, 212; Arabic language use by, 101–2; archives of, 4, 7–8; areas of settlement of, 83; blasphemy and martyrdoms of, 33, 39, 86n8, 91–99; borderland fighting of, 169, 185–88, 203–8; circumcision practices of, 114n67; in Cordoba, 86–87; as court concubines, 105–6; feasts and celebrations of, 89, 141–43; intercommunal relations of, 99n34, 137–40, 149n59; interfaith marriages of, 105–6, 144–45; on Islamic doctrine, 115n68; as merchant travelers, 190–91, 204; pretending to be Muslim by, 67; as slaves, 145–46. *See also* borderlands; boundary making; People of the Book

Church of St. John (Damascus), 3

Church of St. Zoylus (Cordoba), 86

Church of the Three Martyrs (San Pedro) (Cordoba), 84, 86

circumcision, 89, 114, 166, 214

civil war of 1009–1031, 219n

clients. *See mawālī*; patron-client relationships

Cohen, Anthony, 23

Cohen, Jeffrey Jerome, 21

Cohen, Mark, 15n27

Colin, G. S., 164n102

A Common Justice (Simonsohn), 7

concubinage, 50, 78, 84, 105–6, 116

construction of Umayyad authority, 35–36, 77–80, 209–11; under 'Abd al-Rahman I, 40–43; under 'Abd al-Rahman II, 39, 43–50; adherence to Maliki madhhab in, 46, 71–77, 78; border establishment in, 171–79; boundary making in, 65–69; centralized administration in, 43–45; debate and consensus building in, 46–55; defining belief and unbelief in, 53n37; defining insiders and outsiders in, 35–36, 40; dynastic legitimacy in, 36–38; *hasham* (army) in, 43, 44n13, 110; ibn Hafsun's rebellion in, 38–40, 59–69, 77–78, 172, 176; judicial practice in, 70–71, 78–80, 156; juridical tradition in, 45–46; at Madinat al-Zahra', 38, 69, 79–80; *mawālī* in, 40–41, 55–59;